MICROSOFT

OFFICE 365

ALL-IN-ONE

FOR BEGINNERS & POWER USERS 2022

The Complete Microsoft Office 365 A-Z Mastery Guide for All Users Updated for 2022 (Word, Excel, PowerPoint, Access, SharePoint & OneDrive)

FRITSCHE KING

CONTENTS

CHAPTER SEVEN -- 139

TAKING ADVANTAGE OF THE PROOFING TOOLS-- 139

CHAPTER EIGHT -- 156

DESKTOP PUBLISHING WITH WORD --- 156

CHAPTER NINE--- 182

GETTING WORD'S HELP WITH OFFICE CHORES--- 182

INTRODUCTION

Microsoft Office Suite is the "come to stay" version of Word processor that can be periodically updated without any threat of software crash or unauthorized version. Office 365 has evolved and transformed to stay relevant in today's business world but despite this, many businesses still use it exclusively for Microsoft Word and Excel only. If you find yourself looking at the other apps and features and wondering what they do, keep reading this guide to Office 365 till the end.

The most commonly used Office 365 apps include Word, Excel, PowerPoint, and Outlook. These applications are essential for creating documents, spreadsheets, presentations, and communicating both internally and externally but these are not all Office 365 entails, other apps like SharePoint, Access, etc. are also included in the Office 365 suite. This user guide has been specially prepared to teach you the in and out of these powerful programs in Office 365 with *Word, Excel, PowerPoint, Access, SharePoint and OneDrive* being the specificity. This is a guide that does not only explain "WHAT" (theoretical application), but also "HOW" (practical application). I am excited because you have just made the right choice.

OVERVIEW OF OFFICE 365

Introduction to Office 365

In the past, Microsoft Office was always sold as box software, so when you buy your new computer, you have the options of buying Office whether Microsoft Office 2007, 2010, 2013, 2016 or other subsequent versions. You could pay $300USD to $500USD depending on the version you request for, and you will get the software on your machine which would be installed into your PC as infinity software, meaning you will pay once and never pay again for the software, this is how Microsoft deals with its previous products for very long time.

In the past years, many companies have started switching over to a subscription model of selling software such as Adobe, Photoshop, and other subscription software; you can't just buy them completely anymore. You purchase a subscription and through that subscription, you always get the latest updated and upgraded version of any other program you subscribe for. So, with Microsoft, they sell box software which also leads to an upgrade in its service rendering for a quick solution to unexpected issues, flexible storage space, and secured information with other benefits only available to its subscribed users.

What is Office 365 Cloud Service?

Office 365 is a collection of different cloud applications which serve different purposes but similar in features. It is important to note that Office 365 has been synchronized as Microsoft 365 which comes with many packages such as:

- **Word:** It is a text editor specifically designed to process text, image, shapes & other features without the need to manually install it on your PC.
- **PowerPoint:** It is the software majorly constructed for presentation purposes.
- **Excel:** This is a calculation framed software used to solve the complexity of statistics, Mathematics, and plotting of graphs with other features in a flexible way.
- **Outlook:** Outlook is an email that is designed to receive incoming messages and also send outgoing messages.
- **OneDrive**: This is an online storage space specifically designed for all Microsoft users to store personal data which can be accessed anywhere around the world. It also comes with a link privilege to share files and other items stored on it.
- **OneNote:** OneNote is a note-taking software
- **To Do:** It is a task management utility that is designed to take your regular activities schedule.
- **Family Safety:** This is also another feature of Microsoft that gives the privilege to monitor your family activities such as setting screen time limits, filtering of content, activities report, and lots more to make sure family members are safe while using the internet with Microsoft.
- **Calendar:** It is used to schedule and share meetings and event times. One can automatically get reminders.
- **Skype:** This is a meeting software which is designed to make video and voice call, chat and share file or screen if need be.

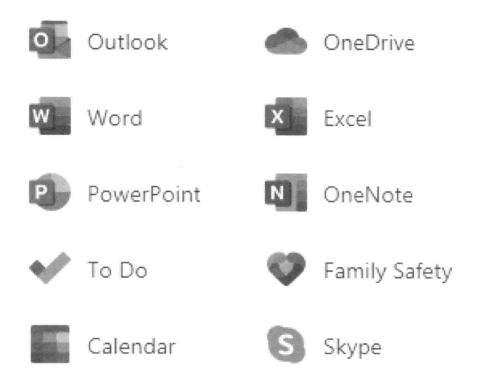

Difference between Office 365 & Microsoft 365

Office 365 is a cloud-based software collection of applications such as Word, Excel, PowerPoint, and more. Microsoft 365 is a bundle of existing services under one license that includes Office 365 with several other services including Windows 10 Enterprise plus Security tools. Sooner or later, Microsoft will be branding its cloud-based productivity suite, Office 365, as Microsoft 365. This amendment in the naming resolution reflects Microsoft's strategy to convert all its products & services under one common name to avoid any confusion among its users by bringing everything under one umbrella.

Types of Microsoft Office 365 Suite

For every Microsoft product and service, there is always an avenue for multiple choice for users. Microsoft Office 365 suite is divided into two categories:

Microsoft Office 365 Subscription Plans	Description
Home Plans Family Personal	Microsoft 365 **Family** costs $95USD to $100USD per year for 2 to 6 people with 1 Terabyte (TB) storage per person. Microsoft 365 **Personal** costs $60USD to $65USD. Only per year package is available for 1 person with 1 Terabyte (TB) storage

	Both plans give access to Microsoft Office applications such as Word, Excel, PowerPoint, OneDrive, 60mins Skype per month, and more.
Business Plans Business Basic Business Standard Business Premium Apps for business	Microsoft 365 **Business Basic** costs $5 per month with access to Office suite packages Microsoft 365 **Business Standard** costs $12.50 per month with access to Office suite packages Microsoft 365 **Business Premium** costs $20USD user per month with access to Office suite packages Microsoft 365 **Apps for Business** costs $8.25USD per month. It is best for businesses that need easy remote solutions, with Microsoft Teams, secured cloud storage, and Office Online. The business plan includes a 300-user limit. Packages are a little different from one another depending on your need.
Enterprise Plans Enterprise 3 Enterprise 5 Firstline 3 Apps for Enterprise	Microsoft 365 E3 costs $32USD per month Microsoft 365 E5 price is not fixed Microsoft 365 F3 costs $8USD per month Enterprise plan includes unlimited user features. All these prices might vary depending on your country's currency and Microsoft update of other features which might affect the price.

Note

i.   **Microsoft 365 for home plans:** are for family usage which gives room for monitoring of family members' activities for the sake of children.
ii. **Microsoft 365 for business plans:** are mainly for organizational usage. It is designed to suit office performances and is also used to secure remote work.
iii. **Microsoft 365 for enterprise plans:** This is similar to the business plan but different in some aspects, enterprise plan gives the privilege

Why should I use Office 365 over previous versions?

It is important to note that the world at large is moving fast beyond human imagination, just as we have our daily experience so also is the advancement of technology moving rapidly.

Over time, Microsoft has found it a bit difficult to release an update on the purchased version since all previous versions of Suite majorly work offline; auto-update will be difficult or impossible to occur to them all from Office 2007, Office 2010, Office 2013, Office 2016 to Office 2019. Microsoft users find it a waste of time to update since everything is working perfectly, which led to the latest version which is online-based known as Office 365. It's a cloud service that works directly from the Microsoft database for security and monitoring purposes. Very soon application installation won't relent any longer due to the rate of technology advancement daily.

Becoming a Microsoft User

Many people find it difficult to create an account with Microsoft, which without an account you can't enjoy the limitless benefits of Microsoft features. Below are steps on how to go about it

- Go to your browser search for **"Microsoft office 365",** make sure it is Microsoft link then click on **"Official Microsoft 365® Site - Formerly Office 365®"**

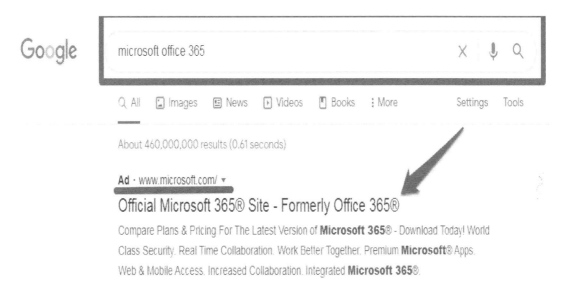

- You will be brought into the Microsoft website, below is a link to **"Sign in",** click on it or you can also locate an image icon at your top right-hand side, you can also click on it

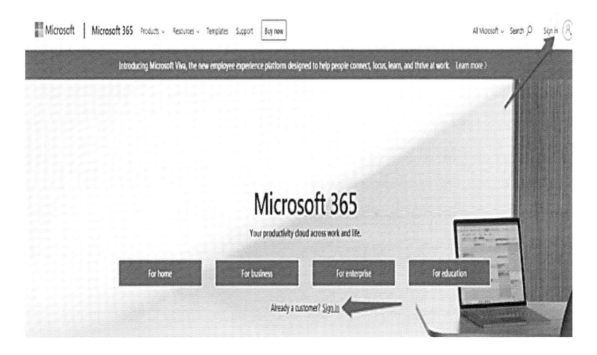

- Or you can directly type Microsoft website into your browser www.microsoft.com. Once the Microsoft website is done loading, look at your right-hand side you will see **an image icon,** click on it to create your user account

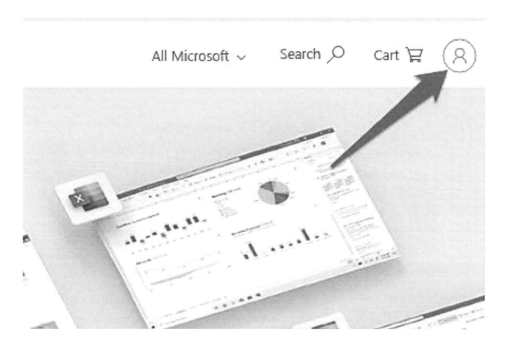

- You will be brought here, simply enter your existing Microsoft account. If you don't have one click on **"Create One".**

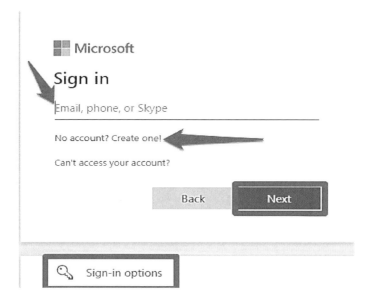

- In case you can't access your account, click on **"Can't access your account"** below create one, a dialog box will appear notifying you that your Windows 10 operating system will receive a security key that will give you access

- Or you want a sign-in option without you having to enter your password for reasons best known to you, simply click on **"Sign-in options"**

- If none of these is your case but want to create an account simply click on **"Create one"**

- Simply follow the instructions to get your Microsoft account opened, once done, you will be brought into Microsoft 365 environment

BOOK ONE

WORD 365

CHAPTER ONE

WELCOME TO WORD 365

Word 365 Installed License Environment

Word 365 Free Web based Environment

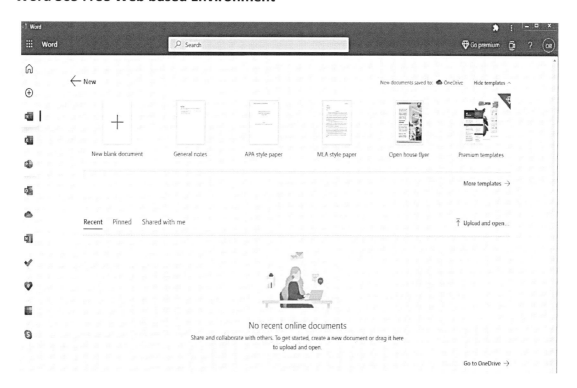

Word 365 interface is designed to perform similar tasks as previous versions with more added features such as online help, latest release, online sharing, and lots more.

Historical Background of Microsoft Word

- **Microsoft Word DOS:** The first version of Microsoft Word was released in 1983, it was named Microsoft Word DOS which stands for "Disk Operating System", with a 16bit system type capacity.
- **Microsoft Word for Windows:** Another version of Microsoft Word was released in 1989 with a different edition.
- **Microsoft Word 95:** After the release of Microsoft Word for Windows which had a lot of limitations, Microsoft Word 95 was released in 1995 to solve the problem of graphics and limited features.
- **Microsoft Word 97:** Microsoft Word 97 was released on November 19, 1996, to solve the limitation of Microsoft Word 95.
- **Microsoft Word 2000:** Microsoft Word 97 was replaced by Microsoft Word 2000 as a new release on July 7, 1999.
- **Microsoft Word 2001/Word X:** Word 2001 was packaged with the Macintosh features. Word 2001 was released in October 2000 and was also sold as an individual product. Word X was released in 2001 and was the first version to run natively
- **Microsoft Word 2002/XP:** Word 2002 was also released in 2001 to replace Microsoft Word 2001 & Word X. It had several of the same features as Word 2000, but a new feature was added called the "Task Panes", which gave quicker information and control to a lot of features.
- **Microsoft Word 2003:** Microsoft Word 2003 is an office suite developed by Microsoft for its Windows operating system. Office 2003 was released on October 21, 2003. It was the replacement of Word XP.
- **Microsoft Word 2007:** Word 2007 was introduced with a graphical user interface called the "Fluent User Interface", ribbons and an Office menu. It was released on January 30, 2007.
- **Microsoft Word 2010:** Microsoft Word 2010 is another version of the Microsoft Office suite for Microsoft Windows. Office 2010 was released on the 15th of April 2010. It is the successor to Word 2007.
- **Microsoft Word 2013:** Word 2013 was released on January 29, 2013, with more updated features and was later replaced by Word 2016
- **Microsoft Word 2016:** Word 2016 was launched on September 22, 2015, with a lot of built-in features such as auto-correct, spelling check, auto-save, and lots more. Word 2016 was later replaced with Word 2019.
- **Microsoft Word 2019:** Word 2019 was released on September 24, 2018, with similar yet upgraded features such as Sign in, share, and auto-resume with other friendly tools. It was later replaced with Word 365.
- **Microsoft Word 365:** Word 365 was released on June 28, 2011, with a similar interface yet different with newly added features such as speech dictation, resume assistant, sharing of documents online, OneDrive cloud storage, and lots more. Word 365 is the latest version of Microsoft Word which functions online; without having a Microsoft account you are not eligible to make use of it.

Exploring Word 365

For simplicity and comprehension, I will be using the free web version to explain Word 365 features for the sake of those who can't afford a license version yet, and for those that can, I will be using both to explain along the line to be able to cover both parts.

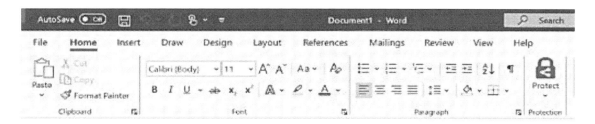

Word 365 comes with simple yet loaded features that autosave itself online into your OneDrive cloud storage

Title bar functionality

The title bar consists of your application name which is **"Word"** and beside it is your current working document which can be renamed, and also the location of your document storage which is OneDrive as seen above.

Exploring tab Functionality

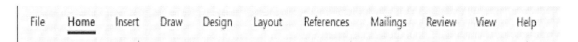

A menu bar is the anchor or entry point that leads to other features. The menu bar names details where you can access such features from:

File tab features

Once you click on "file", it'll display a dialog box that gives an overview of multiple features of what **"File menu"** represent.

Home: Home under **"File menu"** also known as the **"backstage view"** takes you to Word 365 launching page where you can open a new document to work on, locate existing documents and also see your recent works.

Home

New

New blank document   General notes   APA style paper

Info: Info gives the privilege to make use of previous Microsoft Word on your desktop or PC, Protection view and to view, restore or download previous versions of your document.

Info

Open in Desktop App
Use the full functionality of Microsoft Word.

Protect Document
Always open view-only to prevent accidental changes by asking readers to opt-in to editing.

Previous Versions
View, restore, or download older versions of this document.

Save as: This is the feature that makes Microsoft Word 365 save & rename an active document because there is no save button, every work is automatically saved online. You can also click on **"Download a copy"** to download a duplicate copy into your PC, or **"Download as PDF"** directly into your PC, or **"Download as ODT"** to your PC.

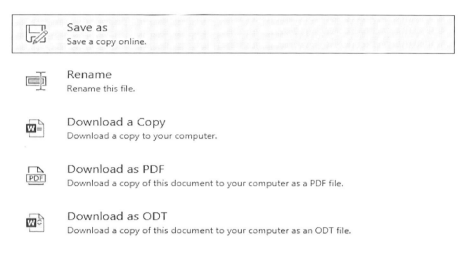

Export: Export gives room for transferring a document into another Microsoft 365 Suite such as PowerPoint. As time goes on, more options will be added to the list.

Export

Print: The print option is designed to covert softcopy into hardcopy format, all that is needed is a connected printer to complete this process of printing.

Print

Share: This is the feature that allows you to share your document with others by inviting them, and you can also embed this document in your blog or website

Share

Share with People
Invite other people to view or edit this document.

Embed
Embed this document in your blog or website.

About: The about option gives the summary of terms and conditions of using Word 365 with third-party notice. Under the about option is where you get your product ID known as "Session ID", and "Build" for any technical support from Microsoft.

About

Terms of Use
Read the terms and conditions of using Word.

Third-Party Notices
Privacy and Cookies

Privacy and Cookies
Learn how Microsoft protects your privacy.

Recommended

The following session details may be requested by technical support.

Session ID   679cd699-875a-40f1-bd72-a1824ebfa4a7
Build   16.0.13904.41003

Home tab feature

"Home" as its name implies, is the default displayed feature of the Word 365 interface which comes with ribbons that are grouped for your command, these can also be categorized as **_Standard toolbar_** for customizing your text and **_formatting toolbar_** for editing your text. Home comes with tools for beautifying text such as:

- **Clipboard ribbon tab:** Clipboard is one of Microsoft tool designed as part of Word 365 to cut, copy and paste an item

- **_Cut:_** Cut removes a selected portion and stores it directly into your clipboard.
- **_Copy:_** Copy duplicates item and stores it into your clipboard.
- **_Format Painter:_** This is a tool used to duplicate a text format into another text format.
- **_Paste:_** Paste displays all cut or copied items to any assigned destination.
- **Font ribbon tab:** Font is a Word 365 ribbon that consists of various tools for editing your text font style, font size, superscript, subscript, color, and lots more.

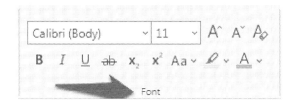

- **_Bold:_** It is a tool that makes your text appear in a bold form, it is recognized by a bold **B** icon
- **_Italic:_** It is a tool that slants or slopes your text, it is recognized by a slant "_I_" icon
- **_Underline:_** It is a tool that rules a line under a selected text, it is recognized by an underlined U icon
- **_Strikethrough:_** It is a tool used to cross through your text, it is recognized by a strikethrough ab icon

- **_Font style:_** It is designed to beautify text style into your preferred choice.

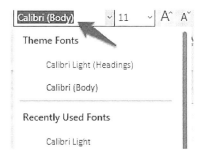

- **Font size:** This is another portion that gives increment and decrement to your text.

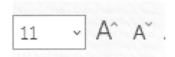

- **Font Color:** It is the tool that changes the color of your text into your preferred choice, it affects the selected text body. It is represented with a capital letter A underlined with red color.

- **Text highlighted color:** This is similar to font color. Text highlighted color affects highlighted text background areas. It is represented with a pen icon underlined with yellow color.

- **Superscript & Subscript:** This is the feature responsible for text positioning, superscript makes text above the text line, while subscript makes text below the text line.

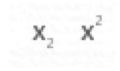

- **Change Case:** It is a feature that gives the privilege to change text into lowercase, uppercase, sentence case, and other formats, it is represented with capital letter A and a small letter 'a' (Aa)

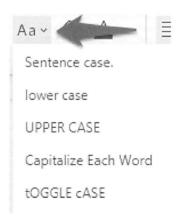

- *Clear formatting:* This helps to remove all formatting from the selection, leaving only the normal text unformatted. It is represented as seen in the illustration below

- **Paragraph ribbon tab:** "Paragraph" is a ribbon tab that other commands are grouped into for specialization. Paragraph features are also known as formatting toolbar for aligning text in an orderly approach. Part of paragraph features are:

- *Bullet's library:* Bullets is a tagged icon that works in form of numerical numbering. In bullets, every symbol icon is the same in listing except there is a need to have sub-list items

- *Numbering library:* Numbering is the opposite of bullets. Numbering comes in forms, numerical order, alphabetical order, and roman figure order

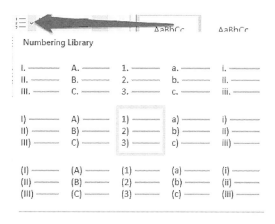

- **Multilevel library:** It is a sub-listing arrangement that consists of a mixture of bullets listing & numbering listing in sublevels.

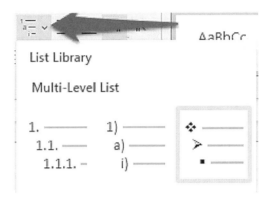

- **Decrease & Increase Indent:** It is designed to adjust the movement of text from a standpoint to another standpoint.

- **Left-to-right text direction:** This is an auto feature that moves an item from the left-hand side position to the right-hand side

- **Right-to-left text direction:** It is the opposite of the left-to-right text direction. It automatically moves text from the right-hand side position to the left-hand side position

- **Left alignment:** It helps to align your content to the left margin

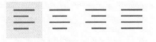

- **Center alignment:** It helps to centralize your content
- **Right alignment:** It helps to align your content to the right margin
- **Justify alignment:** It helps your content to look fit on right and left margin

- **Line spacing:** This is another feature of the paragraph ribbon tab. Line spacing determines the space between lines of text or between paragraphs

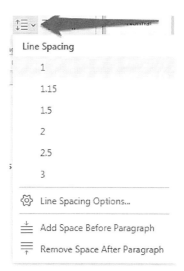

- **Styles:** Style gives your content a consistent polish look. It also comes with multiple options to choose from through the navigation pane

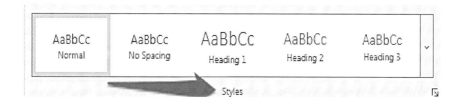

- **Editing:** Editing is a tool that is used to find text, replace text, and also to select text

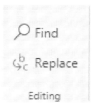

- **Dictate:** Dictate is a new tool added into Word 365 that allows its users the privilege to use speech-to-text.

- **Editor:** Editor is a tool in Word 365 that offers auto spelling & grammar suggestions.

- **Designer:** Designer is a newly added tool that presents a list of potential features for fonts and headings that you can apply to your document to make it professionally presentable. It also gives users the privilege to professionally design complete templates

Insert tab feature

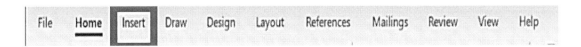

Insert menu bar feature is designed to add, import & customize your content in a lovely way. Insert menu bar has many tools such as:

- **Pages ribbon tab:** This is the controller of your contents, that involves page breaks. Subsequent updates from Microsoft will lead to additional features such as cover page and others.

- **Table ribbon tab:** The table ribbon tab is responsible for table creation based on your preferred choice

- **Picture ribbon tab:** It is a tool that grants access to images from external images on your PC into Word 365 environment.

- **Add-ins ribbon tab:** Add-in is a feature that allows Microsoft users to merge external application features with Word 365

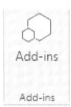

- **Link ribbon tab:** Link makes it possible for link creation into another file, webpage, and lots more.

- **Comments ribbon tab:** This is a feature that adds a note on a selected text, majorly for reference purpose.

- **Header & Footer:** "Header" helps you to repeat content at the top of every page while "footer" helps you to repeat content at the bottom of every page.

- **Symbols ribbon tab:** Symbol comes with various mathematical representations that can be used for different purposes based on the user's preferred choice.

- **Emoji ribbon tab:** Emoji is a newly added feature that is still under development. Emoji is a little facial expression image that was first recognized on smartphones. Microsoft is bringing the possibility of Word 365 emoji.

Note: More features are being updated daily with time, and there will be lesser usage of offline Word application once Microsoft stops it support from previous versions.

Design tab features

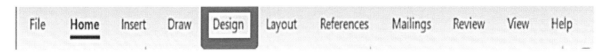

The design tab is an embodiment of document formatting tools and page background styling such as:

- **Document Formatting ribbon tab:** It is a group collection of tools for styling your document
- **Themes:** This is a feature that enables a predefined template format for styling your document content from a professional viewpoint.

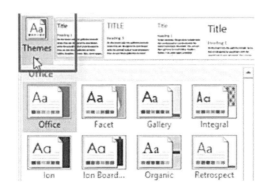

- **Colors:** Microsoft Word predefined templates also come with redefining colors for an individual preferred choice.

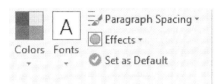

- **Fonts:** Microsoft also comes with a lot of fonts that can sort your preferred choice since individual taste varies. With this, you can redefine your theme font.
- **Page Background ribbon tab:** It is a group of collections used to edit your theme template and also to customize your pages.

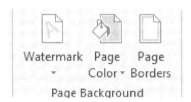

- **Watermark:** Watermark is a great tool used to design your background document with either a text or image depending on the individual preferred choice.
- **Page Color:** This helps you to customize your page document from the default white color to another color of your choice.
- **Page Borders:** It is used to create a variety of line styles, widths, and colors.

Layout tab feature

Layout is Word 365 menu bar that is responsible for page settings such as:

- **Page Setup ribbon tab:** This is the ribbon tab that groups other commands responsible for page configuration such as:

- **Margins:** It is used to set the right and left edge for all pages, it is a manual page setting.
- **Orientation:** Page orientation is divided into two categories, portrait & landscape; by default, your Word settings is on portrait, the landscape is used for different purposes such as tabulation of analysis.

- **Size:** Page size helps to make use of different paper sizes such as A4 (which is Word default paper size), A5, and many more. It is an auto page setting.
- **Paragraph ribbon tab:** This is a manual setup for paragraph settings, it is used to set indent and space.

- **Left & Right Indent:** They both determine how far to move the paragraph away from the left margin and the right margin.
- **Before & After Spacing:** They both determine how much space appears above or below the selected paragraph.

References menu bar:

The references menu bar consists of different Word 365 tools such as Updating table of contents, Footnotes, and Insights

- **Table of Contents ribbon tab:** This is used for the arrangement of contents.
- **Footnote ribbon tab:** Is used to take note for citation of written words.
- **Update Table of Contents:** Word 365 provides an overview of your document by adding a table of content
- **Remove Table of Contents:** You can auto-remove your created table of contents at your wish
- **Footnotes ribbon tab:** Footnote is a written text on the bottom of Word 365 page to reference a sentence; it is majorly used for journals.
- **Insights ribbon tab:** This is a newly added feature that serves as a mini browser to get an insight into a word or statement.

Review tab:

The review menu bar is designed to give a comprehensive detail on your written document such as:

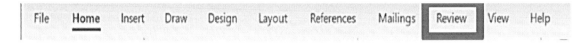

- **Editor ribbon tab:** It is a tool used to check spellings and correct words.

Editor

Review Tools

- **Word Count ribbon tab:** It is a tool designed to auto count words & pages.

Word Count

- **Accessibility ribbon tab:** The Accessibility feature helps to verify your document against a set of instructions that detect possible issues for people who have disabilities. Depending on how severe the issue is, the Accessibility Checker classifies each issue as an error, warning, or tip.

Check Accessibility

Accessibility

- **Translate ribbon tab:** The Translate feature is a tool that helps you to interpret text into a different language. By using Word 365 you are already connected online to get your translated words.

Translate

Translate

- **Comments ribbon tab:** It helps to add a note about any selected part of your content and also, other tools reveal your comment items

New Comment   Delete   Previous   Next   Show Comments

Comments

- **Tracking ribbon tab:** Tracking helps you to keep in touch with your document in case of any changes made by you or other people you shared your document with. It is majorly used to note every single step of added and removed words.

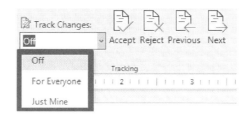

- **Resume Assistant:** It is a newly added feature from Microsoft Word 365 that enables its users to get different templates.

Mailing's tab

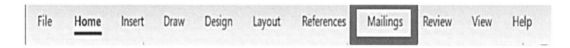

Mailing's tab is a feature used to forward, edit, and select emails.

View tab

The view menu bar is constructed to preview content, read content, zoom in & out, and lots more

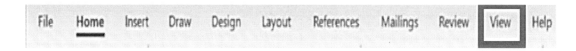

- **Document Views ribbon tab:** This is a new feature added into Word 365 where you can view your content and also make your PC auto-read it
- **Zoom ribbon tab:** Zoom is a tool used for viewing your content into a level that is suitable for you
- **Show ribbon tab:** Show ribbon tab consists of ruler for margin measurement, navigation to search words from your content, header & footer to cite or number pages, with other features.

Help tab:

Help is a newly added feature that provides a solution, contact support, and feedback to Microsoft users.

Editing tab:

Editing is also a new feature from Microsoft; this makes you choose to edit your work, review it for additional touch, or view your document without making any change depending on the users' choice (majorly seen at the top menu of Microsoft Word free web version also in licensed version but not placed above your menu).

CHAPTER TWO

WRESTLING WITH THE TEXT

Manipulating the text

Text manipulation is done in different ways; some of it which are:

Alignment of Text

Text alignment is achieved in four (4) different ways based on an individual purpose of usage:

- **Left Alignment:** By default, all texts are located at your left-hand side; for any reason it is not so, simply click on the arrow indication to return it to your left-hand side or you can highlight it for specialization in a situation where there is more than one line of text. It is also used for heading and footer.

Note: In left alignment, only the left-hand edge will be aligned on the same lines. You can also use **Ctrl + L** as the left alignment shortcut.

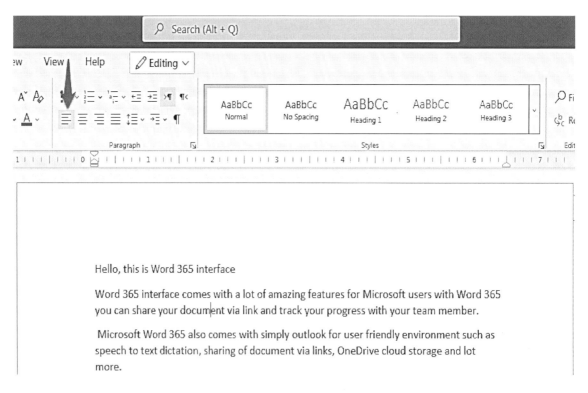

- **Right Alignment:** Right alignment is used majorly for special purposes such as addressing a letter. The arrow in the illustration below indicates the function command responsible for right alignment after you select your text.

Note: In right alignment, only the right-hand edge will be aligned on the same lines. You can also use *Ctrl + R* as the right alignment shortcut

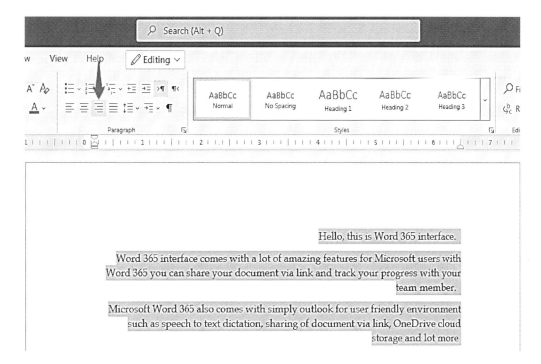

- **Center Alignment:** Center alignment positions your text at the middle of the Word interface; it's majorly used for headings. The pink arrow indicates the command function responsible for center alignment positioning; it is often used for a cover page, quotes, and sometimes headings.

Note: In center alignment, selected text will all be aligned in the middle altogether. You can also use *Ctrl + E* as the center alignment shortcut.

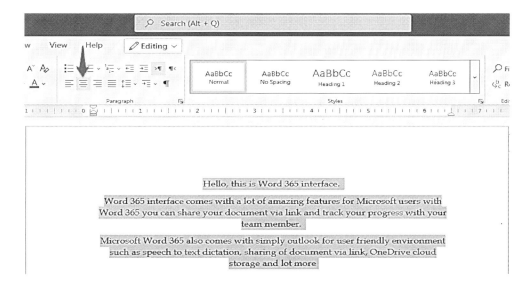

- **Justify Alignment:** Justified text gives your document clean and crisp edges so it looks well organized. Go to the home tab, select the **justify command** as illustrated below.

Note In justify alignment, all selected texts will be justified on the left and right-hand edges altogether. You can also use **Ctrl + J** as the "justify alignment" shortcut.

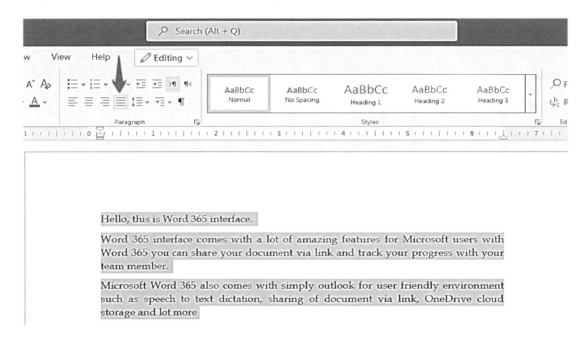

Bolding Text & Adjusting font size

To bold text, select the portion you want to bold, then go to the home tab, select the **B** icon which stands for bold, your text will be in bold format; make sure it is still highlighted then also go to font size as indicated below through the pink arrow, click on it or type the font size you want. You can use **Ctrl + B** as a shortcut to bold text.

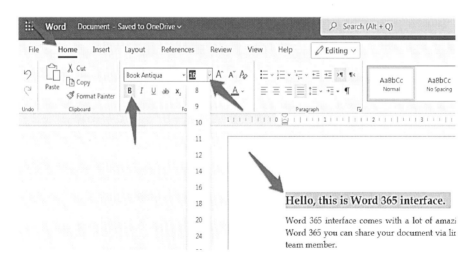

Underlining your text

Go to the home tab

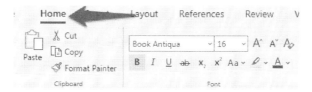

Make sure the text you want to underline is highlighted

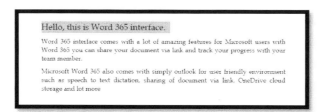

Select the **underlined icon (U)**

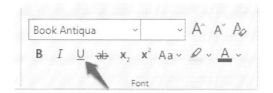

Your highlighted text will become underlined

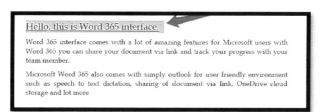

Italicizing your text

Go to the "home tab", select the text to be italicized by highlighting it with your mouse

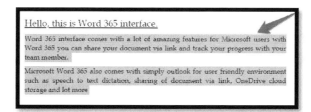

- Go to the "Font ribbon tab" beside your bold icon (**B**), click on **the italic icon (*I*)**

- Then, your highlighted text will become italicized

Selecting Text

You can select text with your mouse by left-clicking and simultaneously dragging through the text you want to select. Your arrow keys can also perform the task by holding the shift key and pressing the arrow key in the direction you want (if it is forward highlighting you want, click on the forward arrow key without leaving your shift key).

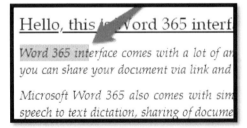

Moving & Copying Text

Moving & copying of text, highlight on the text to be moved

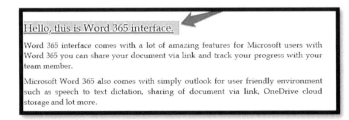

Left-click and hold, simultaneously drag your mouse on the highlighted text and drag it to anywhere you want it to be. In this illustration, drag beside the last line, then drop it.

Word 365 interface comes with a lot of amazing features for Microsoft users with Word 365 you can share your document via link and track your progress with your team member.

Microsoft Word 365 also comes with simply outlook for user friendly environment such as speech to text dictation, sharing of document via link, OneDrive cloud storage and lot more. Hello, this is Word 365 interface.

Changing the font color of your text

To change the look of your text, highlight your text

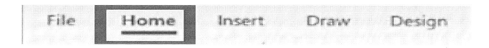

If your Word 365 interface is not on the "home tab" as its default display, simply go to the "home tab" and click on it

File   Home   Insert   Draw   Design

Below the "home tab", select "font color" which is identified by a capital letter A underlined with a red stroke as illustrated with an arrow sign below. Are we together? Right let us continue

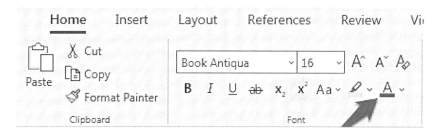

Remember that your text is still selected (highlighted), once you click on "font color", your highlighted text will change to red color.

Hello, this is Word 365 interface.

Choosing more color

You can also click the little arrow beside the "font color" to select your preferred choice, if not found check below for "more colors"

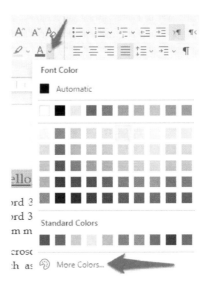

You can also decide to change the *"font style"* known as *"font name"* by selecting *"home tab"*, check on the little arrow beside your current font, dropdown options will be displayed, you can select your preferred choice, but for similarity and understanding purpose select *"Calibri Light (Headings)"*

Your highlighted text will take effect immediately

Before

Hello, this is Word 365 interface.

After

Hello, this is Word 365 interface.

Speaking, not Typing Words

Microsoft Word 365 comes with many added features, one of which is the "Dictate tool" which makes keyboard typing less needed due to time consumption and speaking more needed due to time utilization.

How to use Dictate tools

Go to the *"Home tab"*

At your right-hand side, you will see *"Dictate",* click on it and two options will appear to you *"Dictate"* & *"Transcribe",* select *"Dictate"*

Then, you can start your speech to text typing. Make sure you have an internet connection and the illustrated speaker is turned on from a white icon to a red icon

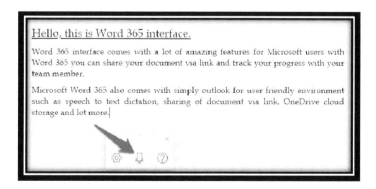

Applying Text Effects to Texts

- Highlight your text

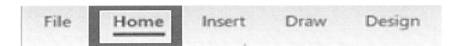

- In the "Home tab"

- Within your "Font ribbon", you will see "text effects", click on the drop-down arrow

- Select your preferred text effect template and click on it, your text will have the same effect of the format immediately

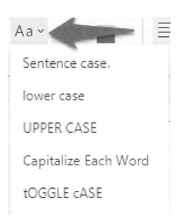

Quick Ways to Handle Case or Capitalization

Change case is a tool for transforming text from small letters to capital letters or a mixture of both with other preferred options. Cases are divided into five (5) segments which are:

- **Sentence case:** Sentence case only capitalizes the first letter of every new paragraph, it is also applicable after a statement ends with a full stop, the next first letter only will be capitalized. To apply sentence case, highlight your text, under the "home tab"

Locate "font ribbon" and select "change case" identified by a capital letter A and a small letter a. Pick "Sentence case"

Then, your text will take effect immediately. Note that every first letter in every paragraph and a new sentence are all in capital letters only, which might affect other words in a statement that should start with a capital letter by default. For example, take a look at the illustration below.

In the first line second paragraph, "Microsoft" carries a small letter 'm' which should always be in capital, not a small letter; that is why it is underlined with a red line, indicating it has a mistake. Right-clicking on the word "Microsoft" will give you the right spelling.

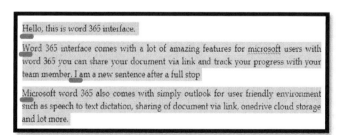

- **Lower case:** Lower case makes every word be in a small letter. To apply lower case, highlight the portion you want to effect lower case into, for this illustration, let's highlight all the text

Go to the "Home tab"

Locate "font ribbon" and select "change case". Pick "lower case"

Then, it will take effect immediately on your text. Note that all the text including the first letter of every paragraph will reflect lower case by default

hello, this is word 365 interface.

word 365 interface comes with a lot of amazing features for microsoft users with word 365 you can share your document via link and track your progress with your team member. i am a new sentence after a full stop

microsoft word 365 also comes with simply outlook for user friendly environment such as speech to text dictation, sharing of document via link, onedrive cloud storage and lot more.

- **Upper case:** Upper case is used to capitalize words. This is majorly used for headings or a title that reflect what a bunch of words represent. To apply upper case, kindly highlight your text

hello, this is word 365 interface.

word 365 interface comes with a lot of amazing features for microsoft users with word 365 you can share your document via link and track your progress with your team member. i am a new sentence after a full stop

microsoft word 365 also comes with simply outlook for user friendly environment such as speech to text dictation, sharing of document via link, onedrive cloud storage and lot more.

Go to the "Home tab"

Locate "font ribbon" and select "change case". Pick "upper case"

Then, it will take effect on your text immediately. Note all text will be capitalized by default

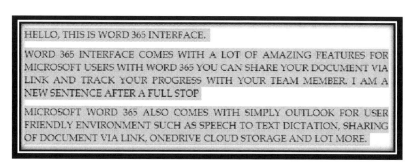

- **Capitalize each word:** this is used to capitalize each word in a sentence. To apply this, highlight all your text or the specific one you want it to affect; based on this guide we will be highlighting all, after highlighting all

Go to the "Home tab"

Locate "font ribbon" and select "change case", pick "Capitalize each word"

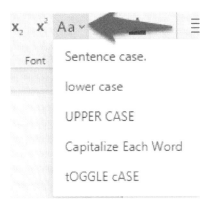

Then, it will take effect immediately on your text. Note all first words will be capitalized by default.

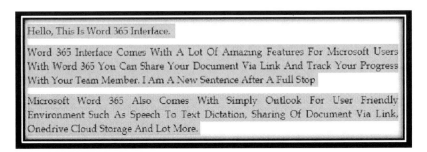

- **Toggle word:** Toggle word is the opposite of "capitalize each word". In the toggle word, every first letter of a paragraph or a letter of a new sentence is in small letters while others are in capital letters. To apply toggle word, simply highlight all your text as usual

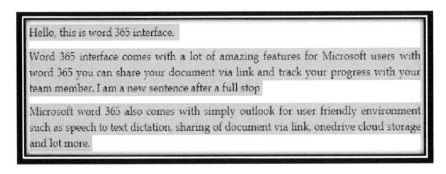

Go to the "Home tab"

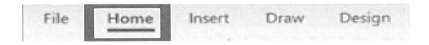

Locate "font ribbon" and select "change case". Pick "toggle case"

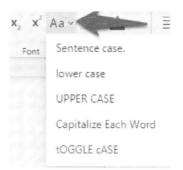

Then, it will take effect immediately on your text. Note that all first letters in each paragraph and a new text after a full stop will start with a small letter.

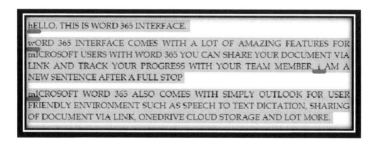

Entering Symbols and Foreign Characters

Symbol as its name implies is a sign or a tag used to list and categorize text. Symbols include a variety of options such as mathematical symbols, currency symbols, copyright symbols, and lots more.

- How to apply it; assuming we want to create a fruit list and the first fruit on the list is orange, point your cursor to where orange is located at the beginning of the letter "O" of orange.

- Now, go to the "Insert" menu" bar

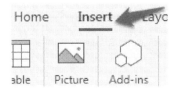

- You will locate your "symbols ribbon" at your right-hand side

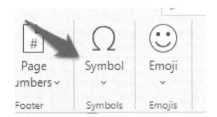

- Click on "Symbol's ribbon" to select your preferred choice

- Once selected, it will affect the cursor position, you can do the same to other items on the list

Creating Hyperlinks

Creating a hyperlink is a great feature of Microsoft Word that redirects you to the web for more info on the linked text. It is majorly used for references.

Linking a hyperlink to a web page

- First, select your text to be linked

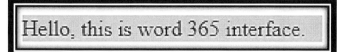

- Secondly, go to "Insert menu bar"

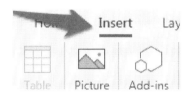

- By your right-hand side, you will see "link", click on it

- Once you click on it, a dialog box will appear (still make sure your link text is highlighted), if your text is still highlighted, it will show automatically on the *"Display text box".* Let us assume we want our link to redirect us into Microsoft website, simply type the website, www.microsoft.com and click the *"Insert option".* This is your result for Microsoft Word 365 web users.

For Microsoft Word 365 license users, this is your result, locate *"Existing file or web page"* by your left-hand side which is titled *"Link to",* select the first option *"Current folder"* under *"Look in",* once selected, look down, you will see another titled bar named *"Address"* enter your redirected address and press *"Ok".*

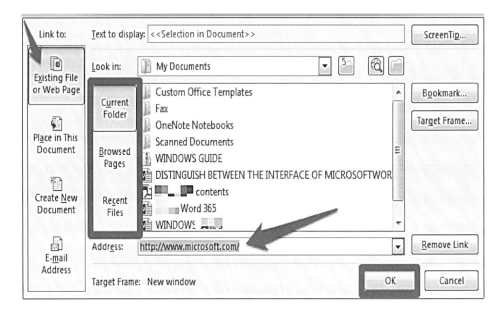

- Your highlighted text will be converted into a blue color with an underline

Hello, this is word 365 interface.

- To redirect into the Microsoft link, kindly press your "Ctrl key + Left-click". You will be redirected to the Microsoft website we inputted

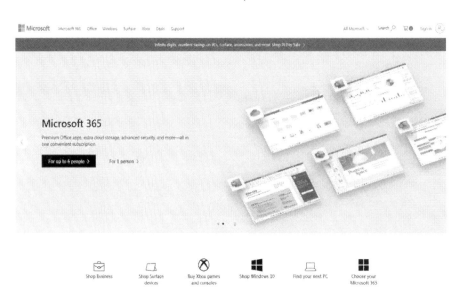

Note: this can be used on any other website of your choice.

Creating a hyperlink to another place in your file.

Note: By now, this feature of linking one file to another has not yet been included on Microsoft Word 365 Cloud version, it's still under improvement, and due to being a free version, some features are withdrawn and only available on Microsoft Word 365 installed application version which comes with a licensed product key that can be purchased from Microsoft official website (**www.microsoft.com**). So, this illustration is based on Microsoft Word 365 licensed version. Are we together? Alright, can we continue? Okay.

- Select the text you want to link into another file

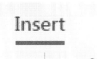

- Go to **"Insert"** in the menu bar

Insert

- By your right-hand side, locate the **"Link ribbon"** click on it

- A dialog box will pop up, select **"Existing file or web page",** then click on **"Current folder"** or **"Browsed pages"** to locate your file, once seen, select it as illustrated in arrow three, it will be automatically selected in the "Address bar". Above is our highlighted text named **"text to display"**, except you highlight it as explained above, it won't reflect on the above dialog box. Click "ok" to see the effect.

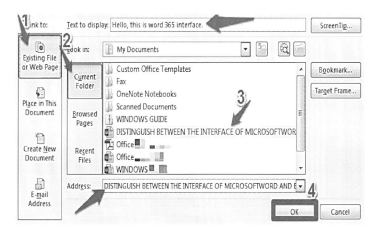

- Below must be your outcome, the highlighted text will change from its normal black color to blue or orange color, press Ctrl and simultaneously left-click on your mouse.

- A dialog box will be displayed warning you that hyperlinks might be harmful to your computer and data, that you should only click those hyperlinks you trusted such as the one you created yourself and other trusted ones. Click **"Yes"** to proceed

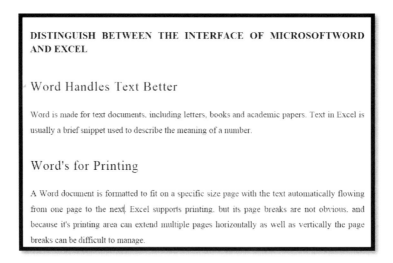

- Your linked file will be opened automatically

> **DISTINGUISH BETWEEN THE INTERFACE OF MICROSOFTWORD AND EXCEL**
>
> Word Handles Text Better
>
> Word is made for text documents. including letters, books and academic papers. Text in Excel is usually a brief snippet used to describe the meaning of a number.
>
> Word's for Printing
>
> A Word document is formatted to fit on a specific size page with the text automatically flowing from one page to the next. Excel supports printing. but its page breaks are not obvious, and because it's printing area can extend multiple pages horizontally as well as vertically the page breaks can be difficult to manage.

Creating an email hyperlink

- Select the text you want to link into another file

Hello, this is word 365 interface.

- Go to "Insert menu bar"

- By your right-hand side, locate **"Link ribbon",** click on it

- Link ribbon dialog box will pop up with multiple options, for this session we are going to create an email link. Don't let us forget our highlighted text at the top side that will still reflect itself as a means of reminding us that we highlighted a text before starting this process of creating an email link which is **"Hello, this is Word 365 interface."**

Below at your left-hand side is your "Email Address", click on it, you will be brought here, enter your **"Email address"** & **"Subject"** and **"Recently used email address"** (This is optional except you have been using email linking before all your previous activities will be displayed here). Once you are done filling, click "Ok"

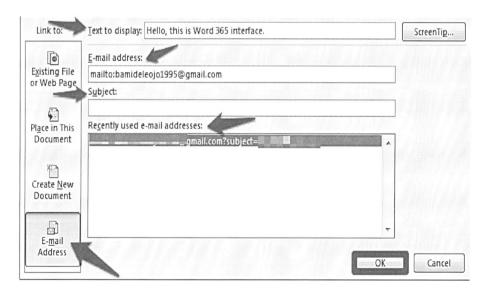

- Your highlighted text will automatically change from black to either blue or orange color as a sign that our process of creating a link via email is successful. To confirm, press Ctrl and simultaneously left-click, your cursor arrow pointer will change to the hand-click icon, then left-click to redirect you to your inserted details.

> Hello, this is word 365 interface.

Removing hyperlink

No effect without remedy, every action on Microsoft Word has a way of maneuvering it. To remove the hyperlink on your affected text.

- Select your affected text that has a hyperlink effect

- Go to "Insert menu bar"

- By your right-hand side, locate **"Link ribbon"** click on it

- The Link dialog box will appear, at your right-hand side as illustrated with the arrow below, click on **"Remove Link"** and hit **"Ok"**

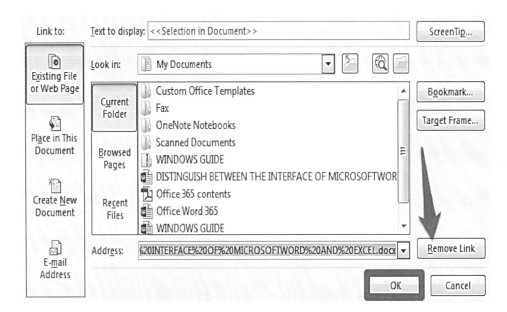

- Your highlighted linked text will automatically be removed from the hyperlink and it will become normal text with your default black color.

Notification

Notification gives more awareness about a newly added feature, which is one of the reasons software companies are all gradually moving online to reduce upgrading and different release.

How to rename your document

- Simply click on **"File"**

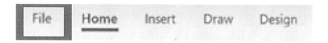

A dialog box will slide in by your left-hand side, look for **"save as"**, click on it

Note that there is no save button on Word 365 free online version, it AutoSaves itself online. Once you select **"Save as"**, a slide will appear beside the blue 'Save as' slide at your right, look for **"Rename"** and click on it.

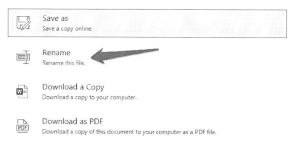

A dialog box will appear titled **"File Name"**, you can rename your document as you wish

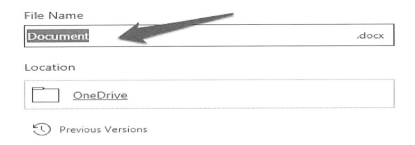

How to Save a document directly to your PC

- Go to "File menu"

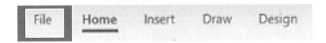

- Select "Save option"

- A dialog box will appear, select the location you want to save, name your document on the "File name box" and click "Save".

Note: saving your document on your PC is only for licensed users, Microsoft Word online free version saves automatically online on OneDrive storage.

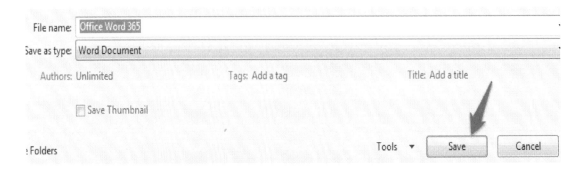

How to Save a document directly to your OneDrive cloud storage

- Go to "file menu"

- You will see multiple options, select "Save as"

- A dialog box will appear, you will see the "OneDrive" option, once you click it, your document will be saved online. If you have many folders on your OneDrive storage, you will be asked to choose the destination you want your work to be saved in, once done, hit "Save".

Where does my document go to?

Your document majorly comes to your PC storage or OneDrive cloud storage. OneDrive cloud storage serves as a physical hard disk drive, while PC storage is your system's hard disk storage. When you put your files and photos in OneDrive, they are always at your fingertip, no matter where you are. It is important to note that your files are private until you decide to collaborate by sharing your documents with your team and edit together in real-time by sending them a link and authorization access to edit.

How to upgrade your Microsoft 365 web free version

Upgrading is only recommended for office usage or personal usage that has more files than the normal 1 Gigabyte free storage capacity can contain in the long run. Once you are among the license subscribers, you will be informed depending on your plan.

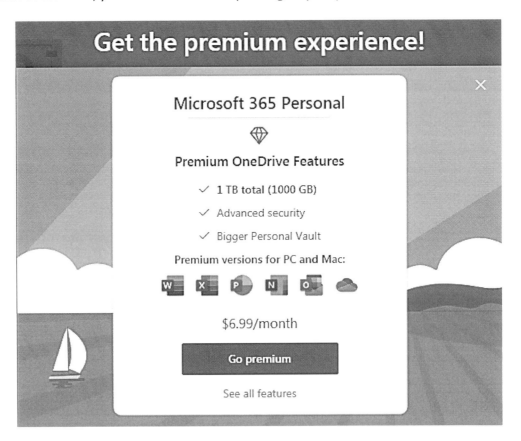

It is advisable to know what you want to achieve with an upgrade in order not to be charged unnecessarily.

CHAPTER THREE

SPEED TECHNIQUES WORTH KNOWING ABOUT

Undoing and Redoing Commands

Undoing and repeating commands are more of erasing and recalling words

To Undo Text

- After typing a bunch of text on Word 365

> Hello, this is word 365 interface.
>
> Word 365 interface comes with a lot of amazing features for Microsoft users with word 365 you can share your document via link and track your progress with your team member.

- You can press Ctrl + Z to undo your text, it will gradually backward your text

> Hello, this is word 365 interface.
>
> Word 365 interface comes with a lot of amazing features for Microsoft users with word 365 you can share your document via link

- Or you highlight the part to be removed and press **"backspace"** from your keyboard to remove it.

> Hello, this is word 365 interface.
>
> Word 365 interface comes with a lot of amazing features for Microsoft users with word 365 you can share your document via link and track your progress with your team member.

- You can also use Word 365 undo icon to backward your text, either way, your text will be undone. Simply go to the **"home tab",** which is your default display interface and by your left-hand side you will see your Undo icon. The first arrow is your undo icon facing backward while the second one is your redo icon facing forward.

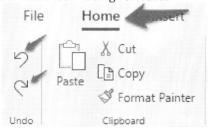

- After typing a bunch of text on Word 365

> Hello, this is word 365 interface.
>
> Word 365 interface comes with a lot of amazing features for Microsoft users with word 365 you can share your document via link and track your progress with your team member.

- You can press Ctrl + Y to redo your text, it will redo what you earlier undo

> Hello, this is word 365 interface.
>
> Word 365 interface comes with a lot of amazing features for Microsoft users with word 365 you can share your document via link

- You can also use Word 365 redo icon to forward your text only if it had been earlier backwarded. Your text will redo when you mistakenly remove or delete some text. To use the redo icon, simply go to the **"home tab"** which is your default display interface, by your left-hand side, you will see your redo icon the first arrow is your undo facing backward while the second one is your redo facing forward.

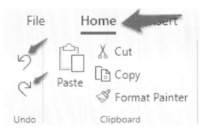

Zooming In and Zooming Out

Zooming In & Zooming Out is a feature of Microsoft Word that makes the Word interface clearer and more readable depending on the user's choice. You see that Microsoft Word is embedded with simplicity and flexibility.

- Go to **"View menu bar"**

- Under *"View menu bar"*, select *"Zoom percentage"*

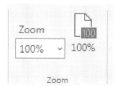

- Once you click on the little arrow beside the *"100%"*, dropdown options of Zooming In & Zooming Out will pop up, select your preferred choice and it will affect the entire interface of your current working document.

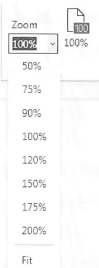

- The other *"100%"*, will return your zooming in & out to 100% default displayed zooming settings

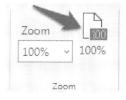

Viewing a File through More than One Window

Viewing of file through more than one Window creates the possibility to work in another Window and not affect your original Window.

Steps on how to apply it

- From your current opened document, go to "View menu bar" by your right-hand side

- It is advisable to purchase a license Microsoft Office installation software because the one online is still very much under progressive development; not all features are on Word 365 web base.

- Under the "view menu bar", click on "New Window" (which is known as document interface), your current document which is opened will be duplicated and named "document:1" by default, except you rename it. Another duplicated one will be named "document:2"

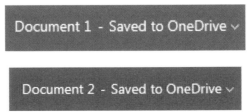

- Any changes in one will automatically lead to the same changes in the other.

Correcting Typos

Errors can be an omission in typing and as long as a human being is concerned, a computer can never use itself, but rather, human determines the behavior of a PC, this is the reason for misspelling and other mistakes made by PC users. Yet, Microsoft researcher team members look for a remedy to this issue, which leads to auto-correct in Microsoft packages.

Steps on how to enable auto-correct

Automatically, auto-correct is always activated on all Microsoft packages. Due to one reason or the other, if it is not, simply follow this simple process:

- Go to "Review menu bar"

- At your left-hand side on "Proofing ribbon", click on "Spelling & Grammar"

Spelling & Grammar

- Once you click on "Spelling & Grammar", auto-correct for error detection are shown one at a time as they occur in your document. You must deal with them one after the other (serially).

Entering Text Quickly with the Auto-Correct

Entering text quickly with the auto-correct command is often used for frequently used words such as an address, greetings text format, letter text template, and other text purposes.

Steps on how to go about AutoCorrect Command

- First, select the text you do use often by highlighting it

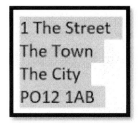

- Go to *"Insert menu bar"*

Insert

- By your right-hand side, you will see "Quick Parts", click on it and select *"Save Selection to Quick Part Gallery"*

Quick Parts

- Make sure your selected text is still highlighted, if not *"Save Selection to Quick Part Gallery"* will not be visible

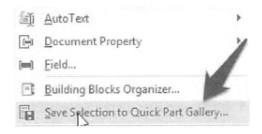

- After you select "Save Selection to Quick Part Gallery", a dialog box will appear with the name "Create New Building Block", there, you can rename the title of the highlighted text, and in the "Gallery" text box, select "Quick Part"

- Make sure this is what you inputted, if you followed and typed the highlighted text as instructed, for understanding purpose, leave the "Description", "Save in" & "Options" the way it is. Once done, press "Ok"

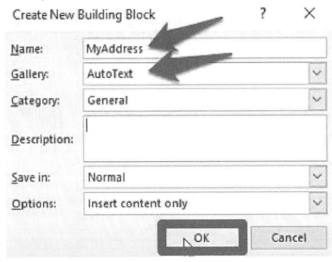

57

How do you assign a shortcut key to bring forth your auto text entry?

- Go to your "file menu bar" which is also known as "file menu"

- Under "file menu", select "Options"

- A dialog box will appear on your left-hand side, select "Customize Ribbon"

- By your right-hand side, "Customize Ribbon" features will appear, below it, you will see "Keyboard shortcuts", click on "Customize"

- Another dialog box will appear titled "Categories", search for "Building Blocks"

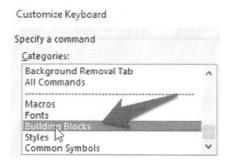

- Once you have located "Building Blocks", click on it, building blocks features will appear beside it at your right-hand side, locate "MyAddress"; based on my illustration on "Steps on how to go about AutoCorrect Command", I renamed the "Name" text box under "Create New Building Block" as "MyAddress" that is why I can locate it here. In case you name yours differently, search for it, or else, go back and follow how I did mine.

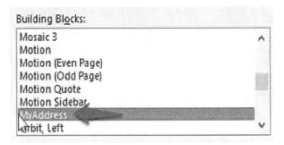

- Once selected, below it is a dialog box where you can assign a shortcut key to it, it is titled "Press new shortcut keys:"

- I will be inserting my preferred shortcut command which is "Ctrl+Shift+M". I will advise you do the same in order not to make any mistake, once you understand it you can repeat the process yourself.

- Once done, look at your left-hand side and click on "Assign"

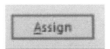

- Above the "Assign" option, your shortcut command will appear on a box titled "Current keys:" as against the previous title- "Press new shortcut keys:"

- Then, click on "Close"

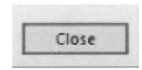

- Also, click on "Ok" on the "Customize the Ribbon and keyboard shortcuts" dialog box that leads to "Keyboard shortcuts"

- Now delete your highlighted text or open a new document to confirm our newly added auto text shortcut key.

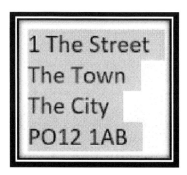

- Once you press "Ctrl + Shift + M" from your keyboard, your auto-text will reappear back automatically.

Tips

Practice makes perfect, try doing something different by changing the address and shortcut to suit your taste and run your newly added shortcut to see if you will get it correctly without following my exact text & shortcut.

CHAPTER FOUR

LAYING OUT TEXT AND PAGES

Paragraphs and Formatting

It is important to note that paragraphs in a document cannot be ignored as far as typing is concerned. A Paragraph has different clicking methods: Single-click, double-click, triple-click, and click and drag

- **Single-Click:** Single-clicking on a paragraph only makes the cursor point on a particular text in the paragraph.

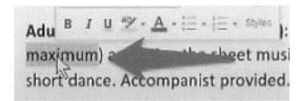

- **Double-Click:** Double-clicking in a paragraph highlights a particular text

- **Triple-Click:** Triple-clicking highlights the whole text in a paragraph as illustrated below

> It is important to note that paragraph in a document cannot be ignored as far as typing is concerned. Paragraph has different clicking methods: Single click, double click, triple click and click and drag

- **Click and Drag:** Click and drag selects within or beyond a paragraph depending on the user's preference.

> **Adult singers (18 years and older):** Please prepare an upbeat song (other than one from the show) and bring the sheet music with you.
>
> **Adult dancers (18 years and older):** Please prepare a short dance (2 minutes maximum) and bring the sheet music with you. Tap dancing is encouraged for the short dance. Accompanist provided.
>
> **Youth singers and dancers (9 to 14 years):** You do not need to prepare a song.

Paragraph Settings

Paragraph Settings help to finetune the layout of the current paragraph, including spacing, indentation, alignment, outline level with other features.

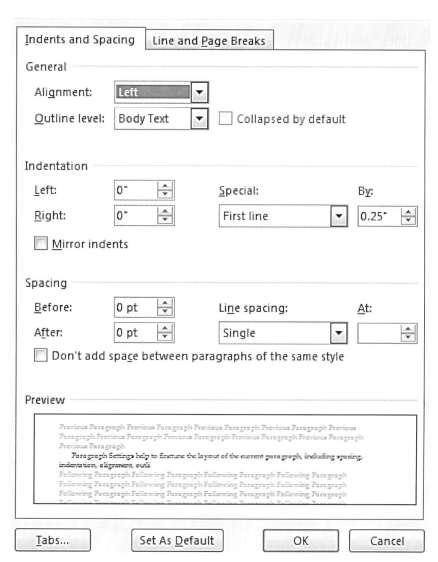

Page Formatting & Cover page

Page formatting is a tool that determines the outlook of your pages such as page margins, page orientation, page size, page columns, and lots more.

- **Page Margins:** Page margin is used to set the sizes for the entire document or the current section. Page Margins gives the privilege to choose from several commonly used margin formats or customize your own. Anyone you select will automatically affect your current working document.

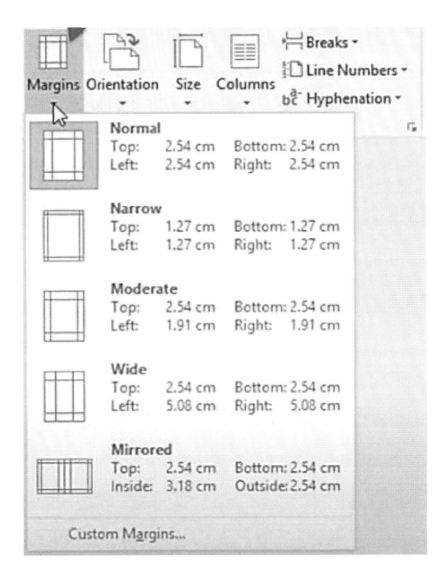

- **Page Orientation:** Page orientation determines the outlook of your page in portrait or landscape format. Anyone you select will automatically affect your current document.

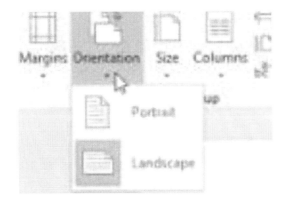

- **Page Size:** Page size comes in various forms but by default, A4 is the standard page size from Microsoft

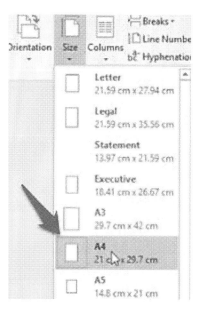

- **Page Columns:** Page columns give you the privilege to slit your text into two or more columns. You can also choose the width and spacing of your columns, or use one of the preset formats

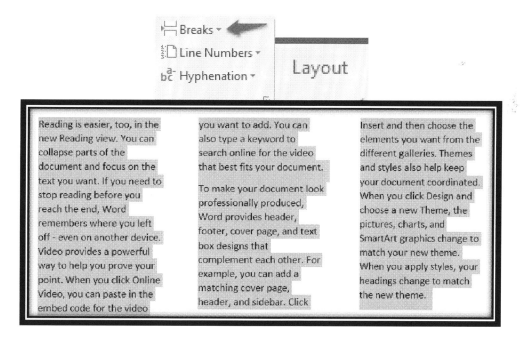

Above is an example of three columns, all you need to do is to highlight the area you want to make changes to, if you don't select it, the whole of your pages will be affected by the columns you choose.

Setting Up and Changing the Margins

Note: By default, Word document comes with default configurations, one of which is the normal margin.

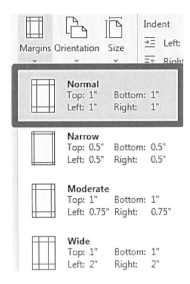

How to change your margins

- Go to "Layout tab"

- By your left-hand side, you will see "Margins"

- Once you click in, your default "Margin" settings will be on "Normal".

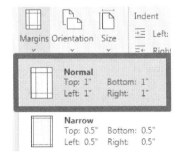

- Scroll through to select other desired options which will automatically affect your active opened document.

Note: Adjusting or changing of margin only affects your opened document, and it remains when you save the effect. For web users, you don't need to save, it automatically saves into your OneDrive cloud storage, while for offline users go to "file menu", and then you will see the save option. OneDrive storage is also available for offline users as long as you are connected to your Microsoft account.

Inserting a Section Break for Formatting Purposes

Before illustrating how to insert a section break format, it is important to know what "section break" is all about. Section break gives a separation between texts and sends the separated one into another page

- Point your cursor to where you want to set a section break

Video provides a powerful way to help you prove your point. When you click Online Video, you can paste in the embed code for the video you want to add. You can also type a keyword to search online for the video that best fits your document. To make your document look professionally produced, Word provides header, footer, cover page, and text box designs that complement each other. For example, you can add a matching cover page, header, and sidebar. Click Insert and then choose the elements you want from the different galleries.

Themes and styles also help keep your document coordinated. When you click Design and choose a new Theme, the pictures, charts, and SmartArt graphics change to match your new theme. When you apply

- Go to the "Layout tab"

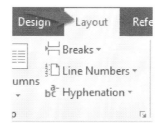

- Select "Breaks"

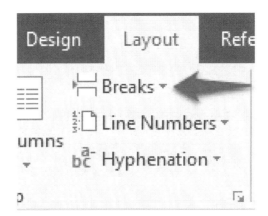

- Then, you can select "Page" to make your text have the section break effect

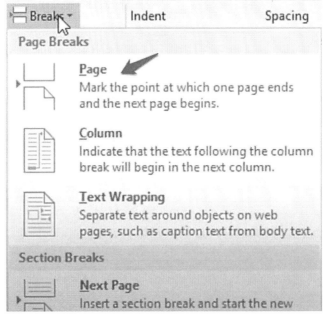

- Once you select "Page", the text where your cursor pointer is located will be automatically separated into a new page

Video provides a powerful way to help you prove your point. When you click Online Video, you can paste in the embed code for the video you want to add. You can also type a keyword to search online for the video that best fits your document. To make your document look professionally produced, Word provides header, footer, cover page, and text box designs that complement each other.

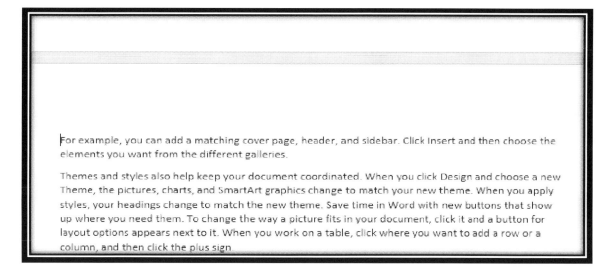

For example, you can add a matching cover page, header, and sidebar. Click Insert and then choose the elements you want from the different galleries.

Themes and styles also help keep your document coordinated. When you click Design and choose a new Theme, the pictures, charts, and SmartArt graphics change to match your new theme. When you apply styles, your headings change to match the new theme. Save time in Word with new buttons that show up where you need them. To change the way a picture fits in your document, click it and a button for layout options appears next to it. When you work on a table, click where you want to add a row or a column, and then click the plus sign.

There is also a shortcut to section break, once you set your cursor to the location you want to part, simply hold down your "Ctrl key" and hit "Enter key" from your keyboard. The point where your cursor is will automatically be parted into another page.

Cover Page

A Cover Page is a front guide of every documentation, project, brochure, and other documents which gives a summarization of what your content entails.

How to Insert a Cover Page on your Document

- Go to "Insert tab"

- At your left-hand side, you will see *"Cover Page"*

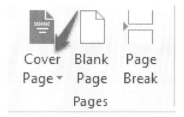

- Click in to see multiple built-in "Cover Page" templates, select your preferred choice

- Once you select your preferred choice, your selected cover page will occupy your front page

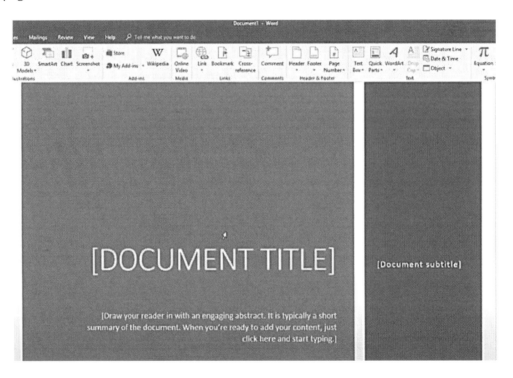

- Then, you can start editing the title page, the writeup below your title, subtitle, and other aspects depending on the template you selected

Indenting Paragraphs

- Go to the "Home tab" which is your default Word 365 interface

- At your right-hand side, locate the "Paragraph ribbon", you will see the decrease & increase indent

What is Decrease & Increase Indent?

Decrease Indent: Decrease indent moves your paragraph closer to your margin

Increase Indent: Increase indent moves your paragraph farther from your margin

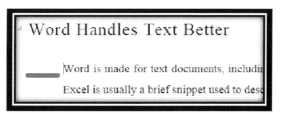

- Once you select increase indent, your paragraph moves to your right-hand side

> **Word Handles Text Better**
>
> Word is made for text documents, includi
> Excel is usually a brief snippet used to des

- And if you select decrease indent, your paragraph will move back to your left-hand side

> **Word Handles Text Better**
>
> Word is made for text documents, including
> usually a brief snippet used to describe the m

- Decrease indent & Increase indent are both used depending on what is required or what the user wants to achieve

Numbering the Pages

Page Numbering is a way of making your content arranged serially for orderliness and reference purposes.

How to Insert Page Numbering

- Go to "Insert tab"

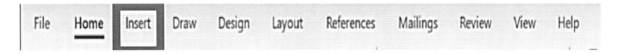

- At your right-hand side, you will see "Page Number" under "Header & Footer ribbon"

- Click on "Page Number", once you click on it, you will be given multiple options on where you want your page numbering to be positioned such as "Top of Page", "Bottom of Page", "Page Margins", "Current Position".

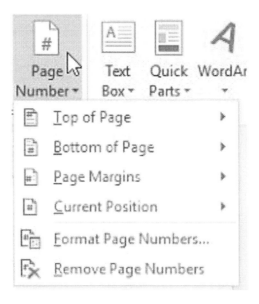

Or you can decide how you want your page numbering to look by clicking on "Format Page Numbers". A dialog box will appear for you to configure your Page Numberings such as "Number format", where you want to start effecting from, and lots more. Once you fill it, press "ok" to effect changes

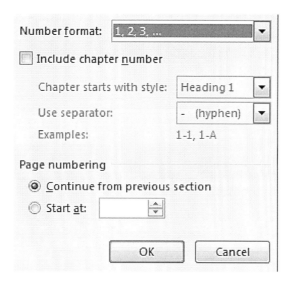

- Assuming you want the "Bottom of Page" option, click on "Bottom of Page" which is the normally used page numbering
- A dialog box will appear beside it, choose the middle numbering format

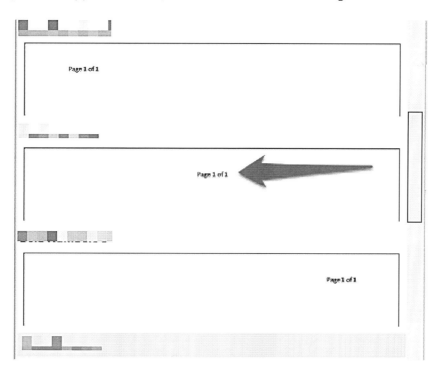

- By default, all your text will automatically be numbered serially

Remove Page Numbering

- Go to "Insert tab"

- At your right-hand side, you will see "Page Number" under "Header & Footer ribbon"

- Click on "Page Number", once you click on it, you will be given multiple options, look for "Remove Page Numbers", click on it, and every page numbering on your current opened document will be removed automatically

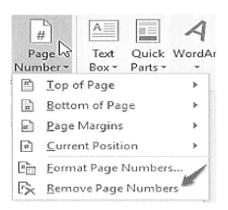

Putting Header on Pages

- Go to "Insert tab"

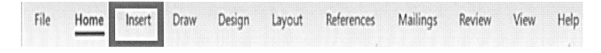

- At your right-hand side, look for "Header"

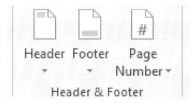

- A dialog box will appear, select your preferred alignment positioning

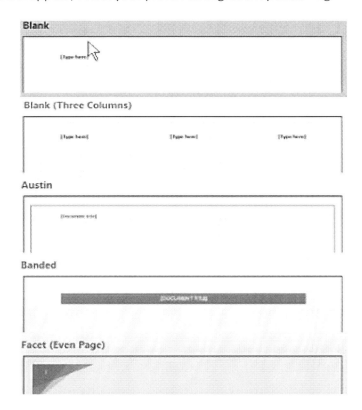

- Once done, you will be brought to your header editing edge to input your text

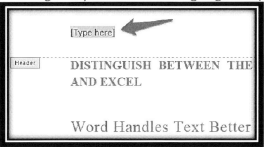

Note: You can also double-click on the top empty edge of your document to make use of the header format.

Removing Header from Pages

- Go to "Insert tab"

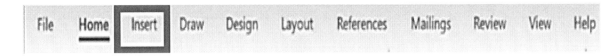

- At your right-hand side, locate "Header" and click on it

- A dialog box will appear below "Header" showing you header positioning, look down the list you will see "Remove Header". Once you click on it, your "Header" will be removed automatically

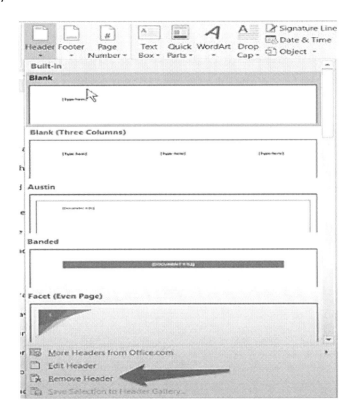

Putting Footer on Pages

- Go to "Insert tab"

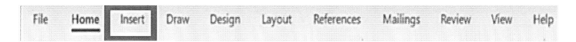

- At your right-hand side, locate "Footer" and click on it

- A dialog box will appear, select your preferred alignment positioning

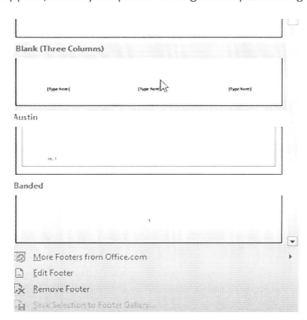

- Once done, you will be brought to your footer editing edge to input your text

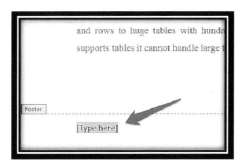

Note: You can also double-click below the page you want to insert the footer, you will be brought to an empty or footer format area where you can input your footer format.

Removing Footer from Pages

- Go to "Insert tab"

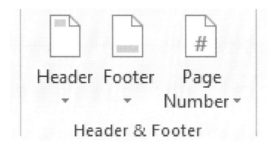

- At your right-hand side, locate "Header", click on it

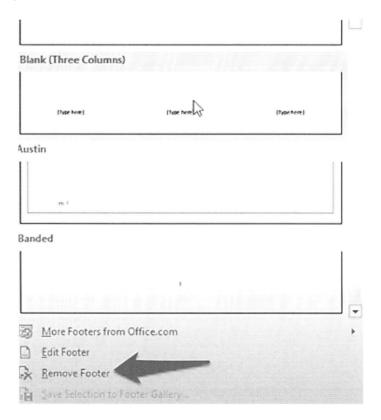

- A dialog box will appear below "Footer" showing you footer positioning, look down the list, you will see "Remove Footer". Once you click on it, your "Footer" will be removed automatically

Line and Paragraph Spacing

Line and Paragraph determine how much space will be allocated between lines of text or between paragraphs. To apply the same spacing to your whole document, use the Paragraph spacing options on the "Design tab".

Adjusting the space between lines

- Go to "Home tab" which is Word 365 default displayed interface

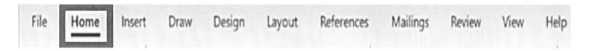

- At your right-hand side, locate "Paragraph ribbon", you will see the "line and paragraph spacing" icon

Paragraph

- Once you click in, you will be shown multiple options for line spacing between text or if your preferred choice is not in the list, click on "Line Spacing Options" to manually decide your choice

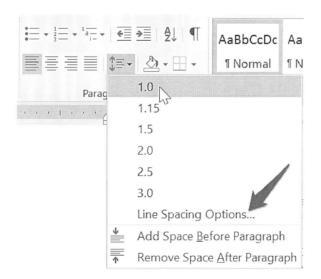

- If you click "Line Spacing Options", a dialog box will appear for you to decide your line spacing measurement "Before" & "After" once set to your preferred choice, hit the "Ok" button below

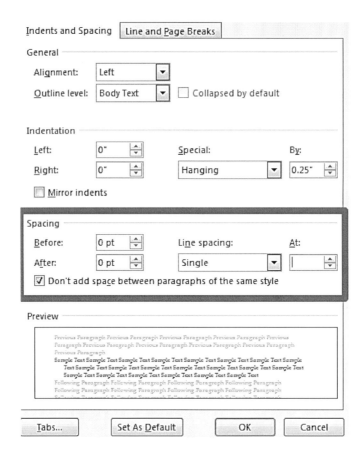

- It will automatically take effect on your opened document.

Adjusting the space between paragraphs

- Go to the "Design tab"

- Look at your right-hand side and select "Paragraph Spacing"

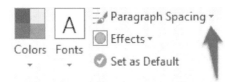

- A dialog box will appear displaying multiple options available for use

- Once you select your preferred choice, the effect will take place automatically on the entire document.

The difference between line spacing under "home tab" & paragraph spacing under "design tab"

Line and paragraph spacing under *"home tab"* adjust text manually, and it is done per paragraph, except you highlight the whole of your document.

Paragraph spacing under the *"design tab"* adjusts text automatically. This affects the whole of your document.

Creating Numbered and Bulleted Lists

Creating Bulleted Lists

- Highlight the portion of text that you want bullet list to take an effect on

- Go to the "Home tab" which is your display settings interface

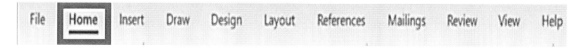

- At your left-hand side in the "Paragraph ribbon", the first tool you will see is the "Bullets list".

- In the "Bullet" list, select your preferred choice from your "bullet library" and click on it

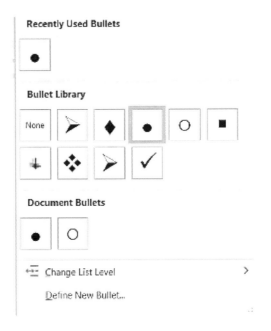

- It will automatically take an effect on your highlighted text

- Or you can click on "bullet list" and select your preferred choice on a free space in the document which also grants you access to be listing your item automatically.

- Once you enter an item and you click on "Enter key" from your keyboard, it will continue the bulleting automatically

Creating Numbered Lists

- Highlight the portion of text that you want the numbering list to affect

- Go to the "Home tab" which is your display settings interface

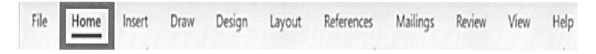

- On your left-hand side, locate the "Paragraph ribbon", the second tool you will see beside the bullet's icon is the "numbering list", click on it.

- You will be given many options to pick from, you can pick the numbering of your choice.

Note: The numbering library consists of number listing, alphabet listing, and roman figure listing, it's not designed for numbers alone.

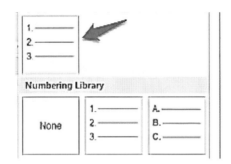

- Immediately you select the number list (you can pick your preferred choice), it will automatically take effect on your highlighted text.

- Or you can check "number list" and select your preferred choice on a free space in your document which also grants you access to be listing your item automatically.

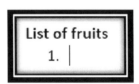

- Once you enter an item and you click your "Enter key" from your keyboard it will automatically continue the numbering.

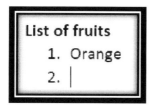

Constructing lists of your own

Either bullets list or numbering list, you can construct your own preferred choice of bullets list or numbering list

For bullets list

- Go to the "home tab" which is your default displayed interface

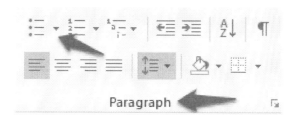

- At your right-hand side, you will see the "Paragraph ribbon", select bullets list

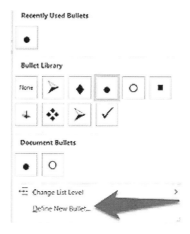

- Select "Define New Bullet"

- A dialog box will appear titled "Bullet character" which comes with design tools for your configuration bullet list, you can make your list as an image format by browsing through your PC to select your preferred image, or mathematical symbols and also set the alignment positioning. Once done with the settings, hit the "Ok" option.

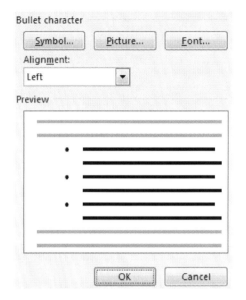

- Your selected image and other adjusted styles will take effect by default

For numbering list

- Go to the "home tab" which is your default displayed interface

- Around the middle area, you will see the "Paragraph ribbon", select the numbering list

- Select "Define New Number Format"

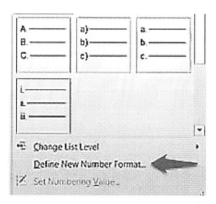

- A dialog box will appear titled "Number format", on the numbering list, you can't add an image or symbol, but you can determine your numbering format, be it alphabet format, roman figure format, or numbering format

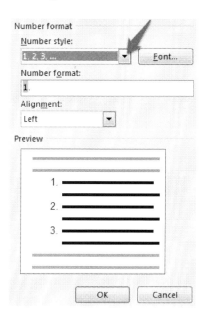

- Since the default numbering is numeric, let's choose the Roman figure to see the effect in a different way

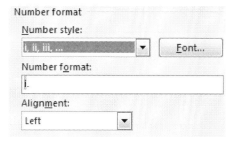

- Once selected, click "Ok"

- By default, the selected roman figure will take effect immediately.

Note: There are other numbering formats available; you can choose something different after trying what we just accomplished.

Managing a multilevel list

- Highlight the portion of text that you want numbering list or bullet list to affect

- Go to the "Home tab" which is your display settings interface

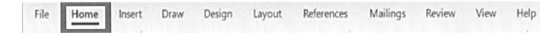

- At your right-hand side in the paragraph ribbon, you will see "multilevel list", as indicated below with a pink straight line

- Once you click on "Multilevel List", a dropdown of multilevel list options will appear

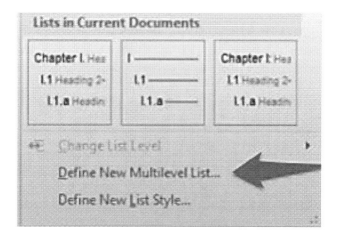

- Select "Define New Multilevel List" as illustrated above and a dialog box will appear named "Click level to modify", you will be instructed to set your multilevel list to your preferred taste.

The first numbering at your left is the first list item, the second is the second item till numbering 9 for the ninth item. Below is the "Enter formatting for number" option where you edit the dropdown (sub-list) item. Once done, click "ok".

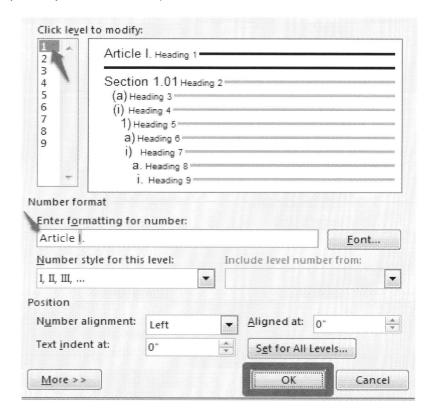

- Now back to our highlighted items

- Let make use of the "Numbering list"

- Select numeric list, double-click on it

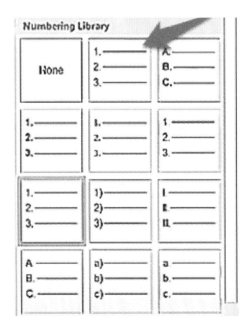

- Once it has been numbered, this will be the outcome of your highlighted items, but this is not what we still want to achieve

- Now, highlight only "Apple", "Blueberry", "Mango", "Watermelon", "Pineapple" (item 2 to 6 on the list).

- Then, press the "Tab" key on your keyboard located by your left-hand side, you will get this result; "orange" will have a sub-list below itself. We are getting closer but we can do beyond this, let's continue

- Now, highlight only "Blueberry" & "Mango"

- Then, press your "Tab" key located on your keyboard by your left-hand side, by default "Apple" will have a sub-list of items which are "Blueberry" & "Mango"

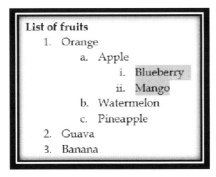

You can also play around it to achieve something different from my illustration. Now, you see how flexible working on Word 365 is.

Working with Tabs

Tab on your keyboard has been a wonderfully used key function, the beauty of it is that it can also be set to suit you.

- Go to your "Home tab"

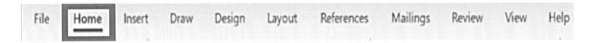

- In the "Paragraph ribbon or group", choose Paragraph Settings.

- Click the Tabs button.

- Set the Tab stop position, choose the Alignment and Leader options. By default, your tab stop is always on "0.5", you can also modify that and the positioning alignment with other aspects too, once done, click the "Ok" option and use your "Tab" key to test your text movement spacing.

Hyphenating Text

Hyphenation is used when a text runs out of space on a line. With hyphenation, text will automatically move down to the next line. When you turn on hyphenation, the text will hyphenate itself by default when running out of space.

- Go to "Layout tab"

- Under the "Layout tab", below locate "Hyphenation"

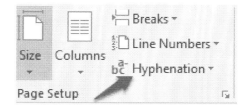

- Once you select "Hyphenation", dropdown options will pop up such as "None", "Automatic", "Manual" and "Hyphenation options"

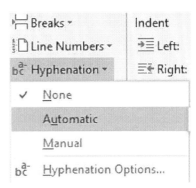

- Once you select "Automatic", it will take effect on your document

> Excel allows you to perform complex calculations where changing one number causes many other calculated numbers to change as well. Excel includes an extensive library of built-in formulas to help you perform those calculations.

Automatically and manually hyphenating

Automatic hyphenating keeps all texts hyphenated, while manual hyphenating gives its user access to edit how text should be hyphenated.

All About Styles

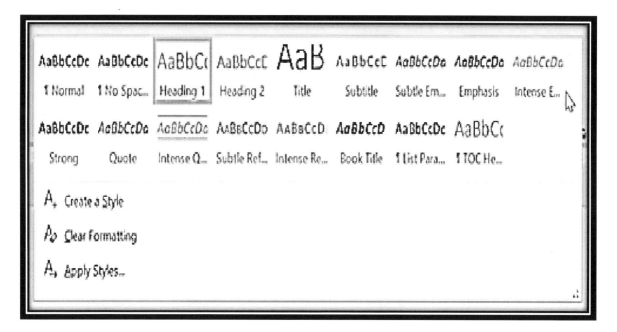

Style is a predefined template used to differentiate between texts such as heading text from body text. Style comes with other options for creating a new style, clearing an existing format, applying styles, and modifying styles.

Style and Templates

Style as said earlier is a predefined template that comes with auto-installed font style, size, and color which makes it a template to be used when the need arises. Note that style, as the name implies is not only for designing text, it can also be used for creating tables of content, headings, and lots more.

Types of Styles

It is important to note that one style is different totally from another with its unique name.

Paragraph styles

These styles control the appearance of a text in paragraph sections and allow you to edit large sections of text. A paragraph style may contain format settings for character style, it's also the overall design of a paragraph. The paragraph style Standard is usually preset for the entire text. Paragraph styles format Indents, and spacings, Line and page breaks, borders and shading, lists, tabs, all character attributes.

Character styles

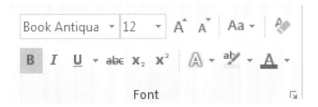

Character style is the appearance of text based on individual choice and is mostly used to format text sections such as highlighting words. Character styles do not format the entire paragraph, but rather, format font, font size, font color, bold, italic, or underlined markings, and so on.

Table styles

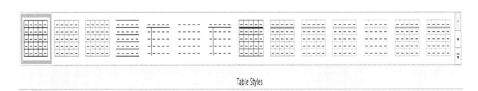

Table styles determine the formatting outlook of your table in terms of individual choice and the purpose of usage can be for creating a calendar, scoring list, items, and lots more.

List styles

List styles in Word format give the appearance that best suits the user, such as importing an image as 'list style', formatting of bulleted lists, formatting of numbered lists, indents, and lots more.

What are the advantages of Word styles when formatting a text?

Preset as well as custom styles make it easier to work on a text document with simplicity and flexibility. This is mostly visible while editing complex documents. Primarily, manual formatting seems easier and quicker, but for longer texts, it's more effective to use Word styles instead of frequently formatting text sections separately. The advantages of using styles in Word are:

- Adaptability
- Simplicity
- Continuity
- Efficiency
- Navigation
- Outlining

Applying Styles to Text and Paragraphs

- Highlight the text to be altered

- Go to the "Home tab" which is your default displayed Word 365 interface

- At your right-hand side, second to the last, you will see the "Styles" ribbon

- Select one of the styles above, you can also click on the dropdown arrow to view other styles, let's assume we choose "Heading 1"

- Your highlighted text will be converted to the selected style which is "Heading 1"

Word's for Printing

A Word document is formatted to fit on a specific size page with the text automatically flowing from one page to the next. Excel supports printing, but its page breaks are not obvious, and because it's printing area can extend multiple pages horizontally as well as vertically the page breaks can be difficult to manage.

- You can also do something similar to your paragraph by also highlighting it

Word's for Printing

A Word document is formatted to fit on a specific size page with the text automatically flowing from one page to the next. Excel supports printing, but its page breaks are not obvious, and because it's printing area can extend multiple pages horizontally as well as vertically the page breaks can be difficult to manage.

- Go to the "Home tab" which is your default displayed Word 365 screen

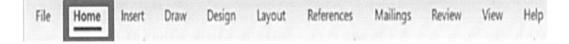

- At your right-hand side, locate the "Style" ribbon

- Now, let select the second heading which is "Heading 2"

- Your paragraph text will change to "Heading 2" styling

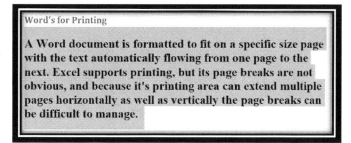

Experimenting with style sets

- Go to the "Home tab" which is your default displayed Word 365 screen

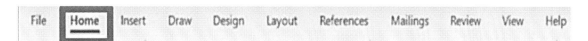

- At your right-hand side, locate the "Style" ribbon, click the dropdown arrow as illustrated below to see other options

- Below is what you will be shown, you can select your preferred choice, or create your preferred choice; that is how style is applied to text.

Creating a New Style

- Go to the "Home tab"

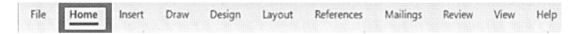

- At your right-hand side, second to the last ribbon, you will see "Styles", select the dropdown arrow as illustrated below

- Different options will be shown to you, among the options choose "Create a Style"

- Another dialog box will pop-up titled "Name", name it according to your choice

- Then, select "Modify" for more modification on your newly created style

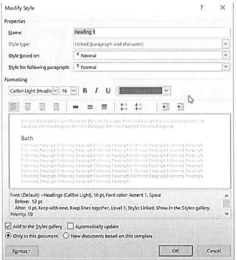

- Once done, click "Ok", your newly created style will be added to the styles list

Modifying styles

Modification is majorly in two ways, you either modify your existing style or your just created style, I just explained **"Creating a New Style"** and I illustrated how to modify it. Here, I will be demonstrating how to modify existing styles

- Go to the "Home tab"

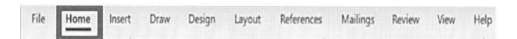

- On your right-hand side, you will see the "Styles" ribbon. Assuming we want to modify "Heading 1", right-click on it, a dialog box will appear with many options, select "Modify"

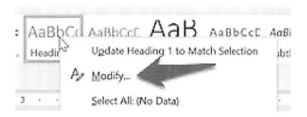

- Here is where your "Heading 1" modification which is one of the existing styles on your list is. You can modify the font style, font size, boldness, color, and many more. For simplicity and illustration purpose, click on "color" and choose "red" color, then click "Ok".

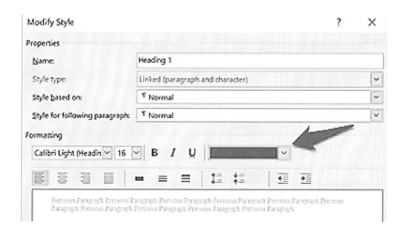

- Note the changes, "Heading 1" which is one of the existing styles will have the effect of color red which we modified it to

Renaming Styles

- Make sure your text that carries a style format is highlighted to recognize the specific style to be renamed

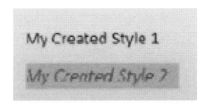

- Go to the "Home tab"

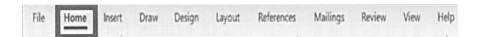

- At your right-hand side, you will see the "styles" ribbon

- Below the "styles" ribbon, click on the little arrow

- A dialog box will appear, indicating your selected or created style

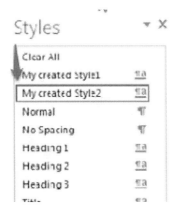

- Below the "Styles displayed box", select the last option titled "Manage Styles". Double-click on "Manage Styles"

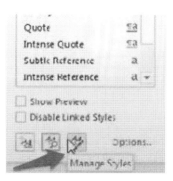

- Another dialog box will appear, make sure your style is highlighted as indicated in the illustration below, then click on "Modify"

- You will be brought to the modification box named "Properties". This is where your selected style can be edited, renamed, and your font size, style, color, alignment, and the rest can be worked upon. Once done hit "ok"

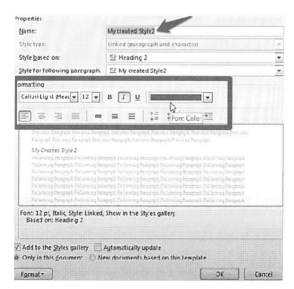

102

- Let's assume I only renamed my style from "My created Style 2" to "My 2"

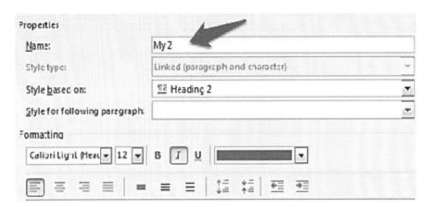

- Once done, click "ok"

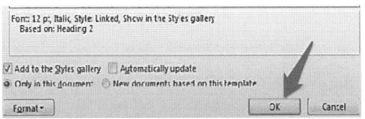

- Your previous displayed box titled "Manage styles" will also affect the new changes, also click "ok" to see your styles ribbon having the same effect

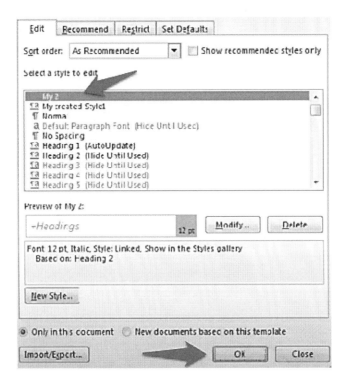

- Now, you will see the changes we made on renaming our style from "My created Style 2" to "My 2"

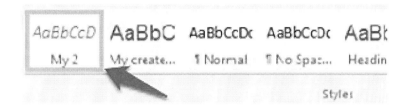

Applying Themes in Word 365

Themes is a multiple template design to suit individual preferred choice, its major purpose is to make Word interface stylish in a unique way. Themes, once selected, automatically changes the whole outlook of your content.

How to Apply Themes

- Go to the "Design" tab

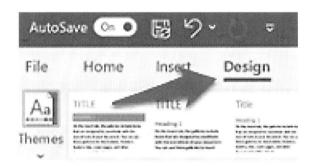

- At your left-hand side, select "Themes"

- Drop-down options of themes will be shown to you immediately

- Select your preferred choice. Each theme has its template style

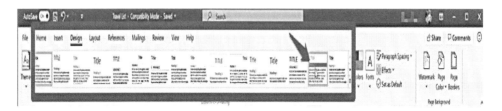

- Assuming we select the above theme where the arrow is pointed, all your headings will also be painted blue color, and any style that was there before will be changed.

CHAPTER SIX

CONSTRUCTING A PERFECT TABLE

Table Jargon

A table is a grid of cells arranged in vertical and horizontal order. It is also a great way to organize information within your document. Tables are useful for different activities such as the arrangement of description items, presenting text information and numerical data, text and image illustration, and lots more. In Word, you can create a blank table, convert text to a table, and apply a variety of styles and formats to existing tables.

Creating a Table

Creating a table has been for different purposes such as for grading, calculating, listing of names, items, and so on. To create a table, simply follow this procedure

- Go to the "Insert" tab

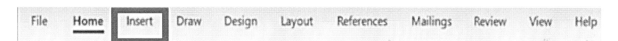

- Below the "Insert tab", you will see "Table", click the little arrow under to get the dropdown table options

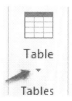

- Once you click on the arrow, you get the dropdown rows and columns which is known as "Table Grid". Select the numbers of rows and columns you want, then, click on the last selection of row and column to display it on your Word document

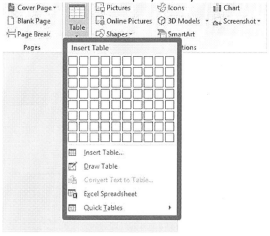

- Assuming we pick five rows and two columns, at the last selection, right-click on your mouse to effect it on your Word document

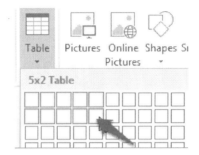

- Here is the result that you will have on your Word document

Styling your table

- Go to "Insert"

- Below the "Insert tab" you will see "Table", click the little arrow to get the dropdown table options

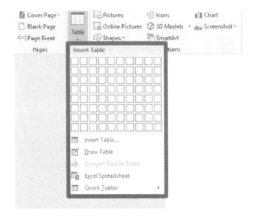

- Once you click on the arrow, you get the dropdown rows and columns which is known as "Table Grid". Select the numbers of rows and columns, then click on the last selection of row and column to display it on your Word document

- Once you have selected the number of rows (horizontal) and columns (vertical), then your table will be displayed in your Word document, let's assume it is four rows and three columns

- Click inside one of the columns, once you do this, it becomes active to receive text

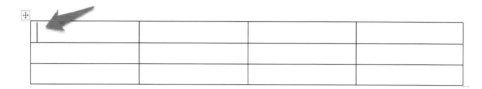

- Immediately, the menu bar will show "Table Tools" which are the "Design" table tab and "Layout" table tab, click on "Design table tab"

Design   Layout

- Under "Design", you will see "table" styles which consist of predefined table styles to use, click on any colorful style to see its effect on your table

Table Styles

- You can also click on the dropdown arrow on your right-hand side to view other table options

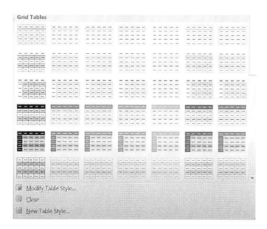

- Once selected, your created table will be transformed into the predefined template

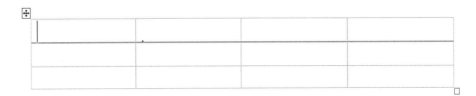

Note: **"Table Tools"** only show up whenever the table cell is active.

Entering Text and Numbers in your Table

- Go to the "Insert" tab

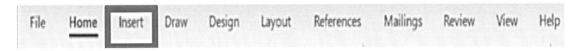

- Below the "Insert tab", you will see "Table", click the little arrow to get the dropdown table options

- Once you click on it, you get the "Table Grid", select the numbers of rows and columns you want, then click on the last selection of row and column to display it on your Word document

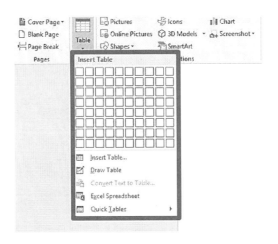

- Once you have selected the number of rows (horizontal) and columns (vertical), then your table will be displayed in your Word document. Assuming it is three rows and five columns, place your mouse cursor on the table to type your text and number

- Then, start typing your words inside

Number	Text	
1	One	
2	Two	
3	Three	
4	Four	

Adding additional rows and columns

- Go to "Insert tab"

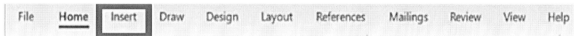

- There, you will see "Table", click the little arrow to get the dropdown options

- Once you click on "Table", you get the "Table Grid", select the numbers of rows and columns you want, then click on the last selection of row and column to display it on your Word document

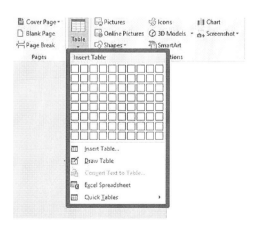

- Once you select the number of rows and columns and you have inputted your texts, there is a possibility of needing an additional table to continue your content, simply place your cursor at the edge of your table as illustrated below.

Position	Type	Location
Computer Engineer	Full-time, two months	Clearwater
Software Developer	Full-time, open-ended	Tampa
UI Designer	Part-time, two months	St. Petersburg

- Once you see the plus sign (+), click on it, another empty single row and column will be created

Position	Type	Location
Computer Engineer	Full-time, two months	Clearwater
Software Developer	Full-time, open-ended	Tampa
UI Designer	Part-time, two months	St. Petersburg

- You can then fill up the empty rows and columns with your desired text

Position	Type	Location
Computer Engineer	Full-time, two months	Clearwater
Project Assistant	Full-time, three months	Coral Springs
Software Developer	Full-time, open-ended	Tampa
UI Designer	Part-time, two months	St. Petersburg

How to use Autofit on Table

Before we go into how to use autofit, what is autofit all about? Autofit is a predefined feature that gives your table the privilege to fit automatically to the text length. How do we use autofit?

- Simply go to "Insert"

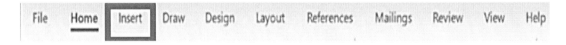

- Below "Insert", you will see "Table", click the little arrow to get the dropdown table options

Table

Tables

- Once you click on "Table", you get the "Table Grid

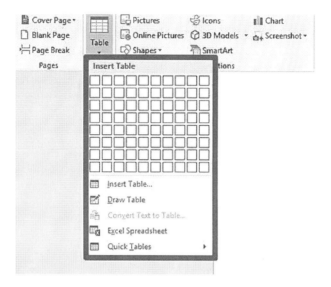

- Create the number of rows and columns for your table, then select it, once it appears on your Word document, you can type your text into it. For us to see how "Autofit" works, I will use my previous table to illustrate "Autofit"

Position	Type	Location
Computer Engineer	Full-time, two months	Clearwater
Project Assistant	Full-time, three months	Coral Springs
Software Developer	Full-time, open-ended	Tampa
UI Designer	Part-time, two months	St. Petersburg

- Once you click any part of your table, a little plus (+) sign will appear on your left-hand side, click on it

Position	Type	Location
Computer Engineer	Full-time, two months	Clearwater
Project Assistant	Full-time, three months	Coral Springs
Software Developer	Full-time, open-ended	Tampa
UI Designer	Part-time, two months	St. Petersburg

- Your table will be automatically highlighted

Position	Type	Location
Computer Engineer	Full-time, two months	Clearwater
Project Assistant	Full-time, three months	Coral Springs
Software Developer	Full-time, open-ended	Tampa
UI Designer	Part-time, two months	St. Petersburg

112

- Then, look above, you will see "Table Tools" appearing since your table is active. "Table Tools" comes with two options "Design" and "Layout"

- Select "Layout". Under "Layout", look for "Autofit"

- Click on "Autofit" and choose the first option which is "Autofit Contents", once you click on "Autofit Contents"

- Your table will automatically resize to your text contents size, you can compare the previous table and the recent "Autofit" to see the changes in size

Position	Type	Location
Computer Engineer	Full-time, two months	Clearwater
Project Assistant	Full-time, three months	Coral Springs
Software Developer	Full-time, open-ended	Tampa
UI Designer	Part-time, two months	St. Petersburg

Aligning your table positioning

- Simply go to "Insert tab"

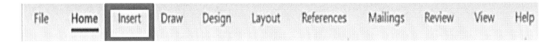

- Below "Insert", you will see "Table", click the little arrow to get the dropdown options

- Once you click on "Table", you get the "Table Grid", select the numbers of rows and columns you want to work with, then click on the last selection of rows and column to display it on your Word document

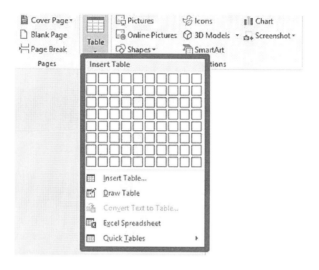

- Once it appears on your Word document, you can type your text into it. For us to see how to align a table, I will use my previous table to illustrate how to align your table

Position	Type	Location
Computer Engineer	Full-time, two months	Clearwater
Project Assistant	Full-time, three months	Coral Springs
Software Developer	Full-time, open-ended	Tampa
UI Designer	Part-time, two months	St. Petersburg

- Once you click any part of your table, a little plus (+) sign will appear on your left-hand side, click it

Position	Type	Location
Computer Engineer	Full-time, two months	Clearwater
Project Assistant	Full-time, three months	Coral Springs
Software Developer	Full-time, open-ended	Tampa
UI Designer	Part-time, two months	St. Petersburg

114

- All your table will be automatically highlighted

Position	Type	Location
Computer Engineer	Full-time, two months	Clearwater
Project Assistant	Full-time, three months	Coral Springs
Software Developer	Full-time, open-ended	Tampa
UI Designer	Part-time, two months	St. Petersburg

- Then, go to your "home" tab

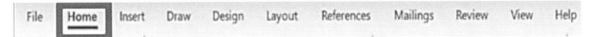

File | **Home** | Insert | Draw | Design | Layout | References | Mailings | Review | View | Help

- By your right-hand side under the "Paragraph" ribbon, there are four types of alignment; left alignment, center alignment, right alignment, and justify alignment. For understanding, we will be using center alignment to see the effect, because by default your table is on left alignment; simply click the "**center alignment**" which is the second alignment icon from your left

Paragraph

- You can press the shortcut, "Ctrl + E" on your keyboard, your table will be moved to the center point. Once you select center alignment as illustrated, here's what it will look like

For further information about any of these new jobs, or a complete listing of jobs that are available through the Career Center, please call Mary Walker-Huelsman at (727) 555-0030 or visit our website at www.fpcc.pro/careers.

Position	Type	Location
Computer Engineer	Full-time, two months	Clearwater
Project Assistant	Full-time, three months	Coral Springs
Software Developer	Full-time, open-ended	Tampa
UI Designer	Part-time, two months	St. Petersburg

To help prepare yourself before applying for these jobs, we recommend that you review the following articles on our website at www.fpcc.pro/careers.

Manual Method of Inserting a Table

- Simply go to your "Insert tab"

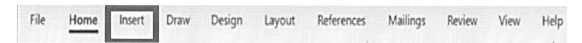

- Under "Insert", locate "Table" and click on it

- A dropdown option will be displayed choose "Insert Table"

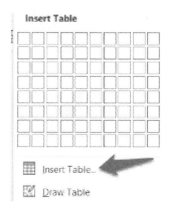

- Another dialog box will appear where you can insert the number of rows and columns to be displayed in your document. By default, manual insert for columns is five, while for rows is two, these can be adjusted at wish. You can also decide to choose "Autofit to contents", "Autofit to window" or "Fixed column width", then, hit "Ok" to effect your changes

- If you did not edit the manual insert table, below is the result you will get

How to delete columns and rows

Since I have shown you how to insert tables, now let us look at how to delete or remove that which was inserted. Assuming we have five (5) rows and seven (7) columns, and all we need is only four (4) rows and six (6) columns, simply click on row 7 on the table as an indication of where we want to delete

1.				
2.				
3.				
4.				
5.				
6.				
7.				

- Look above, you will see "Table Design" and "Layout", choose "Layout"

- Under "Layout" on your left-hand side, you will see multiple options on the "Rows & Columns" ribbon such as "Delete", "Insert above", "Insert below", and other options. Click on "Delete"

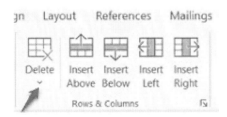

- A dropdown menu will be displayed, select "Delete Rows" from the options, your rows that was seven (7) in number will become six (6)

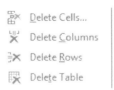

- This should be your result. **Note**, anywhere your cursor is within your table is where the delete will take effect from

1.				
2.				
3.				
4.				
5.				
6.				

How to Merge Cells in a table & Designing a table style

Beyond explanation, it is also important to understand the little element that the big element is made up of. "Cell" is the inputted part where your text and number are inserted into. So, why merge cells? Merging of cells is mostly needed for various reasons such as naming your table, constructing a calendar.

The month and year (for example, January 2022) need to occupy the first rows in a bold and large format to give a clear update on what the table is all about as seen in the image below

January 2022						
Sunday	Monday	Tuesday	Wednesday	Thursday	Friday	Saturday
						1
2	3	4	5	6	7	8
9	10	11	12	13	14	15
16	17	18	19	20	21	22
23	24	25	26	27	28	29
30	31					

Then, how do we merge cells?

- Since I have shown you how to insert tables, Let's assume we want to create something similar to the calendar format above. For us to merge our table, if you count the rows, you will notice it is seven (7) in number, while the columns are eight (8) in number including the heading (January 2022). This is also an opportunity to create a calendar with Office Word document. After creating your table, input the text and number in its various location

January 2022						
Sunday	Monday	Tuesday	Wednesday	Thursday	Friday	Saturday
						1
2	3	4	5	6	7	8
9	10	11	12	13	14	15
16	17	18	19	20	21	22
23	24	25	26	27	28	29
30	31					

- Then, place your cursor at the beginning of "January 2022"

January 2022						
Sunday	Monday	Tuesday	Wednesday	Thursday	Friday	Saturday
						1
2	3	4	5	6	7	8
9	10	11	12	13	14	15
16	17	18	19	20	21	22
23	24	25	26	27	28	29
30	31					

- Once your cursor is blinking at the beginning of January 2022, simply hold down "Shift key" on your keyboard with the "forward Arrow" at the right-hand side of your keyboard. It will be highlighting your first row, once your highlighting gets to the last row, release your hand from the "Shift & "Arrow keys" on your keyboard, below is where the highlighting of your rows should stop

January 2022						
Sunday	Monday	Tuesday	Wednesday	Thursday	Friday	Saturday
						1
2	3	4	5	6	7	8
9	10	11	12	13	14	15
16	17	18	19	20	21	22
23	24	25	26	27	28	29
30	31					

- After highlighting it, go to the "menu bar", click on "Layout"

| File | Home | Insert | Draw | Design | Layout | References | Mailings | Review | View | Help |

- Under "Layout" look at your left-hand side, you will see the "Merge" ribbon, click on "Merge cells"

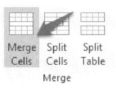

Merge Cells | Split Cells | Split Table

Merge

- By default, your highlighted row will be merged as one, you will also notice the column lines that separate the entire table is no longer applicable to the "January 2022" row

January 2022						
Sunday	Monday	Tuesday	Wednesday	Thursday	Friday	Saturday
						1
2	3	4	5	6	7	8
9	10	11	12	13	14	15
16	17	18	19	20	21	22
23	24	25	26	27	28	29
30	31					

Designing a table style

- Now, to make it look fashionable, simply click on "Design"

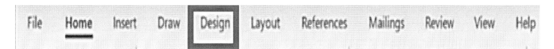

- Then select your built-in table template, you can click the little dropdown arrow for other options of your choice; remember we want it to look like the blue template shown earlier

- You will be shown other table design options, the arrangement might be different but the table design remain the same, once you select it, your table will possess the template

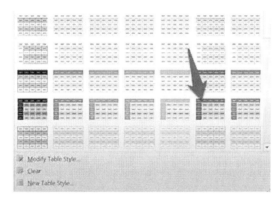

- Now, you see we are closer to what you saw earlier, don't forget to apply "Autofit Content" under "Layout" to make it look professional and similar to what I did, which I also applied into what you are seeing. You can revisit chapter seven to see how to apply "Autofit Content" to your created table

January 2022						
Sunday	Monday	Tuesday	Wednesday	Thursday	Friday	Saturday
						1
2	3	4	5	6	7	8
9	10	11	12	13	14	15
16	17	18	19	20	21	22
23	24	25	26	27	28	29
30	31					

- Now, let us do the final part, make sure your "January 2022" is highlighted. Simply to go your "Home tab" and under the "font" ribbon, select "**Bold**" if yours is not bolded. It is recognized with a **B** icon. Also, increase the "font-size" to "20" to get the same result

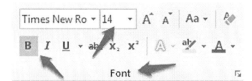

- Then, go to the next ribbon which is the "Paragraph" ribbon, select "center alignment" as illustrated below or you press the shortcut keys "Ctrl + E" from your keyboard to also get the same result

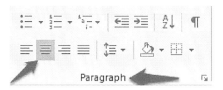

- Your highlighted text which is "January 2022" will move to the center, aligned to the middle, and also increase in size only if it is still highlighted

January 2022						
Sunday	Monday	Tuesday	Wednesday	Thursday	Friday	Saturday
						1
2	3	4	5	6	7	8
9	10	11	12	13	14	15
16	17	18	19	20	21	22
23	24	25	26	27	28	29
30	31					

How to Split Cells in a Table

Splitting of cells means dividing a Cell into multiple cells. Splitting cells is the opposite of merging cells. We will be using our calendar table to illustrate how to split a cell in a table by following these procedures:

- Assuming we are splitting back "January 2022" that was merged, simply highlight "January 2022", and click on "Design" in the menu bar to change its blue displayed design to black & white which is the default table color (black & white has nothing to do with splitting) just for us to be able to see the changes on the splitting of cells

January 2022						
Sunday	Monday	Tuesday	Wednesday	Thursday	Friday	Saturday
						1
2	3	4	5	6	7	8
9	10	11	12	13	14	15
16	17	18	19	20	21	22
23	24	25	26	27	28	29
30	31					

- Once you change your table template back to black & white, as long as you followed the illustration that led to me adding a table template, you get this as your result

January 2022						
Sunday	Monday	Tuesday	Wednesday	Thursday	Friday	Saturday
						1
2	3	4	5	6	7	8
9	10	11	12	13	14	15
16	17	18	19	20	21	22
23	24	25	26	27	28	29
30	31					

- Note that I still highlighted "January 2022" since it's what we merged before. Also, note that you can also split other areas of your table rows and columns which I will be illustrating soon. To proceed with the splitting, simply go to "Layout" on your menu bar

- Then, select "Split Cells"

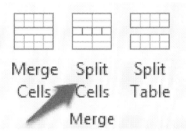

- A dialog box will appear, asking for how many rows and columns you want the highlighted area to multiply into. Note, your button might not be like the illustration below, depending on your operating system, therefore, don't be surprised by any changes you observe

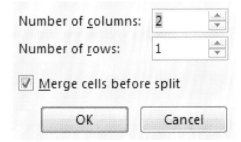

- Choose your preferred number, assuming we want to use the default numbering which is 2 columns and 1 row, your selection will reflect on your result and the highlighted "January 2022" will be moved to one cell since another cell has been created, but it will still maintain its alignment and other features format applied to it

January 2022						
Sunday	Monday	Tuesday	Wednesday	Thursday	Friday	Saturday
						1
2	3	4	5	6	7	8
9	10	11	12	13	14	15
16	17	18	19	20	21	22
23	24	25	26	27	28	29
30	31					

Moving columns and rows

It is possible to move your table around to any location on your document by simply following this simple step:

- For comprehensive understanding, let us use our created calendar table. As explained earlier, point your mouse cursor into your table in the next cell after number "31" as illustrated below, then, a plus (+) sign will appear at the top left corner, use your mouse cursor to hold it down and drag it to anywhere you want to place it within your document.

January 2022						
Sunday	Monday	Tuesday	Wednesday	Thursday	Friday	Saturday
						1
2	3	4	5	6	7	8
9	10	11	12	13	14	15
16	17	18	19	20	21	22
23	24	25	26	27	28	29
30	31					

Decorating your table with borders and colors

Borders are the lines that form table edges. With borders, you can decorate your table and design it to your preferred choice. How to decorate your table with borders and colors will be explained step by step below

- To save time because of the process of creating another table, we will be using our calendar table. Highlight your heading cell which is "January 2022" or you point your cursor into the "January 2022" row. Note you can use any cell, just for a well-ordered work, we will use the heading cell (January 2022)

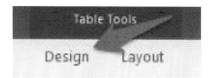

January 2022						
Sunday	Monday	Tuesday	Wednesday	Thursday	Friday	Saturday
						1
2	3	4	5	6	7	8
9	10	11	12	13	14	15
16	17	18	19	20	21	22
23	24	25	26	27	28	29
30	31					

- Then, the table options will appear named "Table tools", under it is "Design" and "Layout", click on "Layout"

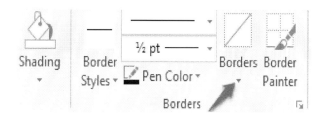

- At your right-hand side, locate "Borders"

- Click on "Borders" to select a different line style format to replace the default borders. For example, we could choose a triple line border

124

- We can also change the line weight to one and a half point ($1\frac{1}{2}$ pt)

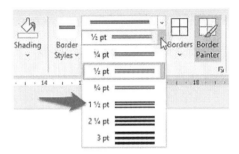

- We can also change the border color by picking the orange color

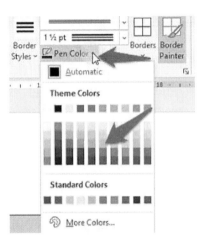

- Once your color has been selected, the "Border Styles", "Line Weight", "Line Styles" and "Pen Color" will have the effect of your chosen color. Note that your "Border Painter" is selected automatically

- Once your "Border Painter" is selected, your mouse cursor will change to pen cursor, simply place it on the line edge you want your triple line and color to affect. Note, if you place it wrongly, you will need to select "Border Painter" again

January 2022						
Sunday	Monday	Tuesday	Wednesday	Thursday	Friday	Saturday
						1

- But there is also another way out without having to click and wrongly place line edges; simply click on "Borders"

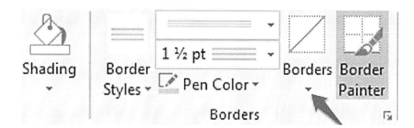

- Then, select what area you want your border to cover such as "Bottom Border", "Top Border", "Left Border", "Right Border" and so on. We will be clicking on "All Borders"

- Once "All Borders" has been selected, your created calendar table will be formatted on your active cell which is "January 2022" where your mouse cursor is pointing.

January 2022						
Sunday	Monday	Tuesday	Wednesday	Thursday	Friday	Saturday
						1
2	3	4	5	6	7	8

NOTE: If you want the remaining rows and columns to also be formatted, then, you need to highlight the entire table to perform such an operation.

- You can also add shade color on the background of "January 2022" by changing the white background. To do this, click on "Shading"

- Select your preferred color. For illustration, I will pick the gray color to achieve a color blend.

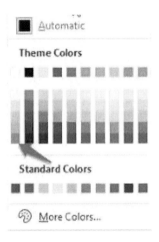

- Your outcome if you choose the same color with me, will be the illustration below

January 2022						
Sunday	Monday	Tuesday	Wednesday	Thursday	Friday	Saturday
						1

Exploring more on Borders

In continuation of ***"Decorating your table with borders and colors"***. It is important to note that there is also more to Border Style

- Still on our created calendar table illustration

January 2022						
Sunday	Monday	Tuesday	Wednesday	Thursday	Friday	Saturday
						1

- Click on "Design" table tools

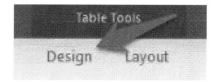

- At your left-hand side, you will see a dropdown arrow, click on it

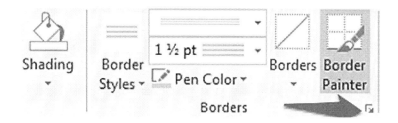

- You will be brought here, where all our formatted styles are reviewed and edited. It consists of "Borders settings", "Page Border settings" and "Shading settings". If you remember, previously, we choose an orange color, that is why you are seeing orange color and one and half width. Click on the "Shading" option

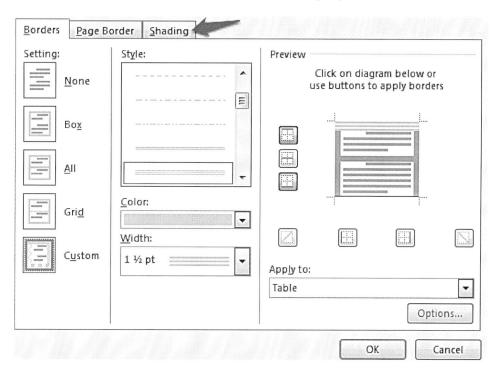

- Once you click on "Shading", you will be brought to this page, where you can set your "Shading Patterns", "Style", "Color" and "Apply to". Under "Apply to", select "Table", then click "Ok" to see the effect

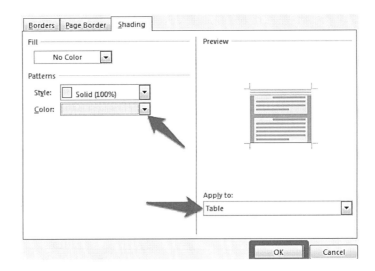

- Here is what your result will be if you do exactly as I did

January 2022						
Sunday	Monday	Tuesday	Wednesday	Thursday	Friday	Saturday
						1
2	3	4	5	6	7	8
9	10	11	12	13	14	15
16	17	18	19	20	21	22
23	24	25	26	27	28	29
30	31					

Using Math Formulas in Tables

This is the unbelievable part of Word; many thinks once you want to do any mathematical calculation you need to use other Microsoft products such as Excel to be able to do your calculation. Every Microsoft App has its uniqueness but can interchange some features within such other since all the applications are all Microsoft packages. Sooner or later, everything will come together uniquely, just as there is now "My Add-ins" that gives other apps the privilege to interact with the Word environment.

So, how do we use mathematical formulas in our table? Below is the step-by-step procedure on how to go about it:

- Create a table format as taught earlier, type the below information

Mick Scores	
Math	60
English	80
ICT	55
Physics	75
Total	

- Once done, click your mouse cursor directly to your empty cell which is where your total summation will be, make sure your mouse cursor is blinking on the empty cell for your summation

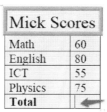

- Now, go to "Layout" in your menu bar, click on it

- Look at the last tool on your right-hand side you will see "Formula" with an "fx" icon, click on it

- A dialog box will appear, with a default formula "=SUM(ABOVE)"

=SUM, represent add up (+) your figures together. (ABOVE) represent add the numbers in the column above the cell you are in. (LEFT) represent add the numbers in the row to the left side of the cell you're in. (BELOW) represent add the numbers in the column below the cell you're in. (RIGHT) represent adds the numbers in the row to the right side of the cell you are in.

Your "Number format" represents your figure settings. For example, $100 can be $100.00 depending on how you want your number format to look.

Your "Paste function" is an added formula feature by Microsoft to perform more complex calculations by default. You can just click the "Ok" option to just perform your normal summing calculation.

- Your "Mick Scores" will be summed up automatically

Mick Scores	
Math	60
English	80
ICT	55
Physics	75
Total	270

How to move or drag a table

- Assuming we are using the "Mick Scores" table,

Mick Scores	
Math	60
English	80
ICT	55
Physics	75
Total	270

- Place your mouse cursor on any cell, mine was placed on the "total score 270", a little plus (+) sign will appear at the left side, use your mouse cursor to pin it down then drag it to any position on your document

Mick Scores	
Math	60
English	80
ICT	55
Physics	75
Total	270

How to enlarge or reduce your table

- Assuming we want to enlarge the "Mick Scores" table

Mick Scores	
Math	60
English	80
ICT	55
Physics	75
Total	270

- Click on any cell in your table, for illustration, I will change my mouse cursor from "Total Scores" to "Mick Scores" which is the heading. Once your mouse cursor is blinking in any cell you choose, you will notice additional features joint together with your table, one is your top left cross arrow which has been discussed, while the other is a "little white box" below your table on the right-hand side as indicated with a pink arrow.

Mick Scores	
Math	60
English	80
ICT	55
Physics	75
Total	270

- Once you hold down the "little white box" with your mouse cursor, drag it down to enlarge it or upward to reduce it.

Mick Scores	
Math	60
English	80
ICT	55
Physics	75
Total	270

Enlarged

Mick Scores	
Math	60
English	80
ICT	55
Physics	75
Total	270

Reduced

Using a picture as the table background

- Let's create an empty table as you were taught earlier by checking on the "Insert" tab to locate your "Table" and create columns and rows

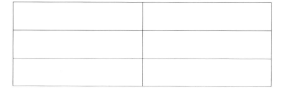

- Next, insert text inside your cells, type "Island", "Animal" and "Nature" on each cell by your left-hand side

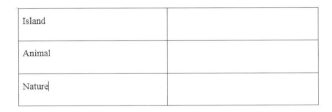

Island	
Animal	
Nature	

- Now, place your mouse cursor in the first empty cell on the right side

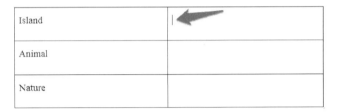

Island	←
Animal	
Nature	

- Make sure your cursor is blinking, then go to your "Insert tab"

- In the "Insert tab", you will see the "Illustrations" ribbon, select "Pictures" which is the first option

- You will be directed into your PC storage to locate the location of your picture manually, after getting it, then select it and click on the "Insert button" below. Note, you can also get the same image I used as long as you are running Microsoft operating system just go to your "Picture's folder"

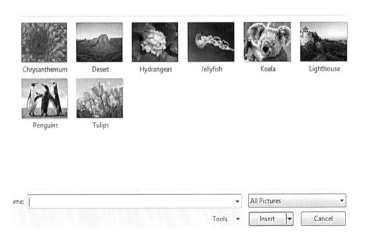

133

- Once your picture has been selected and inserted, the cell where your mouse cursor is blinking will display the picture. Note your picture might increase the table size, simply reduce it by 'reducing the little arrow dot', you can also rotate your picture by moving the curved arrow at the top of the picture

- Let's do the same to the other two empty cells

- Looking at it, you will notice it wasn't properly positioned, this is where additional adjustment is needed; simply click on any cell to make the little plus (+) arrow appear at the top left-hand side

- Once done, click on the plus (+) arrow above, all your table cells will be highlighted

- Then, in your menu bar, and click on "Layout"

- Make sure your table cell is still highlighted, then under "Layout" you will see the "Alignment" ribbon, select "Align Center" which is the middle icon, click on it

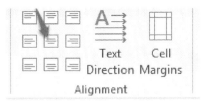

- All your entire table cells will automatically be centralized; you can compare the previous table with this adjusted table and see the difference

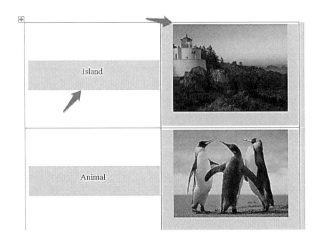

Drawing a table

- Go to "Insert tab"

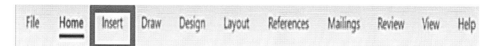

- Under the "Insert tab", select "Table"

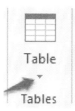

- It will display the "Table Grid", under it, select "Draw Table"

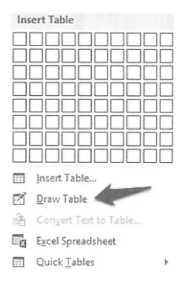

- You can design your table as desired as seen in the illustration below

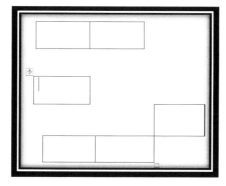

Drawing diagonal lines on tables

- You can draw any table of your choice and also add additional lines into your table as illustrated below. Note that your cursor will always change to a pen icon whenever you are working with the "Draw Table" Tool

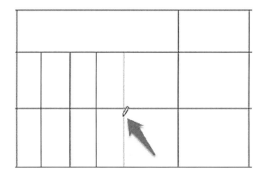

Wrapping text around a table

- Create a table of your choice as you were taught earlier, you can decide to replicate the one I'm using for illustration, two (2) rows, and three (3) columns. Make sure your cursor is blinking inside the one cell

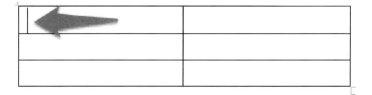

- Next, look above and locate "Table tools". Under "Table Tools", click on "Layout"

- Then, locate "Properties" and click on it

Properties

- Once you click on "Properties", a dialog box will be opened titled "Table" properties, under "Table", locate "Text wrapping", by default it is on "None", simply select "Around" and then press "Ok"

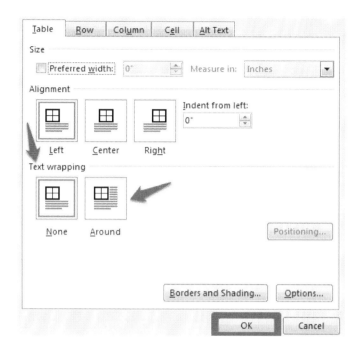

- Then, you can move your table to the center position and start typing or you can drag it into the middle of a text without having any issue with it, just as in the illustration below

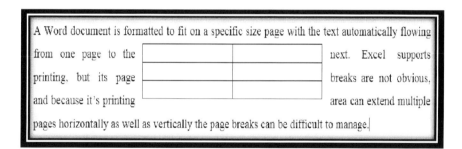

A Word document is formatted to fit on a specific size page with the text automatically flowing from one page to the next. Excel supports printing, but its page breaks are not obvious, and because it's printing area can extend multiple pages horizontally as well as vertically the page breaks can be difficult to manage.

Tips

Now you see and understand how flexible and simplified Word 365 is. Simply do something different from what we have achieved, and let see how comprehensive you get what has been explained to you so far.

CHAPTER SEVEN

TAKING ADVANTAGE OF THE PROOFING TOOLS

Correcting Your Spelling Errors

Computer software such as Word processing has been a wonderful tool for effective means of simplifying human needs. While trying to construct words, typographical errors can occur, this led Microsoft corporation to look for a means to reduce the possibility of typographical errors while typing. Luckily, Word comes with several and different tools that can help you proofread your document and correct any mistake. Many don't know how helpful Word 365 is when it comes to autocorrect and spelling checking. To know how to autocorrect or scan your document against typographical errors, simply follow this step-by-step procedure below:

- Make sure you are currently on your document to be corrected

- Go to the "Review" tab

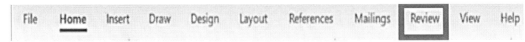

- At your left-hand side, look for "Spelling & Grammar" and click on it

A dialog box will appear on your right-hand side which will start spelling check from the first error to the last, the first typographical error was "Resoucres" instead of "Resources", so if it was intentionally typed, you click on the "Ignore" option. If not, select the corrected word in the suggestion box, then click on the "Change" option to continue to autocorrect other words.

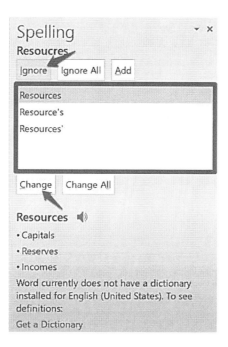

- Once you are done selecting the right suggested words, click on the "Change" option which will take you to the next misspelled text. In this illustration, the next is "Marcom", instead of "Marcum". Note that if the dictionary feature is installed on your Word 365 and it is a similar word in the dictionary, it will be explained below, if not, click on the "Get a Dictionary" option.

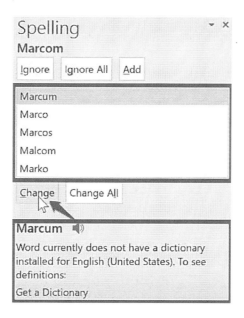

- It is important to note that the spell-checker is not perfect, sometimes it will say a word is spelled wrong when it is not, such as people's names, street names, and other unique proper nouns. If that happens, you have a couple of different options;
- The *"Ignore"* option will skip the word one time without changing it.
- The *"Ignore All"* option will skip the word every time it appears in your document.
- While the *"Add"* option will add the word to your inbuilt dictionary permanently, so it never comes up as an error again. Just make sure the word is spelled correctly before you go with any of these options.

Correcting misspellings one at a time

- By default, Word is designed to mark spelling and grammar errors while you type, that is what the little red and blue wavy lines as seen in the illustration are for, so, you can check your document manually (like I have just shown you), or you can refer to the marks, and make corrections as you go.

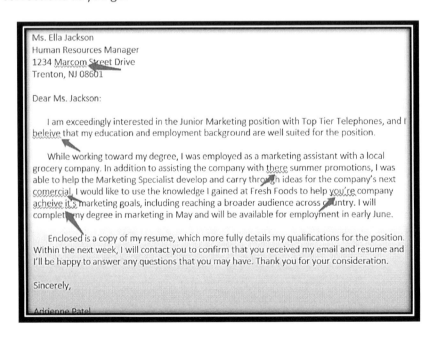

- Red means that there is a spelling error. To correct it, all you have to do is to right-click, then choose the proper spelling from the appeared menu after which the red curly line will be erased.

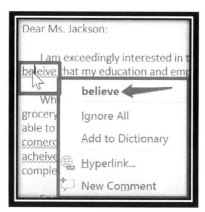

- Here is the corrected text "believe" instead of "beleive"

- Blue means that there is a kind of grammatical error. In this example, it looks like I used the wrong word in the context of the sentence. I should have used **"their"** instead of "there"

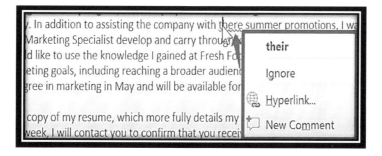

Customizing Spelling & Grammar Check

"Word" can be pretty good at picking up on errors like this, but there are certain things that it is set to ignore by default, including sentence fragments, poor sentence structure, and other common grammar mistakes. To include these things in your grammar check, you will need to adjust the default proofing settings. To do this;

- Go to the "Backstage view" which can be accessed through your "File menu"

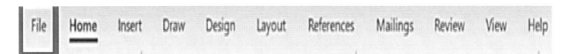

- Click on "Options" in the left pane

- Then, navigate to "Proofing" in the dialog box

- To customize your grammar settings, look for "Writing Style" near the bottom of the Window. Then click the "settings" option located on the right side

- And another dialog box will appear, here you can choose to set it to check Grammar Only, or Grammar & Style, which will cause Word to be strict about the style of your preferred choice. You can also turn specific items on or off to better suit your needs, for example, if you want Word to check for sentence fragments and run-ons, you can turn them on. Make sure you click the "Ok" button once you are through with the changes.

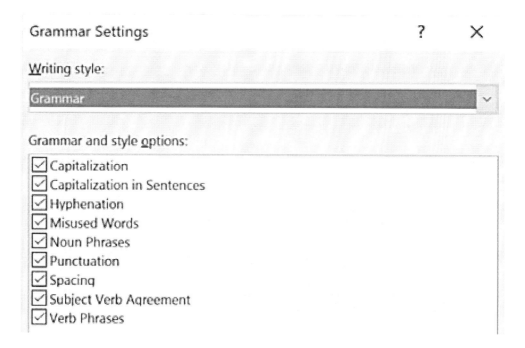

Preventing text from being spell-checked

- To do this, go to the "Backstage view" which can be accessed through your "File menu"

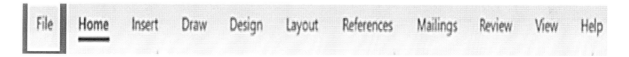

- Click on "Options" in the left pane

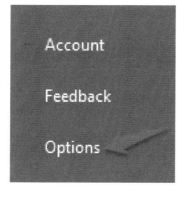

- Then, navigate to "Proofing" in the dialog box

- There are still lots of other ways that you can use to customize your settings depending on your preference. For instance, you can stop Word from marking spelling and grammar errors while you type.

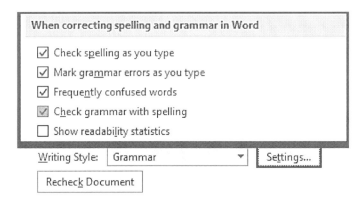

- You can also turn off frequently confused words, like *"**there** vs. **their**"*. Keep in mind, your spelling and grammar choices only apply to your copy of Word. So, if you ignore any error, or add a word to your dictionary (for example, your name), those wavy lines will reappear when you send the document to someone else. You can avoid this issue by hiding spelling and grammar errors in this particular document. Just check the two boxes near the bottom of the Window. When you are done, click "Ok" and now, the errors are hidden.

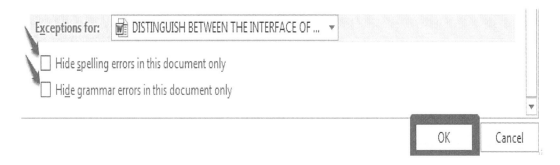

145

Finding and Replacing Text

Finding and replacing text is one of the Word features that give the privilege to replace text by finding it within a bunch of text without any complication, to know how to find and replace words, follow these simple procedures:

- Go to the *"Home"* tab

- Under the *"Home"* tab, kindly locate *"Replace"* click it or press *"Ctrl + H"*

- A dialog box will appear, enter the word or phrase you want to locate in the *"Find what"* textbox. Also, in the *"Replace with"* textbox, enter the text or phrase you want what you found to be replaced with. For example, I can search for "Thank you" and replace it with "Thanks" on my document.

- To update all instances at once, choose "Replace All"

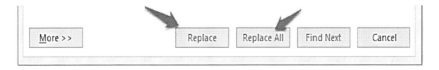

Finding the Right Word with the Thesaurus

Before I explain how to use "Thesaurus", it is important to know what "Thesaurus" is. Thesaurus is a tool that is specially designed into Word by Microsoft for getting the synonyms of whatsoever you are looking for by giving you a bunch of suggestions. For example, you can look for "benefit" and you will be given multiple suggestions of synonyms for "benefit" such as "advantage", "profit", with a classification of which part of speech such words fall under.

Now, how do we make use of Thesaurus? Simply follow these steps:

- Go to your "View" tab"

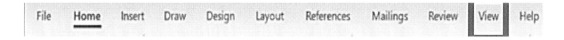

- Under the "View" tab, at your left-hand side, locate "Thesaurus" and double-click on it

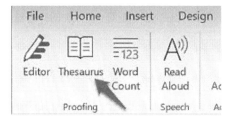

- A dialog box will appear at your right-hand side opposite your Navigation pane dialog box which is located at your left-hand side if activated

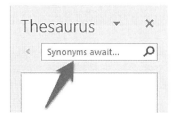

- Then, you can type your word or phrase into the "Search" bar. For example, we can look for "Environment" on our "Thesaurus pane" and see what our result will be. You can also type another word of your choice and also see what your result will be

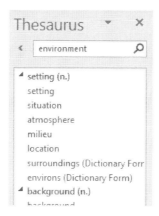

Proofing & Converting Text Written in a Foreign Language

- Go to your "Review" tab

- Under the "Review" tab, at your left-hand side, click on "Translate", this will allow you to translate your content into different languages of your choice

- Now, once you click on "Translate", you will be given two options, one is the "Translate Selection" which enables you to select the specific part of your document to be translated, while the other option is the "Translate Document" which creates a translated copy of your document with Microsoft Translator

- Assuming you select "Translate Selection", a dialog box will appear at the right-hand side where you can select your text or type it inside in the provided textbox

- Let also assume that I select a portion from my text

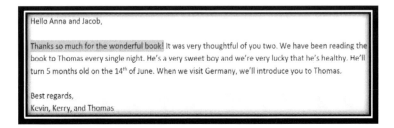

- It will automatically reflect on my translator pane. From English to German based on what I selected. To make use of other languages, click on the present language it will show you other language options

- You can also translate the whole paragraph

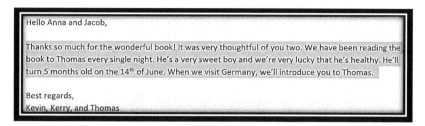

- Your text will also be interpreted

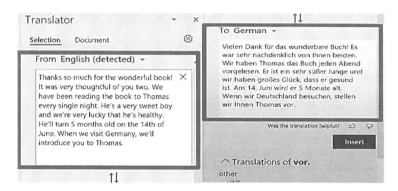

- Then, you can copy the translated copy by highlighting it, right-click, and pick the "copy" option.

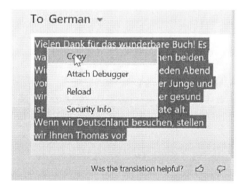

- This can also be pasted into your document.

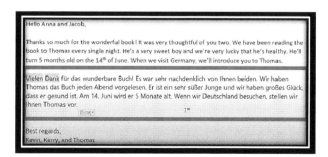

- Let's also see the other option which is "Translate Document". Just click on the other side of your "Translate pane" which is "Document", an instruction of what it is- "Create a translated copy of this document with the Microsoft Translator service" will be written below. Always note that you can change your language anytime you wish by clicking on the current language to select your choice.

- Once you click on "Translate", it will process the translation of your document. Note that you must be connected to the internet via modem, router, Wi-Fi or any means of connection for it to work effectively without bouncing back.

- It will be converted to "German" which is the selected language. Note, the translated document will be opened on a "New document" and your original document will be intact.

151

- Once completed, check the new document to see the translated document

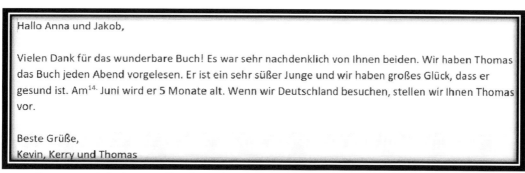

Hallo Anna und Jakob,

Vielen Dank für das wunderbare Buch! Es war sehr nachdenklich von Ihnen beiden. Wir haben Thomas das Buch jeden Abend vorgelesen. Er ist ein sehr süßer Junge und wir haben großes Glück, dass er gesund ist. Am14. Juni wird er 5 Monate alt. Wenn wir Deutschland besuchen, stellen wir Ihnen Thomas vor.

Beste Grüße,
Kevin, Kerry und Thomas

- You can minimize one for the other to preview

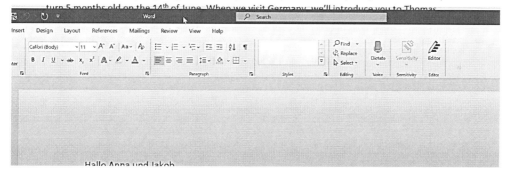

Hello Anna and Jacob,

Thanks so much for the wonderful book! It was very thoughtful of you two. We have been reading the book to Thomas every single night. He's a very sweet boy and we're very lucky that he's healthy. He'll turn 5 months old on the 14th of June. When we visit Germany, we'll introduce you to Thomas.

Hallo Anna und Jakob,

Making use of the Navigation Pane

For simplicity and flexibility, it is important to note that you can have your search bar pane through navigation pane side by side while typing in Word environment, simply follow these step-by-step procedures to achieve that:

- Go to the "View" tab

- Under the "View" tab, at your left-hand side look for "Navigation Pane" make sure it is ticked, if not, do so to see the effect on your document.

- Here is the result; the below "Navigation" dialog box will automatically appear on the left-hand side of your document permanently except you untick it from the "View" tab. It enables you to see your listed "Headings", slide "Pages", and search "Result" instantly.

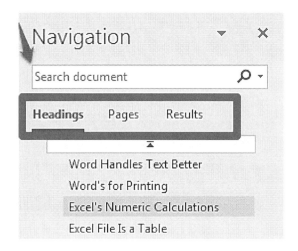

Choosing Language Option

- Go to the "File menu"

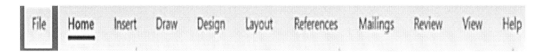

- At the displayed interface, click on "Options"

- A dialog box will appear on your left-hand side, select "Language"

- Then, "Language" features will also appear on your right-hand side, below towards your left-hand side is the "Display Language" option, while at your right-hand side is the "Help Language" option. You can choose from the available languages by scrolling through to see other options.

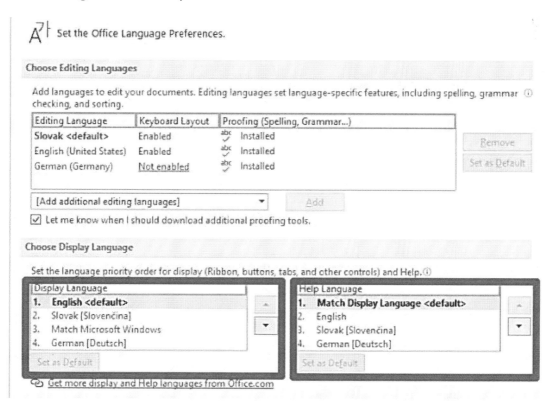

- Once done press, the "Ok" option

- Then, you will be instructed to restart Office so that your language changes can take effect.

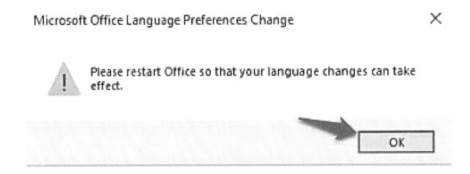

- Take note of your Word 365 interface before restarting your PC, it's by default in the English language

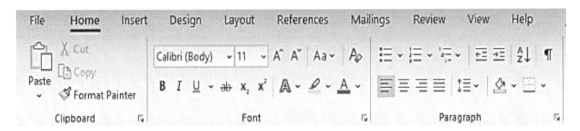

- And here will be the outcome after your PC has been restarted, everything will automatically be in the German language.

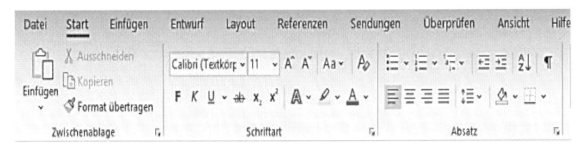

CHAPTER EIGHT

DESKTOP PUBLISHING WITH WORD

Experimenting with Theme

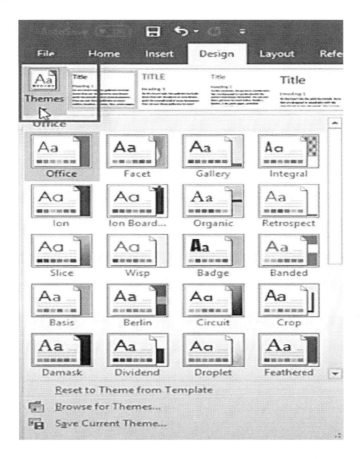

Themes are a predefined style template format that adds to your document content. Each theme uses a unique set of colors, fonts, and effects to create a consistent look. To access your various themes, all you have to do is to go to the "Design" tab, on your right-hand side you will see the word "Themes", click on it and you will be shown different unique themes interface to pick from and each theme as sub-template format.

Decorating a page with a border

- Go to the "Design" tab

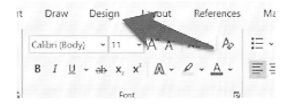

- Under "Design", at your right-hand side, you will see the "Page Background" ribbon, select "Page Borders"

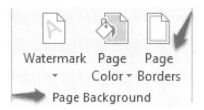

- Once you click on "Page Borders", a dialog box will pop up which is your "Page Border" configuration. On the left-hand side is the "Setting" option for various page border templates. By the side of the "Setting" option is the "Style" option where you can choose the kind of lines you prefer. Below "Style" is the "Color" option where you can determine which color fits into your page document border.

Below the "Color" option is the "Width" option which is the only component that controls the border thickness. Below the "Width" option is the "Art" option that reflects different kinds of art designs to be used for your framework, while at your right-hand side is the "Preview" option which gives you what your outcome configuration will look like before you click on the "Ok" option.

The "Apply to" option is where you determine where your effect should take place such as "Whole document", "This section", "This section first page only", and "This section all except the first page." Your choice determines your outcome, once done hit the "Ok" button to see your changes.

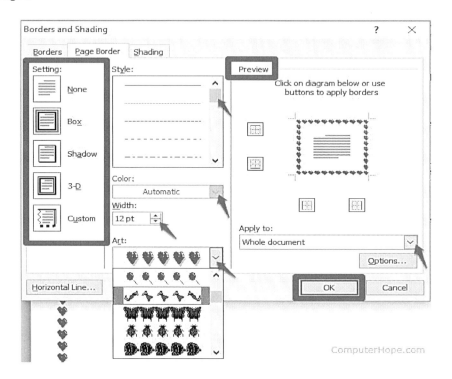

Putting a Background Color on Pages

- In the menu bar, click on "Design"

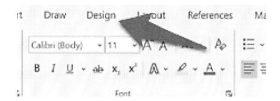

- Under "Design", at your right-hand side, you will see the "Page Background" ribbon, select "Page Color"

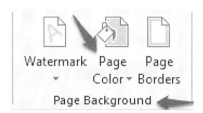

- Under "Page Color", a dropdown box will appear with different kinds of colors. If your preferred color was not found, there's a "More Colors" option below, click on it

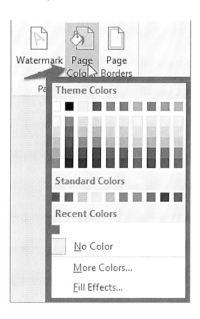

- After clicking the "More Colors" option, you will be brought here under "Standard" where you can randomly select your preferred color which was not found on the page displayed color. On your right-hand side is where your chosen color will be previewed. If you previously choose a color, it will be shown as "Current" with that color, while the newly selected will be shown as "New" with the color you selected as illustrated below.

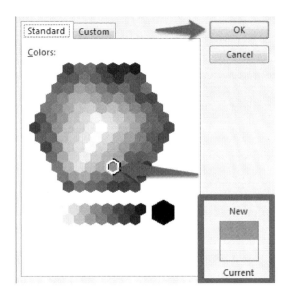

- You can also explore more colors on "Custom" which is an advanced color selection option where you can see the mixture of Colors Red, green, and Blue that was added together to make your preferred color. The illustration below shows that "Yellow color" was picked, and the mixture of it was calculated underneath as "Red: 221", "Green: 221", and "Blue: 35" which resulted in the color yellow.

Note also that beside the color picker, there is a black arrow (   ) which is used for adjustment of any preferred color, once done click the "Ok" button.

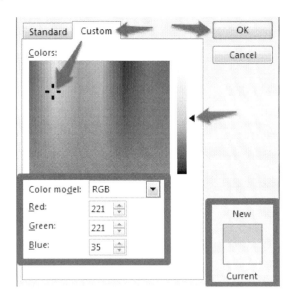

Getting Word 365 help with Resume Assistant

With Word 365, there are limitless possibilities to what you can access, that is why I am glad that you made the right choice for purchasing this valuable book which enables you to know some hidden features of Word 365. It is important to note that Word 365 has made it possible for third-party software to partner with them for flexibility and simplicity of technology

159

advancement in our day-to-day life. To make Word 365 assist you with cover letters, simply follow these procedures

- Go to the "Review" tab

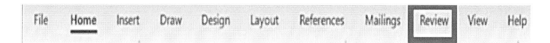

- Under the "Review" tab, look at your right-hand side, you will see "Resume Assistant", click on it

- A dialog box will appear on your right-hand side, click on "Get started" to proceed

- Another way to create a "Resume" is to go to your "file menu", click it

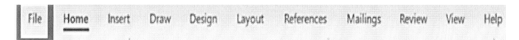

- Click on "New", then, you will be shown multiple template options to pick from, or you can also search online, this will require a data connection

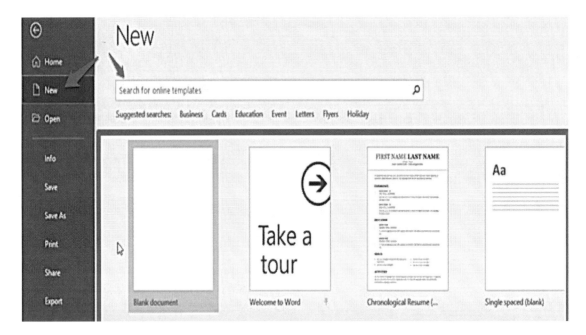

- You can also scroll down to see other "resume" options

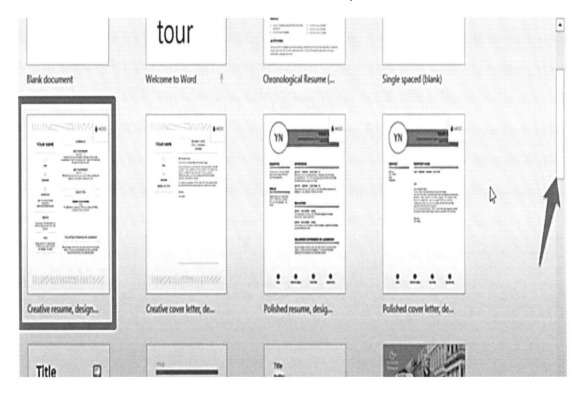

- Once you find your preferred choice, select it and see more information about it, then you can click on "Create"

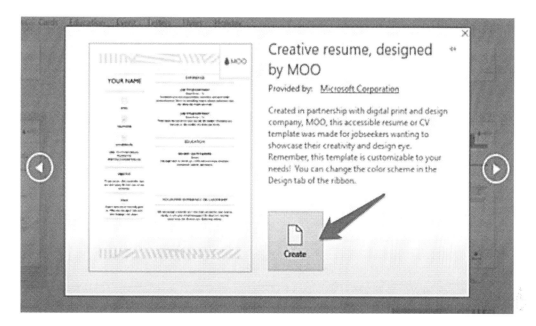

- Once you click on "Create" it will automatically create a template on your Word 365 for you to work on, and your "Resume Assistant" will also appear on your right-hand side for further assistance

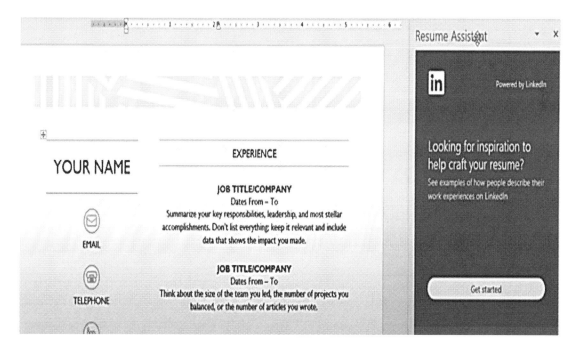

- At your right-hand side on your "Resume Assistant", you can click on "See examples" to see the role and industry format you are looking for

- Or you can go to **https://www.linkedin.com/** (this is optional) which is a third-party affiliation to Microsoft. Once you get to the website, you either "Sign in" with your "Linkedin" account or you "Join now" to register afresh. Never enter your Microsoft account details, remember it is a third-party affiliation not owned by Microsoft.

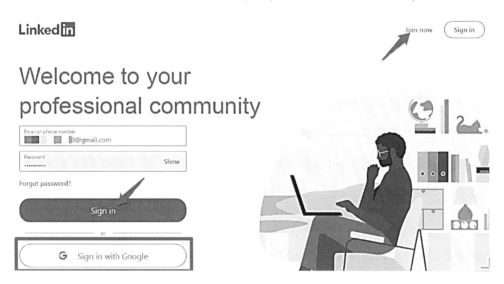

- To join, click on "Join now" at your top right-hand side as illustrated above, then a new page will be brought to you to fill up your registration form

- And if you already have an existing account with "Linkedin", enter it by clicking on the "Sign in" option to explore more on the third-party website, which is specifically designed for professional life where you can showcase what you are up to professionally, and it's also a way of meeting people around the world.

Getting Word 365 help with cover letters

- Go to your "file menu" click it

- Click on "New", then, you will be shown multiple template options to pick from or you can also search online, this will require a data connection

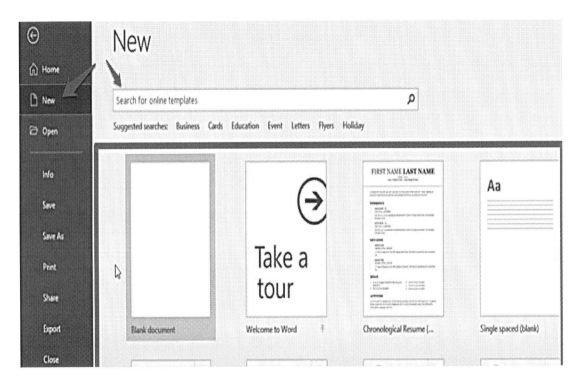

- You can also scroll down to see other "cover letter" options or type "cover letter"

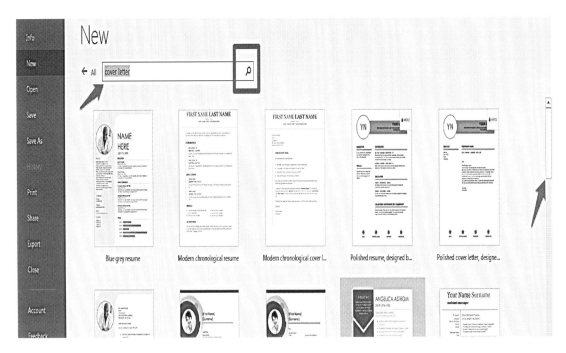

- Once you locate your preferred choice, select it, a pop-up box will appear where you can create it.

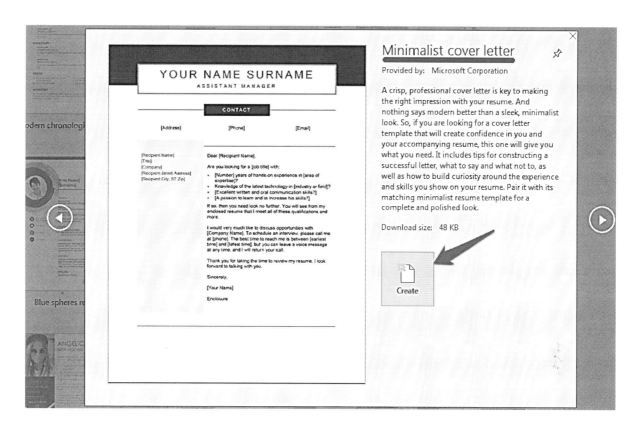

Making Use of Charts, Shapes, and Photos

- Go to your "Insert" tab

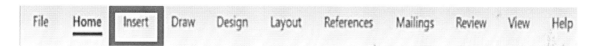

- Under the "Insert" tab, locate the "Illustrations" ribbon

Before we proceed, let's begin by defining "Chart".

What is a Chart?

In a simple word, Chart is a spotted pattern and trend in data used to estimate the graphical scaling by inserting a bar, area, or line chart.

How to Insert "Chart"

- Select "Chart" in the "Illustrations" ribbon

- A dialog box will appear consisting of the "All Charts" features such as "Column", "Line", "Pie", "Bar", "Area", and other charts. It's majorly used to view the estimation of data after it has been concluded.

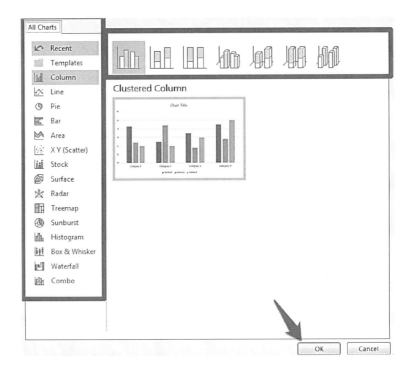

What is a Shape?

Shapes are predefined tools that are used for different purposes such as block arrows shapes, start and banner shapes, equation shapes, and others. To make use of "Shapes", follow these simple procedures below:

- Go to your "Insert tab"

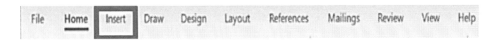

- Under the "Insert" tab, locate "Illustrations", in the "Illustration" ribbon, you will see "Shapes", click on it

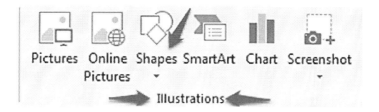

- "Shapes" will show its dropdown features where you can select from. Let's assume we select "love shape" under "Basic Shapes" where my mouse cursor is pointing.

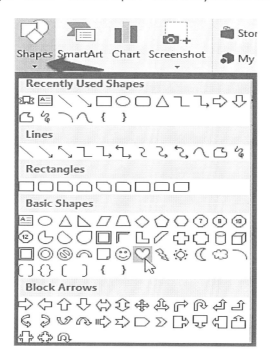

- Once the love shape has been selected, you can now double-click and drag your mouse cursor to make it more visible.

- You can also add more touch to your "love shape" by making sure your mouse cursor is placed on your "love shape", thereby, showing dots around it

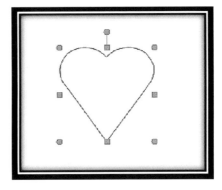

- Then, look above, you will see "Format", click on it

- And you will be shown different colors. You can also click on the dropdown arrow as indicated below to also see other options

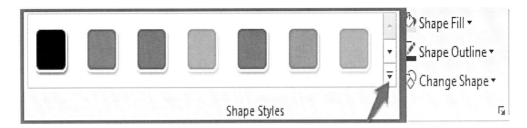

- Select your preferred choice and it will automatically take effect on your selected "love shape".

Now, let's discuss Photos which is also known as Pictures

What is a Picture?

A Picture is a static image used for different illustrations and purposes. Now, how do we insert pictures into our Word document?

- Go to "Insert" in your menu bar

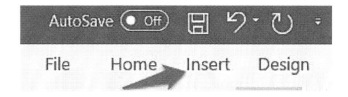

- Under the "Insert" tab, locate the "Illustrations" ribbon. In the "Illustrations" ribbon, select "Pictures"

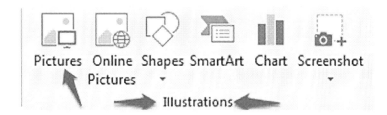

- Once you click on "Pictures", a dialog box will pop up and direct you to your PC storage, locate the folder where your pictures are stored and click on your preferred image, then click "Insert"

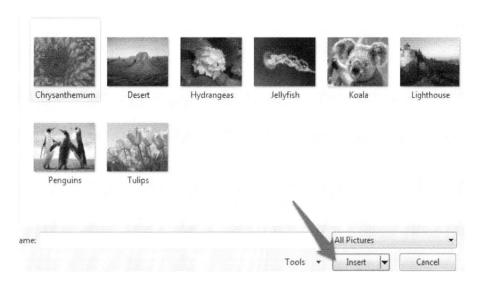

- Then, your image which is also the same as a picture will reflect on your Word document immediately. If you remember earlier when treating how to make use of "Table", I taught you how to resize your image at the dots areas and rotate it if need be, using the curved arrow icon as illustrated below

Positioning and Wrapping Objects Relative to the Page and Text

Positioning and wrapping objects to the page and text can be achieved with the help of "Text Box", which is another hidden feature. Many times, we come across some impossible mathematical images in students' textbooks and keep wondering how did this happen? It is simple, it happens with the help of Word unknown tools. With "Text Box", you can position your words in any area of your document by wrapping your content into it and place it wherever you want your text to be fixed. Then, how do we locate "Text Box"?

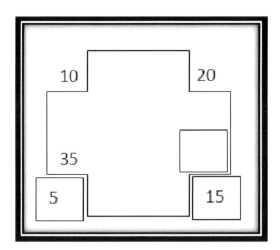

Working with Text Boxes

- Go to the menu bar, select the "Insert" tab

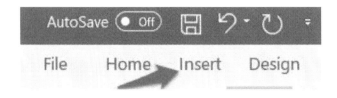

- Under the "Insert" tab, at your right-hand side, look for "Text Box"

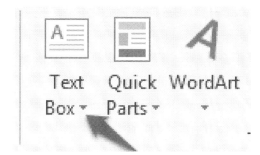

- Once you click on it, you will see "Text Box" options, just pick the first option which is "Simple Text Box"

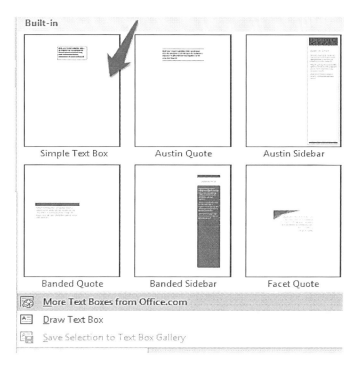

- Once selected, it will appear on your document with a bunch of texts telling you what "Text Box" is all about

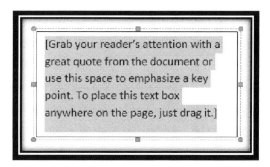

- Simply delete the highlighted instruction and insert your own words or number inside. Never forget that dots are used for resizing, it can be used to enlarge or reduce your "Text Box"

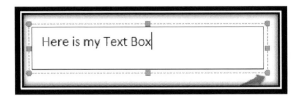

Here is my Text Box

- You can also hide the lines in your "Text Box" by editing it, make sure your "Text Box" dots are still showing, look up, and select "Format". The "Format" tab only appears whenever any editable object is selected

Format

- Then, under "Format", click on "Shape Outline" and select "No Outline", by default, your "Text Box" outline will be hidden

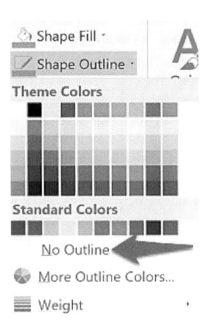

- Here is your result

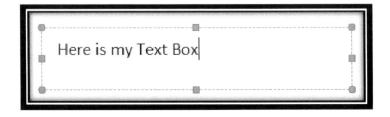

Here is my Text Box

- Then, click outside your "Text Box", you won't notice any line, as if the line never existed, whereas, it's still there but hidden. Whenever you click on the text, the dots will reflect that there is a "Text Box" on this text, you can also drag it as you were taught earlier by hovering on the dots at the edge, still, your mouse cursor shows plus (+) arrow, then you can drag and drop it in any area on your document.

> Here is my Text Box

Drop Cap

Drop Cap is used to create a large format of text at the beginning of a paragraph

- To make use of "Drop Cap", simply highlight your text (a single letter)

A Word document is formatted to fit on a specific size page with the text automatically flowing om one page to the next. Excel supports printing, but its page breaks are not obvious, and because it's printing area can extend multiple pages horizontally as well as vertically the page breaks can be difficult to manage.

- Go to "Insert" in your menu bar

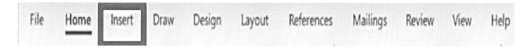

- Under the "Insert" tab, look for "Drop Cap" click on it

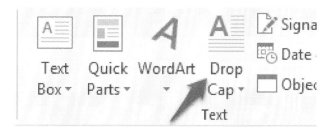

- Once you click on it, dropdown options will appear, select "Dropped" and your first letter at the beginning of your paragraph will receive the effect.

- **Note**: when it comes to "Drop Cap", if you highlight the first letter on the paragraph your mouse cursor is indicating, that is where your "Drop Cap" will take effect. Click outside the transformed text to make the dots and lines hidden.

A Word document is formatted to fit on a specific size page with the text automatically flowing from one page to the next. Excel supports printing, but its page breaks are not obvious, and because it's printing area can extend multiple pages horizontally as well as vertically the page breaks can be difficult to manage.

Watermarking for the Elegant Effect

Watermarking is a great way to show that a document requires special treatment without distracting from the content. How do we make use of Watermark? Simply follow these step-by-step procedures:

- Go to "Design"

- Under the "Design" tab, look at your right-hand side, you will see the "Page Background" ribbon, above it, is the "Watermark" option, click on it.

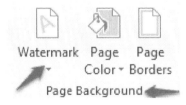

- Once you click on "Watermark", multiple options will be displayed, some are in diagonal format, and some are horizontal. Any template you click on will automatically reflect on your document. You can also customize your watermark. Select your preferred choice, or you choose "Custom Watermark" to customize your preferred choice

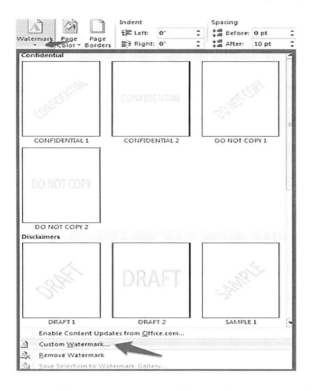

- Assuming we choose "Custom Watermark" by clicking on it, a dialog box will appear. There are three options to "Custom Watermark" which are: "No watermark", for no effect, "Picture watermark" for image effect, and "Text watermark" for text effect. Choose the preferred "Text" and "Language" you want to insert as well as "Font" format, "Size", "color" and "layout", once done, click the "Ok" button.

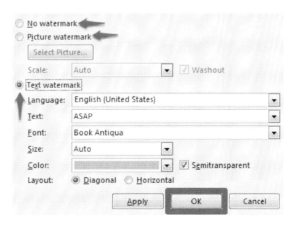

All the changes will automatically reflect on your document.

Putting Newspaper-Style Columns in a Document

- Go to the "Layout" tab

- Under the "Layout" tab, you will see the "Page setup" ribbon, within it you will also see your "Columns", click on it

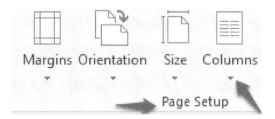

- You will see "Columns" dropdown options; let's pick "Three" because if you check any Newspaper, you will notice that on a page, the contents are normally divided into three columns.

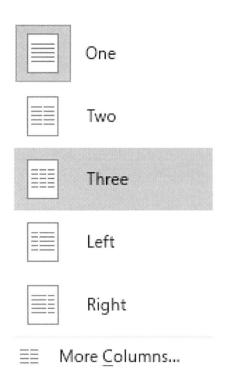

- Make sure you have content; else you won't see the effect of the "three" columns that you selected

DISTINGUISH BETWEEN THE INTERFACE OF MICROSOFTWORD AND EXCEL

Word Handles Text Better

Word is made for text documents, including letters, books and academic papers. Text in Excel is usually a brief snippet used to describe the meaning of a number.

Word's for Printing

A Word document is formatted to fit on a specific size page with the text automatically flowing

page breaks can be difficult to manage.

Excel's Numeric Calculations

Excel allows you to perform complex calculations where changing one number causes many other calculated numbers to change as well. Excel includes an extensive library of built-in formulas to help you perform those calculations.

Excel File Is a Table

An Excel file displays as rows and columns

of columns and thousands of rows. Although Word supports tables it cannot handle large tables as well as Excel.

Word Supports Footnotes

Because word is page oriented it supports features, such as footnotes and table of contents that don't make sense for a table. Other page-oriented concepts, including centering text horizontally on a page, are very easy in Word, but make no sense in Excel.

Landscape Document

It is important to note that a Word document can be in two formats which are "Portrait" and "Landscape". By default, your Word document is in "Portrait" format. How do we now switch between Portrait & Landscape?

- Simply go to "Layout"

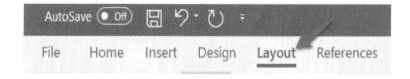

- Under "Layout", look for "Page Setup ribbon" select **Orientation**

- You will see two options under "Orientation", which are "Portrait" & "Landscape". As I said earlier, a Word document by default is in "Portrait" (vertical format), once you switch it to "Landscape" as illustrated below, your presently opened Word document will be in horizontal shape.

Printing on Different Paper Size

To print on a different paper size,

- Simply go to "Layout"

- Under "Layout", look for "Page Setup" ribbon, select "Size"

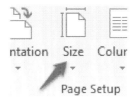

- Under "Size", multiple options will be displayed. By default, your Word document paper size is on "A4", you can choose other options or click on "More Paper Sizes"

- Under "More Paper Sizes", you can set your paper "width" and "height" to your preferred taste, once you are done, press "Ok" to see the effect.

Showing Video in a Document

To show video in a document, follow these steps

- Go to "Insert"

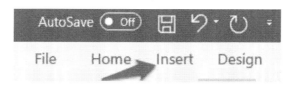

- Under the "Insert tab", on your right-hand side, you will see "Online Video Media", click on it

- A dropdown dialog box will appear with two options: "Online Video" which will refer you online (this requires your data connection) and "Video on My PC" (data connection not needed) which is the video from your PC storage. Once you choose your preferred choice you are good to go in watching your video through the Word environment

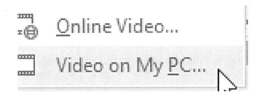

CHAPTER NINE

GETTING WORD'S HELP WITH OFFICE CHORES

Highlighting Parts of a Document

Highlighting parts of a document has been one of the quickest ways to perform your formatting tasks, such as bolding a text, increasing the font text size, changing text font, and other features. When it comes to effecting changes on some areas of your document content, the only option available is to highlight the parts of your document content.

How to Highlight a Text

There are only two ways of highlighting texts, which are: Mouse highlighting (click and drag) and Keyboard highlighting (Shift key + Navigation key).

Mouse highlighting (Click and drag)

- Place your mouse cursor at the beginning of your text area where you intend to start your highlighting from

Word is made for text documents, including letters, boo

usually a brief snippet used to describe the meaning of a

- Once your pointer has been placed at the beginning of where you want to highlight, simply right-click on your mouse and hold down (if you are using a desktop, which has an external mouse) or left-click on your mouse and hold down (if you are using a laptop which has an internal mouse), then, start dragging it to the last edge where you want to stop.

Word is made for text documents, including letters, books an

usually a brief snippet used to describe the meaning of a num

Keyboard highlighting (Shift key + Navigation key)

- Place your mouse cursor at the beginning of your text area where you intend to start your highlighting from

> Word is made for text documents, including letters, boo
>
> usually a brief snippet used to describe the meaning of a

- Once it is rightly positioned, hold down the "Shift" key on your keyboard and simultaneously press the "Navigation key" depending on the direction you want to navigate it. There are four Navigation keys, "Upward navigation", facing up; "Downward navigation", facing down; "Backward navigation", facing the back direction, and "Forward navigation" facing front. Below is an illustration of the "Shift" key together with the "Forward" navigation key

> Word is made for text documents, including letters, books an
>
> usually a brief snippet used to describe the meaning of a num

Commenting on a Document

Commenting on a document is a great way of referring to it later and understanding your reason for particular tagged content.

Entering comments

- Select the content you want to comment on by highlighting it

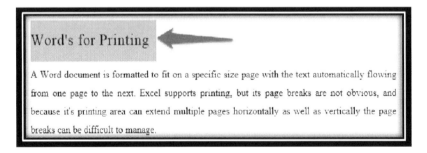

- Once your text has been selected, simply go to the "Review" tab

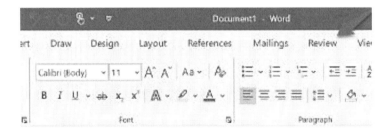

- Under the "Review" tab, you will see "New Comment" below it

- Enter "New Comment" by clicking on it, your highlighted text will be colored and another dialog box will appear on your right-hand side, the little "speech bubble rectangular shape" is a symbol or a referrer to your "comments box" at your left-hand side

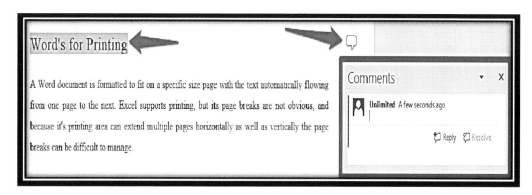

Replying to comments

- Input your text inside the "Comment box", since our text is centered on "Printing", I will be typing "Printing Instruction", note below is another session to also "Reply" on your comment, just like an online post.

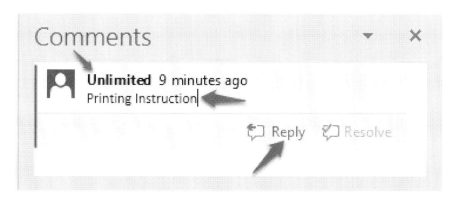

Note: don't be confused with the name "Unlimited" it is my PC name that I used, yours might not be "Unlimited", what your PC name is stored as is what will reflect on your comment session and your comment duration period after dropping your comment will be noted.

184

- You can reply on "Comment" with any word assuming I typed "More details on printing procedures" as my "Reply".

Note that on a single comment, your "Reply" does not have limits.

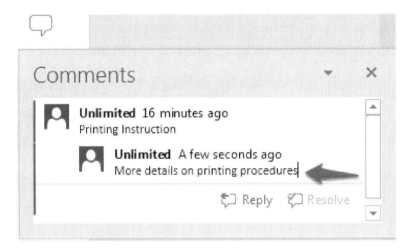

Resolving comments

- Highlight the comment or reply to be resolved or right-click on it to resolve it

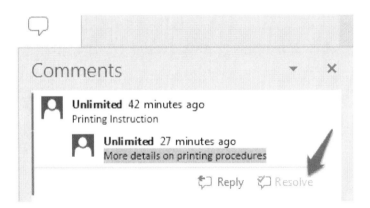

Viewing and Displaying Comments

- Go to the "Review" tab

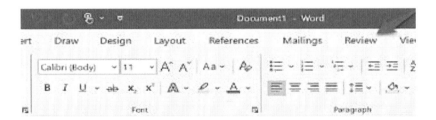

- You will see "Show Comments"

- Or on your document, you will notice a little speech rectangular icon, once you click on it, it will display your comments

- Your comment box will be displayed again for viewing or editing purpose

Tracking Changes to Documents

Keeping track of changes made to your documents is especially useful if the document is almost done, and you are working with others to make a revision or give feedback on your progress.

Working with Track Changes

- Simply go to "Review"

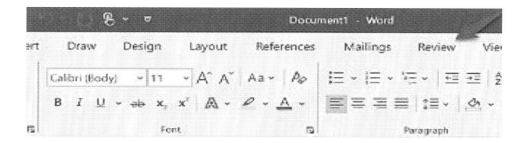

- Under "Review", at your right-hand side, you will see "Track Changes", click on it

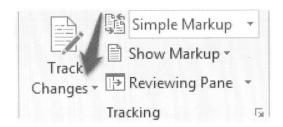

- You will be given two options "Track Changes" & "Lock Tracking"

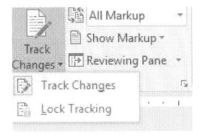

- Once you select "Track Changes", your content will be automatically monitored and tracked, and any changes made will be signaled with a red straight stroke as illustrated below with the additional words

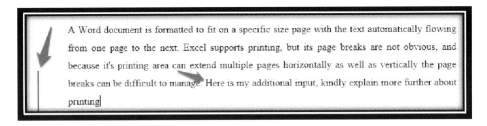

- You can also select "Lock Tracking" and a dialog box will appear requiring you to enter your "password" for prevention against unauthorized corrections which without the password, the other authors won't be able to add any changes.

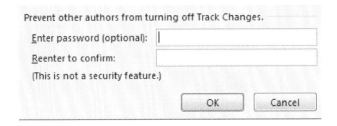

Reading and reviewing a document with revision marks

- Go to the "Review" tab

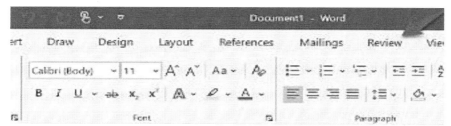

- Under the "Review" tab, at your right-hand side, you will see "Reviewing Pane", click on it

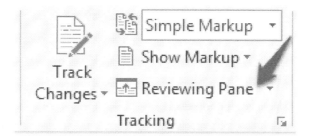

- Once you click on it, you will be given two options either to "Review Pane Vertically" or "Review Pane Horizontally". Assuming we choose "Review Pane Vertically", all your added words will be reviewed.

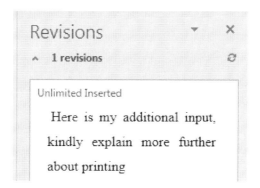

Marking changes when you forgot to turn on revision marks

- Go to "Review"

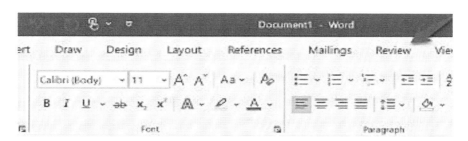

- Under the "Review" tab at your right-hand side, you will see "Sample Markup", click on it and select "All Markup"

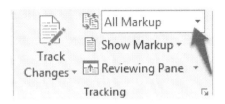

- Then, all your added texts will be marked with a red color and also underlined, as a way to make one know the added content from the one that was previously there before adding additional words.

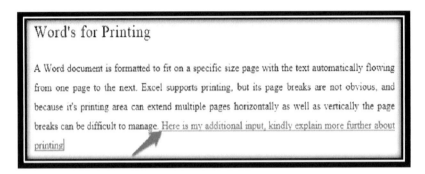

Accepting and rejecting changes to a document

- Simply go to "Review"

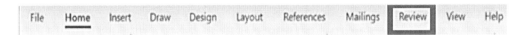

- Under "Review", at your right-hand side, you will see "Changes", above it is the "Accept" & "Reject" options

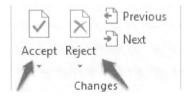

With the "Accept" option, you can move to the next track changes by selecting your preferred options under the "Accept" option

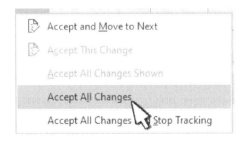

While the "Reject" option Undo changes and immediately moves to the next track changes. You can also select your preferred options under "Reject" just as in "Accept"

Printing an Address on an Envelope

- Go to "Mailings"

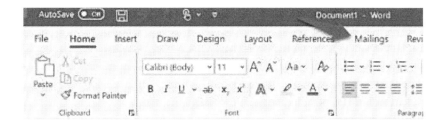

- Under the "Mailings" tab, at your left-hand side, you will see "Envelopes", click on it

- Simply fill in all the required details such as "Delivery address", "Return address", "Add to document" if need be. Once everything has been verified, click on "Print"

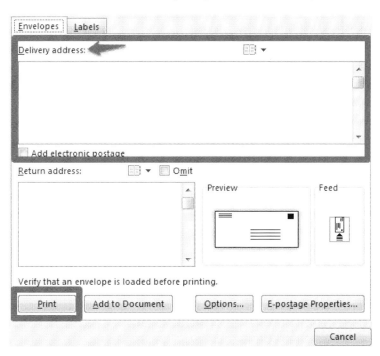

Printing a Single Address Label (or a Page of the Same Label)

- Go to "Mailings"

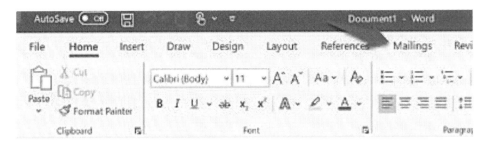

- Under "Mailings", on your left-hand side, you will see "Labels", click on it.

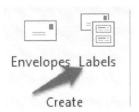

- Then, you can start filling the required input such as "Address", "Use return address" if need be (also select the amount of "Row" & "Column"), then click on your "Print" once you are done with labeling address.

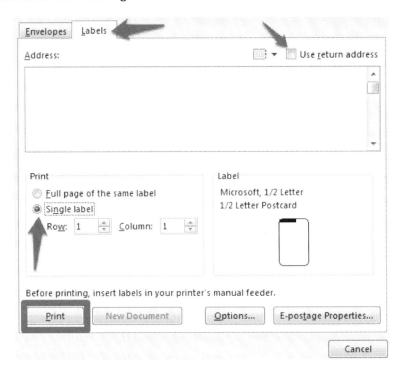

CHAPTER TEN

KEYBOARD SHORTCUTS

Frequently used shortcuts

Shortcut	Function
Ctrl + A	Highlight all your content
Ctrl + B	Applying bold to selected text
Ctrl + C	Copy content into the Clipboard
Ctrl + D	Font dialog box
Ctrl + E	Centralized text
Ctrl + F	Navigation for searching
Ctrl + G	Go to a page, section, line number
Ctrl + H	To replace a text
Ctrl + I	Applying italic to selected text
Ctrl + J	To justify your text
Ctrl + K	Insert hyperlink to content
Ctrl + L	Align text to the left
Ctrl + M	Move paragraph
Ctrl + N	Create a new document
Ctrl + O	Open a document
Ctrl + P	Print out document
Ctrl + R	Align text to the right
Ctrl + S	Save document
Ctrl + U	Applying underline to selected text
Ctrl + V	Paste the copied contents from the Clipboard
Ctrl + W	Close current document
Ctrl + X	Cut the selected content
Ctrl + Y	Redo the previous action
Ctrl + Z	Undo the previous action
Ctrl + [	Decrease the font size
Ctrl +]	Increase the font size
Esc	Cancel a command
Ctrl + Alt + S	Split the document Window
Ctrl + Alt + S	Remove the document Window split

Access Keys for ribbon tabs

Shortcut	Function
Alt + Q	Move to the "Tell me" or Search field on the Ribbon to search for assistance or Help content
Alt + F	Open the **File page** to use Backstage view.
Alt + H	Open the **Home tab** to use common formatting commands, paragraph styles, and the Find tool.
Alt + N	Open the **Insert tab** to insert tables, pictures and shapes, headers, and text boxes.
Alt + G	Open the **Design tab** to use themes, colors, and effects, such as page borders.
Alt + P	Open the **Layout tab** to work with page margins, page orientation, indentation, and spacing.

Alt + S	Open the **References tab** to add a table of contents, footnotes, or a table of citations.
Alt + M	Open the **Mailings tab** to manage Mail, Merge tasks and to work with envelopes and labels.
Alt + R	Open the **Review tab** to use Spell Check, set proofing languages, and to track and review changes to your document.
Alt + W	Open the **View tab** to choose a document view or mode, such as Read Mode or Outline view. You can also set the zoom magnification and manage multiple document Windows.
Alt or F10	Select the **active tab** on the ribbon, and activate the access keys
Shift + Tab	Move the focus to commands on the ribbon.
Ctrl + Right arrow	Move between command groupings on the ribbon
Arrow keys	Move among the items on the Ribbon
Spacebar or Enter	Activate the selected button.
Alt + Down arrow key	Open the menu for the selected button
Down arrow key	When a menu or submenu is open, it's to move to the next command
Ctrl + F1	Expand or collapse the ribbon
Shift+F10	Open the context menu
Left arrow key	Move to the submenu when the main menu is open or selected

Navigate the document

Shortcut	Function
Ctrl + Left arrow key	Move the cursor pointer one space at a time to the left
Ctrl + Right arrow key	Move the cursor pointer one space at a time to the right
Ctrl + Up arrow key	Move the cursor pointer up by one paragraph
Ctrl + Down arrow key	Move the cursor pointer down by one Paragraph
End	Move the cursor pointer to the end of the current line
Home	Move the cursor to the beginning of the current Line
Ctrl + Alt+ Page up	Move the cursor pointer to the top
Page down	Move the cursor pointer by scrolling the document down
Ctrl + Page down	Move your cursor pointer to the next page
Ctrl + Page up	Move your cursor to the previous page
Ctrl + End	Move your cursor to the end of the document

CHAPTER ELEVEN

MICROSOFT WORD TIPS & TRICKS

Dark Mode

Do you know that you can turn on "dark mode" in Microsoft Word from the default background interface which is in white mode? The Dark mode is specifically designed for sight adjustment, majorly for the night users and other purposes.

To Enable Dark Mode

- Simply go to the top left-hand corner and click on your "File menu"

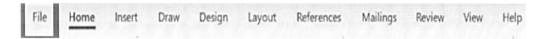

- Once you click on "File menu", scroll down, at the bottom left-hand corner, click on "Account"

- Once you click on "Account", you will see your "User Information", below it is "Office Theme" by default, it is on "Colorful theme", click on the little dropdown arrow as illustrated below to see other options, next on the dropdown list is "Dark Gray", let's select it and see its effect.

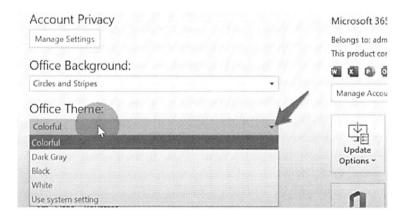

- "Dark Gray" makes your Word background interface a little bit dark

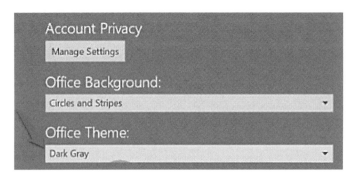

- You can select "Black" to get the "Dark mode" if you wish. Note that any change in your themes will also affect other Microsoft Suites such as Excel, PowerPoint, Outlook, and others.

- Here will be your Microsoft Word displayed interface

Changing the white document interface

Every of your theme settings or your customized theme settings can only affect the outlook, not the document content itself. To also change your white-board known as your document content area, simply follow these steps below:

- Go to your "Design tab"

- Under "Design", at your right-hand side, locate "Page Color" and click on it

- Then, you can select "Theme Colors" to "Black"

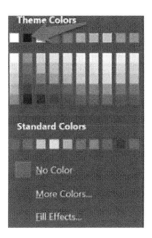

- Once you select "Color Black", your document content area will be on Black

Note: Your dark document content area has nothing to do with your printing out the document, it will print out your standard white format and black texts, your themes selection, and design document content, it only affects your Word interface not with the copies to be printed.

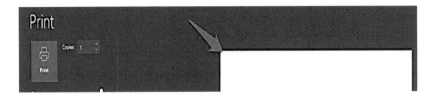

Turn Word Document into Interactive Web Page

- Go to the menu bar, and click on "File"

- Once you click on "File", scroll down and look for "Transform", once seen, click on it

- This will automatically open a pane at your right-hand side in your document where you can select any "Web Page" template of your choice

197

- Once you get your preferred choice, click on it and you will see the preview above

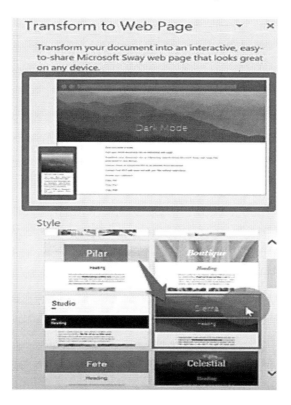

- Then, click on the "Transform" option to make changes

- You will be instructed about your preferred choice, that your document will be transformed to a Microsoft Sway web page. Once you are sure about your decision, simply click on "Transform" to proceed

- Once done, your web page transforming template will automatically open on your web browser

- You can also edit your web page by clicking on "Edit" which gives you the privilege to modify your web page template.

- You can also review the "Navigation"

- And also "Share" the link with others

Converting Photo or Text PDF into Editable Word Document

Convert from PDF with ease and edit your files without any restrictions, you can also do the same to an image text with Word 365, you are limitless.

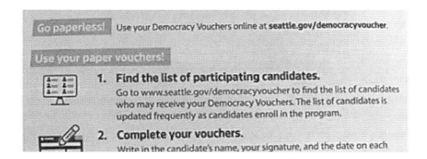

To see how this works;

- Simply go to the "File" menu

- In the "File" menu, a pane will appear by your left-hand side, click on "Open"

- At your right-hand side, "Open" features will appear, locate the document to be converted, whether an "Image text" or "PDF text"; if not found, navigate to where you have your file in your "Folders" to browse it or click and drag it into Word environment.

- You will get a "Microsoft Word Notification" that Word is about to convert your PDF to an editable Word document. The resulting Word document will be optimized to allow you to edit the text, so, it might not look exactly like the original PDF or Image-text especially if the original file contained lots of graphics. Note that for an effective result; make sure you have a data connection. Once you agree with the "Microsoft Word Notification" by pressing "Ok", then your PDF or Image-text will be displayed as an editable Word document

- Below will be your outcome, after the extraction of the text, which will be placed on your Word document for further self-editing.

Go paperless! Use your Democracy Vouchers online at seattle.gov/democracyvoucher.

Use your paper vouchers!

1. Find the list of participating candidates.

   Go to www.seattle.gov/democracyvoucher to find the list of candidates who may receive your Democracy Vouchers. The list of candidates is updated frequently as candidates enroll in the program.

2. Complete your vouchers.

   Write in the candidate's name, your signature, and the date on each voucher. You can assign one or more vouchers to participating

Copy and Paste Multiple Items on Clipboard

Most of us are familiar with copy and paste but not aware of copying multiple texts differently and then see all your copied text while pasting it. Let me illustrate

- Assuming, I type "Copy me!", "Copy this!", and "Copy that!"

- Then, I copy it separately and I press "Ctrl + V" which is to paste, my result will only affect my last text which is "Copy that!"

- What if I want to paste the first text or the second text locally? Word will help with this by going to your "Home tab", below it, you will see your "Clipboard ribbon", there is a dropdown arrow indication, click on it to view all your different copied text

- Below is your outcome, where you can manually select the preferred text you want to paste by clicking on it, which in return will be pasted wherever your mouse cursor is pointing at (the blinking position).

Note: This is not limited to text, image also can be copied and pasted

Use formulas to calculate values

It is rarely known that Word performs mathematical calculations with different formulas like "Microsoft Excel", I will be showing you the possibilities

- Assuming, I have created my tabulated figures and all I need to do next is to sum it up without having to manually calculate it myself or with my PC calculator

Using formulas in Word

Word can do formulas too!

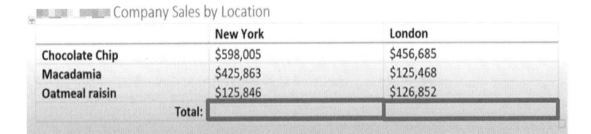

Company Sales by Location	New York	London
Chocolate Chip	$598,005	$456,685
Macadamia	$425,863	$125,468
Oatmeal raisin	$125,846	$126,852
Total:		

- Look to the "menu bar" and select "Layout"

- Once selected, at your left-hand side, locate "Formula" and click on it

- Once you click it, a dialog box will appear where you can perform your arithmetic, this has been explained in "chapter seven", but for further understanding and the rareness of it. I have to show you more about it.

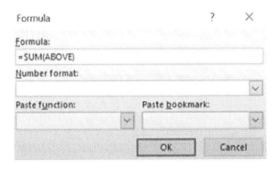

- Note, this is not only limited to summing up values, you can also click down below the illustrated apart and see all of the different formulas you can apply to your calculation. Calculating is not only about the summation of figures, other formulas can also perform other tasks such as getting your "Average" figure, "Max" for maximum figure, "Min" for minimum figure, and lots more, just scroll through the "scroll bar"

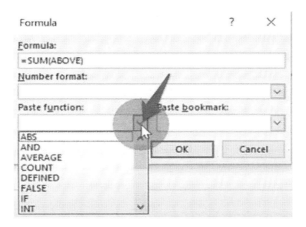

- I am going to stick to "=SUM(ABOVE)". To know more about what the symbols represent, kindly check back on "Chapter Seven" on the topic **"Using Math Formulas in Tables".** After you click on the formula you want, click "Ok" to see the effect

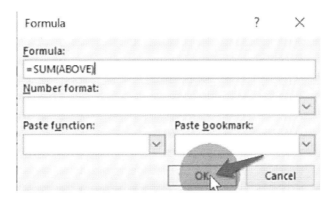

- Below is your total summation, make sure your cursor is on the cell where your total figure will be pasted, because if not you won't get your expected result

Sales by Location

	New York
	$598,005
	$425,863
	$125,846
Total:	$1,149,714.00

Assignment

From the table on pg. 241, calculate the total summation for "London" using the just explained procedure and do your manual calculation also for comparison.

Sort lists Alphabetically

- Do you know that you can sort lists in Microsoft Word and you can also sort lists in various ways? First of all, I will type some largest city in the World as illustrated below

- Secondly, the list will be automatically sorted out alphabetically. To do this, select (highlight) the list

- And then, go to your "Home tab"

- At your right-hand side, click on the "Sort" icon which is represented with "upward A & downward Z with a downward arrow". After you click on it

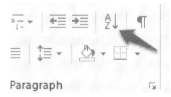

- A dialog box will appear titled "Sort Text"; make sure at your right-hand side you select "Paragraph", while at your left-hand side you select "Text", also click on the "Ascending" button for us to get our alphabetical order arrangement. Below it, you will see "My list has" which shows options, "Header row" and "No header row". For this illustration, I have no header row, which means I will click on "No header row". Once done, click on the "Ok" button.

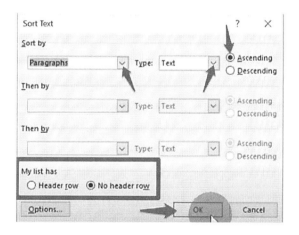

- You will notice your highlighted list will automatically rearrange itself alphabetically.

Sort in Word

Sort lists Numerically

Sorting out lists is not only limited to alphabetical arrangement alone, but you can also sort out lists numerically by following these steps:

- Highlight your numbers to be sort

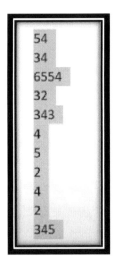

- Assuming, you want to rearrange the above numbers, simply go to your "Home tab"

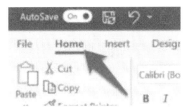

- At your right-hand side, click on the "Sort" icon which is represented with "upward A & downward Z with a downward arrow". After clicking it

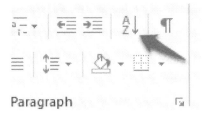

- A dialog box will appear titled "Sort Text", make sure at your right-hand side you select "Paragraph", while on your left-hand side you select "Number", also click on "Ascending" for us to get our numerical order arrangement. Below it, you will see "My list has" which shows options "Header row" and "No header row". For this illustration, I have no header row, which means I will click on "No header row", once done click "Ok".

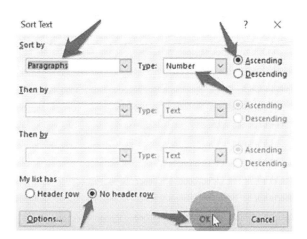

- You will notice your highlighted list will automatically rearrange itself numerically in ascending order.

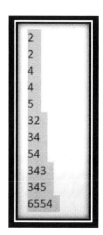

Sort lists by Date

You can also sort out your listed dates in ascending order, without the use of Microsoft Excel. I know you are amazed by a lot of interesting Microsoft Word features. Now you understand, when I said, this is the right book you have purchased for your self-improvement. So, let us also see how sorting out dates works.

- Highlight your dates

- To rearrange the above numbers, simply go to your "Home tab"

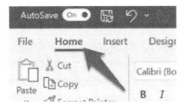

- At your right-hand side, click on the "Sort" icon which is represented with "upward A & downward Z with a downward arrow". After you click on it

- A dialog box will appear titled "Sort Text", on your right-hand side, select "Paragraph", while on your left-hand side, select "Date". Also, click on "Ascending" for us to get our alphabetical order arrangement. Below, you will see "My list has", which shows options, "Header row" or "No header row". For this illustration, I have no header row, so, I will select "No header row". Once done, click on the "Ok" option.

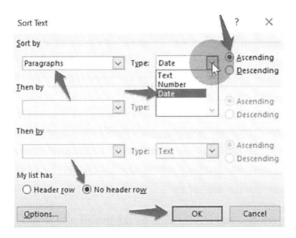

- You will notice that your highlighted date will automatically rearrange itself in an ascending way

Collaborate with others via a link

Easily share your documents to work together with others as a team by using a link to send your document. In the past, if you wanted to work with others on a document, you have to email them by sending an attachment of your document for editing. They do the editing, send it back to you, and then, you have to merge all the edits which might consume a lot of time, especially when you are trying to see what has been added or removed; what a stressful process! Luckily, things have gotten a lot easier

- Simply look at the top right-hand corner of your Word 365, you will see a "Share" option, click on it

- This opens a "share" dialog box which gives the access to share your document via a link. By default, it is on "Anyone with the link can edit"

- You can click on the default settings which is "Anyone with the link can edit", you will be shown other options such as "People in your domain with the link", "People with existing access", and "Specific people". Below are other functions you can tick or untick; "Allow editing", "Set expiration date" for termination of your shared link, "Set password" against unauthorized co-authors, you can also set "Block download" at your wish. Once you are through with your configuration, click on "Apply"

- If the above illustration is not what you need, press the "Cancel" option beside "Apply". After you click on apply, you will be brought here, type in the co-author email, you can also add some write-up with it, then send it, or you can also copy the link to your document depending on your preferred choice

Collaborate with others via mentioning someone's name

Easily share your documents to work together as a team with others by using "@" mentioning others to get their attention in responding to you as it is on your Facebook, whenever your name is mentioned, you are notified about it. To see how this works,

- highlight any part of your text document you want to inform others about

- Then at the top corner of your right-hand side, click on "Comments"

- You see a dropdown option, click on "New Comment"

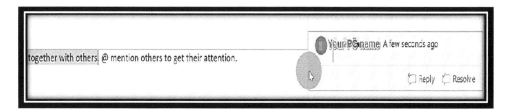

- Once you click on "New Comment", your highlighted text will be colored and another dialog box will appear at your right-hand side with your PC name or your Microsoft account name at the top of the "comment box"

- If you want to get someone's attention, simply start with an at "@" symbol, then you will be shown people within your list to be mentioned on your comment, which they are also going to be notified about

- Once you type or select the name of the person you want to add to your comment, you are going to be informed on granting access into your commented document by selecting either you "Share and notify" or "Don't share" button

- Once you select "Share and notify", their names will appear at your comment session, then, you can now type what you want them to do about your comment when your notification reaches the other end

Pinning a Document

Another hidden feature on Word 365 is the "pin" feature that enables you to quickly pin down a document and get back to the content in the future.

- To pin a document, simply go to "File menu"

- This brings us to the backstage within your "Home view"

- Look at your right-hand side, you will notice all your recently opened documents

- When you click on any of the recently opened documents, on your right-hand side, you will see two icons, the first one is the "share" icon which I have explained earlier, while the second one is the "pin" icon. Click on the "pin" icon to pin your preferred document

- Once you have clicked on "pin" to pin down your preferred document, simply click on the title "Pinned" to see your pinned document.

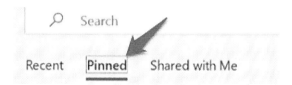

Rewrite suggestions

Another newly added feature of Microsoft Word 365 is the "Rewrite Suggestions" which gives its subscribers access to rephrase words. Let's see how it works

- Assuming I typed the below sentence

I'm **always working** to **continuously improve** my videos.

- Now, you highlight the area which you want to rephrase. Let's assume it is "always working" in the above illustration

I'm **always working** to **continuously improve** my videos.

- Right-click on the selected text, a dialog box will appear, locate and click on "Rewrite Suggestions"

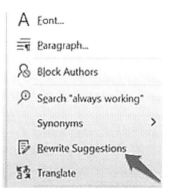

- Once you click on "Rewrite Suggestions", another dialog box will appear at your right-hand side with a suggestion of my highlighted text instead of "always working to" you can say "constantly working to" or "working all the time to"; I will click on "constantly working to"

- Then my highlighted text will be replaced with "constantly working to".

I'm **constantly working to continuously improve** my videos.

Assignment

Simply get another word replacement by using your "Rewrite suggestions" to rephrase "continuously improve" as illustrated below

I'm **constantly working to continuously improve** my videos.

Table of Contents

Microsoft Word has made it extremely easy to insert "table of contents"

- Simply go to the "References" tab

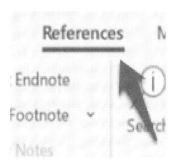

- Under "References", at your left-hand side, you will see your "Table of Contents", click on it

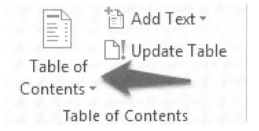

- Dropdown options of "Table of Contents" will appear where you can pick your preferred choice

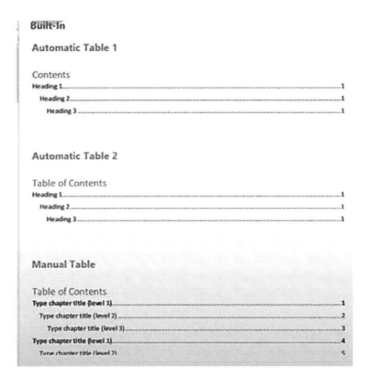

- To customize your own "Table of Contents", make sure you first highlight your headings then, go to the "Home" tab and select your "heading style" on all your headings or titles, once done, position your cursor in your document area where you want your "Table of Contents" to appear on

- Then, you can go back to your "References" tab to select your preferred "Table of Contents" as illustrated earlier

- Then, your highlighted headings and selected heading style will enable your "table of contents" to display automatically. As you go through your document to add more words, some of your "Table of Contents" might change in numbering due to newly adjusted words

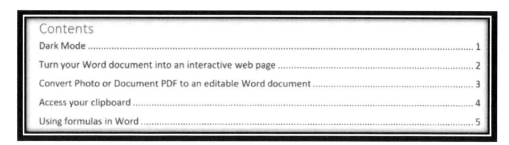

- You can keep your "Table of Contents" updated by clicking inside the top left-hand corner of your created "Table of Contents". A little displayed dialog box will popup named "Update Table"

- When you click on "Update Table", a dialog box will appear titled "Update Table of Contents", requesting you to select one of your preferred options between "Update page numbers only" and "Update entire table"

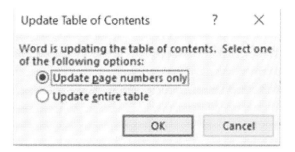

Citations and bibliography

Citation and bibliography on Microsoft Word are used to give credit to a source of information by citing the article, book, or other sources it comes from.

How to Insert Citation

To insert your citation, simply follow the steps below

- Firstly, construct a bunch of text to be cited

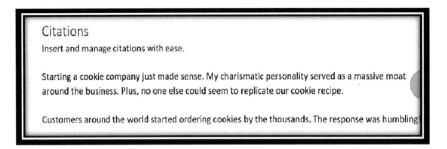

- Go to the "References" tab

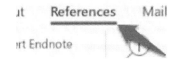

- At your right-hand side, locate "Insert Citation" and click on it

- Once you click on "Insert Citation", you will see dropdown options, choose "Add New Source" by also clicking on it

- Clicking on "Add New Source" will automatically open another dialog box titled "Create Source"

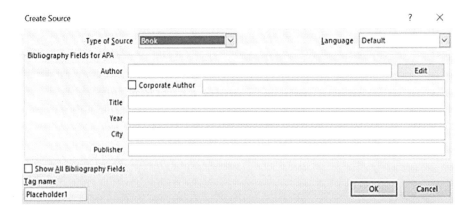

- Here, you can add all necessary information related to your source of information. For example, "Type of Source" will give you a dropdown of suggested lists to choose from about your citation, once you fill every required question, you can then click the "Ok" option

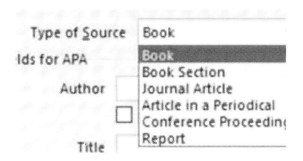

- Once you are done, your citation will automatically be added to your text

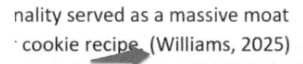

How to Create Bibliography

- To also create your bibliography, you can first get your "Style" format. Assuming, we choose the first option which is APA style

- Next, let also click on "Bibliography"

- A displayed dropdown list of "Bibliography" will appear, for understanding purpose, I will select "Works Cited"

Works Cited

Chen, J. (2003). *Citations and References*. New York: Contoso Press.
Haas, J. (2005). *Creating a Formal Publication*. Boston: Proseware, Inc.
Kramer, J. D. (2006). *How to Write Bibliographies*. Chicago: Adventure Works Press.

- Then, your configured bibliography will appear below

Works Cited

Williams, J. (2025). *How the ▨▨ ▨▨ Company took over the food industry*. New York: Stratvert
Publishing.

- You can also update subsequent citation by clicking on the "Bibliography" table and at your top left-hand corner, you will see "Update Citations and Bibliography"

Conclusion on Word 365

Wow, am glad you were able to make it through this practical guide (Book 1) on Word 365. Now that you have gone through the process of learning, you can now see the power behind reading the right book. I believe you have no more worries about Word 365 again.

I encourage you to also use this knowledge to contribute towards the wellbeing of humanity in your unique way, which in turn, your value will be appreciated in a greater way than you can ever imagine, how do I know this? This is the foundation of how Bill Gate, the founder of Microsoft started his pathway in life.

Can you compare before you went through this guide, and now after going through this guide? Now you fully understand what I meant by practical guide for all, irrespective of your career path.

Kindly, share with us your experience of this guide, looking forward to hear from you soon.

BOOK TWO

EXCEL 365

INTRODUCTION

Excel Office 365 is a new update patching into an excel program and it uses a more powerful tool that can allow you to create a document in a better way and to work with others conveniently. Excel 365 permits you to put together a lot of information from various people and sectors into a single worksheet, above all, you will be permitted to work with two or more persons on a similar worksheet at the same time which in turn improves efficiency and leads to a new vision for an organization as information is shared with all relevant personalities within the organization. In the same vein, it introduces an Excel pivot that can let you convert Excel into a driving force that can combine considerable volumes of data from numerous sources and construct a connection between them.

It is the free version of Excel that allows you to use a web browser by signing up for a Microsoft account with a new email or an existing email address with monthly or yearly payment to have access to Excel 365 features as well as the privilege to update to the latest version and effective security updates and bug fixes.

Above all, it securely stores all your document into the cloud with 1 TB of one cloud storage, nevertheless, you can access this cloud anywhere.

Do not get it twisted, Online Excel remains Microsoft Excel with a few differences from the traditional Excel. For instance, you run Excel on your computer by navigating to the start menu, search for Excel and click on it to open it, while Excel Online runs on the cloud and it can only be accessed with your web browser over the Internet by using Outlook.com or Gmail.com.

Once you acquaint yourself with the traditional Excel, you will find Online Excel interface very easy to work with because they are very similar in major aspects, though with little but significant differences, and thus there won't be a problem using Excel 365.

This is a well-designed user guide for all levels of users that is produced to grant you the prerequisite skills and knowledge you need to produce an accurate worksheet be it from a blank document or template with the necessary formulas for all data and text values input.

CHAPTER ONE

OVERVIEW OF MICROSOFT EXCEL

Origin of Excel

Microsoft has been in existence since early 1980 but it began to come into the limelight in 1987/1988 when Excel version 2.0 was released. It started to gain significance during the release of Excel version 5.0 with the inclusion of VBA (Visual Basic for Application) which opened many opportunities for crunching data and present the result to offices and organizations for use.

The present version of Excel is the newest release of Excel version 2019 and Excel 365 which because of their capability and the change they bring to every business demand has helped them to gain popularity and be used in the universe. Using Excel with other Microsoft applications will do greater leveraging because there can only be little that will be unachievable when they come together.

Meaning of Excel

Excel is a spreadsheet application with the major purpose of organizing and carrying out calculations on data. It is a tool for recording, analyzing data, and representing such data on a graph or chart. It is the most potent electronic application for data analysis and documentation. It comprises several rows and columns, which in turn comprises data or pieces of fact through which you can build a formula or edit it.

Relevance of Excel

The relevance of Excel cannot be overemphasized, this makes it a preferable spreadsheet application over other spreadsheet programs, and this is the key reason why it always finds expression in both small and big offices. To say the fact, we can't talk about all Excel relevance, but we will touch the essential ones.

Among what makes Excel relevant are the following:

1. It is used in keeping track of expenditures you made and for monthly budget preparation.
2. Effective modeling and practically analyzing every data
3. It is used to create a formula and edit the formula.
4. Good for finance and accounting analysis.
5. It is used to create a check and balance of a report and checkbook.
6. Performing work easier and faster.
7. Performing better in making a concise and accurate prediction.
8. Virtually developing the new feature on every new release for proper calculation such as CONCATENATE and TEXTJOIN in Excel 2019.
9. It is used in storing and manipulating data.

What Is Excel 365?

Excel 365 is an online-based version of Excel with a monthly or yearly subscription which you can operate on the Web or Cloud and thereby grant you the privilege of getting new features anytime there is a new release of any kind. It permits you to save your document both on the Cloud and hard disc or storage device.

Differences Between Excel 365 And Traditional Excel Such As (2013, 2019 And Others)

Talking about Excel 365 and traditional Excel, there may be many similarities, nevertheless, there are few differences, they may be few, but significant. Let us delve into those differences in a jiffy:

PRICING METHODS (EXCEL 365)
It involves continuous monthly or yearly payments. It is just like leasing a house, immediately you stop paying, you stop enjoying the features, though it may be a continuous payment, yet, it is very little compared to an exorbitant one-time purchase.

	Monthly cost	Annualized cost	Number of users
Office 365 Personal	$7	$84	1
Office 365 Home	$10	$120	6
Office 365 Business	$8.25	$99	5 PCs/Macs for 1 user

TRADITIONAL EXCEL (2016, 2019, etc.)

It involves a one-time purchase and when you pay for it once, you enjoy it forever, nevertheless, you will not enjoy the new features unless you will have to pay for such. For instance, when new versions come, perhaps version 2022, 2025, etc. to enjoy any feature that comes with the newer version, you are going to pay an exorbitant price that comes with it.

UPDATED VERSIONS AND FEATURES (EXCEL 365)

It always stays updated whenever there is a release of newer versions or features including security updates and bug fixes. For instance, if there is a release of Excel 2022 or 2023 in the future, you will be informed when it is out and you will get the features of such version to your application with a single click on the **update** option and it will be downloaded to your system. In short, no need for any future payments aside from the monthly and yearly payments you have been paying.

TRADITIONAL EXCEL (2016, 2019, etc.)

It does not stay updated, when there is a release of a newer version, you will not even get to know, unless other users tell you. Besides that, you will have to pay another exorbitant amount before you can enjoy any newer features or versions including security update and bug fixes. In short, before you can enjoy a new feature, you will have to make a substantial payment again unless if your version will not be updated and you continue with the older version and features.

DOCUMENT SAVING TYPES (AUTOSAVING OR AUTO RECOVER)

EXCEL 365

It has an Autosaving format of saving a document, by saving automatically to OneDrive. When you are working with Excel 365, you do not have an issue with system crash or power breakdown and thus, you have nothing to lose, even if the system you are using gets destroyed or gets lost. In short, it has an ever-reliable saving format because you can access such documents anywhere in the world.

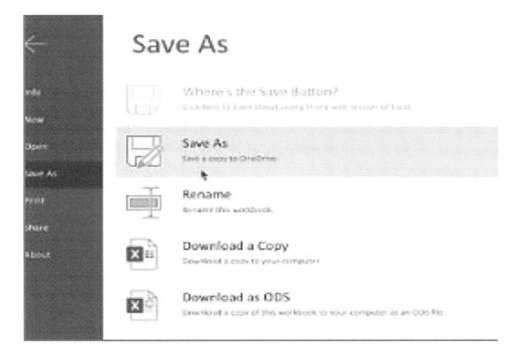

TRADITIONAL EXCEL (2016, 2019, etc.)

It has an Auto recover format of saving a document, by helping you recover the document you forgot to save maybe as a result of power breakdown or other things which may necessitate auto recovering of a document. Note that you have to meet the conditions of auto recovering before it can recover such a document. Nevertheless, it has a limitation, if the system crashes or gets lost; any document recovered or saved to that system has gone with it.

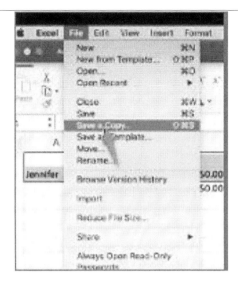

COLLABORATION (EXCEL 365)

You can collaborate and work with others through co-authoring feature which permits people to work together on a single document at the same time from anywhere in the world. This is done with an invitation via a link. To do this, single-click on "share" and enter their e-mail contact.

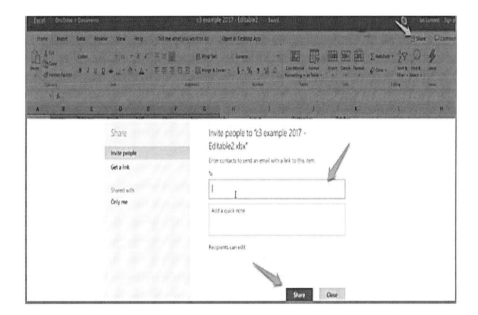

TRADITIONAL EXCEL (2016, 2019, etc.)

You can't collaborate with others, you are the only person that can work on the document unless you send the document to another email, and still, you can't work together on it at the same time with the person you sent it to.

SUB RIBBON MENU (EXCEL 365)

The sub ribbons of Excel 365 are not many; they involve basic tools for data analysis. They have a similar menu tab and you will notice they are the same but, immediately you click on each tab or ribbon, you will notice that they are little, each contains the basic tools.

TRADITIONAL EXCEL (2016, 2019, etc.)

It has full sub ribbons, it includes all the tools for data analysis and when you click on each tab or ribbon, you will observe it contains every tool you need for data analysis.

Similarities Between Excel 365 And Traditional Excel (Such As 2013, 2019 And Others)

Let us check the similarities between them, though we can't mention all, yet, we will mention the major ones.

1. Both are downloaded into the computer
2. Both are spreadsheets for recording and analyzing data.
3. The Window screen and menu tab are almost the same.

Importance of Excel 365

Excel 365 comes with a lot of benefits, but we will just make mention of the few essential ones which are:

1. Instant communication in and out of the organization: Excel 365 helps to forward instant messages to co-workers and invite them for online meetings to rub minds together on a particular document and work on it at the same time to reach a meaningful conclusion.
2. Security mindset priority: your Excel 365 document is scanned every minute, 24 hours a day to fight against malware of any type, and thus safeguard your document and information.
3. Cost-conscious and flexible: aside from pay as you go, that is, paying stipends for the service you are receiving from Excel 365, you can as well stop the payment when you do not need the service anymore, and also make payments again anytime you need the service again. This allows for immediate flexibility according to the trend.
4. 24 hours accessibility: having a consistent internet provider grants you access to the document, program, and other information on your Excel 365 program.

CHAPTER TWO

START YOUR EXPLOIT WITH EXCEL

Creating and Opening A New Excel Workbook

Before we go into creating a new excel workbook, what is a workbook? The workbook is an excel document that contains one or more worksheets that you can use to arrange your data. A workbook can be created from a blank document or an available template.

To create Excel workbook from a blank document, you have to:

- Navigate to the **start menu** and **scroll down or** you type **the name and** then click on **Excel** to launch it.

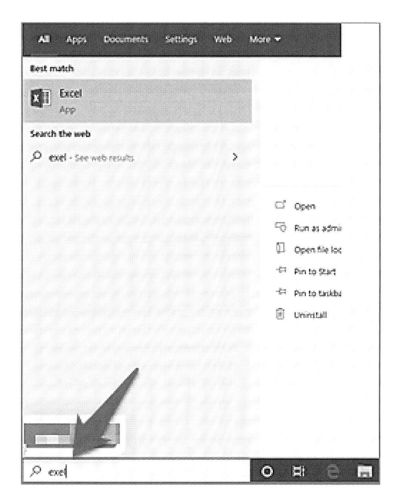

- Click on **New**, then click on **Blank Workbook**

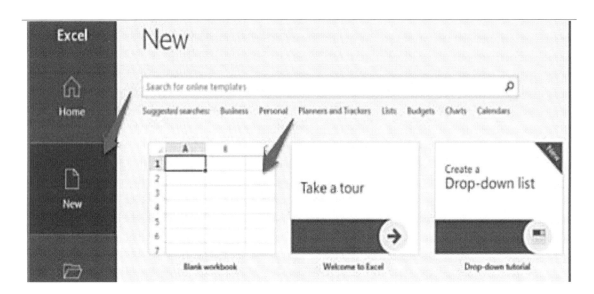

- Click on **each cell** and begin to **input data.**

To create Excel workbook from a template, after you must have opened the Excel program, kindly:

- Search for the **desired template** by scrolling through the templates or type its name in the search box for the online template and then double-click on the desired one.

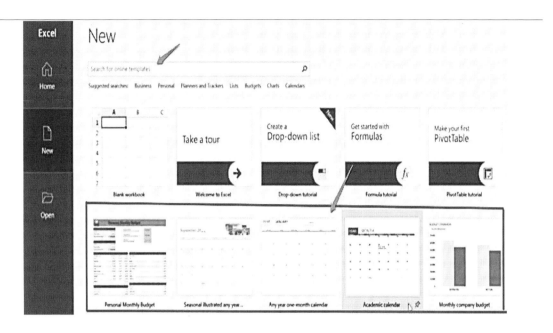

- Click on **each cell** and begin to input your data.

Note: Excel connects you to the online database with more than thousands of databases you can make use of.

Getting Familiar with The Excel Interface

Excel interface comprises of several keys which you can use together to produce a meaningful assignment, such as:

(1)   **Excel document:** Excel document is called **a workbook**; the default name is **book 1**.
(2)   **Excel ribbon:** it is broken into tabs, such as File, Home, Insert, and so on, they are used to perform specific commands. When you click on each tab, you will be able to see the various sub-grouping**.**

(3)   Name and formula bar:
a. **The name box** is located at the upper left side above the Excel column and it usually displays the address of the current cell.
b. **The formula bar** is located after the **name box** to the right side and it is used to display the content of the current cell.
(4)   Column, row, and cell:
a. **Columns** are the cells arranged vertically in the spreadsheet.
b. **Rows** are the cells arranged horizontally in the spreadsheet.
c. **A cell** is the intersection of row and column; it is represented by a rectangular box.
(5)   Worksheet navigation key: this is a button that permits worksheet forward and backward movement within a workbook with a single click on each button.
(6)   Status bar: it tells you the current mode of each worksheet such as:
a. **Ready mode:** it means you have not entered anything into the worksheet.
b. **Enter mode**: this means you are currently typing something into the worksheet.
c. **Edit mode**: it means you are correcting the current cell that has data inside. This is done by double-clicking on the cell to be corrected.
(7)   Plus icon: this is a link to add more worksheets to your workbook. The more you click on it, the more worksheet you will be having within your workbook.
(8)   Worksheet: this is the whole workspace where you can insert the numbers, letters, and formulas to carry out intended calculations.
(9)   Scroll bar: it is the bar that navigates you to any other position within the worksheet and also an indicator of your current position.
(10)   Zoom Slider: it is used to adjust the worksheet view by increasing or reducing the zoom ratio of the worksheet.

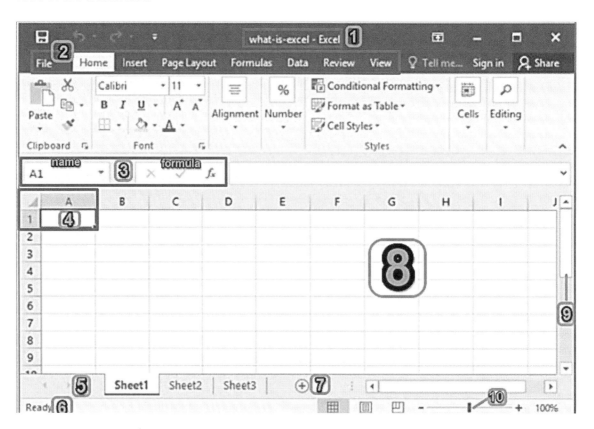

233

Understanding Rows, Columns, And Cell Addresses

Row carry headings with numbers, they are in the vertical level of the worksheet, and are identified with **numbers 1, 2, 3,** and so on. It ranges from 1 to 1048576.

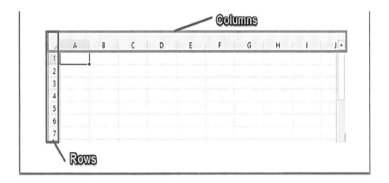

Column carry headings with letters, they are in the horizontal level of the worksheet, and are identified with **letters A, B, C,** and so on. It ranges from A to XFD.

A cell is a rectangular box that represents a point of intersection between columns and rows. This point of intersection is called cell reference, and it is used to address each cell. There are over thousands of rectangles (cell) inside a single spreadsheet.

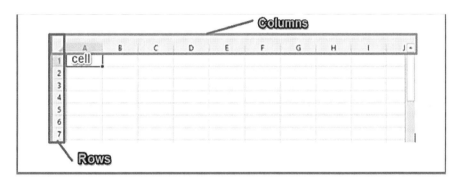

Cell range is the group of two or more cells. Cell range is addressed by **the first** and **last cell** in the cell range. For instance, the selected cell here is (A1:A8)

Workbooks And Worksheet

Excel Workbook is simply a file, or a document, or a book that consists of one or more worksheets with countless kinds of connected information. The workbook contains many worksheets with the drive to organize and arrange relevant data in a single place but in a different grouping which is known as a worksheet. Workbooks can hold unending amounts of worksheet depending on the size and magnitude of the data.

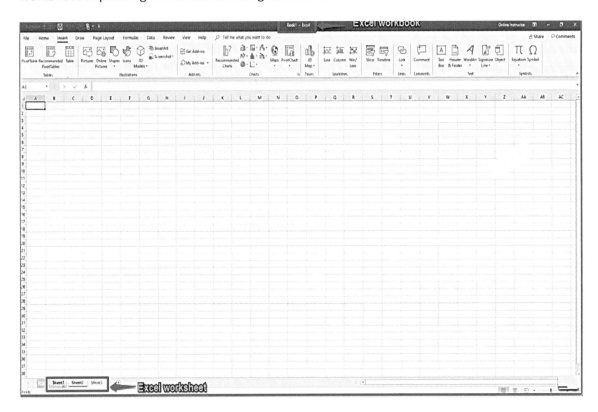

Excel worksheets can be likened to a single work page or spreadsheet in which Excel users can write, edit, and control data while the collection of such is what is referred to as a **workbook**. Though the worksheet is a single work page, it is a complete work page that contains a box of rectangular cells which is the intersection of rows and columns that you can use to reference each cell (Address). You can have as many as possible worksheets inside the workbook because there is no limit to the number of the worksheet that can be inside the workbook.

Entering Data in The Worksheet Cell

Data can be inserted in various ways in Excel. You can insert your data in a single cell, in many cells, or even more than a single worksheet at once. The data carries different forms such as texts, numbers, dates, or time.

Note: perhaps you cannot enter or edit data in a worksheet, such a worksheet might have been protected to avoid data being changed unintentionally either by you or another user. A locked/protected worksheet will allow you to view what is inside the cell but will not permit you to type or edit the cell.

To **unprotect the worksheet**:

- Go to the **Review tab.**
- Move to the **Changes** group and then to the **unprotect sheet** option and below, click **OK.** If it has a password, you will have to input the **password** before you can unprotect it.

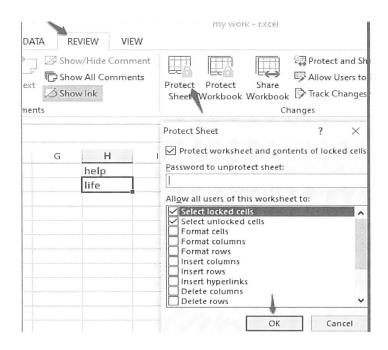

The Basic Knowledge of Entering Data

To enter data into an Excel worksheet, you have to understand what you have to avoid and what you have to practice to avoid frustration and difficulty later on and such basic knowledge will make using Excel tools, functions, and features very easy to use. The following are what you should put at the top of your mind as you begin entering data into the worksheet:

(1) **Do not leave an empty row or column as you are entering associated data:** any empty row or column inside a range of data or data table obstructs appropriate use of several Excel features such as charts, specific functions, pivot tables, and so on.

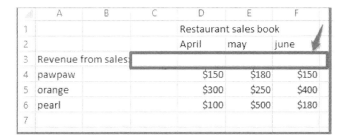

The nonexistence of empty spaces aid Excel to select related data when using a range of features such as sorting, filtering, or Auto sum.

(2) **Do not use figures as column headings and do not put units with the data:** simply use heading at the top of the column, not figures such as 200, 300, and 400, etc. when you use word heading such as equipment, advertising, etc. and not figures, it will make sorting easier

	A	B	C	D	E	F
1				Restaurant sales book		
2	Revenue from sales:					
3				2018	2019	2020
4	pawpaw			$150	$180	$150
5	orange			$300	$250	$400
6	pearl			$100	$500	$180
7	Total income			=SUM (D3:D6)		

If you use numbers as row and column headings, such may be mistakably included in the calculations, and also, using formula and function may not give adequate result when it includes all numbers in the calculation.

(3) **Keep unconnected data separately:** it is expedient to keep similar data together and at the same time it is very paramount to separate every unconnected data. Ensure to put a blank row or column between unalike data range on the worksheet so that excel will choose the correct connected ranges or tables of data.

(4) **Excel aligns texts to the left and numbers to the right:** this is the default alignment of the data which gives you the clue if you have input your data correctly and if it is formatted correctly in the worksheet.

(5) **Using cell references and named ranges in using formulas:** endeavor to use cell references and named ranges when you are using formulas so that the formulas and whole spreadsheet will be error-free and accurate.

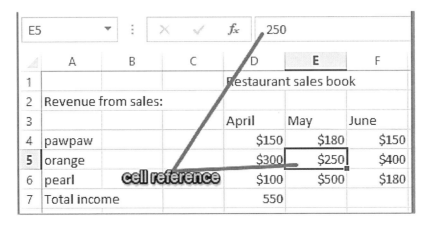

Tips: cell references recognize the position of the data by combining the row of numbers and column of letters (a single cell) while named ranges are used to recognize a range of cells in a worksheet (multiple cells combine).

(6) **Use of percent and Unit (currency, temperature, distance, and other units) symbols:** do not type percent and units' symbol along with numbers because Excel will recognize them as text,

therefore, ensure you enter all your numbers to the worksheet then after the insertion of the numbers you can format the cell to display the accurate figures either as a percentage, currency or other units. Nevertheless, some Excel recognizes the British pound (£) and dollar ($) currency sign if you type them along with numbers in the cell, but every other currency symbols are not recognized and thus they will be interpreted as text, though, this is not the same for all Excel versions. To prevent such occurrence, enter the amount first then later format the cells to input currency instead of typing currency symbols along with the amount.

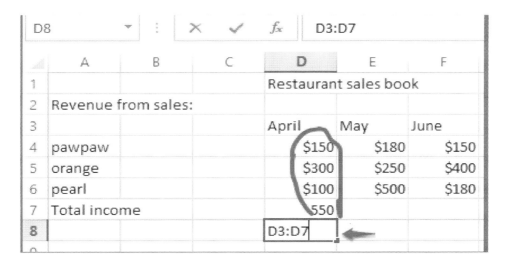

(7) **Pointing at the data:** pointing to the Excel data in a cell to enter the reference into the formulas minimizes the risk of error that may be caused by typing the wrong cell reference or address and range name misspelling.

(8) **Select the data to be sorted:** Excel has an interest in the exact range of cell data you need to sort and therefore identifies those related areas of data, even if there are:

a. Empty rows and columns between areas of related data.
b. No empty rows and columns between areas of related data.

Notes: Excel automatically excludes rows with field names from sorting. However, letting Excel choose the sorting area can be risky particularly when large data is involved.

238

Typing Your Text

The first assignment inside the worksheet is entering some headings into the rows and columns. Before you can make any data input into the worksheet, you have to make your preferred cell in which you want to input data an active cell by clicking on the cell first before typing. For instance, let us open a new blank workbook and enter some text:

1. Click **cell A2** to make it an active cell and type **Skateboarding**, press **"Enter"** to go down to another cell to make it an active cell. If you observe the text you just inserted, it seems like it stands in both A2 and B2 cells, but really, it is only in cell A2, B2 simply permits the rollover because there is no data in it. Believing the text is in cell B2 is a delusion.

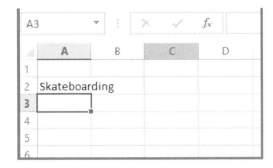

2. Let us continue and type Basketball, then press **"Enter"**.

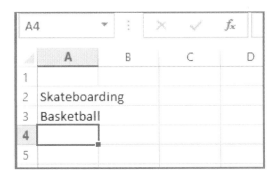

3. Repeat the above process to enter the remaining sport types in column A as shown below.

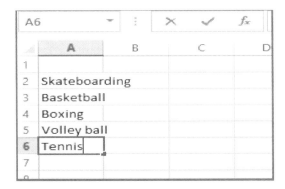

4. Click on **cell B1** and type **China**, then press **Tab** to navigate the cell to the right to make it an active cell.

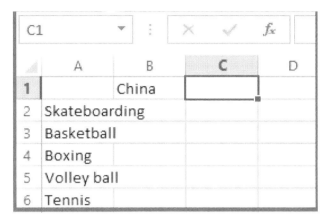

5. Enter the remaining country names in **row 1** as shown below.

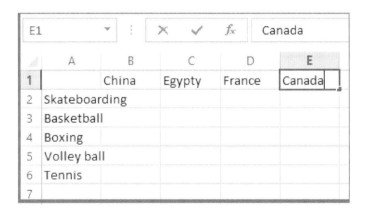

Tips: you are not restricted to use the enter or tab keys to make the cell active, you may use the arrow keys to click on each cell you want or in moving up, down, right, or left.

Typing Numeric Value

Typing number is the same way you type letters or text, by just clicking on the cell and make it active, then type the number inside. The only exception is that of the alignment, that is, the numbers will align themselves to the right side of the cell while letters align themselves to the left side of the cell, both alignments are by default. To examine how to type numbers, let us continue with the above text exercise by:

1. Clicking on **cell B2** to make it active, then type **15300,** and press **Enter** or the **down arrow**. If you observe very well, some of the texts in the left cell are not visible anymore, it is because cell B now has information inside and it has to show superiority of ownership over the texts that should not be in cell B, though some of the texts in cell A are still there.
2. Enter the remaining figures in the other cells to complete the illustration as shown below.

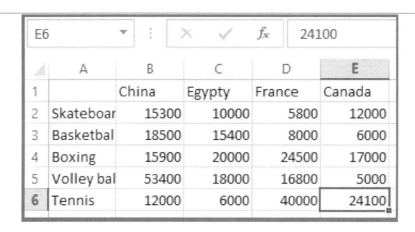

Note: to be sure of what is inside a cell (contents), click on such cell, and go to the **formula bar** at the uppermost of the worksheet to check the data contained in such active cell.

Typing Dates and Time Values

In Excel, dates are referred to a special data because immediately you insert those numbers into the cell inside the worksheet, Excel recognizes the format to which they come and instantly converts them to date. For example, 20-2, numbers like this will be converted to 20-February, from that henceforth, you can use such a date to carry out calculations.

Let us check the scenario by continuing with the previous worksheet by:

1. Clicking on **cell A8** to make it an active cell, then type **Sport at,** then tap **"Tab"** to move to the next cell.

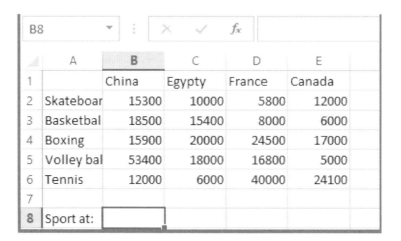

2. Type **20/03** to the active cell you have made above in (1), this number will be identified as a date and will be formatted as a date accordingly. Though you can change the format type at the latter period if you desire.

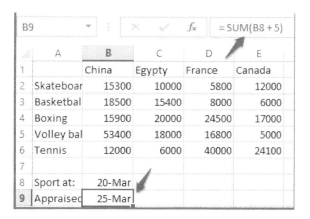

	A	B	C	D	E
		China	Egypty	France	Canada
1		China	Egypty	France	Canada
2	Skateboar	15300	10000	5800	12000
3	Basketbal	18500	15400	8000	6000
4	Boxing	15900	20000	24500	17000
5	Volley bal	53400	18000	16800	5000
6	Tennis	12000	6000	40000	24100
7					
8	Sport at:	20-Mar			
9					
10					

3. Click on **cell A9,** and type **appraised,** then tap **"Tab"** to move to the next cell (B9).

	A	B	C	D	E
1		China	Egypty	France	Canada
2	Skateboar	15300	10000	5800	12000
3	Basketbal	18500	15400	8000	6000
4	Boxing	15900	20000	24500	17000
5	Volley bal	53400	18000	16800	5000
6	Tennis	12000	6000	40000	24100
7					
8	Sport at:	20-Mar			
9	Appraised:				

4. Go to the **formula box** and Type = **B8 + 5** and press **Enter. B8 + 5** is a **formula** that is referencing the date you typed above in cell B8. Formulas are used in the spreadsheet to carry out calculations just like the formula we used here by adding 5 to cell B8 (which signifies 5 days to the date).

B9 f_x = SUM(B8 + 5)

	A	B	C	D	E
1		China	Egypty	France	Canada
2	Skateboar	15300	10000	5800	12000
3	Basketbal	18500	15400	8000	6000
4	Boxing	15900	20000	24500	17000
5	Volley bal	53400	18000	16800	5000
6	Tennis	12000	6000	40000	24100
7					
8	Sport at:	20-Mar			
9	Appraised	25-Mar			

Note: examine the alignment of your date, it should be to the right of the cell just like numbers. If the alignment is at the left, it means the date is invalid to Excel and it is not recognizing it as a date and thus, you have to take cognizance of how you enter your dates.

Taking Advantages of Flash Fill And Autofill Commands By Entering Specific Lists and Serial Data

Worksheet at times includes specific sequences of numbers drawn out of longer sequences. Entering and formatting these longer sequences will take a long time and therefore Excel has offered features like Flash Fill and Autofill to make such long tasks easier and faster. Let us quickly check how to use those features by starting with the Flash Fill.

A. **Combining data with Flash Fill:** let us begin the illustration by:
1. Opening the worksheet and input employer names; start with the First name, followed by the last name, and Establishment name in row 1 and other rows after you must have made those cells active.
2. We will assume all employers have the same format of email address which we will take as first name.last name@establishment.com.
3. We will now try to produce an automatic email address with Flash Fill by putting the first email manually. Simply click on **cell D2** and type Albert.dent@goldminers.com.

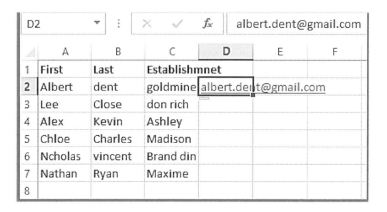

4. Now let us check the function of Flash Fill by navigating to the **Data tab** and click on the **Flash Fill** ribbon, Excel will operate it automatically, but ensure cell D2 remains cell active before you click on Flash Fill. Once you have done that, Excel will input the remaining employees' email by creating their email addresses based on the first email address's format.

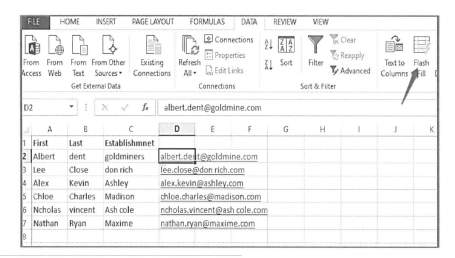

5. If you observe row 3 and row 6 email addresses. You will notice that their establishment names have two words and spaces between them and thus those spaces were included in their respective email, let us get to correct the error.

6. Navigate to **column D** and click on **cell D3**, erase the email address inside it and type lee.close@donrich.com, the space between don and rich has been removed, now go to Flash Fill, and ensure you are still having D3 as the active cell, then click on Flash Fill to apply the same formulas to the remaining email address and you will perceive that no company name will have space in the email address again irrespective of whether there is space in their establishment name or not.

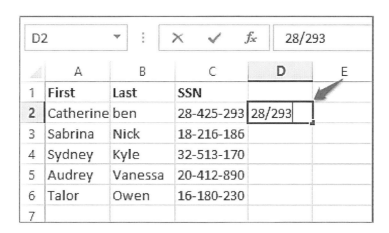

Note: remember you have to enter one cell manually and use it as a formula, to let Excel know what you are trying to do.

B. **Extracting data with Flash Fill**: as you have combined data with Flash Fill, you can as well extract data with Flash Fill. How? Let us check the below illustration:

1. We are having a first name, last name, and security serial number (SSN), but the security number is not real and the actual SSN ought to be the first two (2) numbers and the last three (3) numbers of the initial SSN. Now we will be using Flash fill to extract the real SSN by clicking on **cell D2** and type **28/293** which represents the first two and last three digits of the first SSN to tell Excel what you are trying to do and what you want to do to the remaining ones.

2. Ensure **cell D2** remains the active cell, now move to click the **Flash Fill** button, and you will notice Excel has grabbed the actual digits we want to extract and even add the Separator line to the digits, this is the power of Excel using Flash Fill.

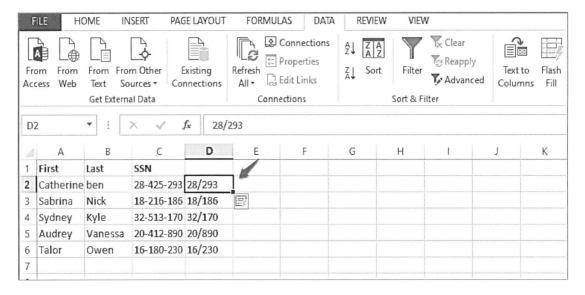

C. **Auto Fill command:** identifies a specific category of data such as consecutive numbers, dates, days of the weeks, and months of the year and therefore, instead of entering all these data manually, simply enter one or two pieces of such data and Excel will quickly fill the remaining data with the AutoFill command. To enjoy the AutoFill command, kindly observe the following processes:

1. Click **the cell** that will be the first in the sequences. For instance, list the month, and the day you want. For illustration, start with February, Wednesday, or a consecutive number such as 3.
2. Then enter the first item in sequence into the cell as stated above in (1).

3. Move to the **next cell** perhaps in row order or column order and enter the second item in the sequences such as March, Thursday, and 6, so that Excel can perfectly understand the flow of the sequences.

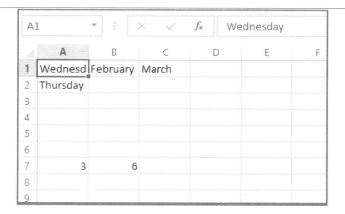

4. You can now select the **cell or cells** you have inserted your data into, either you will select one of the two cells or both cells by a click on one cell or dragging over the two cells.
5. Then click on the **AutoFill** handle and double-click to begin dragging it to the direction you want those sequences to appear on the spreadsheet.

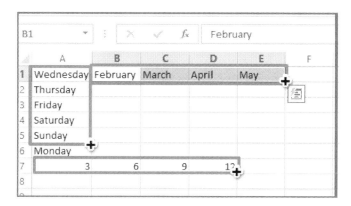

Note: **AutoFill** handle is the small green square located at the lower-right corner of the cells you selected. It is inactive until it changes to a black plus (+) sign, then you can drag it by double-clicking it. The more you drag the AutoFill handle, the more the serial data will be appearing in a pop-up box. AutoFill options appear immediately you start entering serial data, and it gives you the option to either copy or fill the cell without transferring the data along with the format.

Probably you want to enter the same item into many empty cells, drag over the cells to select those cells, then type the text or numbers you want to duplicate to other cells into the first cell in the sequence and press **Ctrl + Enter**. You can as well select those cells by holding down the Ctrl key and continue clicking on where you want the item to enter.

Applying Formatting to Numbers, Dates, Money, And Times Values

Formatting in Excel simply means changing the appearance of the numbers, dates, and times to your taste. For instance, if you type 23/3 in a cell, Excel will change it to a date format and it will be displayed as 23-March in the cell, in the same vein you may type 11.15a, Excel will interpret it as time and show it as 11:15 AM. This format may not tally with your preference and thus you have to change it by formatting such data. To format numbers, times and dates kindly:

- Click **cell C2**, hold down the Shift key, and then click on **C7** to select a range of dates.

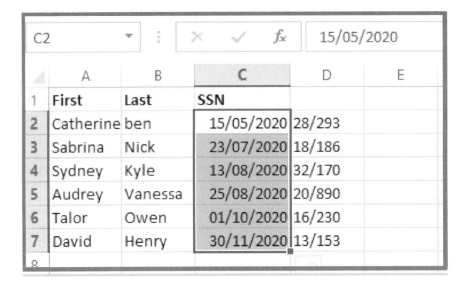

- Move to the **Menu bar** and click on the **Home tab,** then move to the **Number** group to see a number format.
- In the number group, click on the **Long date** option to change those selected short dates to a long and more explicit format.

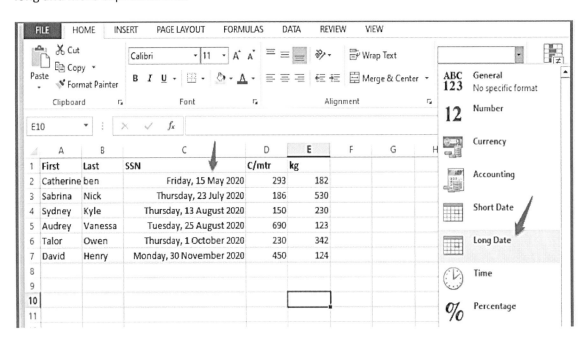

- For currency, select the range of cell D2 to cell D7, move to the **Number** group, then select **Currency**. The currency here is naira (#), you can check other currencies by moving to the "more number format" option to select your preferred currency.

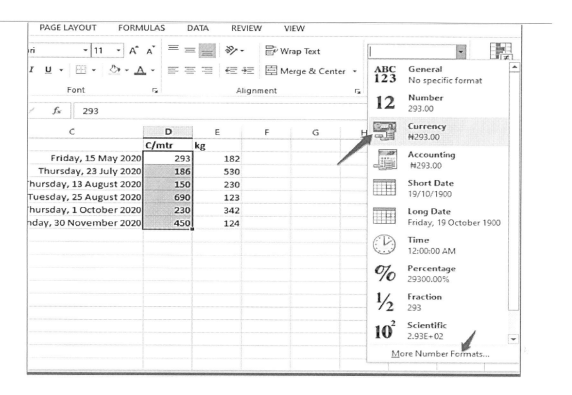

- On the Number bar, click on **Currency,** pick your preferred currency, and tap **Ok**.

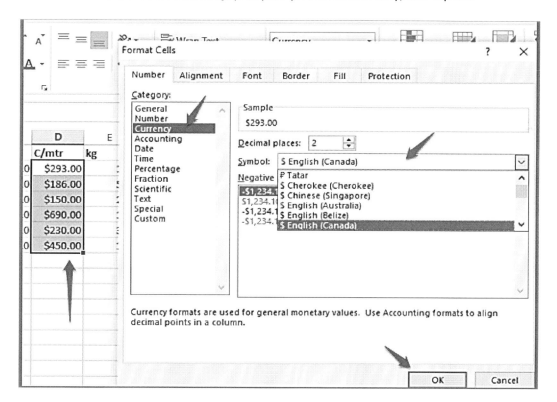

- Select a range of **Cell E2 to E7** and move to the **Number** group, then select **Number** to show numbers in two decimal places. You can still go to "More Number Format" for more options.

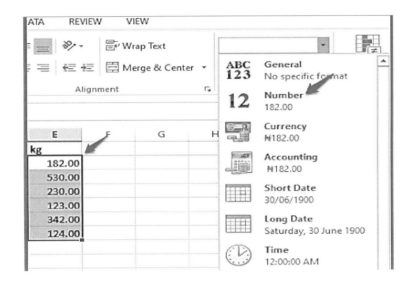

Note: you can press **Ctrl + 1** as a shortcut to access the "More Number Format" dialog box.

Essential Guide to Data Validation

Data validation is a special feature made by Excel that permits users to control what they enter into the cell. Data validation can help you to enter data in a preferred specified format, restrict the kind of data to be entered into the cell, and can be used to create a drop-down as well.

Let us now check types of data validation rule:

1. **Allowing whole numbers and decimal only:** to restrict the type of data that will enter into the cell such as whole numbers and decimal, you have to:
a. Pick **the cell** you want to restrict its data.
b. Move to the **Data tab** and select **data validation** to bring forth the data validation dialogue box.

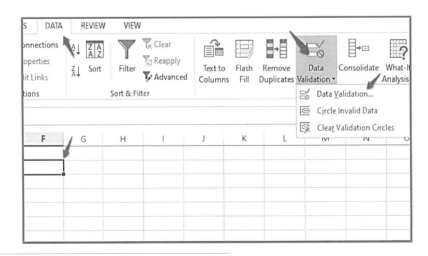

c. Pick the **Data type** under "Allow" such as whole numbers and decimal.

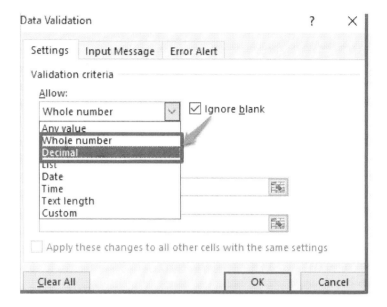

d. Then establish the measures by choosing under **"Data"** perhaps it is between, equal to, and so on.

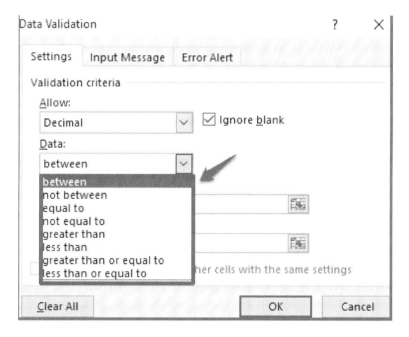

e. Supply further information that is required for restriction guidelines such as "Minimum" and "Maximum". For instance, a filling station attendant with a customer number between 5500 to 10000 will set the minimum as 5500 and maximum as 10000. After that, tap on **Ok.**

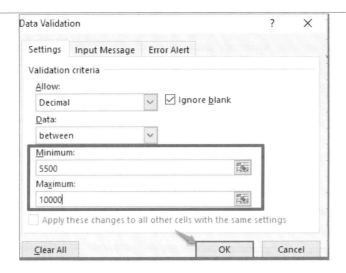

Note: immediately your data entry goes against the validation rule, there will be a prompt warning that the data doesn't match validation restrictions defined for the cell.

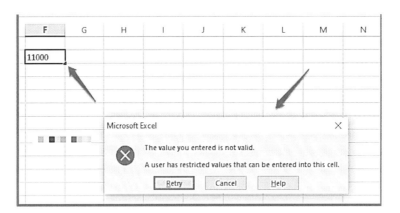

2. **Setting rules for text character length**: rules can be set for a particular text character length to limit the length of the text that can occupy the cell. To do that:
a. Select the cell or cells that will receive the restriction guideline.
b. Move to the **Data tab** and click on **Data Validation** to open the data validation dialogue box.

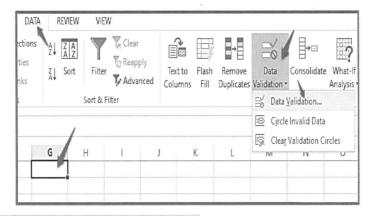

c. Pick **"Text length"** under "Allow".

d. Establish befitting measure under the **"Data"** option.

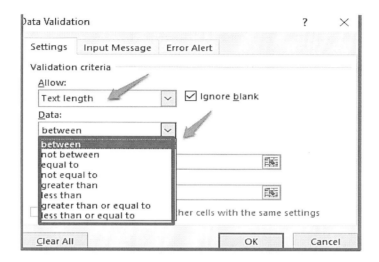

e. Supply further information which will stand as a restriction guide. For example, you might want the applicant's username to be within a range of 7 to 15 length in character. Input 7 in the minimum box space and 15 in the maximum box space.

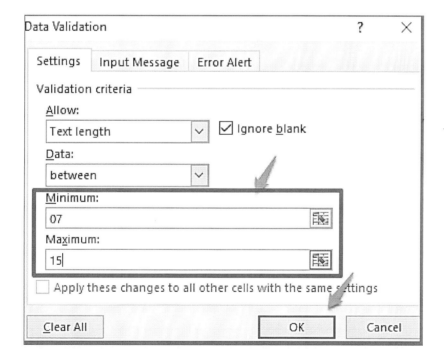

3. **Validating dates and times:** you may set a data validation rule to both the date and time to restrict specific entry into the cell. To achieve that, kindly:

a. Choose the cell or cells that will receive the validation rule.

b. Move to the **Data tab** and click on the **Data Validation** to open the Validation dialogue box.

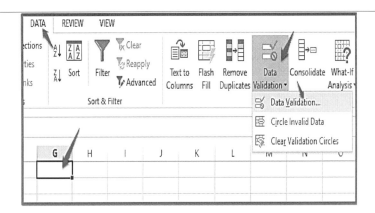

c. Pick the **"Date"** or **"Time"** option under **"Allow"** depending on the restriction item you want to incorporate first.

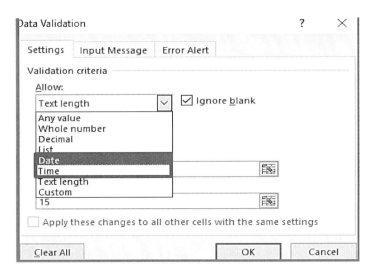

d. Pick the accurate measure that suits your preference under "Data" options.

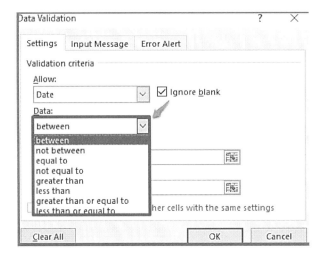

e. Supply further details needed for guideline restriction. For instance, you can choose to set employees' leave periods within the limit of a specific week in a month (10th of June to 17 June). Set the **start date** as June 10 and the **end date** as June 17.

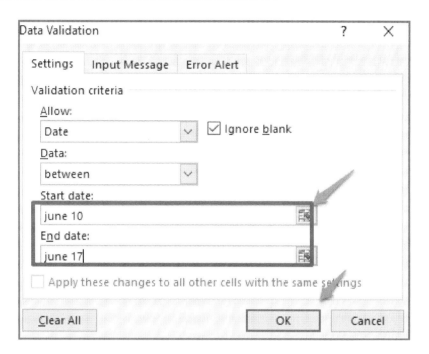

Note: Data validation guide helps Excel users to frame what they will enter within the restriction limit in such a way that it will not go beyond standard settings to avoid an error that may occur through data entry.

CHAPTER THREE

IMPROVING YOUR WORKSHEET

Editing Your Worksheet Data

Editing worksheet data simply means editing the contents of what is inside a cell either by clicking on each cell and editing it straightway or by typing data into the formula bar to edit what is inside the active cell. Any time you are editing your cell, Excel will be in editing mode.

How does Excel react in Edit mode? Some Excel users can't differentiate between Edit mode and Ready mode, Excel reacts in these two ways in Edit mode.

- In Edit mode, the "Arrow key" reacts differently, instead of moving the cursor from one cell to another cell, it will be moving from word to word within a cell.

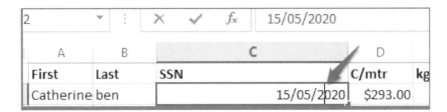

- You can't apply special formatting or adjust the alignment of cell content in Edit mode.

How do I enter Edit mode?

To navigate into edit mode, use one of the following methods:

- Click the cell that contains the contents you want to edit, then proceed to click **the formula bar**.

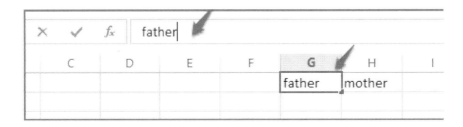

- Double-click on **the cell** that has the data you want to edit and press **"F2"** on the keyboard.

Navigating Around the Worksheet

To move around inside a worksheet, you have to make use of the cell cursor otherwise known as active cell indicator, which is the dark shape that surrounds the active cell. However, you can move round in the worksheet and alter the position of the active cell by:

1. Clicking on the cell you want to make active via the mouse.

2. Clicking on any of the four arrow keys on the keyboard to move the cell cursor in the direction of where the arrow is pointing till you get to your cell destination.

To navigate around the worksheet easily and speedily, you have to master the following shortcuts to fast-track your movement within the worksheet:

CODE	DIRECTION
Enter key	Moving to the next line near the left side.
Tab key	Moving from one cell to another in the right direction.
Shift + tab	Moving from one cell to another in the left direction.
Arrow keys	Moving cells in the direction of the arrow keys.
Home	Moving one cell to the beginning of the row that has the active cell.
Ctrl + Home	Moving one cell to the beginning of the worksheet
Ctrl + End	Moving one cell to the last cell in the worksheet.
Page down	Moving one screen down.
Ctrl + Page down	Moving to the next sheet in the workbook.
Page up	Moving one screen up
Ctrl + page up	Moving to the previous sheet in the workbook
Alt + Page up	Moving one screen to the left
Alt + Page down	Moving one screen to the right

Note: to scroll back to the active cell, perhaps you can't see it anymore on the screen, simply press **Ctrl + Backspace**.

Giving Your Worksheet A New Appearance

Programing your worksheet for a new and better look will even give you a vibe to work more on the worksheet. You have to structure your worksheet in such a way that you will be able to know which column and row you are inputting your data. The subsequent sub-topics under this chapter describe more on how to change the appearance of your worksheet for a better display such as rows and columns hiding, freezing and splitting of rows and columns, and so on.

Freezing and Splitting Columns and Rows

Freezing: Freezing is used to lock particular rows and columns while splitting helps to generate separate Windows for the same worksheet. Freezing and splitting are needed when you have navigated deeper into the worksheet to the extent that you can't see data tags on the first row and column which therefore makes it difficult for you to figure out where to input the data on the worksheet. For instance, if you have navigated deeper to W30 or C50, for you to make an area of the worksheet obvious as you have gone too far in the worksheet, you have to make use of Freezing and splitting.

Splitting: Splitting works better than freezing because you can drag the split line to another place whenever you split. Also, you can quickly get rid of both horizontal and vertical split by double-clicking on it, but all these do not apply to

freezing (though it is only freezing that will make the top row and first column stand firm without moving, thereby, permitting you in return to view the row and column tag anywhere you are in the worksheet).

How do I freeze or split rows or columns on the screen? No qualms, follow the processes below:

1. Click **the row** that is exactly below the row you desire to freeze or split, or the column exactly at the right side of the column you desire to freeze or split.
2. Move to the **View tab**, click on **The Split Button** to split the row or column. You can take hold of the split bar, which has a small division marker that is exactly above the vertical scroll bar and exactly at the left side of the horizontal scroll bar. In splitting, you will be able to know the position of the split bar because the pointer arrow turns to two when the pointer is on the split bar.

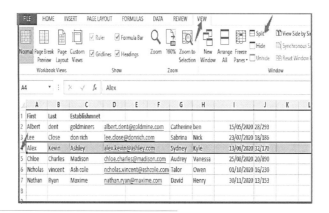

3. Click and drag **the split bar** when it turns to two arrow division to split the screen horizontally or vertically.

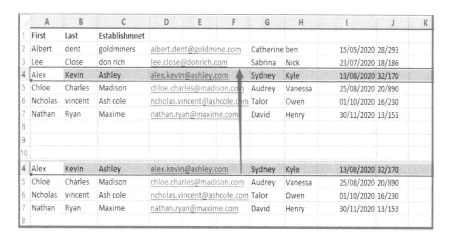

4. For freezing, kindly click on **The Freeze Panes** button**,** then choose either **the top row or first column** which are the 2nd and 3rd options respectively. Immediately you are done freezing and splitting, there will be a line that will be displayed on the screen which signifies those rows and columns have been frozen and split.

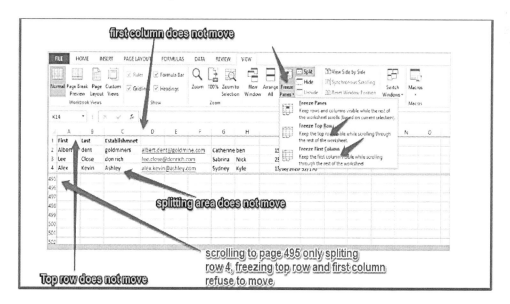

Note: Every other thing will move inside the worksheet except the frozen and split area.

Can I unfreeze and unsplit what had been frozen and split before? Yes, you can, by:

- Clicking on **the split button** once and then double-clicking either of the two bars to remove it. Drag the split bar to the top of the right or left side of the worksheet Window to unsplit rows and columns.
- Kindly click on **Freeze Panes** under the **View tab** and then proceed to pick **Unfreeze Panes** to unfreeze rows and columns.

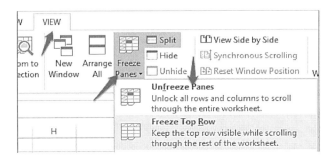

Hide and Unhide The Columns and Rows

Hiding rows and columns at times might be the best approach when you observe that you are having about thousands of rows and columns. It may be very disturbing to work in such a crowded environment, then, hiding such rows and columns will come forth as the only best option.

(1) **How can I hide a row?** This is the way:

a. Click on **the exact row (s)** you want to hide to select them.

b. Right-click on **the row(s)** after they have been selected and pick **hide** from the drop-down menu or you can press **Ctrl + 9** as the shortcut.

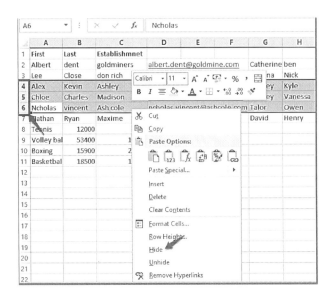

You will notice rows 4, 5, and 6 are not there anymore.

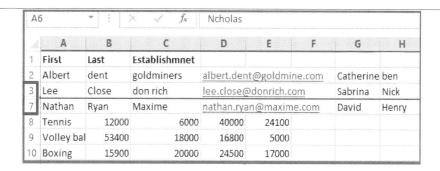

(2) Now, you have hidden rows, what if you want to unhide what you had hidden above? Let us dive into that:

a. Select **the rows** on both sides of the hidden rows (the row at the top and the row below the hidden rows).

b. Right-click on the selected rows and pick **unhide** from the drop-down menu or you can press **Ctrl + Shift + 9** on the keyboard as the shortcut.

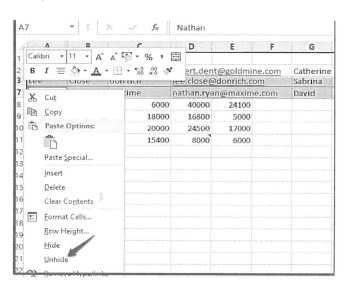

(3) However, this pattern to unhide rows can't work for the first row on the worksheet because it only has a row beneath and does not have any row above, as a result, to **unhide hidden row 1,** you have to use a different pattern:

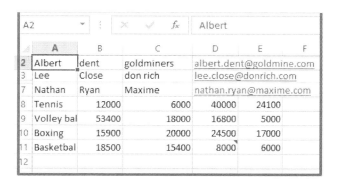

a. You will perceive row 1 of this spreadsheet has been hidden, now to unhide row 1, you will have to move to the cell selection box beside the formula bar at its left side, type A1, and press the **Enter key** so that Excel will understand you want to perform certain functions with A1.

A1		⋮	✕ ✓ *fx*	Albert		
	A	B	C	D	E	F
2	Albert	dent	goldminers	albert.dent@goldmine.com		
3	Lee	Close	don rich	lee.close@donrich.com		
7	Nathan	Ryan	Maxime	nathan.ryan@maxime.com		
8	Tennis	12000	6000	40000	24100	
9	Volley bal	53400	18000	16800	5000	
10	Boxing	15900	20000	24500	17000	
11	Basketbal	18500	15400	8000	6000	

b. Go to **the Home tab,** click on **Format cell** ribbon, then pick **Hide & Unhide** from the Format cell drop-down, and lastly click **unhide rows** option from the drop-down list.

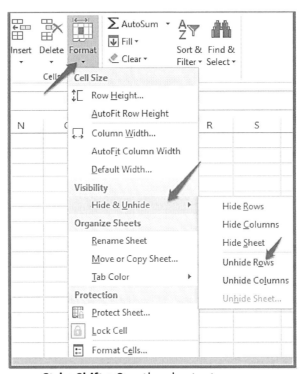

NOTE: You can simply press **Ctrl + Shift + 9** as the shortcut

(4) The Hide and Unhide Column is the next one. Though the patterns look similar, they are different. Let us quickly move to how to hide a column:

a. Let's attempt to hide **column D** as an example. Click on the **D identifier** which is above cell D1 to select the whole column as illustrated below.

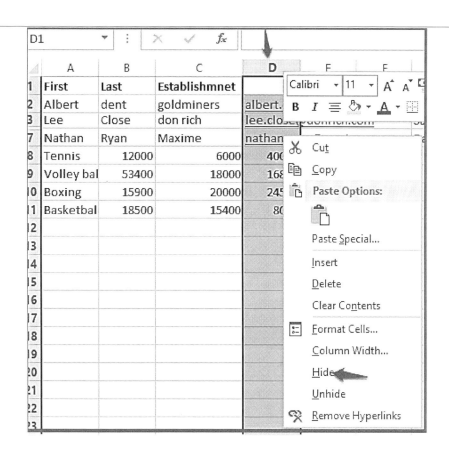

b. Right-click on it and pick **Hide** from the context menu or you can use shortcut **Ctrl + 0 (zero).** You will notice that column D has disappeared.

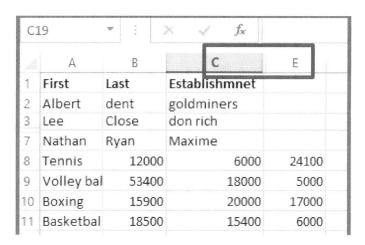

(5) To unhide the above-hidden column, you have to:

a. Select **the column** on both sides of the hidden column and then right-click on them.

b. Pick **unhide** from the drop-down menu or you can make use of the shortcut by pressing **Ctrl + Shift + 0 (zero).**

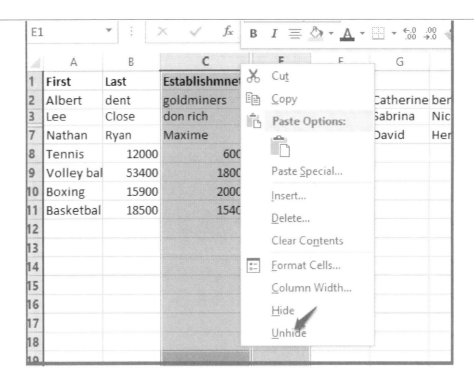

Note: probably you hide the first column, follow the same process we used in (3) above to unhide row 1 to unhide column A also;

a. Click into the **cell selection box** and input **A1.**

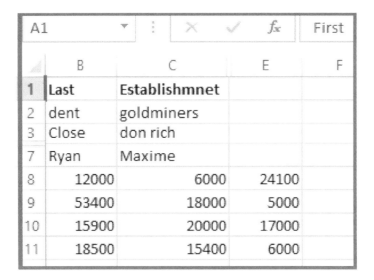

b. Navigate to the **Home tab,** and pick the **format** ribbon, and then choose **"unhide column"** from the drop-down menu.

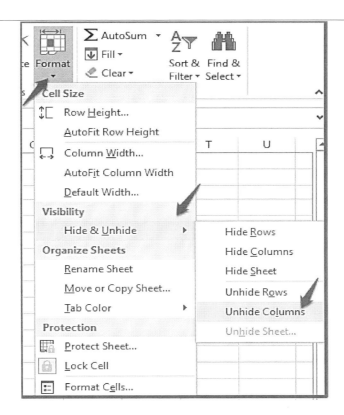

(6) **Unhide all rows and columns:** Let's assume you hid many numbers of rows and/or columns, it is not prudent to unhide them one after the other as such will take a lot of time and effort, unless you are not unhiding them all.
To unhide many rows and columns at once;

a. Highlight all the cells in the worksheet by pressing row and column identifiers or you press **Ctrl + A,** whichever you prefer.

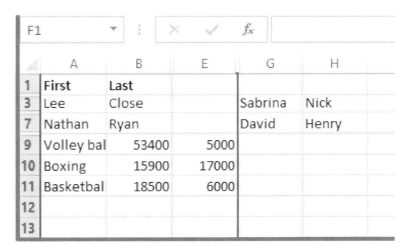

b. Right-click on **row and column identifiers** and pick **unhide** from the pop-up menu or you press **Ctrl + Shift + 9** to unhide all hidden rows and columns.

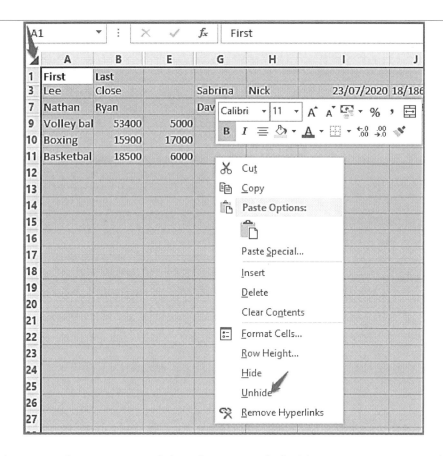

Note: perhaps you observe your worksheet is too crowded with contents, attempt to hide some rows columns to enjoy working with your worksheet.

Comments for Documenting Your Worksheet

Comments are the notes that are associated with a cell in the worksheet. They are used to give prescriptions to your worksheet. Those prescriptions give more details to the contents inside the cell, especially if it happens to be the cell with special numbers and formulas.

Comments are very easy to identify, they do have a little red triangular shape which will be displayed at the corners of each cell that has comment(s).

What do I have to know about comments? The following are the essential things you suppose to know about worksheet comments:

1. **Inserting a comment:** the first thing you can do when it comes to comment is inserting a comment. How can you do that?
a. Tap the cell you want to attach a comment to.
b. Move to the **Review** tab and click on the **"New comment"** option.

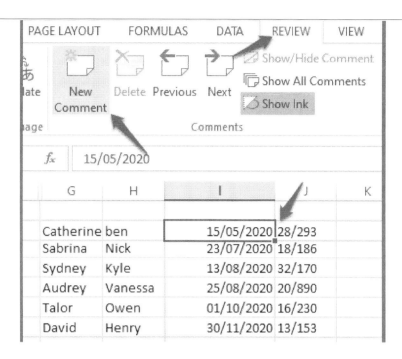

c. Insert your comment into the rectangle pop-up box that shows up after you click on the new comment option.

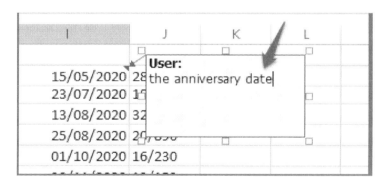

d. Click on **any cell** when you are done inserting your comment.
2. **Viewing a comment:** simply direct your mouse pointer to the little red triangle to view the comment in the pop-up box.

G	H	I	J	K
herine	ben	15/05/2020	28/293	
rina	Nick	23/07/2020	18/186	
hey	Kyle	13/08/2020	32/170	
rey	Vanessa	25/08/2020	20/890	

3. **Finding comment:** go to the **Review** tab, tap on the **previous or next** button to move from one comment to another comment to find the one you are looking for.

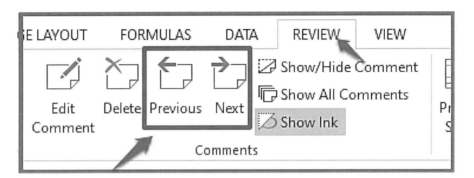

4. **Editing a comment:**
a. Select **the cell** with the comment.
b. Move to the **Review** tab and tap on the **Edit comment** button to edit the comment inside the pop-up box.

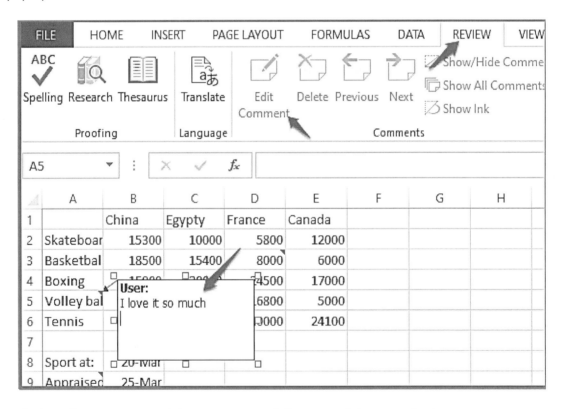

5. **Deleting all comments:** To delete comments, follow one of these methods:
a. Highlight all the cells with comments, go to the **Review** tab and tap on the **Delete** button.

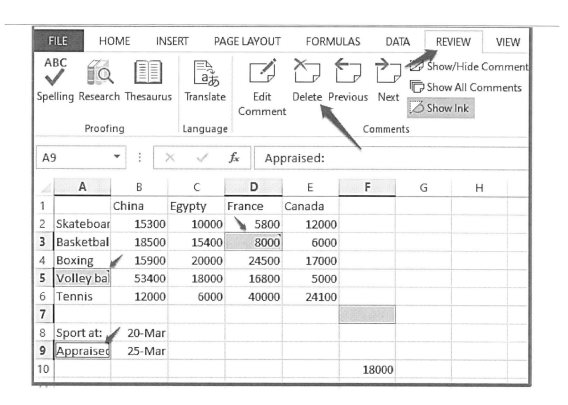

b. Alternatively, you can select all the cells with comments, go to the **"Home"** tab and then click on the **Find and Select** button.

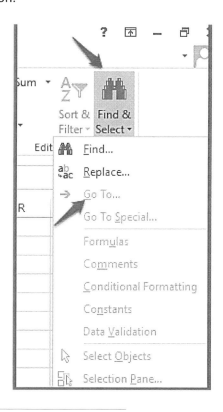

Under the **Find and Select** option, select **Go to** and tap the **Special** button.

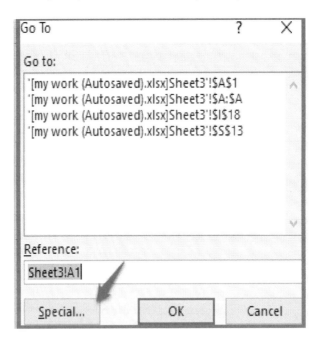

In the "Special dialog box", select **Comments** and tap **Ok**.

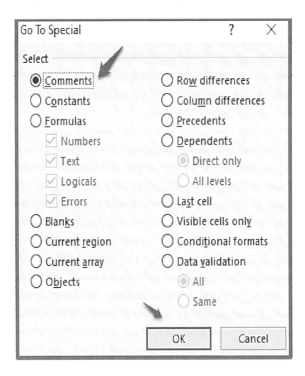

Tips: you can insert your name to the comment(s) you enter by clicking the **Office** button, select **Excel** options, and then proceed to pick a popular category from the Excel Options' dialog box where you will enter your name in the username text box.

Selecting Cell (S) In A Worksheet

You select cells most times in Excel to apply formatting effect to them or to perform a specific operation such as copy and the likes on the selected cell.

1. **How to select an individual cell:** you can select an individual cell by simply left-clicking on it. Immediately you do that, it will become an active cell, and the signal is that such cell will be surrounded by a thick box.

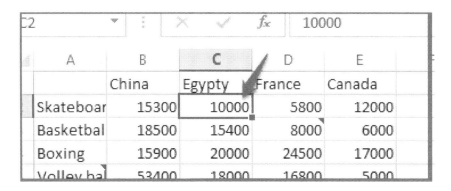

Alternatively, you can move arrow keys from one cell to another to select an individual cell. You can enter data in them immediately they become an active cell and you can as well edit the data you put in them by pressing F2 on the keyboard.

2. **How to select multiple individual cells:** multiple individual cells can be selected just by holding down the Ctrl key and then continue to click on the individual cells that you want to select.

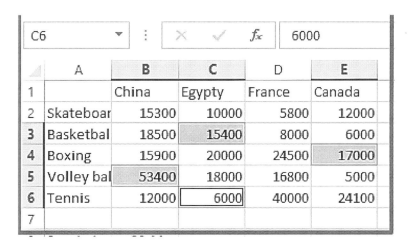

Note: as you continue to select them; those selected cells will be turning to a shaded cell to specify their selection. The last active cell is also part of the selected cell but it will not indicate immediately.

3. **How to select range of cells:** to select a range of cell, you have to:
a. Left-click via the mouse on the cell that will be the first in the range you want to select.

b. Press and hold down the Shift key.

c. As you hold down the Shift key, move to the last cell in the range and left-click on it. For instance, you want to select cell C2 to cell G2, just left-click cell C2, then hold down the Shift key and move to cell G2 to left-click as well.

Alternatively, left-click via the mouse on the first cell in the range of the cell you want to select, hold the left side of the mouse, do not release it, and then drag the mouse cursor to the last cell in the range. For instance, you want to select cell B2 through B6, left-click cell B2 and immediately without releasing the mouse, drag the mouse to cell B6.

4. **How to select all cells:** you can select all the cells in the worksheet by:
a. Navigating to the uppermost of the row and leftmost of the column in the worksheet.

b. Tap on the square area that has a shaded triangle at the top of the first column and the left side of the row, instantly, all cells inside the worksheet will be highlighted.

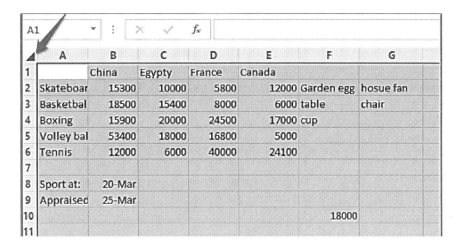

Alternatively, press **Ctrl + A** as a shortcut on the keyboard to select all the cells in the worksheet.

Deleting, Copying, And Moving Data

It is expedient at times to delete wrong input of data or incorrect data and in the same vein moving and copying data within and outside the worksheet can't be overemphasized.

1. **Delete your cell contents by:**
a. Highlighting the cells to be deleted, and then press the **Delete** Key on the keyboard.
    OR
b. Right-click the selected cells and pick the **clear contents** option or move to **the Home tab,** choose the **clear button** option, and lastly pick **clear contents.**

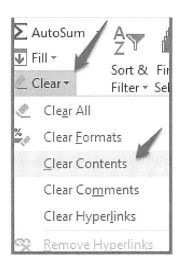

Note: Do not use the delete button on the home tab to delete cell contents because using it will delete cell contents and also the cell itself along with it.

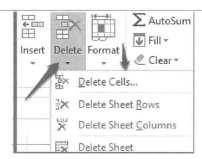

2. Moving and copying the cell contents are very similar, but has a little difference. To move and copy, kindly:

a. Select the cell you want to move or copy its content.

b. Right-click on the cell and pick **cut** or **copy** depending on which of it you want to do.

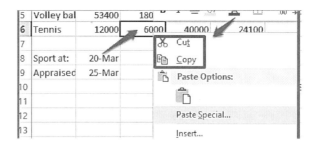

c. Go to the cell that will be the receiver of what you are moving or copying and right-click.

d. Pick **paste** from the pop-up menu, if you pick the **cut** option to cut the contents, the paste option will move the contents, and if you pick copy the content, the paste option will copy the contents.

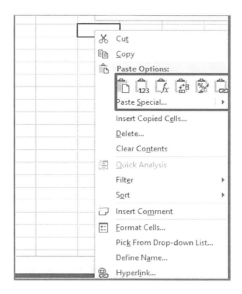

After you have selected the cell, and you are about to move or copy its content, then;

a. Move the pointer to the edge of the selected cell block (that is the cell that has the data inside), and wait till the pointer turns to a four-headed arrow.

b. Then double-click and start dragging to the receiver cell. You should hold the Ctrl key as you drag the four-headed arrow to the receiver cell to copy the contents, but if you want to move the contents, you should not hold the Ctrl key.

Managing the Worksheets in A Workbook

You can manage your worksheet inside the workbook by the way you handle the worksheet. Such management has to do with how to add, rename, delete and move amidst the worksheet inside the workbook.

Let us look at some ways of managing the worksheet:

1. **How to move a worksheet inside a workbook:** you can move from one sheet to another sheet in a workbook by clicking on each worksheet tab at the bottom of the screen.
   OR click on the navigation scroll button at the left side of the worksheet tabs.

2. **How to rearrange worksheet:** worksheet can be rearranged with its tab by simply double-clicking to drag the worksheet tab to a new position. While you are dragging, you will see a little black arrow and a page icon that will appear to indicate the position of where your worksheet can be dropped to.

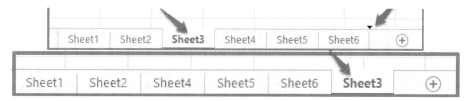

   OR by:
a. Navigating to the **Home Tab**, go to the "Cells" ribbon and select **Format**.
b. Then choose **move** or **copy** from the drop-down menu, the dialog box will be displayed.
c. Tap the position of the sheet where you want to drop your worksheet and tap **Ok.**

3. **How to select worksheet(s):** click on the worksheet tab to select a worksheet.
- You can as well select many worksheets at the same time by holding down the control key and continue clicking on the worksheet tabs to be selected.

- You may also select all the worksheets by right-clicking on the worksheet tab and pick "**Select All Sheets**" from the popup menu.

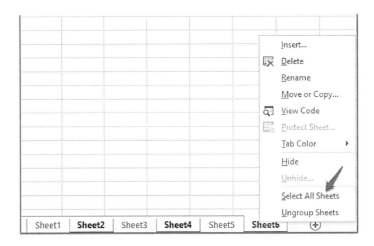

4. **How to rename a worksheet:** to rename a worksheet, you have to:
a. Go to the **Home** tab, move to the "Cells" ribbon and select **Format**.
b. Then select **rename** from the drop-down menu and insert a new name as desired.

Alternatively, simply right-click the **worksheet tab** and pick **rename** from the pop-up list.

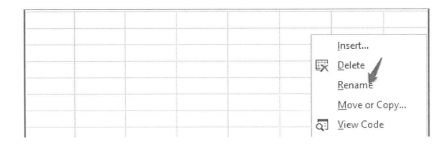

Then insert a new name and tap **Enter** to see its effect

5. **How to copy a worksheet:** copying a worksheet is very easy, just hold down the Ctrl key and double-click on the worksheet you want to copy and drag it to another position.

6. **How to add a new worksheet:** click on the **new worksheet icon (+)** that is located at the right side of the worksheet tabs, and a new worksheet will come forth.

7. **How to colorize your worksheet:** add color to your worksheet by following these steps
a. Highlight the worksheet and move to the **Home** tab, go to the "Cells" ribbon and select **Format**.
b. Select **tab color** from the drop-down menu and pick the color you want on the submenu.

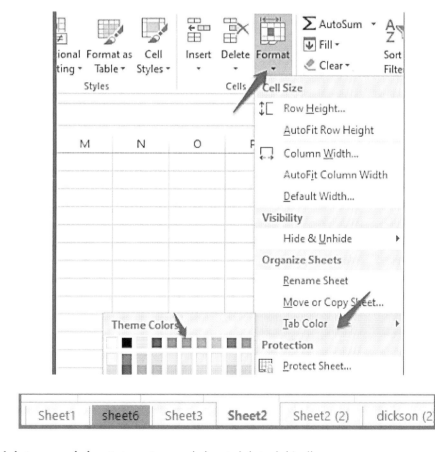

8. **How to delete a worksheet:** to get a worksheet deleted, kindly:
a. Select the worksheet you want to delete, go to the **Home** tab, locate the **delete** option under the "Cells" ribbon, and then select **Delete sheet** from the drop-down list.

You can also delete a sheet by right-clicking on the **worksheet tab** and pick **Delete** from the options.

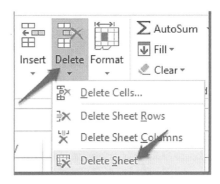

Restricting Others from Meddling with Your Worksheets

There are ways provided by Excel for a user to prevent others from meddling with their worksheet even if they access your PC. The two ways are worksheet hiding and protection.

Let us buttress more on these two ways. We'd start with hiding the worksheet, and then protecting the worksheet.

Hiding Your Worksheet

Observe the following steps to hide your worksheet so that others will not know it even exists except you

a. Select the **worksheet,** move to the **Home** tab, and locate the **Format** button under the "Cells" ribbon.
b. Select **Hide & Unhide** from the drop-down menu, and lastly, pick **Hide Sheet** from the drop-down list.

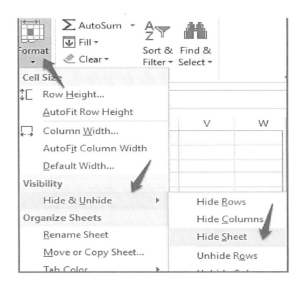

Shortcut: right-click the **worksheet tab** and pick **"Hide"** from the pop-up list.

You can as well unhide the sheet you have hidden previously by this method:

a.   Move to the **Home** tab and tap on the **Format button.**
b.   Then pick the **Hide & Unhide** option from the Format drop-down list and select **Unhide Sheet** from the list that pops up.

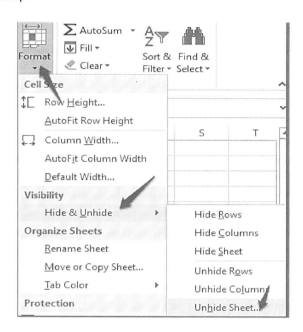

c.   Immediately you click on **Unhide Sheet**, a dialog box will come up, kindly click on the **worksheet name** you want to unhide and tap **Ok.**

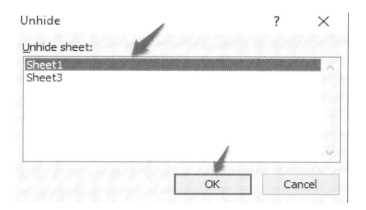

Protecting Your Worksheet

As I have said earlier, protecting one's worksheet means preventing it from any form of editing and formatting from unauthorized users. What are you preventing? They are your cell contents, rows, and columns of your worksheet, addition or removing of any row and column and so on.

Let us examine how to protect one's worksheet from an unauthorized editor:

a. Select the **worksheet** to be protected.
b. Move to the **Review** tab and tap on the **Protect sheet** button, and you will be provided with a sheet protector dialog box.

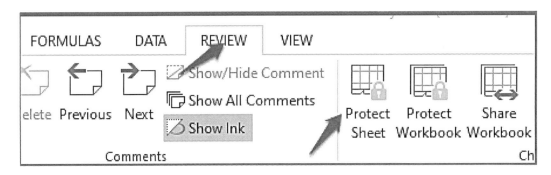

c. Input a **password** in the password space provided in the Protect Sheet box so that only those you authorize by giving them the password to unprotect it will have access to it.

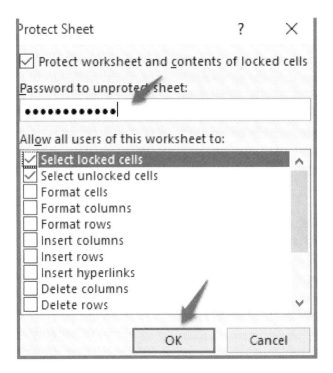

d. In the Protect Sheet box, go to **"Allow All Users of This Worksheet To:"** list, click what you want other users to do like **format cell** if you want them to format it. You only have to deselect **the "Selected locked cell"** to prevent anyone from adjusting anything on the worksheet because initially, by default, all the worksheet cells have been locked, and by deselecting the **"Selected locked Cell"**, you excellently prevent any cell from been edited.

e. Tap **Ok** to effect the changes. Perhaps you entered the password in (c) above, you will have to enter it once requested for again, then you can tap **OK**.

Note: you can unprotect the sheet you have previously protected by following these simple steps:

a. Move to the **Review** tab and click on **Unprotect Sheet**.

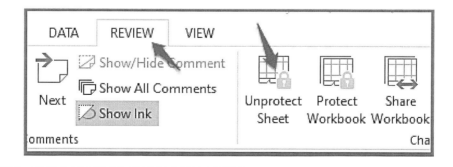

b. Input the **password** you have previously attached to it when you were protecting it.
c. Then tap **Ok**

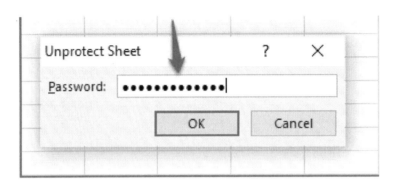

CHAPTER FOUR

COMPUTING DATA WITH FORMULAS AND FUNCTIONS

About Formulas

Excel formulas have been very helpful when it comes to numbers computation. There are certain things you will not be able to do with Excel unless you know how to structure formulas for such decisions. Excel formulas start with equal to (=), for instance, 8 + 4 = 12, that is, Excel formulas and the result. Yours is just to structure the formulas, Excel will do the computation and provide the result.

Referencing the Cells Via Formulas

Each formula you are using in Excel will be referring to some specific set of cells. Though Excel is referring to the cells, it is indirectly referring to the data or contents inside those cells to make use of them in the calculation. Let us quickly check the below illustration to get a glimpse of it:

Assuming cell C2 has 48 and cell C3 has 52, and a formula is structured in cell C4 in reference to cell C2 and C3, for example, C2 + C3, the result it will bring after you press **Enter** is 100 which is the addition of the contents that are inside cells C2 and C3. Though, Excel will not refer to the number in itself, but the cell number, therefore, if the number in cell C2 is changed to 30 and cell C3 is changed to 20, automatically, the result will be changed to 50 as well.

We need to study the illustration below to have the full understanding of how Excel goes in referring to cells and how it eventually makes use of the contents when it comes to formulas:

The example is about a small enterprise that forwarded its records to the worksheet with the agenda of checking the flow of income:

i. **Column B** is about the sales made and it shows all incomes from various sources.

ii. **Column C** is about the purchases made and it shows all expenses made to various sources.

iii. **Column D** is the actual profit, and it is derived by removing all the expenses from all the sales made.

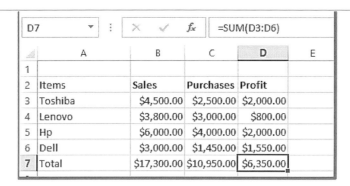

The image below gives details of how the data in the worksheet is computed:

i.   Column D shows the amount of profit from various sources calculated by subtracting the Column C (purchases amount) from Column A (sales amount).

ii.   The **Total** derived in Row 7 is the SUM function of the amount in column 3 to column 6.

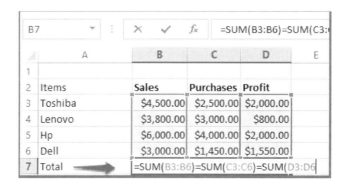

Referencing Formula Results in Subsequent Excel Formulas

Excel carries out its computation by referring to the previous formula results in the cells. Let us quickly examine the worksheet below which shows records of individual account types:

a. **Column E** displays the total aggregate savings of individuals.
b. **Column F** shows how much individual saved on average by using formula result of Total in Column E divided by 3 which stands for the total number of accounts opened by each individual.

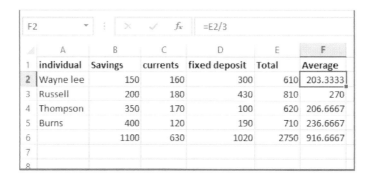

The average point in column F is derived from the formula of total calculation results divided by the average account type which is 3.

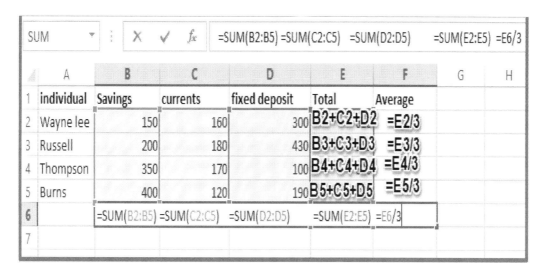

Operators and Precedence of Excel Formulas

Excel users have to understand the use of operators in Excel as it indicates the kind of calculation you are about to carry out on the data as you begin to exploit the formula. There are four (4) types of Excel Operators. Let us buttress on each of them to get you acquainted with them.

1. **Arithmetic type:** This is the kind of operator that carries out basic math functions such as multiplication, subtraction, division, and many more.

Arithmetic Operators

Symbols	Meanings	Illustrations
*(asterisk sign)	Multiplication	=6*2 or = A1 * 3
+ (plus sign)	Addition	=4+6 or = B2 + 4
- (minus sign)	Negative Subtraction	=-5 = 10-4 or = E3-2
/ (right slash)	Division	=10/2 or = D7/5
% (percentage)	Percent of	=20%
^ (caret)	Exponentiation	=10^2

2. **Text concatenation type:** this is an operator that joins one or more values together to produce a single piece of text.

Concatenation Operator

Symbol	Meaning	Illustration
& (connector)	Connecting two value together	= Total no & B3

3. **Reference type:** this is the operator that gathers a range of cells and refers them for calculation.

Reference Operator

Symbols	Meaning	Illustration
: (column)	It is called range operator. It is used to show the range of two or more cells by referencing those cells for computation	=SUM(D5:D8)
' (comma)	It merges multiple cell range and computes their value together to give one value	=SUM(C5:C6, G3:G7)
#	It is used to signify inadequate space, and once the cell is stretched, it will show the actual data inside	###### =SUM(D2##)
@	It indicates the indirect intersection of data items or cells in a formula	=@G1:G8 =SUM (Wednesday selling: Saturday selling)
() space	It is used in combining the intersection of two blocks of cells, those two blocks of the cell will overlap, if not there will be an error message.	(A1:D4 B2:C3)

4. **Comparison type:** this is the type of operator that compares one value with another and establishes reasonable outcomes, either True or False.

Comparison operator

Symbols	Meanings	Illustrations
= (Equal sign)	Equal to	= C1 = F1
< (less than sign)	Less than	= D4 < B2

>(greater than sign)	Greater than	= B2 > D4
<=(less than or equal sign)	Less than or equal to	= E8 <= A7
>= (greater than or equal sign)	Greater than or equal to	= A7 >= E8
<>	Not equal to, it only gives returns of either True or False	= D3 <> 8

The Order of Operator Precedence in Excel Formulas

There are specific orders to which Excel performs its operation, which is why you have to order your data correctly to get an accurate result for your computation. Note that Excel starts its operation from left to right.

Symbols	Details
:	Colon is used in separating all the cells you are referencing into two and gives them one reference for formulas.
'	The comma is used to collect numerous cell references into one reference.
-	Negation like -4.
%	Percentage.
^	Exponentiation or raise to the power of.
*& /	Multiplication and division.
+ & -	Addition and subtraction.
&	Two values connectors or text joint
= < > <= >= <>	Comparison.

Changing Excel Order with Parenthesis

Excel grants you the right to adjust the order by which it calculates by enclosing part of the values or formula you want to calculate into the parentheses. Let us take this scenario for example:

= 8+2*3, you should know Excel will multiply 2 by 3 before adding it with 8 in accordance to its operator order. However, if you want the addition to be done first, you can dictate to Excel your order by structuring the formula like this =(8+2)*3, this structure will cause Excel to attend to the values inside the parentheses before multiplying the result by 3.

Let us consider the example of the table in the next page, Excel will have to add D3+1000 first, after then it will divide the result with the sum of B2 through to B4, but without the parentheses, Excel will take 1000 and divide it by the sum of B2 to B4. That is the power of parentheses.

=(D3+1000)/(B2:B4).

D4	▼	⋮	✕	✓	*fx*	=(D3+1000)/(B2:B4)

	A	B	C	D
1	individual	Savings	currents	fixed deposit
2	Wayne lee	200	160	300
3	Russell	200	180	5000
4	Thompson	600	◈70	10
5	Burns	400	120	190

Foreknowledge of Entering A Formula

Getting yourself familiar with the basic understanding that involves entering a formula will help you to discover other Excel formulas and make the best exploits through it. The following are the steps you should acquaint yourself with before jumping to the pool of formula entering:

1. Select an empty cell where you will put the formula so that the value inside the cell before will not be erased.
2. Double-click the cell to write inside it.

B7	▼	⋮	✕	✓	*fx*	

	A	B	C	D
1				
2	Items	Sales	Purchases	Profit
3	Toshiba	$4,500.00	$2,500.00	$2,000.00
4	Lenovo	$3,800.00	$3,000.00	$800.00
5	Hp	$6,000.00	$4,000.00	$2,000.00
6	Dell	$3,000.00	$1,450.00	$1,550.00
7	Total			

3. You may decide either to write directly into the cell or you move to the formula box above and write the formula there, whichever option you take you will later arrive at the same result.
4. Before you start typing, you have to start with the **equal sign (=)** always, to tell Excel you want to perform a specific function, otherwise, everything you type into the cell will be recognized as values and not a formula.

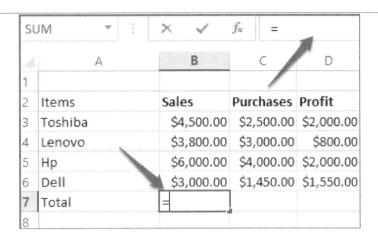

5. The accepted format of entering a formula is as **=(B3*5).** It simply means Excel should find the product of the value inside cell B3 and 5.

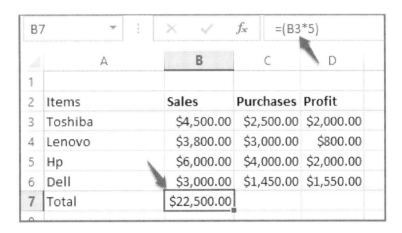

Note: perhaps you want to use the same formula for every other cell in the same row, simply drag down the plus icon (auto command) and the formula will be assigned to other items in the cells based on the formula concerning their column.

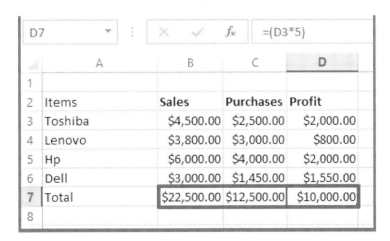

The Fast-Track Method to Observe in Entering A Formula

Excel is capable of calculating mass formulas at once if you get it right with its pattern and method. If you can observe the following patterns of entering a formula, you will never have any problem in getting a speedy result from the Excel formulas you enter:

1. **Make all your system processors available for Excel computation**: Setting all your processors for the task will increase the speed with which Excel works because it will have sufficient processor to handle all the data. You can set up your processor by:
a. Moving to the **File menu** to click on it and then tap on "**options**" from the drop-down list.

b. Click on **Advanced** from the Options drop-down menu and scroll down to where you can locate "**formulas**".
c. Then pick the "**Use all processors on this computer**" option, such will make your Excel calculation work faster than using the partial processor.

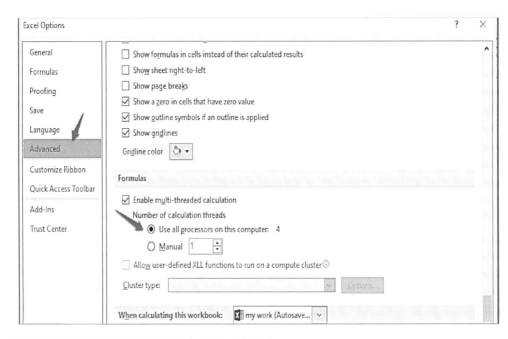

2. **Do not put the final parentheses to a function:** you should not waste time in putting a close parenthesis to your formula; Excel will do that for you automatically. For instance, = **SUM (D3+D4) or =SUM (D3+D4)*5,** just press **Enter,** Excel will add the parentheses and give out the result.

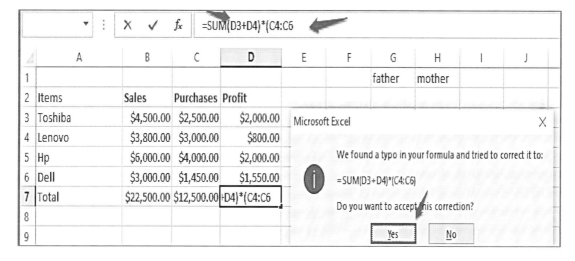

Though this tip will not work if you have more than one set of parentheses (it may be more than one parenthesis, but must not be than one set of parentheses) inside a formula, nevertheless, it will still guess the structure of what you want to type, you only need to press **Yes** if that's what you wanted to type.

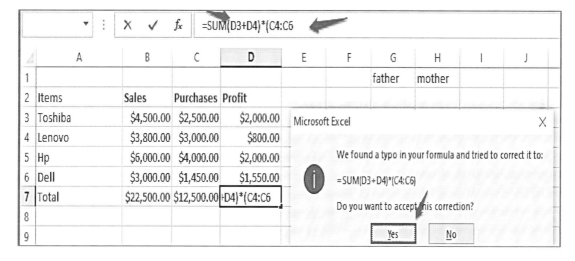

3. **Double click on the Fill handle to copy down the formulas:** when you add formulas together perhaps on the same column or inside the table, you may copy the formula used in the first row to the last row of the same column or table. Simply tap on the **Fill handle** located at the lower right corner of all your selections in Excel, immediately it turns to a plus sign **(+).** Provided the formula in the row sits next to the other row in the same column with a complete set of data in other cells, just double-click the **Fill handle** and drag it over to copy the formula down to the bottom of the last column or table.

D3		:	×	✓	*fx*	=SUM(B3+C3)

	A	B	C	D
1				
2	Items	Sales	Purchases	Profit
3	Toshiba	$4,500.00	$2,500.00	$7,000.00
4	Lenovo	$3,800.00	$3,000.00	$6,800.00
5	Hp	$6,000.00	$4,000.00	$10,000.00
6	Dell	$3,000.00	$1,450.00	$4,450.00
7	Total	$22,500.00	$12,500.00	$35,000.00

4. **Move the "formula prediction box" out of your way:** at times during insertion of formula, the formula hint may be blocking your view or blocking other data that you may want to include into the formula. When you perceive such, just recall you can move the hint box to any other place inside the worksheet by moving the cursor to the edge of the box till there is a four-headed arrow.

=AVERAGEIF(

	D	E	F	G	H	I
	fixed deposit	Total	Average			
160		300	660	=AVERAGEIF(		
180		5000	5380	AVERAGEIF(range, criteria,[average_range])		
170		10	780			
120		190	710			

Then click and drag to any other position in the worksheet and continue to input your formula. Note that the hint box will still be predicting formulas for you wherever it is in the worksheet.

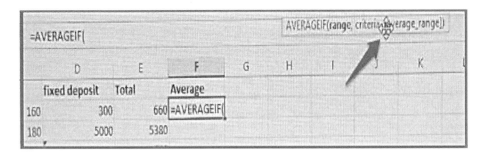

5. **Enter a formula automatically by creating a table:** when you create an Excel table, you can enter a formula faster than if you are using normal worksheet cells. Immediately you convert your data to a table, any formula you insert into the first row will be copied down to the extreme bottom of the table automatically. Excel table makes work faster and averts errors as well. To create an Excel table, simply follow this procedure:

a. Select all the cells that involved.

b. Then press **Ctrl + T** to draw the table over the selected cells.

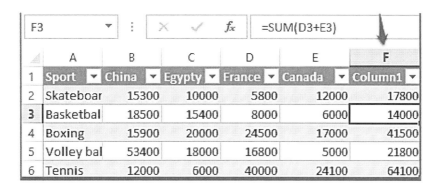

- Excel will update every cell formula of that same column like that of the first column automatically without applying any command.

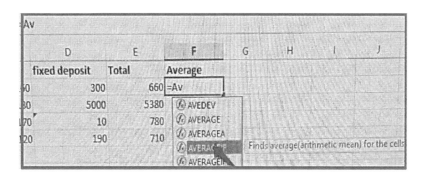

6. **Take advantage of Auto commands, arrow key, and the tab key to enter a function:** As you are about to enter a formula,
a. Insert **an equal (=) sign** and start typing, Excel will begin to pair the text you are entering against the huge list of the functions which is accessible in Excel. The list will correspond with the first letter you type.
b. Scroll down with the arrow key and check the function you want. Immediately you sight the function you want, just make the arrow key remain on it and then press the **tab** key, immediately, such function will be selected.

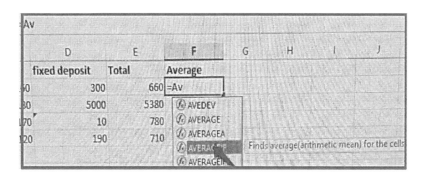

7. **Move a formula and retain its references:** know that you can copy a formula to another position and such formula address will be adjusted to the new position, but at times, the

situation may demand that you will have to retain the formula's address for an essential reason. To do that, kindly drag and drop the value to another position, its address will remain untouched and unchanged.

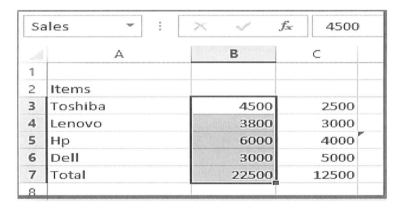

8. **Making use of named range makes formulas convenient and clear:** With named range, formula is easy to use, for instance using pounds or dollars always make cells' addresses more complicated. Making use of name range saves a lot of time and thereby makes formulas work faster. Creating a named range is as simple as ABC. Kindly:

a. Select the cells you wish to name
b. Move to the **Name box** beside the formula bar and type the name you want to use, and then press **Enter**, automatically, the cell range will name them. Hence, you can make use of it in the formula by pointing on the name range as you are structuring a formula.

Note: you may also move to the **Name box** and click on the drop-down arrow to pick the name from the name box and apply it to the cell you selected.

Reference Cells in The Worksheet by Clicking on The Cells

You can click on the cells inside the worksheet to enter their references instead of typing them into the box. Let us examine the steps that are involved:

1. Click **the cell** that will be the receiver of the cells you want to reference.
2. Input an **equal (=) sign** to the cell above in (1).
3. Click **the cell** or drag it over to the groups of cells you want to make reference to, then, the names or references of those cells will enter into the receiver cell instantly after the equal sign.

4. Press **ENTER** to create cell references.

Inserting A Cell Range

A cell is referred to by the intersection of the column letter and its corresponding row number e.g., B2. Cell range or range of cell is called a group of adjacent cells because they are arranged next to each other, and they are separated with the use of column.

There two ways of inserting a cell range, these are:

1. Typing a cell range into the formula box.

2. Dragging the cursor across the cells to be included within the range of cells.

Note: There are also two cell ranges, they are:

a. An adjacent range of cell (e.g. A3:A6), and
b. Non-adjacent cell range (e.g. C2:D6).

Creating Cell Range Name for Formulas' Use

Cell range name is the easiest way of entering data for formulas. Entering cell addresses one after the other is a very strenuous task (such as C3 + C4 + C5 + C6 + C7) and also, it may not be accurate as D4:D6. It is the cell range name that is very dependable and convenient for formulas' use. To create a cell range name, check the below guides for guidance:

1. Select the range of cells you want to name.
2. Click the **formula bar** and pick the **Define Name** button to command for the New Name dialog box.

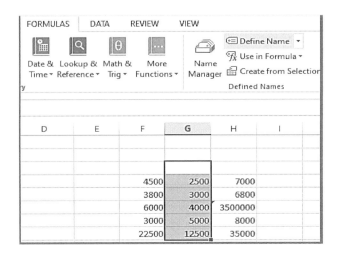

3. Insert a brief and concise name in the provided box.
4. Move to the **Scope** drop-down list, select the **worksheet name** if the use of the range name will not go beyond the worksheet to which it is created from, but, select **Workbook** if you have the intention of using the name range you have just created in another worksheet.
5. Then click **OK** for confirmation.

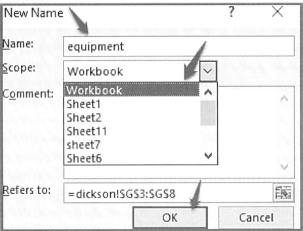

Note: range name reference does not change when you copy a formula with range name address from one cell to the other. A range name consistently refers to the same set of cells, and that is one of its merits.

To make use of the name range created above in a formula, simply:

a. Tap on the **Formula** bar at the place where you want to make use of the cell range name and pick the "**Use in Formula**" button.
b. Then choose **a cell range name** from the drop-down menu.

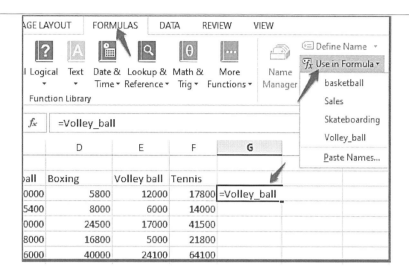

Alternatively, you can also do this:

a. Move to the **formula** button and click on it, then tap on the **"Use in Formula"** option.

b. From the **"Use in Formula"** option drop-down, pick **Paste Names,** and a paste Names dialog box will come forth.
c. Choose a cell range name and tap **Ok**.

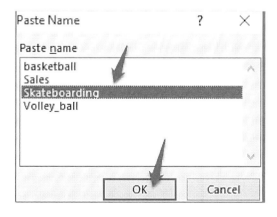

Handling the cell range name: the cell range name belongs to you; you have all the chance to adjust it to your taste whether you want to rename or delete it. To rename or delete a cell range name, follow these processes:

a. Tap on the **Formulas** bar and click on the **"Name Manager"** button, then, the Name Manager Dialog box with a list of cell range names shows up.

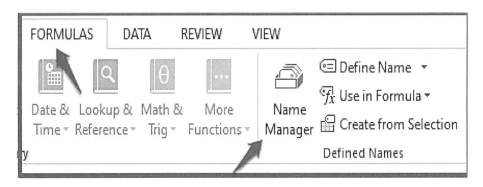

b. Simply click on the cell range name you want to adjust.
c. **To delete**, move to the top where the **Delete** button is and tap on it to delete the range name you want to delete, and then tap on **Ok** to effect the changes.

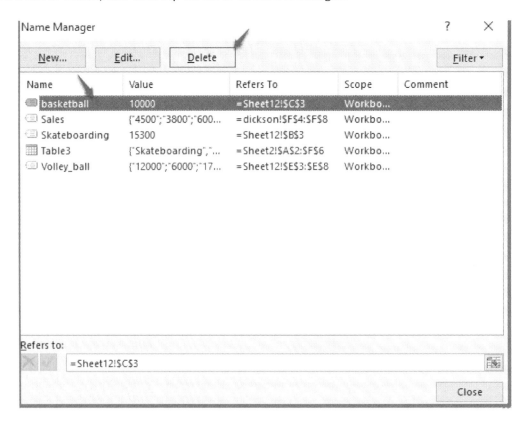

d. **To rename**, click on the **Edit** button at the top and insert the name of your choice in the Edit Name dialog box, then tap **Ok**.

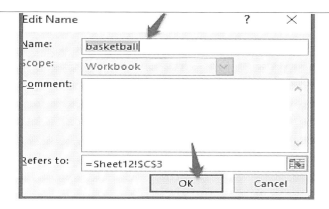

Pointing to Cells in A Worksheet for Formula Purpose in A Different Worksheet

You are permitted to use the cell content of another worksheet of the same workbook for your formulas since the worksheet contains the data and the contents you need for formulas computation. For example, Worksheet 1 has expenditure items for the whole month with the total aggregate amount; likewise, worksheet 2 has all income items with the total aggregate amount. If it happens that the profit establishment will take place in worksheet 2 with a formula, definitely you will need some figures in worksheet 1 before you can arrive at an exact profit figure and thus, you have to point to those cells in worksheet 1 for calculation. Let us check the below example for more comprehension of how to point to cells for the use of formulas in other worksheets.

a. Inside **Worksheet 2** where you want to use a formula, structure it as if you want to enter a formula by starting with **=SUM(D3+D6)-AVERAGE(**

SUM	▼	:	X	✓	f_x	=SUM(D3+D6)-AVERAGE(		
	A	B	C	D	E	F	G	H
1								
2		Skateboard	Basketball	Boxing	Volley ball	Tennis		
3		15300	10000	5800	12000		=SUM(D3+D6)-AVERAGE(	
4		18500	15400	8000	6000	14000		
5		15900	20000	24500	17000	41500		
6		53400	18000	16800	5000	21800	Sheet2	
7		12000	6000	40000	24100	64100		

b. When you need to enter contents of worksheet 1, click on **worksheet 1** tab to move into worksheet 1, immediately you move to sheet 1, you will see sheet1 with an Exclamation mark (sheet1!) in front of the formulas which you are typing in sheet 2
c. Click on the **cell or group of cells** that has the contents you want to make use of by dragging over them or by typing the range in front of (sheet1!) without going back to worksheet 2 where you started the formula. For this illustration, type (E4:E6).
d. Immediately you select the cell(s), it will reflect on the formula box as a continuation of worksheet 2 formula inside sheet 1.

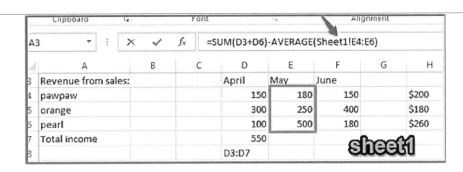

e. After the selection, close the parentheses and press **Enter**. Immediately you tap the enter key, you will be moved from sheet 1 to sheet 2 where you will see the result of the formulas you completed in sheet 1. Nothing will show again in sheet 1.

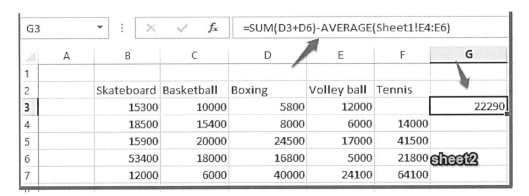

Ways of Copying Formulas from One Cell to Other Cell

Excel provides a means of copying formulas from one cell to other cells instead of typing formulas again. Since the formula is of the same pattern, Excel will only amend the cell reference but will still be the same pattern of the formulas. Copying formulas from one cell to another is the easiest and fastest means.

To copy Excel formulas from cell to cell, kindly:

a. Choose **the cell** that has the formula you want to pass across to others.

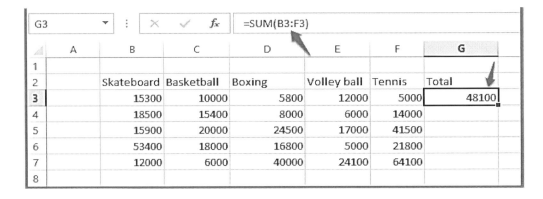

b. Place the cursor to the lower part at the right side and wait till it turns to a black plus sign (+) so as to make use of it in **Autofill handle by dragging it** over the cell you want to copy the formulas to.

c. Release the mouse button to finish the process, and then go back to the cell that you copied it to, click on it and check if the formula pattern is correlated with what you want, because at times, you might have missed something in the formula and it will reflect on the subsequent result.

Discovering and Adjusting Formulas Error

Making an error in Excel formulas can't be overemphasized. One mistake inside Excel formulas can pollute all the calculations inside the worksheet. When a formula error occurs in Excel, you will discover by the presence of a small green triangle at the upper left side of the cell. Once you discover an error, the next action is an amendment. There are various errors that users can make in Excel formulas; let us quickly check those frequent errors that can occur during Excel formulas:

Frequent Message Error for Entering Wrong Formulas

Error symbols	The actual mistake
#NAME	Using a range name that is not well defined such as adding certain symbols to the range name. check the name and restructure it.
#NULL	Referring to a cell range that is not entered correctly.
#DIV/0!	Wrongly divide the number by something that does not exist, like zero.
#REF	Referring to a range name that does not exist
#VALUE	This occurs a lot, it occurs when formulas are being miswritten or you used incorrect functions.
#NUM	Using unacceptable and incorrect argument.

To amend any formula blunder you committed in Excel, there are ways of adjusting errors; we will look at them one after the other:

Discover More About the Error and Adjusting It

a. Select the **cell with signal error** (small green triangle at the upper left corner of the cell).
b. Then click the **Error Checking button** to know more about the error and a means of correcting it.

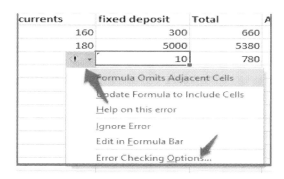

300

Tracing Cell References

This is meant for a crowded worksheet that is loaded with a lot of formulas even formulas from the neighbor worksheet. Tracing the cell reference will give you a hint of how the formulas are structured, and the error contains also a means of restricting the formulas. To trace cell reference, Excel has two types of cell tracer. Both show a connection about the cell you used in carrying out the formulas. A cell tracer shows a blue arrow in tracing the connection that exists between the formulas. Let us quickly run a quick check on the two cell tracers that are available in Excel:

1. **Tracing Precedent:** tracing a precedent helps Excel Users to discover those cells you used in arriving at the result of the formula. It points an arrow to all the cells that contain the data used in arriving at the result of the formula. To make use of Trace precedents, simply:
a. Select the **cell(s)** that has the formula inside and move to the **Formulas** tab.
b. Inside the formulas tab, click on the "**Trace Precedent**" button to check the cells that contribute to the formula and check if there should be a necessary adjustment to the data inside those cells.

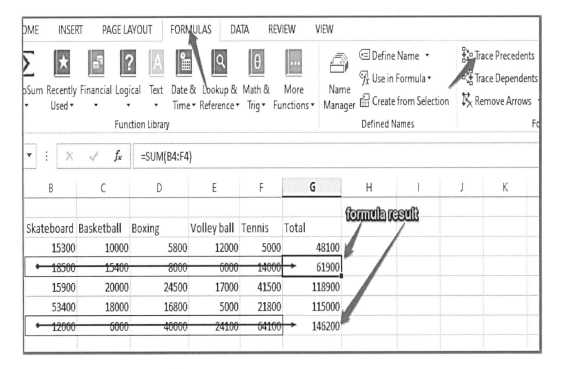

2. **Tracing dependents:** this is just the exact opposite of tracing precedent. Here the cell may have a formula or value inside, but its value or formula is used in producing formula result in another cell. And thus, cell tracer will trace from the cell selected (that is the cell that contributes to another cell formula result) to the cell where its formula or value is used (the cell with the total formula result). To make use of the Trace dependents, you have to:
a. Select **the cell** you want to trace its dependence.
b. Maneuver to the **formulas** bar and pick the "**Trace dependent**" button, check the relationship and amend any necessary item that needs amendment.

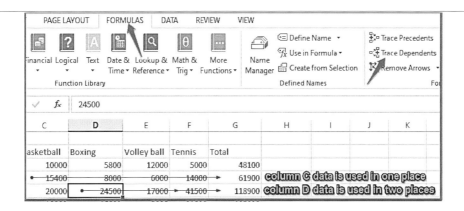

Immediately you are done tracing the cells in either option (precedent or dependent), and you are also done establishing the connection you want to establish, you can proceed to remove the cell tracer so you can have a real worksheet back by: following these steps:

a. Move to the **formulas** bar and tap on the "**Remove Arrows"** button below the precedent and dependent arrow.
b. Select either **Remove Precedent or Dependent** depending on the one you want to remove.

Making Use of Error Checkers Button

Error checker will move to the worksheet and check for any available error, once it detects the error, it will pass the details to you inside the dialog box, and then you can make the necessary adjustment.

How do I run the Error Checker? By:

o Maneuver to the **formulas** tab and tap on **Error Checker** Button.
o You will see the state of the error and the causative factor. Tap on **"Edit in Formula Bar"** inside the dialog box and adjust it there.

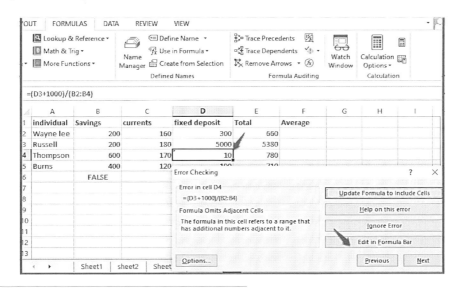

o Then click on **Resume** when you are done adjusting.

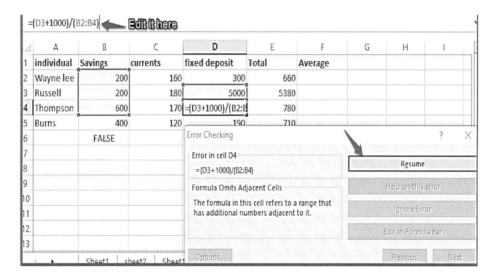

Note: immediately you done adjusting one error, you have to click on the **Resume** option so that every other key will be active again, then click on the **"Next"** button to check the worksheet's next error, but if the error needs no adjustment, tap on the **Ignore** button and you will be moved to the next error.

Stepping into A Function

A function is an embodiment of a formula that you can use in Excel. Excel has a lot of Functions, though areas of their use depend on the Excel user's discipline, nevertheless, there are general functions that cross all disciplines such as **AVERAGE, SUM, PRODUCT,** and other most used functions. They are all located in the formulas tab. This guide will explain more on the general workable functions and how to make them find expressions in formulas to Excel users.

Understand the Use of Argument in Function

Argument is any information you supply after the insertion of a function for instance, let us use SUM function and give it a correct argument, =SUM(B3:B7); (B3:B7) is an argument, though some function does not require an argument, for example, **=TODAY() and =NOW(),** these two functions require no argument, both of them are used to get actual date and time, that is why the parenthesis is empty.

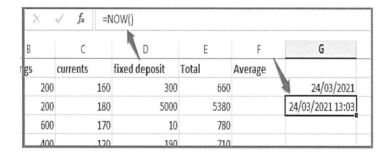

303

Note: using more than one argument for a function needs a comma, for example, =LARGE(B2:B4, 3).

Checking Out the Necessary Argument for A Given Function

At a time, you may not know the specific argument for the function you are about to use, no qualms, for any function you want to insert, simply:

- Click on a cell and input the equal (=) sign.
- Insert the **function** and get the parentheses opened like =AVERAGE (double click on the Function replica in the guessing box.

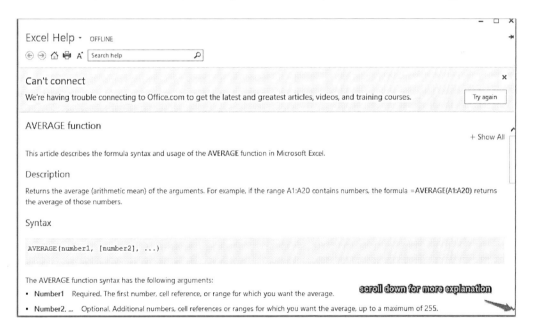

- Immediately, Excel will activate a hint of all the arguments that are available for the function you have entered, follow it to explore any Function that you do not know its argument.

Excel Help · OFFLINE

Search help

Can't connect

We're having trouble connecting to Office.com to get the latest and greatest articles, videos, and training courses. | Try again

AVERAGE function

+ Show All

This article describes the formula syntax and usage of the AVERAGE function in Microsoft Excel.

Description

Returns the average (arithmetic mean) of the arguments. For example, if the range A1:A20 contains numbers, the formula =AVERAGE(A1:A20) returns the average of those numbers.

Syntax

```
AVERAGE(number1, [number2], ...)
```

The AVERAGE function syntax has the following arguments:
- **Number1**   Required. The first number, cell reference, or range for which you want the average.   scroll down for more explanation
- **Number2, ...**   Optional. Additional numbers, cell references or ranges for which you want the average, up to a maximum of 255.

Note: those arguments in the bracket are optional, while those that are not in the bracket are required arguments for example = **NETWORKDAY(2/4/2021-4/6/2021, [today]).**

ENTERING A FUNCTION FOR BUILDING A FORMULA

You can either insert a function either by typing it in the formula bar or inviting Excel to guide you through, let us quickly examine the two ways:

1. **Typing into the formula bar or directly into the selected cell:**
a. Select **the cell** where you want the formula to be created.
b. Type the equal (=) sign directly into the cell after the selection of the cell or in the formula bar
c. Type the **function,** open parentheses and insert your argument, then close the parentheses and press **Enter.**

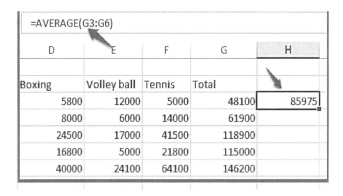

Note: you may enter the function in small letters to fast-track your speed, Excel will change it to upper case automatically.

2. **Invite Excel to guide you in inserting the function:**
a. Select **the cell** where you want the formula to reflect.
b. Maneuver to the **formulas** tab and select the **Insert Function** to open the Insert function dialog box.

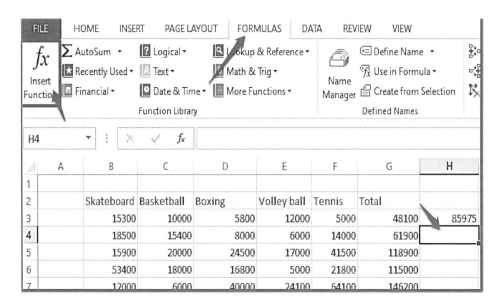

305

c. Choose a category from the **"select a category"** option which includes the most recently used, show all, and other categories.

d. Then choose a function from the **"Select a function"** list and tap **Ok**, another dialog box will appear where you will select the cells to be included in the formula.

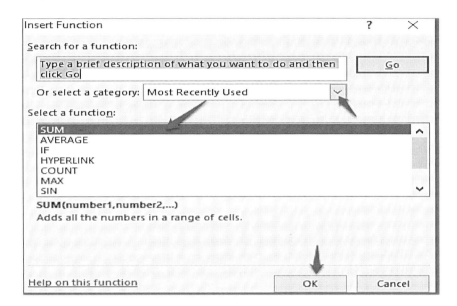

e. Select **the cells** you want to include by typing the cell address into the provided box or by clicking the first cell then drag it over the cell you want to include in the formula

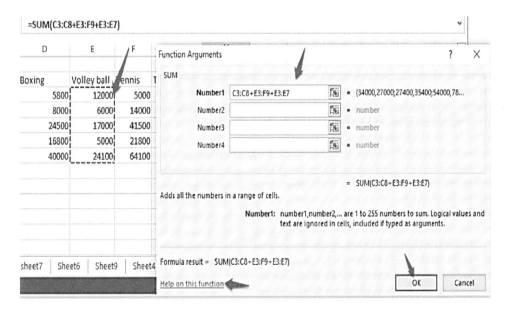

Note: each function has a separate box for the second Window dialog box. If you do not have an understanding of a specific function, call on Excel to help you out by clicking on the "Help on this function" located at the bottom left of the "Insert Function Dialog Box" and Excel will proffer a way out.

Glancing Through Generally Used Function

GENERALLY USED FUNCTION	DESCRIPTION
SUM	Addition of total cells listed in the argument.
AVERAGE	The average value of the cells recommended in the argument.
PRODUCT	The product or multiplication of the listed cell in the argument.
MAX	The largest value out of the listed cell in the argument.
MIN	The smallest value out of the listed cell in the argument.
COUNT	It represents the total number of cells listed in the argument
STDEV	Computation of a standard deviation per the sample of the cells listed in the argument.
STDEVP	Computation of a standard deviation per all the cells in the argument.

Using COUNT and COUNTIF To Count Data Item in A Cell Range

The **COUNT** function is used in counting the number of the data item you have in a selected range of cells, take for instance, =COUNT(B3:B7)

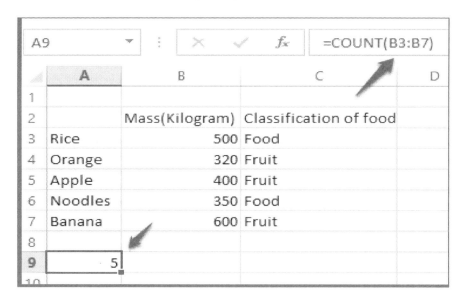

While COUNTIF function works very close to the COUNT function with the exception that the COUNTIF function adds A CRITERION to the argument. It counts how many cells are in the range of selected cells and how many have a particular value, and therefore to use the COUNTIF function you will be having two arguments (Cell range, and the Criterion). The criterion will be enclosed with quotation marks. Take for example, to know how many fruits are in the classification of food, the formula will be structured like this, =**COUNTIF(B3:B7, "Fruit").**

307

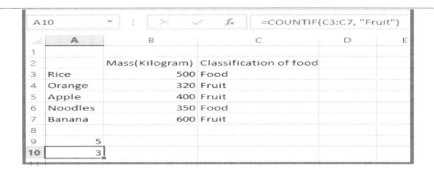

Joining Text with Value with Concatenate

Concatenate Function is about value combination from different cells and merging such into a single cell for a particular purpose, take, for instance, having a three-column name joined together to produce a single full name. The structure of the Concatenate function is like this: **=CONCATENATE(text1, text2,text3,…….).** In combining texts, you have to include space that will be between the quotation marks as an argument for the below example; this is a formula for three (3) names that will combine to be the full name**=CONCATENATE(A3," ", B3," "," ", C3).**

Using Average for Averaging Point Value

The **AVERAGE** function is used in determining the average point of a given data of a selected cell or a cell range. Let us take the below table as an instance by using the AVERAGE to estimate the average point score of the four students in three subjects. This is the structure of the AVERAGE function, **=AVERAGE(cell range).**

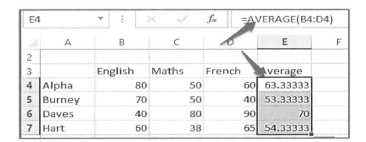

Excel exempts empty cells in the cell range during counting, but it regards zero (0) as part of the range and therefore computes for zero (0).

PMT For Estimating Periodic Payment of Loan

Have you borrowed a specific amount of money or you are about to take a loan but you are confused about the time it will take to repay the loan or how much can even borrow, no qualms, that is what PMT caters for, it describes the particular amount you can borrow at various interest rates and how much you will be paying on such loan yearly or monthly by dividing the yearly rate by 12 months to get the amount to be paid on monthly basis. To make use of the PMT function for calculating periodic payment, kindly observe this formula structure: =PMT(Interest rate, number of payment, amount of loan), let us check the structure worksheet for how PMT looks like:

D4	▾	:	X	✓	fx	=PMT(A4,B4,C4)	
	A		B		C	D	E
1							
2	Interest rate	▾	No. of Payment	▾	Amount of loan	Yearly Payment	Monthly payment
3	3.00%		120		$5,000	-$154.45	-$12.87
4	3.00%		120		$8,000	-$247.12	-$20.59
5	3.00%		120		$4,000	-$123.56	-$10.30
6	3.00%		120		$6,000	-$185.34	-$15.44
7							

Explicit explanation:

- **Interest rate**: do not put a percentage to the interest rate for it to be accepted as a number. After you are done typing the interest rate, move to the **Home** tab under number and go to percentage to format the column. That is, column (A).
- **No of payment:** The no of time to redeem the loan is 10 years, long time loan payment ought to be paid every month, for the case of the loan in this illustration, it is 10 years, multiply it by 12 months in a calendar year, it equals 120 times in 10 years. That is column B.
- **Amount of the loan:** insert the loan amount directly to column C, which is the amount you are calculating for what you want to borrow.
- **Yearly payment of the loan:** this one will be having a formula in this structure: =PMT(A3, B3, C3), it is in column D.
- **Monthly payment of the loan:** to get the amount to be paid every month, you have to divide the yearly payment with a 12-month calendar in formula (=D3/12) for cell E3.

Project Time Measuring with NETWORKDAY and TODAY

Networkday and Today measures the period of days to come, probably for a specific program, assignment, budget planning, etc. It is mainly concerned with workdays only and thus, excludes weekend (Saturday and Sunday), and therefore, the result of NETWORKDAY is for workdays alone. To make use of NETWORKDAY, structure its formula like this: =NETWORKDAY(Start date-End date).

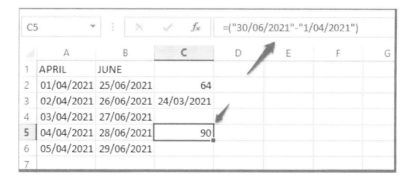

TODAY's function structure is like this: =**TODAY()** because it does not argue.

Note: to get the number of days between two dates, simply remove the latest date from the earlier date by using the minus sign. It will give you a total of the days between the selected dates without removing Saturday and Sunday, =″30/6/2021″-″1/4/2021″. The enclosed quotation is for date identification to Excel.

LEN For Counting Text Character

LEN function in Excel is referred to as the length Excel function as long as it is used to ascertain the length or character of a given word, cell numbers, and many more. To get an in-depth understanding of this function, let us make use of it with the SUM function. =SUM(LEN(A2),LEN(B2)).

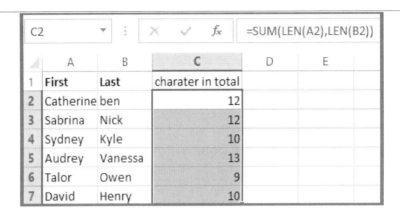

Note: LEN A2= 9 and B2= 3, the total is equal to 12, you will now use the auto-fill handle to copy the pattern of the formulas down.

Compares the Range of Values with LARGE And SMALL

LARGE and SMALL is used to compare which value is largest and which one is smallest within a given range, let us take for instance, the total number of the bag sold in the market.

- 100: maximum bag sold in one month in the market (**MAX**).
- 8: the least bag sold in one month in the market (**MIN**).
- 93: the second maximum bag sold in one month in the market (**LARGE**).
- 10: the second least bag sold in one month in the market (**SMALL**).

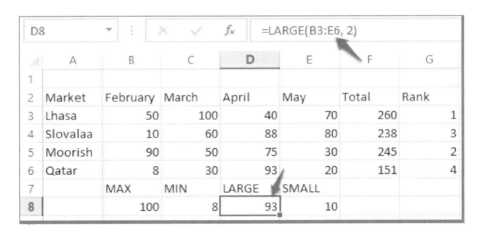

While you are having LARGE and SMALL, you may still at times have to use MAX and MIN. Let us check the use of the four functions in a jiffy with the above worksheet as an example:

1. **MIN:** it gives you the least number or value of the bags sold in the market throughout the whole four months with a given range of =**MIN(B3:E6).**

2. **MAX:** it gives the largest number or the values of the bags sold in the market throughout the four months with a given range of: =MAX(B3:E6).

3. **SMALL**: it gives you the nth position of the smallest value in the list. It will have two arguments, the first argument is the cell range and the second argument is the position of the nth lower value, which maybe 2nd or 3rd position, and the formula will be in a structure like this =**SMALL(B3:E6, 2) or =SMALL(B3:E6, 3)** depending on the nth position.

4. **LARGE**: it will give you the nth position of the largest value in the list. It will have two arguments as well, which are the cell range and nth position either 2nd or 3rd and the formula will be structured like this: =**LARGE(B3:E6, 2) or =LARGE(B3:E6, 3).**

5. **RANK:** it ranks the list of the data; the RANK function has three-arguments which are as follows:

G5			f_x	=RANK(F5,F3:F6,0)		
	A	B	C	D	E	F	G
1							
2	Market	February	March	April	May	Total	Rank
3	Lhasa	50	100	40	70	260	1
4	Slovalaa	10	60	88	80	238	3
5	Moorish	90	50	75	30	245	2
6	Qatar	8	30	93	20	151	4
7		MAX	MIN	LARGE	SMALL		
8		100	8	93	10		

Using cell G5, second-ranking

      a. The cell address with the value you are using for ranking. F5=245

b. The cell range with which you will match the value in deciding the ranking, F3:F6

c. The order of ranking, 0 for descending order, up to down, while 1 is for ascending order, down to up). 0

Text Capitalizing with PROPER Function

The **Proper** function is used to change editing text to upper, lower, or proper case. Excel does not have to confirm change case like MS word, though Excel's change case is not automatic like MS word but at the same time it is not difficult, it just requires some little processes. To change the case of the text you have used before, kindly:

- Create a momentary new column to the right of the column that has the text you want to change its case, which you will later delete when it completes its mission. To create the column:
  1. Select **the column** to the right where you want the new column to be situated.

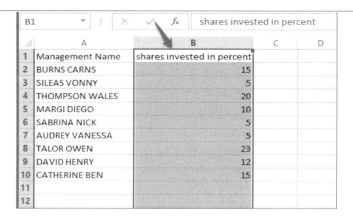

2. Right-click on the **selected column** and pick **Insert**.

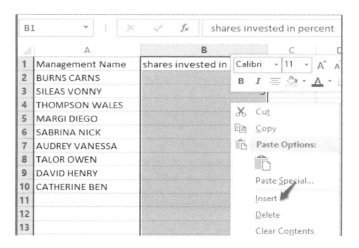

- Immediately you are done with the insertion of the new column, tap on the **first column** on the column you have just created which is direct to the right side of the text you want to change its case.

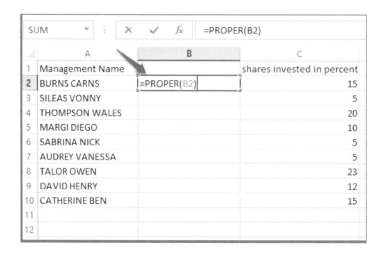

- The column we want to change is in the upper case, but we want to change it to proper case. Now in the column, tap above in (b), insert a formula of this structure there: =**PROPER(B2)**. Perhaps we want to change it to a lower case, we would have replaced the **Proper** with **Lower** because we can only have upper, proper and lower. Immediately after the insertion of the formula, tap on the **Enter** key on the keyboard to initiate the process.

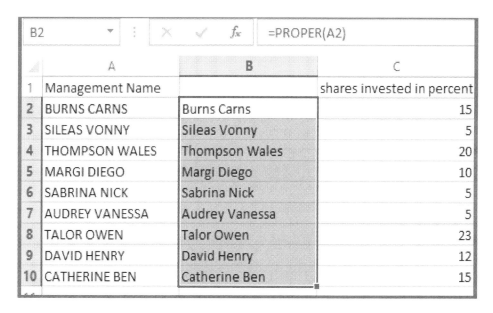

- If you observe, you will notice the text from the first cell A has been copied into the first cell of the new column (B) we created but in the proper case we desire.
- Then use the auto-fill handle to copy down the process for the other names by dragging down the black arrow to the last name on the list.

B2			f_x	=PROPER(A2)	
	A		B		C
1	Management Name				shares invested in percent
2	BURNS CARNS		Burns Carns		15
3	SILEAS VONNY		Sileas Vonny		5
4	THOMPSON WALES		Thompson Wales		20
5	MARGI DIEGO		Margi Diego		10
6	SABRINA NICK		Sabrina Nick		5
7	AUDREY VANESSA		Audrey Vanessa		5
8	TALOR OWEN		Talor Owen		23
9	DAVID HENRY		David Henry		12
10	CATHERINE BEN		Catherine Ben		15

- At this moment, we have gotten the proper case in column B, all we have to do now is to copy the contents in the new column by selecting the names in the new column and press **Ctrl + C** to copy it.

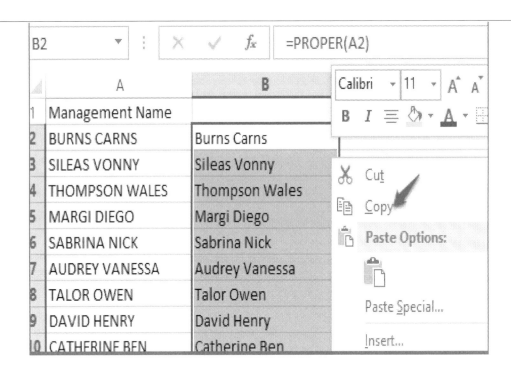

- Then right-click **the beginning of the column** that you want to change, here, we have it as cell A2, tap on the **Paste** special menu for the values you copied.

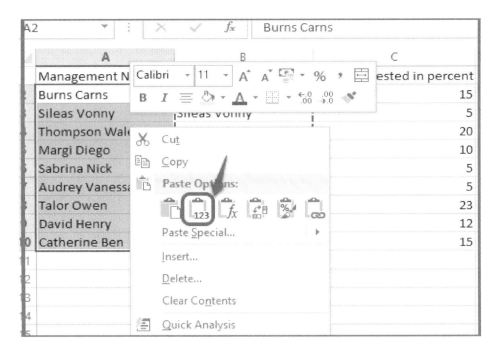

- Now it is time to delete the momentary column that you used to format column A. this is done by selecting the column and right-click it, then pick the **Delete** option.

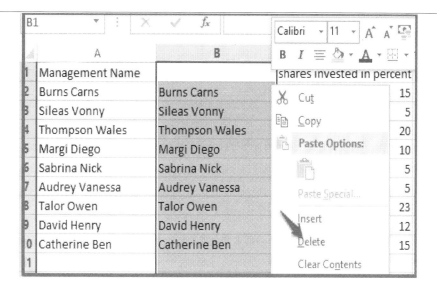

- Column A is now having a set of **Proper cases** you want.

A	B
Management Name	shares invested in percent
Burns Carns	15
Sileas Vonny	5
Thompson Wales	20
Margi Diego	10
Sabrina Nick	5
Audrey Vanessa	5
Talor Owen	23
David Henry	12
Catherine Ben	15

LEFT, MID, AND RIGHT for Data Extraction

LEFT, MID, AND RIGHT are called text functions because they are made purposely to extract certain parts from a word or a group of words. As a means of explanation, you may need to extract the first two letters of a word, the last four letters, or the 6 letters from the middle of the sentence in LEFT, LAST, AND MID functions respectively.

- The **LEFT** function is used for middle extraction; let us put it to practice by starting with the left function.

=LEFT(text, num-chars) or =LEFT(cell address, num-chars)

Text: this is the word or group of words you type or the cell reference where you want to extract your sub word.

316

Num-chars: These are the numbers of characters you choose to extract from the left part. For instance, let us draw out 4 characters in the text "reference", the outcome is "Refe".

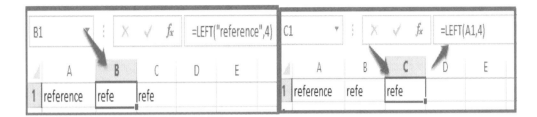

- Over to the **RIGHT** function, it is the exact opposite of the LEFT function, its structure is like this:

=RIGHT(text, num-chars) or =RIGHT(cell address, num-chars)

The explanation with the **LEFT** function is the same, except that you will extract from the right part. For instance, =**RIGHT("right choice", 3)**. This will give us the word "ice", which occurs to be the first three letter from the right.

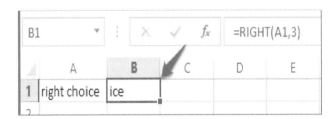

- The third function is the MID function and it is used in drawing out part of the middle letters from the text. It is will be in a structure like this:
=MID(text, start-num, num chars) or =MID(cell address, start-num, num chars)
Text: the text within where you wish to draw out words from.
Start num: this is the number position where to start the extraction from.
Num-chars: this is the number of characters it will be from the start-num.

Let us take for instance; we want to draw out the word **"key"** from the text **"the key of diligence"**. The formula will be structured like this = **MID("the key to diligence",5,3)**

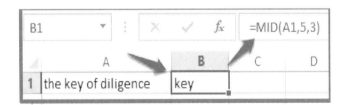

a. **5: start-num** which happen to be the position of the starting point, we will count five (5) characters ("the" is 3 characters, space is recognized in MID function making it four-characters, from the beginning, in short, the 5th number start from K).
b. **3: num chars**, the total character to draw out from the text is 3 from the starting point which is K, and counting 3 characters from K will be the word "key".

317

IF For Analytical Identification

The IF function is the most recognized used function for analytical comparison between a particular value and your expectation. True return means your expectation is right and if it is otherwise, then your expectation is wrong.

For instance, =IF(D1=8, "True", "False"), It means IF D1=8, then it's True, but if otherwise, return False.

You can use the IF function to estimate text and values, it is called nest IFfunction, let us buttress more on the illustration below. IF(A4>B4," surplus" ", deficit").

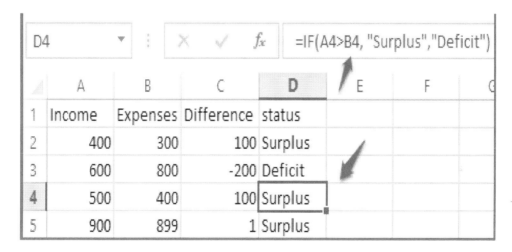

The above illustration is saying IF(A4>B4, then return surplus, IF otherwise return deficit).

CHAPTER FIVE

CONSTRUCT WORKSHEET FOR EASY COMPREHENSION

Spreading Out Worksheet in An Orderly Manner

As you lay your bed, you shall lie on it, so they say. The same principle applies to the worksheet, if you learn how to manage the worksheet effectively, you will enjoy the result, even before and after you print it out, it will be wonderful and more comprehensive.

Managing a worksheet has a lot to do with how you arrange your worksheet and its contents, such as number formatting probably with percentage or dollars will make the reader understand the actual value of what you put inside the worksheet. Other worksheet management are change character, decorating with color and others that we will be discussing in length in this chapter.

Numbers and Text Alignment in Rows and Columns

The default alignment of the text in the worksheet is to the left, while that of the number is to the right; both default alignments can be adjusted if the need arises. The data inside the cell can be adjusted to the left, right, or middle or from bottom to center, top, and vice versa. You may as well justify cell data. At the time you have to change the alignment of the subject heading so that its look within the cell will be outstanding and that of the worksheet at large.

To change the alignment of the text and number, kindly do the following:

1. **For horizontal alignment** (left to right or side to side alignment.).
a. Select **the cells** that need alignment.
b. Move to the **Home tab** and click on **the respective button** (left align, center align and middle align button).

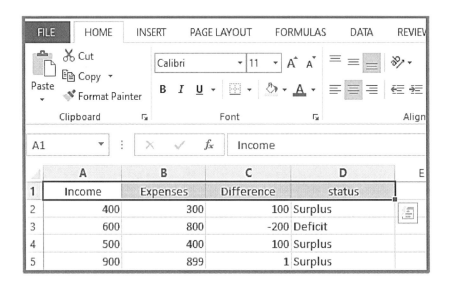

ALTERNATIVELY,

- Tap on the **Alignment** group button and pick the **Format Cell Alignment** option from the drop-down list.

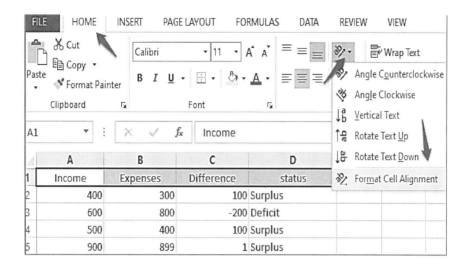

- Tap on the **Alignment** tab inside the format cell dialog box.
- Click on the **Horizontal section** and pick your desired alignment including justify that will fit your letter to the cell.

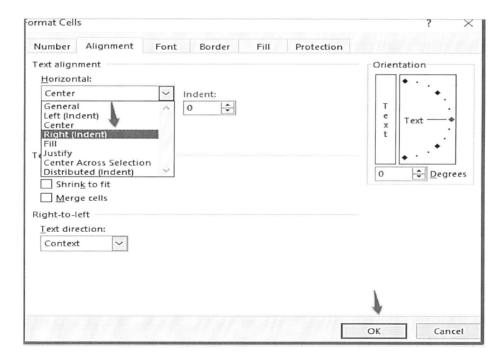

2. **For vertical alignment** (top to bottom or bottom to top):
a. Select the **cells** that need alignment.

b. Move to the **Home tab** and click on **respective alignment** (top align, middle align, and bottom align).

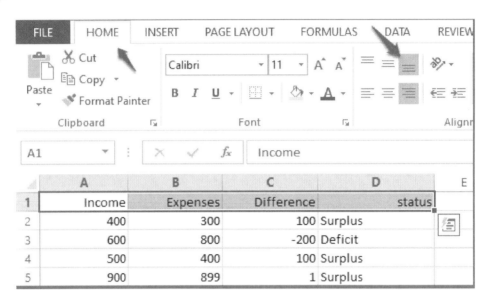

ALTERNATIVELY,

- Tap on the **alignment group button** and pick the **format cell** button from the drop-down list.

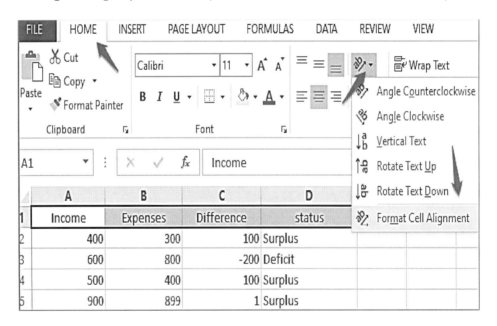

- Tap on the **Alignment** tab inside the format cell dialog box.
- Click on the **vertical section** and pick your desired **alignment** including justify that will fit your letter to the cell.

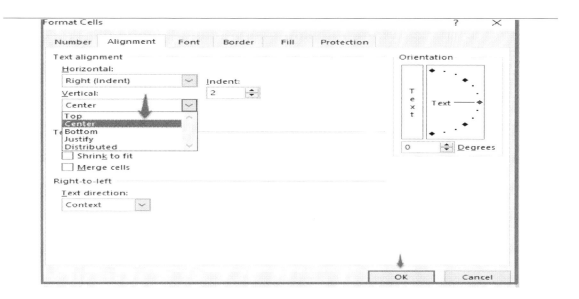

Text Merging and Centering Over Multiple Cells

Text is centered at times to show the information contained in the cell outstandingly or to create a sense of beautification. It helps you to present pieces of text over multiple columns. For example, the words "Local Government Chairman" is centered over five separate cells. To center and merge cells, do the following:

1. Drag your mouse over those cells to select them.

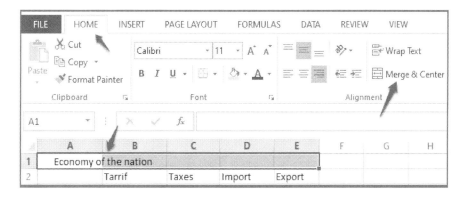

2. Maneuver to the **Home** tab, and then choose the **Merge and Center** button.

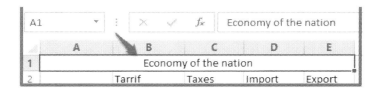

Note: when merging and centering, you will write the text to be merged in one cell, make sure the cell to its left and right side are empty; otherwise, it will be showing you that it's an error.

How do I "unmerge and uncenter" the cells that have been previously merged and centered? You can do that by following these simple steps:

- Click on the "**Merge & Center**" option from the **Home tab**.
- Pick **unmerge cells** from the "Merge & Center" drop-down list.

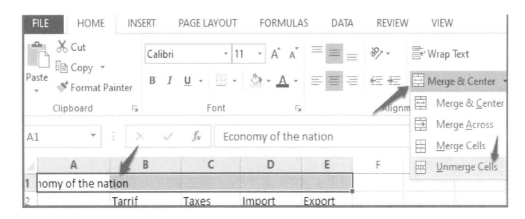

Delete and Insert Rows and Columns

There is always a motive behind deleting or inserting rows or columns, you have to insert a new row or column when you have skipped a particular heading or subject. Rows and columns are mainly deleted when they are not needed anymore.

To insert a new row, kindly do these:

a. Select **the row** that will be below the new row you are about to create.
b. Click on the **Home tab** and tap on the **Insert** button.

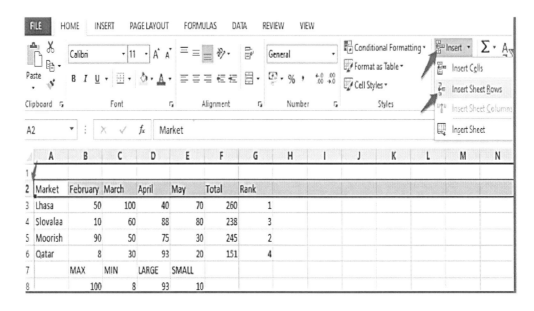

c. Then pick the **Insert Sheet Rows** option from the insert button drop-down menu as seen above.

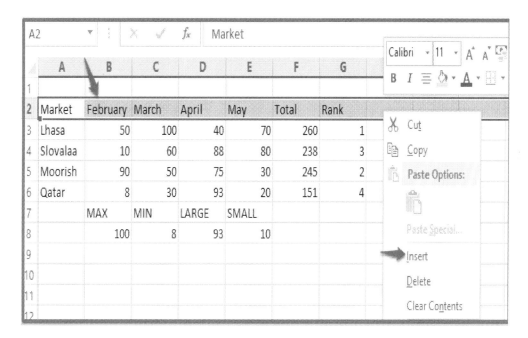

	A	B	C	D	E	F	G	H
1								
2								
3	Market	February	March	April	May	Total	Rank	
4	Lhasa	50	100	40	70	260	1	
5	Slovalaa	10	60	88	80	238	3	
6	Moorish	90	50	75	30	245	2	
7	Qatar	8	30	93	20	151	4	
8		MAX	MIN	LARGE	SMALL			
9		100	8	93	10			

ALTERNATIVELY,

a. Right-click on **the row** which will be below the new row you want to create.
b. Pick **Insert** from the drop-down menu.

How do I insert a column? By simply:

• Selecting **the column** that will be to the right of the new column you want to create.

324

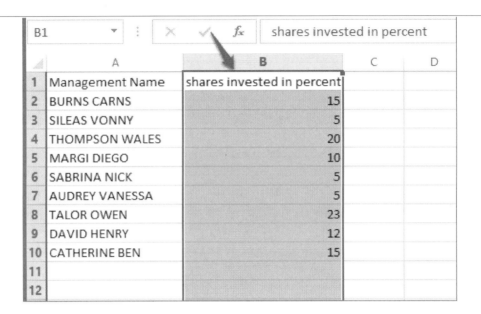

- Click on the **Home** tab and tap on the **Insert** button.
- Then pick the **Insert Sheet Column** option from the insert button drop-down menu.

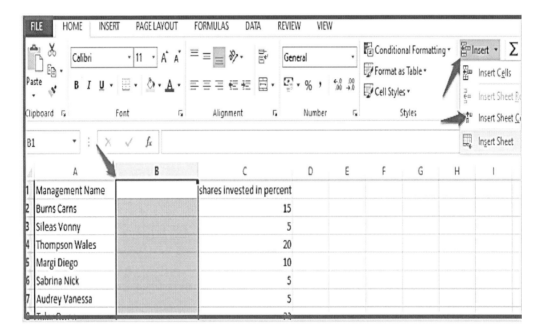

ALTERNATIVELY,

- Right-click on **the column** which will be to the right of the new column you want to create.
- Click on **Insert** from the drop-down menu.

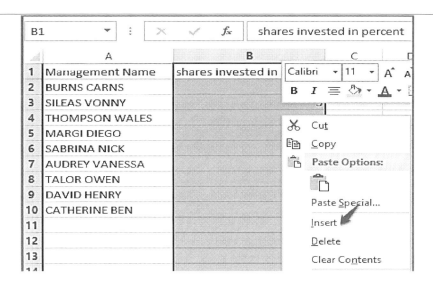

Deleting rows or columns

To delete rows or columns, you have to:

1. Select the **row** or **column** you want to delete or you can drag over the rows and columns and then right-click over them.
2. Pick **delete** from the drop-down list.

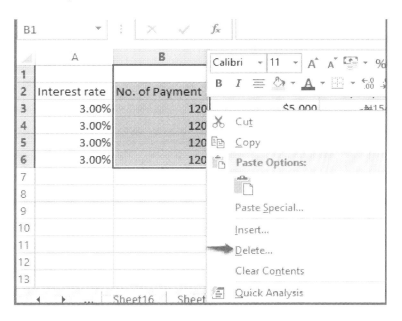

ALTERNATIVELY,

After the selection of the rows or columns to be deleted:

a. Move to the **Home** tab and tap on the **Delete** button.

b. Click on the **Delete Sheet Columns** or **Delete Sheet Rows** from the drop-down list.

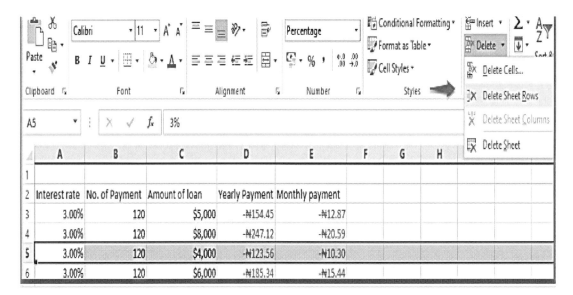

Note: you will see the Insert row and column options when are done inserting rows and columns, tap on it and pick the same format or different ones to the new columns and rows you have created from the pop-up menu.

Be careful not to delete a row that you will still later need because Immediately You Delete It, It Is Gone Forever.

Adjusting Rows and Columns Size

Excel programs the cell box (rectangular column and row box) to be 8.4 characters wide and 15 points high to column and row respectively. But at some point, Excel programming may not work when it comes to entering certain data which are wider than 8.4 in character and higher than 15points in height, as a result, Excel has made diverse preparations as a way of adjusting the sizes of columns and rows depending on what each user has to insert in the cell.

Adjusting the Height of The Rows

The following are the things to note in adjusting the height of the rows:

1. **Adjusting a single row**
a. Click over the **row** number to select the row that needs adjustment.
b. Place the mouse pointer into the boundary between two rows number with which the selected cell should share a boundary with.
c. Shift the pointer a little to change the pointer to a black plus (+) sign, then double-click and drag the boundary between the rows up and down to the measurement you are looking for.

d. As you are shifting the boundary, there will be a prompt pop-up note giving you a hint about the row height measurement you have just reached and to guide you to the measurement you are aiming to reach.

e. Then release the mouse button after you double-click to complete the process.

2. **Adjusting Multiple rows height at once:**

a. Click on the **multiple rows** you want to adjust or drag over them for selection.

b. Then double-click and drag the boundary between one of the selected cells and all the other rows selected with it will be adjusted to the new measurement. Immediately, release the mouse after the double-clicking.

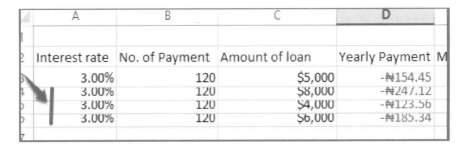

ALTERNATIVELY,

*   Maneuver to the **Home** tab and tap on the **Format** button.

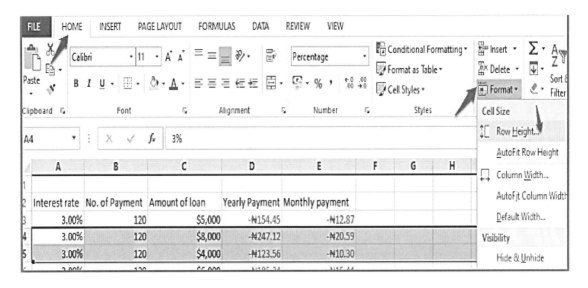

*   Select the **Row Height** option, and then insert the **row height** you prefer in the Row Height dialog box.

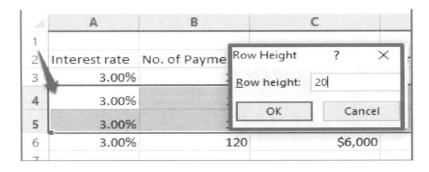

3. **Adjusting cell entry to Autofit the row height:**
   You can adjust your row height automatically to make the data entry fit inside the cell accurately and so that row size will contain the data entry appropriately. Adjust your row height to fit in your data entry by:
a. Moving to the **Home** tab and tap on the **Format** button.

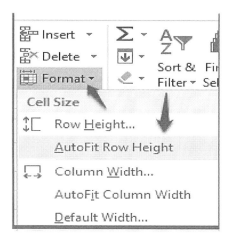

b. Then choose **AutoFit Row Height.**

Adjusting the Column Width

To adjust the column width, below are the steps.

- **Adjusting a single column:**
1. Select **the column** to be adjusted.
2. Place the mouse pointer into the boundary between two column letters with which the selected cell shares a boundary with.
3. Shift the pointer a little to change the pointer to a black plus (+) sign, then double-click and drag the boundary between the columns up and down to the measurement you are looking for.

	A	B	C	D
		Width: 17.86 (130 pixels)		
1				
2	Interest rate	No. of Payment	Amount of loan	Yearly Payment
3	3.00%	120	$5,000	-₦154.45
4	3.00%	120	$8,000	-₦247.12
5	3.00%	120	$4,000	-₦123.56
6	3.00%	120	$6,000	-₦185.34
7				
8				

4. As you are shifting the boundary, there will be a prompt pop-up note giving you a hint about the column width measurement you have just reached and to guide you to the measurement you are aiming to reach.

5. Then release the mouse after double-clicking to complete the process.
- **Adjusting multiple columns:**
- Click on the **multiple columns** you want to adjust or drag over them for selection.
- Then double-click and drag the boundary between one of the selected cells and all other columns selected with it will be adjusted to the new measurement immediately you release the mouse after double-clicking it also.

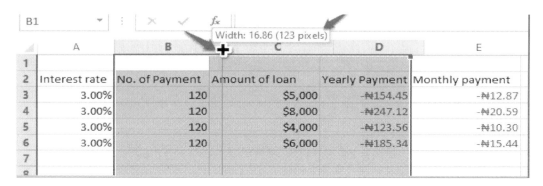

ALTERNATIVELY,

a. Maneuver to the **Home** tab, and tap on the **Format** button.
b. Select the **Column Width** button, and then insert the column width you prefer in the Column dialog box.

- **Adjusting cell entry to Autofit the column width:**
  You can adjust the width of your columns automatically to make the data entry fit inside the column accurately and so that the column size will contain data entries appropriately. Adjust your column width to make data entry fit into it, by:
  o Moving to the **Home** tab and tap on the **Format** button.

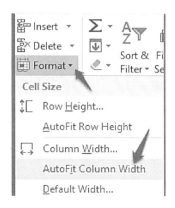

  o Then choose the **AutoFit Column Width.**

Furnishing A Worksheet with Borders and Colors

Worksheet cell is arranged in a gridline format. The gridline is mainly for proper arrangement of your Excel work and thus, when you print Excel work, the grid background will not reflect. Nevertheless, if you prefer that your Excel work should look more presentable and meaningful, you must create something creative within the area of your Excel work, particularly an area that catches the reader's attention such as column heading, aggregate heading, and other essential parts. At the same time, it is of utmost importance to use color to decorate the background of your Excel work to add more life to your work.

Quick Way of Formatting Worksheet with Cell Style

Formatting simply means the appearance of things to make it better. For instance, formatting a worksheet is a way of changing its appearance for better improvement such as text, color, and drawing a table to surround your cells.

The most pressing thing about formatting is that the look and appearances you desire can come out in a jiffy with a little process. It does not take much time, and indeed it is a quick way of formatting a worksheet. There are two ways to format the worksheet either by choosing from thousands of built-in cell styles that comes with Excel or by customizing your cell style to suit your taste.

Making Use of Excel Built-In Cell Style

With Excel built-in cell style, you have limitless access to the collection of cell styles which you can apply to your subject headings or title to capture the attention of the reader. To pick from Excel cell style collection, simply:

* Choose the **cells** to be formatted.
* Move to the **Home** tab and tap on the **Cell style** button, to make the cell style collection open.
* Pick a preferred cell style from the available collection of cell styles to add value to your Excel work.

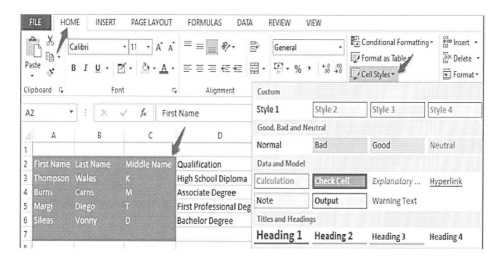

How can I remove cell style from the cell? By:

a. Selecting the cells with the formatting effect and move to the **Home** tab and tap on the **Cell style** button to make the cell style collection open.
b. Pick the **Normal** style from the available collection (the Normal style is under the group of good, bad, neutral, and normal).

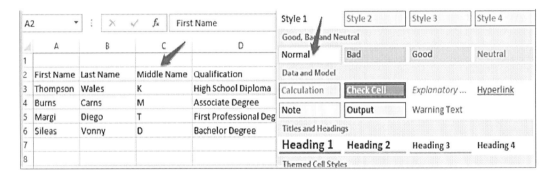

Customizing Your Cell Style

Excel allows for skill development and thus, it grants every user who is innovative an opportunity of building their cell style to suit their personalities. The cell style name you created will be on top of the cell collection under a customized heading for easy identification. To create your style, do the following:

a. Choose the formatting type you prefer for your style in a single cell, such as change case, change font, center alignment or middle alignment, and so on.
b. Move to the **Home** tab and click on the **Cell style** button, then choose the **New Cell Style** option as seen below from the drop-down of **Cell Styles** collection.

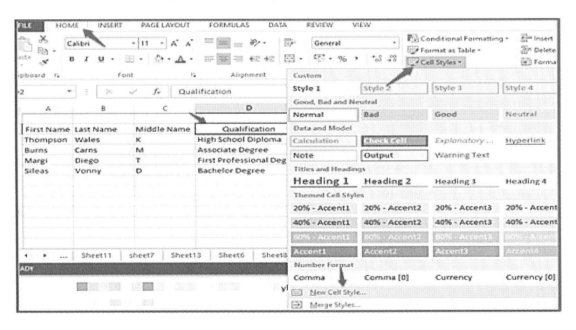

c. The Style dialog box will come forth with the style specification you entered at (a) above, if you wish to change that specification again, you can click on the **format** button to restructure the format at the upper right side of the dialog box.
d. Insert a brief and meaningful name to the style in the Name text box above for your style and tap **Ok**.

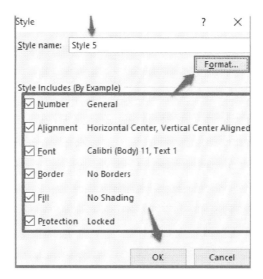

Note: you can remove the manual cell style you created by right-clicking on the name in the cell style collection box and choose the **Delete** option from the drop-down list.

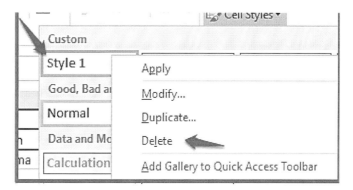

Using Table Style to Format A Cell

Table styles are used to add more decoration to the worksheet data; it gives more neatness and value to the contents inside the cells by creating a wall around them. Check the below steps to explore table style in Excels:

a. Choose the **cells** you want to add table style to.
b. Move to the **Home** tab and click on the **"Format as Table"** button.
c. Then navigate to pick a **table style** from the collection of table styles from the "Format as table" drop-down options.

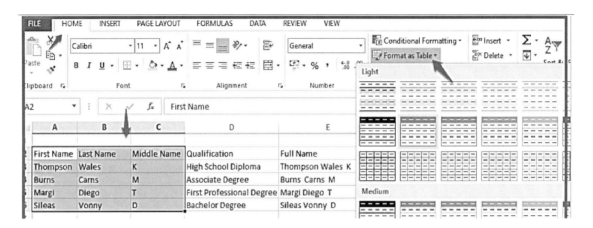

d. Immediately you pick one, you will see a small table style dialog box, tick **"My table headers"** if you have header, label, or title at the top of the column.

e. Tap **Ok** in the "Format as table" dialog box.

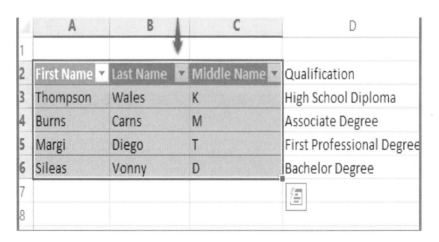

Note: you can improve the design of the table by:

a. Clicking on the **quick style** option or the **table tool** from the Table design.
b. Then select "**More Designs**" to improve the table from the table tool drop-down styles.

You can as well get the table removed from the quick style or table tool as well by moving to the bottom of the table tool and choose "**Clear**" in the table style collection.

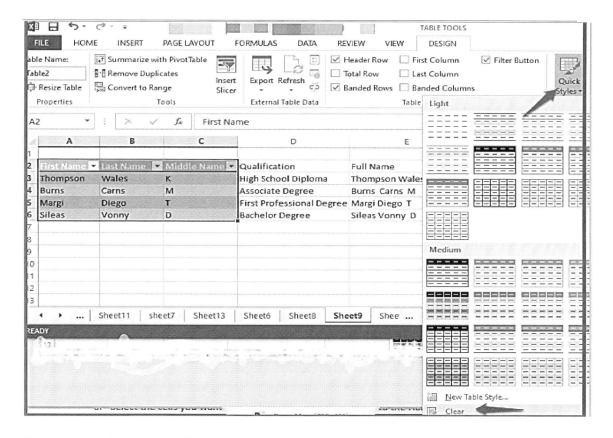

Creating Border on The Worksheet Cells

Borders are the lines that you can use to create a distinct zone between worksheet data and a specific area of worksheet that calls for special attention than the other data. Borders are used to give those items special attention, so that decision can be made with those values rather than glancing through the whole worksheet data. For instance, putting a borderline below the column data for totaling the data item gives the

reader and user a hint of the peculiarities of that area because decision can be made quickly with those distinct zones. Are you confused on how to draw the border on your worksheet, okay, no problem; we have you covered with this one-on-one process:

Create the border using the Format cell dialog box:

- Select the **cells** you want to draw a border around and move to the **Home** tab to select the **Format** button.
- Then select the **Format Cells** options from the Format button drop-down list to open the Format cell dialog box.

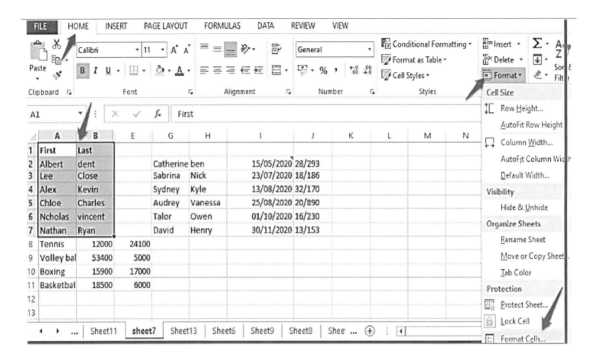

- Tap on the **borders** tab inside the Format cell dialog box and select a border style for the cells you have selected in (a) above.
- Click on the "**Preset**" button to show the preview of the border you chose and for the border to be reflected in the worksheet.

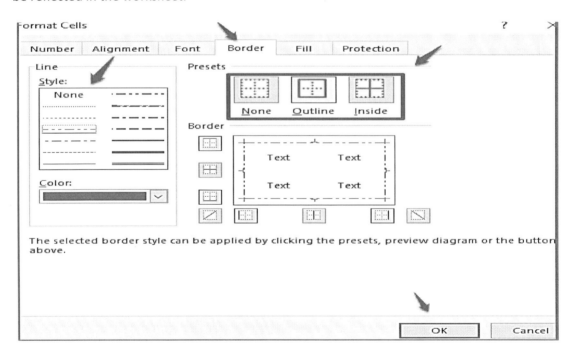

Note: border gives you the chance to use varieties of lines and colors for border, which makes it worthwhile.

337

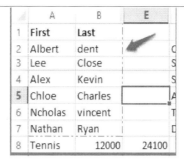

Using drawing to add a border to the worksheet:

1. Moving to the **Home** tab and click on the **Border** button.
2. You can either choose **Border or Border Grid** from the border button drop-down list.

3. Before you draw the border, you can pick the **border style and color** from the border button drop-down list.

4. Then drag over to the position where you want to see your border. As soon as you are done with the border, tap on **Esc** to release the border pen.

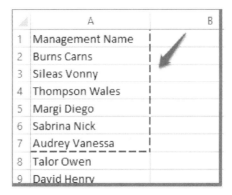

Note: You can remove the border from the cells. This can be done by:

- Selecting the cells with border, from the **Home** tab, tap on **Border**
- Then choose the **No Border** option from the border button drop-down list.

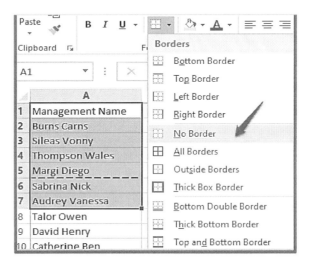

Colorize Your Worksheet

Colors add value and life to an object. Excel color is used to improve the Excel background to entice the interest of the reader to review it. When you are adding color to the worksheet, you have to pick a nice color, some colors are too harsh, do not pick such. To add color to Excel background, do the following:

- Select **the cells** where you want to put the color and tap on the **Format** button.
- Choose **Format cell** from the format button drop-down list and the format cell dialog box will come forth.

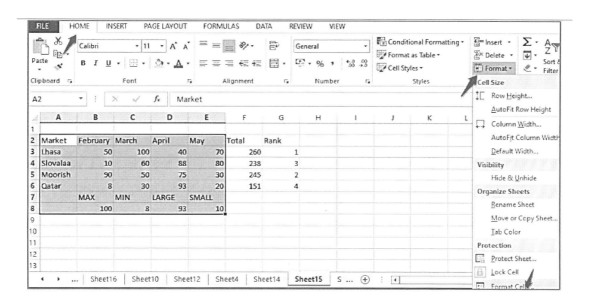

- Select the **Fill** bar from the Format cell dialog box and choose an appropriate color from the collection, then click on **Ok**.

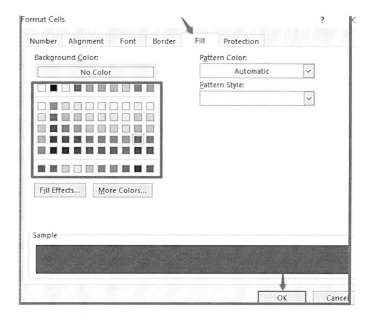

Be Prepared to Print A Worksheet

You have to prepare yourself ahead of printing a worksheet, don't just press Ctrl + P to print anyhow, there are certain steps to follow before you eventually print so that you will not end up printing what you do not want to print. The first process of printing is to check if the worksheet is rightly arranged on a single page so that you will not have a page break and end up printing a half page. To do that, you have to check these two sides of the worksheet (the bottom and right side of the worksheet) to confirm if the contents you are about to print is rightfully set very well.

340

Setting Up A Worksheet to Fit the Page

Setting up a worksheet to fit the page for printing is very expedient so that you will not end up printing what you do not expect. Excel starts its printing from the first column and first row (A1) to the last cell with data to the right side. To avoid page break of any kind and printing the actual document without wasting paper resources, you have to take worksheet page set-up with seriousness.

Note: before you click on print, check the **page layout** of your worksheet by clicking on the **View** button and tap on both **page layout** and **page break preview** to see the glance of what you are about to print.

Printing section of the worksheet: you do not have to print the whole worksheet; you only have to print the useful part with contents that you need. To print a section of the worksheet, kindly:

- Select **the cells** you want to print and move to the **Page Layout** tab.
- Click on the **"Print Area"** button and select **"Set Print Area"** from the drop-down menu, and Excel will be authorized to print the only selected area.

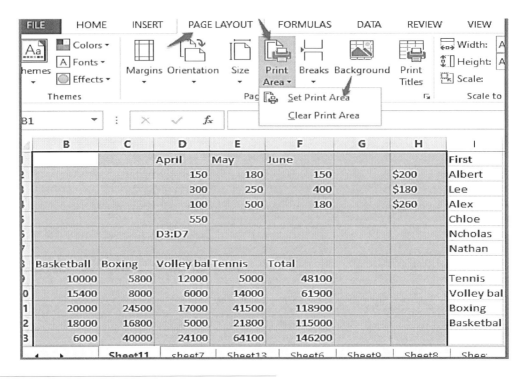

- If you check your worksheet, you will notice an appearance of the box around the area you have selected for printing giving you an indication of the area you want to print.

Note: if you do not like to print the cells you have selected again, you can remove it by choosing **"Clear Print Area"** from the **"Print Area Button"** drop-down list.

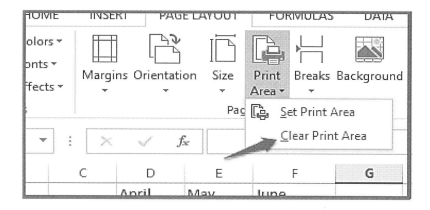

Printing a landscape worksheet:

The landscape is a horizontal printing, Excel users switch to landscape any time they perceive that the worksheet is too wide more than what portrait can accommodate. The beauty of landscape printing is that it permits Excel users to print a worksheet with a wider coverage which is not feasible with portrait printing. Print in a landscape format by simply doing these:

a. Move to the **page layout** tab and tap on the **Orientation button.**
b. Then, select **landscape** from the drop-down menu.

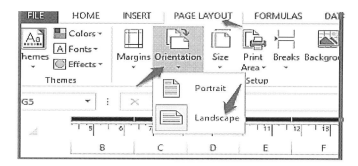

Dealing appropriately with the page break:

Page break is simply the same spot of the start point of one area and the endpoint of another area. There are ways to handle page breaks so that you will not want to have page breaks on page 10 and you will be having it on page 8. Let us quickly check how to manage page break:

- **Viewing the actual position of the page break by:**
1. Navigating to the **View** bar and tap on the **Page Break Preview** button.

2. Inside the **Page Break Preview** view, under **"In this view"**, you will see all the worksheet page numbers and their respective dashed lines which signify the point where each page break will occur.

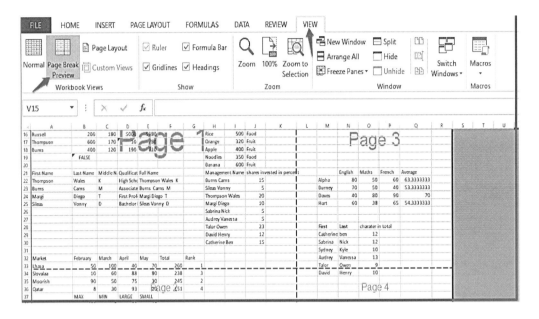

- **Adjusting the position of the page break:**
1. Inside the "page break preview view", double-click to drag the dashed line to adjust the page break position. Immediately you succeed in moving the page break, the previous dashed line will not be there anymore, but that point will be replaced with a solid line, and as a result, the page will not beak at that point anymore but on the new page break page position that you have just created. Be careful not to adjust the page break too much so that your contents worksheet will not be shortened.

- **Inserting a page break:**
1. Select the cell below the point where you want the horizontal break to take place and right to where you want the vertical break to set in.
2. Move to the **Page Layout tab** and click the **Break** button.

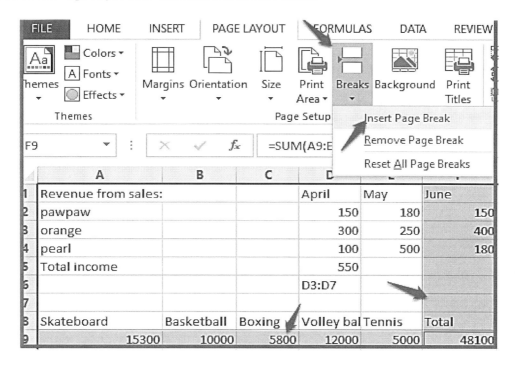

3. Select the **Insert Page Break** from the break button drop-down list and then drag the page break to adjust its location.

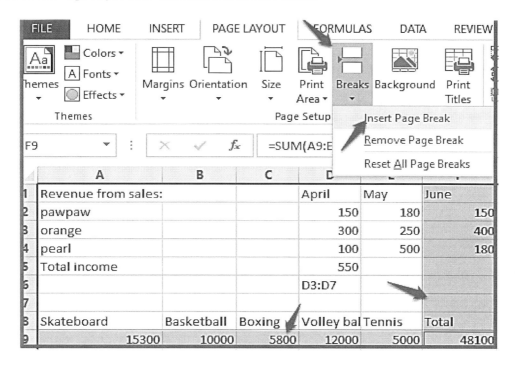

- **Removing a page break:**
1. Select **the cell** below and to the right of the page break and navigate the **Page Layout** tab to click the break button.
2. Choose **"Remove Page Break"** from the Break button drop-down menu.

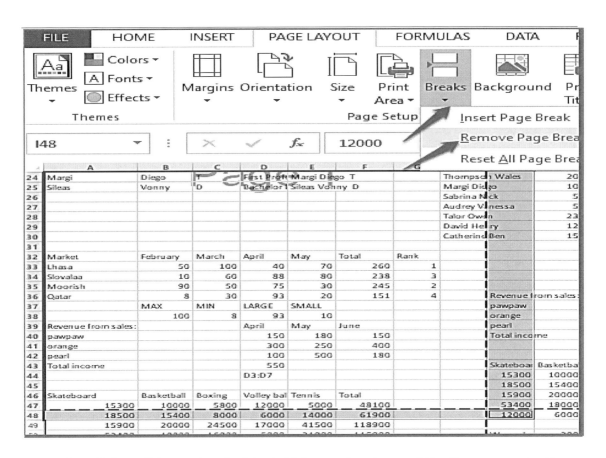

- **Removing all the solid page breaks (the initial page break you shifted):** move to the **Page Layout Tab** and tap on the **Break** button, then choose "Reset all the page breaks".

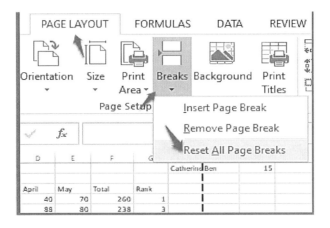

Present A Worksheet in An Attractive Manner

Your ultimate objective is how the work you want to print will get the attention of those people who will read it. You can adjust your worksheet more to make it the best one out there by navigating to the page-set up box. To access the page-set up box, move to the **Page Layout Tab** in the Page set-up group and click on the drop-down arrow.

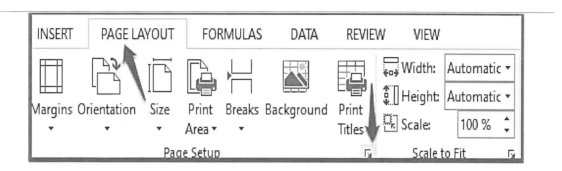

What can I do with the page set-up box? The following are certain things you can adjust inside the page set-up box:

1. **Numbering your worksheet page:** to number your page,
- Maneuver to the **Page** tab inside the page set-up box and insert **1** into the "First-page number text box".

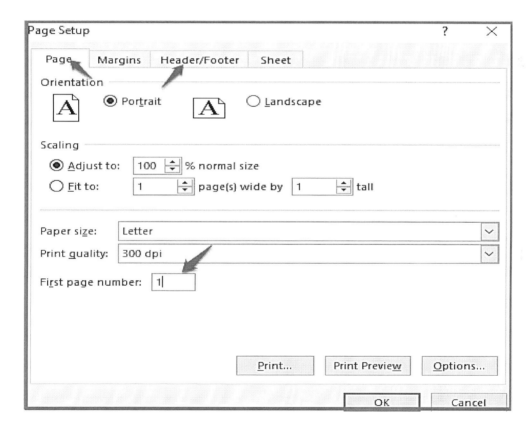

- then move to the header and footer tab and tap on either **footer or header** and pick **"page 1 of?"** from the drop-down list, that is page 1 of (?) the total worksheet pages. You will enter the number of the page number and the total number you are having in your worksheet to the header or footer.

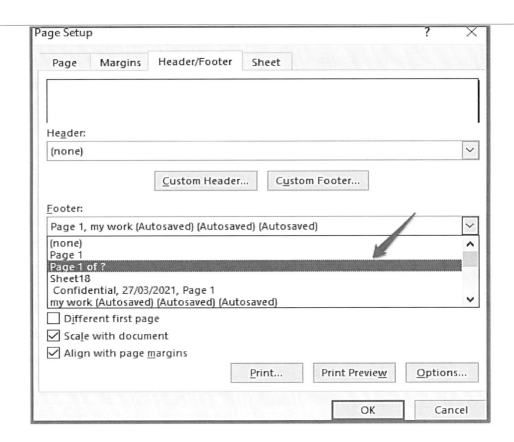

2. **Including headers and footers on page:** tap on the **header and footer** tab on the page set-up dialog box and then click on the "**Custom Header or Custom Footer**" option which will open you up to enter some actions such as, format text, sheet name, page numbers, file name, date, and your name.

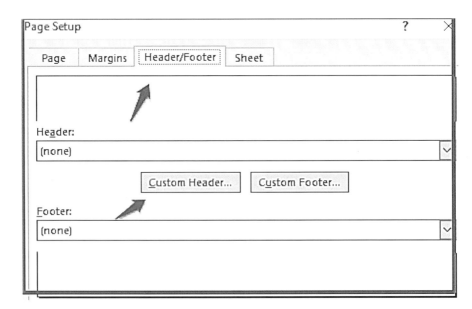

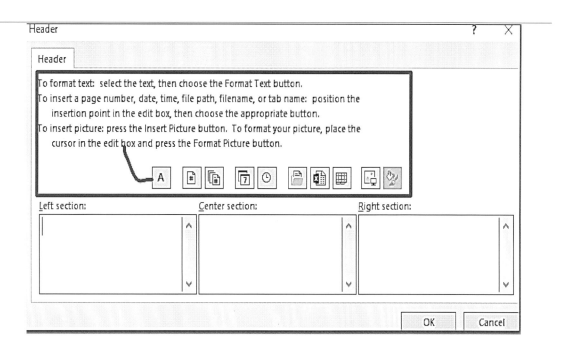

3. **Aligning worksheet page to the center:** click on the **Margin** tab inside the page set-up dialog, where you can either pick horizontal or vertical or both to center the page of the worksheet so as to center it accurately at the center of the sheet.

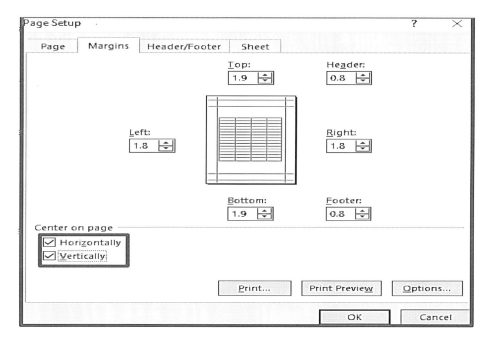

4. **Adjustment for cell gridline, column letters, and row numbers:** Excel neither print the gridline nor columns letters and row numbers by default, the features that give your worksheet an arrangement, but if you choose to print them, you can do that by clicking the **Sheet** tab inside the page set-up dialog box and select whatever feature you desire in the check box.

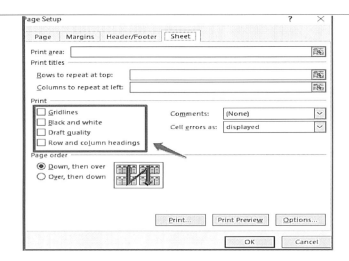

Repeat Rows and Columns Heading on Every Page

Perhaps your worksheet has multiple pages, and Excel does not print title page to every other page by default, and thus if you do not want your worksheet to look absurd because of missing heading on subsequent rows and columns because if the reader finds it difficult to see the title heading, they will as well find it difficult to get the main contents, then you are obliged to set the repeat row and column headings for document that has more than one page. To activate the repeated row and column headings on every page, you have to:

- Move to the **Page Layout** tab and tap on the **Print Titles** icon, in a jiffy, you will see the page setup dialog box open.
- Tap on the **Sheet** tab in the page setup dialog box.
- Locate **row and column references** under the print title.
- Click the reference selector button that relates to the type you set to be repeated. For example, "Row to repeat at the top" and for column "Column to repeat at the left" in the box provided for each heading.

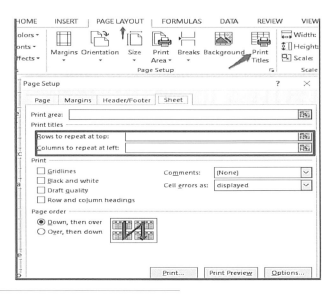

- Select the rows and columns with the references or addresses you need either by typing their address or by dragging over them if they next are to each other.
- By now, the respective headings you selected as the cell range must have been listed in the print title section under respective headings.

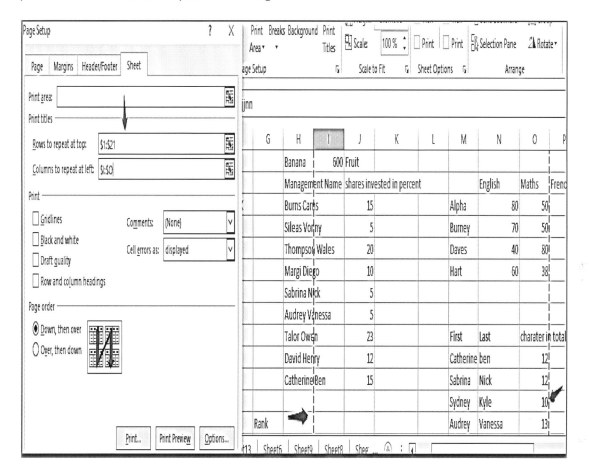

- This is the pattern you will be repeating if you want to set up repeating row and column heading from step (d) – (f).
- Tap **Ok** as soon as you are done with the page setup dialog box.

Tips: Before printing a document, check the print preview button in the page setup dialog box to confirm, if the row and column heading repeat themselves on the pages you selected.

Removing Row and Column Headings

To remove row and column headings, do well to:

- Click on the **sheet** tab in the page setup dialog box.
- Clear all the cell addresses in the rows to repeat at the top and column to repeat at the left in their respective box.

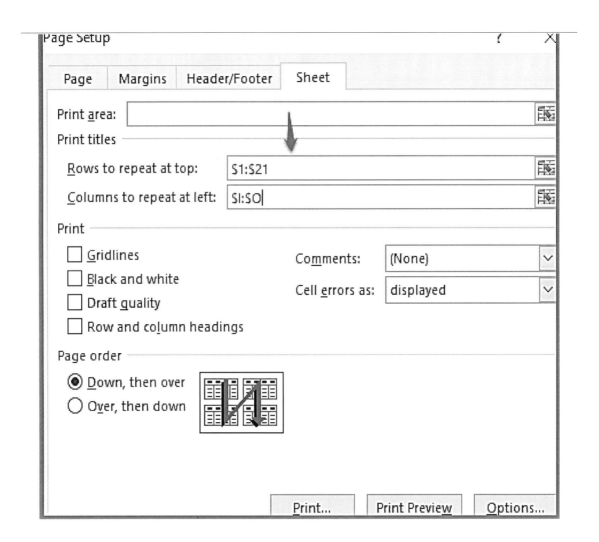

CHAPTER SIX

TOOLS AND TECHNIQUES FOR DATA ANALYSIS

What Are the Sparklines?

Sparklines are the tiny lines that live inside a cell; they show the variation in the dataset. Sparklines are of three types; line, column, and Win/Loss, compares to Excel graph. Sparklines are not graphs; they reside in the cell as a cell background. Let us quickly create one sparklines chart:

a. Select the **exact cell** where you want the chart to show up.
b. Click on the **Line, Column, or Win/loss icon** to open up "create sparklines" dialog box from the insert bar.

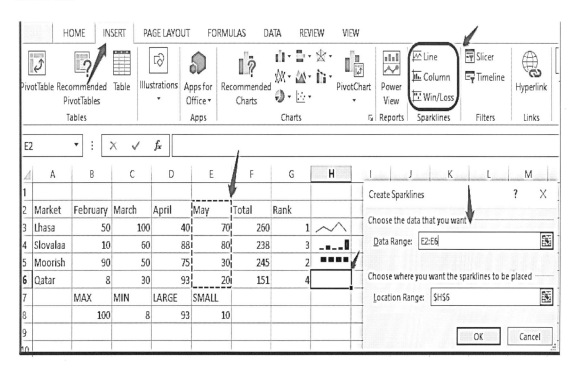

c. Input the range of cells name or drag over a row or column in your worksheet to select the cells from which the data is to be analyzed.
d. Tap on **Ok** to create the sparklines inside the Create Sparklines dialog box.

To remove the sparklines, click on the **Sparkline** and tap on the **Clear** button.

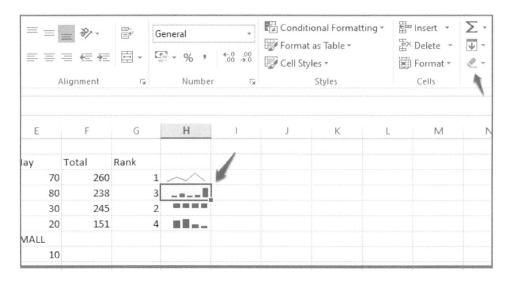

The sparklines' appearance can be improved by moving to the **Design tab** to locate the **sparklines tool** where you can pick some features to change the sparkline's appearance such as bar color, line color, and other various types of sparklines that you can pick as well.

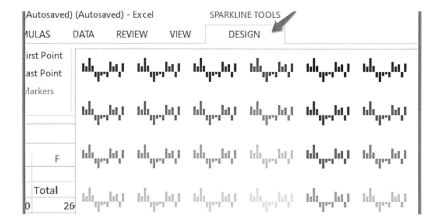

Conditional Format Application for Certain Data That Need Important Attention

The major aim of conditional formatting is to apply a conditional format to data and check if they will meet specific condition or criteria and call attention to it on meeting such condition setup, such as risk-tasks and budget item, it will then tell Excel to highlight those data. For instance, select blue for meeting positive criteria and red or black for meeting negative criteria. Conditional formats give you more understanding of the data. To understand the application of conditional formatting, follow this step-by-step guide listed below:

1. Select the **range values or cells** you want to apply conditional formatting to.
2. Move to the **Home** tab and click on the **"Conditional Formatting"** button.
3. Pick **Highlight cells rule or Top/bottom rules** from conditional formatting button drop-down list:

a. **Picking highlight cells rules:** this is a rule that is demanding attention from a data that is lesser or greater than a certain value or that falls to a specific range of data or numbers. For example, you may decide to highlight a product that has less than 150 in any quantity.

b. **Picking Top/bottom rules:** request for attention from any data that falls within a specific number or percentage within the range of the selected cells.

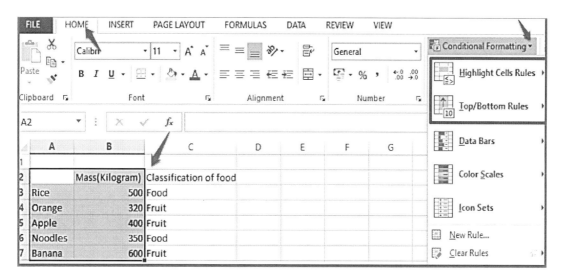

4. Pick an option for the headings you choose above in (3).

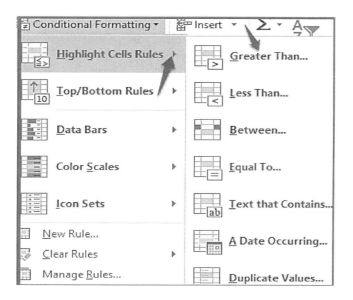

5. Set specific data rules for the cells you selected on the left side of the dialog box. For instance, greater than or less than, texts that contain a specific word or figure, and so on.

6. Select the specific attention you want each data that meet up with the condition to show. For instance, showing blue or red for meeting up with positive criteria or showing red or yellow, for meeting up negative criteria for easy identification, and you may as well refuse to use color at all.

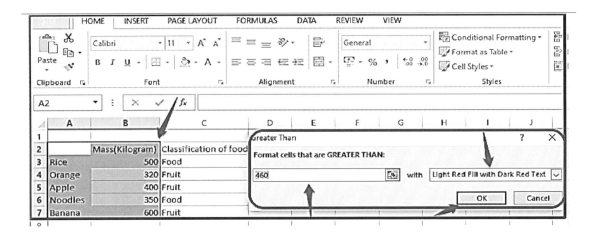

7. Tap on **Ok** to authenticate the process.

   How do I remove conditional formats? It is not difficult, kindly:

a. Select **the cells** that have conditional format and move to the **Home** tab to click the **Conditional Formatting** button.

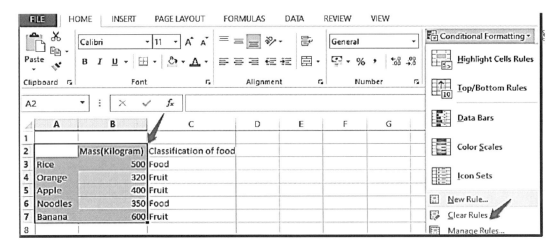

b. Pick the **Clear rules** option, then select "**clear rule from selected cells**" from the clear rule drop-down list.

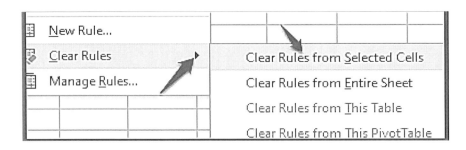

Taking Care of The Information List

Excel is not all about preparing a document for office use alone, at times you have to use Excel to prepare a document for your consumption, even if it is for office use, such document may be prepared on occasion for a later use and such has to be arranged very well so that it will not be confusing next time you are to check it and thus, sorting has to come up for arranging document such as customer information and sort them maybe in numerical or alphabetical order.

Filtering is also used to separate essential documents to the safer side, that is, selecting the necessary information by hiding other data and keeping the information required available.

Sorting List of a Data

Sorting data means to organize a full detailed worksheet row based on the data in the column, take for instance, you may logically organize a list by the first name. Data may be sorted numerically, alphabetically and in various other means to meet your need. When sorting, you can choose to sort a column or multiple columns.

To sort a column: if you want to sort a single column, kindly ensure you attach a header to each column for perfect identification and an effective function of Sorting;

o   Select **any cell** which will represent other cells in that same column for sorting. Select the cell that has the data type you want to sort, and Excel will update it with other cells in the column.
o   Move to the **Data** tab and tap on **Sort & Filter** group, then pick the **Sort type**, probably A-Z(ascending to descending) or Z-A(descending to ascending).

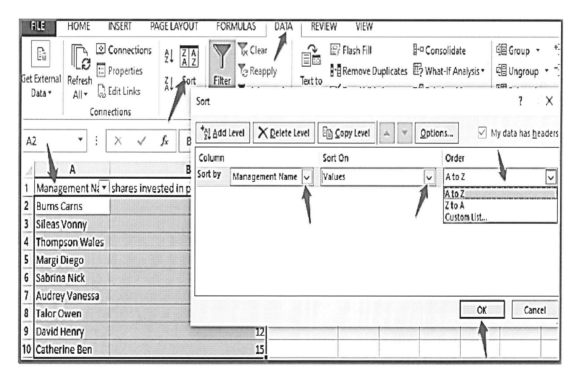

o Tap on a **column heading** and pick "**sort by**" perhaps by the headings and the order you prefer, from top to bottom or bottom to top.

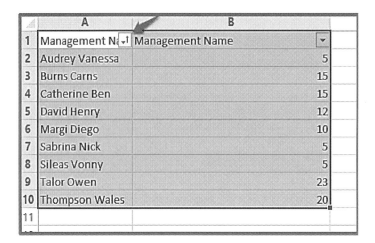

To sort multiple columns: if you want to sort more than one column, kindly:

- Select the **first cell** in the first column
- Maneuver to the **Data** tab to open the "**Sort**" dialog box.
- Inside the Sort dialog box, indicate the column you want to sort under the column for the first column and keep on tapping on "**Add level**" to keep on getting as many as the number of the column you want to sort, and then select the **Sorting order** you will prefer for all the column you have selected.

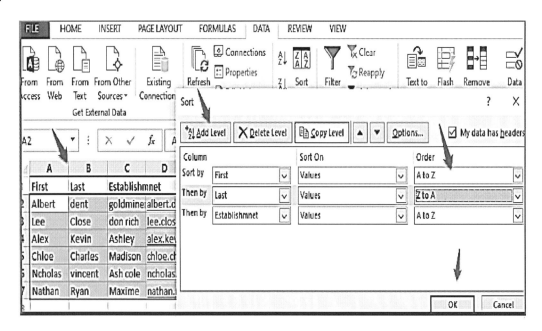

- Tap **Ok** for authentication.

Filtering List of Data

Filtering list of data is used to analyze data and pick out only the rows that meet the filter condition and thus hide all the other data, provided the data that satisfy the criteria for the filter is established. Filtering will clean up the list of data except for the types of rows of data you demand and at the end of the filtering criteria, the list would have shortened down the worksheet data, so, you can view only the information you desire to see. To filter a list of data, endeavor to the following:

- Ensure you attach a header row for each column to make filtering work effectively.
- Select the data you want to filter, move to the **Data** tab, click on **Filter** under the Sort & Filter group.

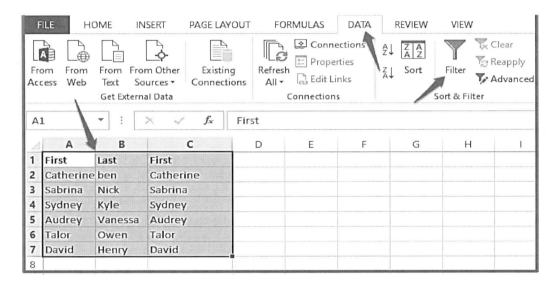

- Tap on each Filter arrow you want to filter and navigate to **Text Filters** to open the options that are available under filter.

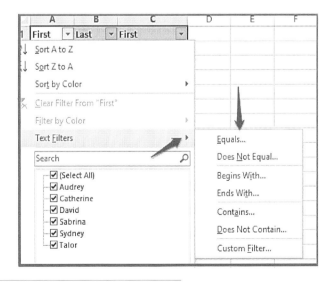

- Tap on the option you want and the Auto filter dialog box will open, supply the condition of the data you are looking for, and tap **Ok**.

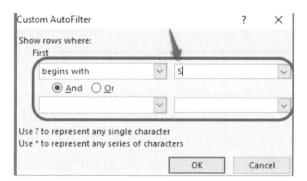

- As soon as you click **Ok**, the filtering will show only the row that meets the criteria with the cells that have that data.

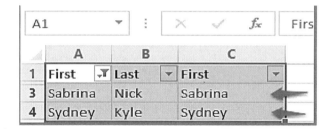

How can I clear all the filters from the worksheet, and get the total information back?

Move to the **Data** tab and click on the **Clear** button from Sort & Filter group.

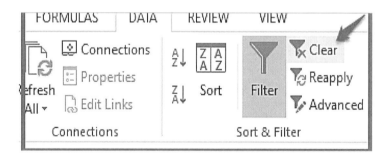

Exploiting Goal Seek Command

Goal seek command is simply a technique of data analysis that focuses more on the result by using the result to formulate an analysis that will help in getting the raw data which will give one the actual result one wants to achieve. Goal seek command is an order you give Excel to experiment result to get the raw data based on the result you desire to achieve coupled with necessary Excel argument.

Goal seek analysis input value in the place of raw data, for instance, you want to borrow money, you know how much to borrow and you have the ability to pay off the loan, and also know the period you will use to pay off the whole loan, but you do not know the exact rate of interest that you will pay in acquiring such loan, Goal seek command will help you in that area. Let us do the computation of interest rate to pay in acquiring a loan with the PMT function with the following guideline:

- Enter the respective elements into the worksheet, for instance:
- B1= Loan amount, B2= period of the payment monthly, B3= Rate of interest, B4= month payment.
- Enter the **respective value** for each element above in (1), for instance,
- Cell C1= $120000, that is the amount you prefer to borrow.
- Cell C2= 180, the number of times to pay off the loan if paid monthly.
- Cell C3= the interest rate we are about to calculate for the loan amount.
- Cell C4= the amount of payment every month, but you are not going to insert it here, it will be used in the Goal seek computation because it is the data result.

	A	B	C
1		Amount of loan	120000
2		Number of payment (Monthly)	180
3		Interest rate	
4		Payment	

- Insert the formula into **Cell C4** by putting in **Cell 4=PMT(C3/12, C2, C1)**, this will give you the formula result for the monthly payment value. In this scenario, you wish to be paying $1200 each month, but you will not enter it, it will be using in Goal seek dialog box for interest rate computation. The formula breakdown:
- **C1** is the loan amount
- **C2** is the period it will take for paying off the loan.
- **C3** is the Interest rate that "Goal seek" seeks to find, and the 12 is 12 months, PMT calculates on yearly basis, and thus you have to divide it by 12 to convert it to a monthly basis. But, because cell B3 does not have anything inside, Excel will assume it to be Zero (0).

C4				f_x	=PMT(C3/12,C2,C1)
	A	B			C
1		Amount of loan			120000
2		Number of payment (Monthly)			180
3		Interest rate			
4		Payment			-$667

- Move to the **Data** tab and tap on **What-if Analysis** and then choose the "**Goal Seek**" button from the What-if Analysis drop-down list.

360

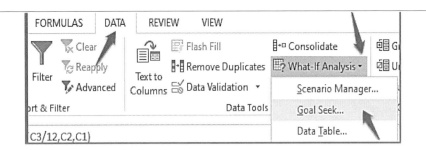

- Once the "Goal Seeks" dialog box opens, insert the **cell reference** that comprises the formula you are looking at, in this case, it is C4.
- Then type the formula result into the "**To Value box**", this is representing -1200 because it is the outflow.
- Insert the **cell address** that comprises the value you want to change inside the **"Changing cell box"**; in this case, it is cell C3.

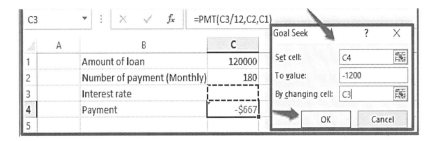

- Tap **Ok** and Goal seek will run the check for you and provide you with the result.

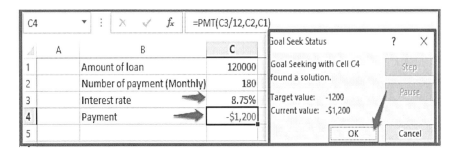

- Then format the cells to display the actual face value by navigating to the **Home** tab, then, click on the **"Number"** group, then move to currency to format it.

	A	B	C
1		Amount of loan	$120,000
2		Number of payment (Monthly)	180
3		Interest rate	8.75%
4		Payment	-$1,200
5			

Analysing Data with Data Table and What If Analysis

Data tables with What-if analysis are combined to address a complex computation. This technique helps to alter the range of data on a single table and extract the cause of adjusting such on the formula results. Goal seeks and data table are almost the same thing except for multiple variables of data that data table uses in carrying out its process and experiment at once.

Using A One Input Data Table for Analysis

One input data table structures its experiment in a single table and provides the results of each formula to be per the change on the input cell in the formula. To get it right at this level, let us use the rate of interest for this scenario by making use of the following set of data below.

◢	A	B	C
1		Amount of loan	$120,000
2		Number of payment (Monthly)	180
3		Interest rate	8.75%
4		Payment	-$1,200
5			

In the above information, we are having:

- The amount of the loan, interest rate on the loan, number of payments every month. The monthly payment value is calculated on the other three (3) elements (it is in red), because it is cash outflow or payment.
- The amount of the loan in cell C1 is $120000, the number of payments every month in cell C2 is 180 times, the rate of interest in cell C3 is 8.75%, and the payment value (monthly) in C4 is calculated based on the first three (3) elements; it has to be in red because it is the cash outflow or payment. It is calculated based on: =PMT(C3/12, C2, C1).

We will be using the above information and analysis to check the number of the monthly payment that will befit you. If your monthly payment capacity will not exceed $1000 compared to $1200 you have been paying before by making use of the data in the above table to formulate different number of payments per month and select the numbers of payment that will give us below $1000.

Let us forge ahead to check what we have to do to formulate different number of payment (monthly) and monthly payment, kindly:

- Insert different number payment (monthly) to column E from above the 180 we are having above because you are paying lesser than $1200, enter the number to column E2 down to column E12.

- Insert, = C4 in cell F1, because it is one row above the value to the column we want to test and thus, it gives reference to cell C4. In referencing, cell C4 you have to refer it, not by inserting the value so that the formula can work but kindly type "=" in F1 and click on C4 to refer it.

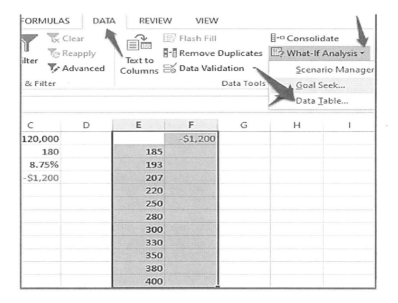

- Now, select the cell in E1 to F12 and move to the **Data** tab, and tap on **What-if analysis**, then click on **Data table** from What-if analysis drop-down to open Data table dialog box.

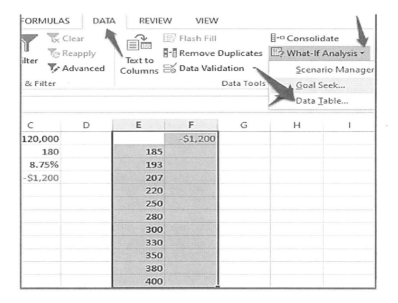

- Inside the **"Data Table"**, give reference to cell C2 in "Column input cell field"; we will be using the column cell field alone because we are calculating with one input data table.

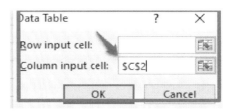

- Tap **Ok**, and the Data table will process the result and insert the data process into their respective cells.

	A	B	C	D	E	F
1		Amount of loan	$120,000			-$1,200
2		Number of payment (Monthly)	180		185	-1184.01
3		Interest rate	8.75%		193	-1160.89
4		Payment	-$1,200		207	-1125.39
5					220	-1097.14
6					250	-1045.28
7					280	-1007
8					300	-986.937
9					330	-962.911
10					350	-950.068
11					380	-934.462
12					400	-926.016

Note: One Input Data table is done with the calculation, by following the calculation, you can pick E8 which gives you 300 of a monthly payment with monthly payment lesser than &1000 ($986).

Clear the Data table you created by:

- Selecting the whole **Data Table** and tap on the **Delete** button. Note that you cannot delete part of the table, that's why you have to select the whole Data Table.

Using A Two Input Data Table for Analysis

As the name indicates, two input data table permits you to test two input elements rather than one input table, taking for instance the above One input unit that we used in calculating the number of the monthly payment in the column, you can as well add another variable such as loan amount to the row so that the computation will cover both sides and be more detailed by combining loan amount and number of monthly payments to meet a specific need. For instance, you may want to combine loan amount and the number of payments that will give you less than $700, it is that computation that will give you the actual loan amount with the period of time that will give you such. Without much ado, let us analyze the data with two input data table by observing this one-on-one process:

- Let us get a diverse number of monthly payments to the column and different levels of the loan amount to the row located above the column one cell above to the right.

	A	B	C	D	E	F	G	H	I	J	K
1		Amount of loan	$120,000			$50,000	60000	70000	90000	105000	120000
2		Number of payment (Monthly)	180		185						
3		Interest rate	8.75%		193						
4		Payment	-$1,200		207						
5					220						
6					250						
7					300						
8					350						
9					400						
10					420						
11					500						
12					550						
13											

- Insert: = **C4 in cell E1** as it represents row above the values in the column. Remember we are working with two input variables and thus, E1 is dependent on both variables (number of monthly payment and amount of the loan), you will not insert C4 directly, you have to reference it, so that the formula can work effectively. Reference it by typing "=" into cell E1 and then move to click on cell C4.
- Then select **cell (E1:K12)**, and navigate to the **Data** tab to click on the **What-if analysis,** then tap on the **Data Table** from the What-if analysis drop-down, to open the Data table dialog box.

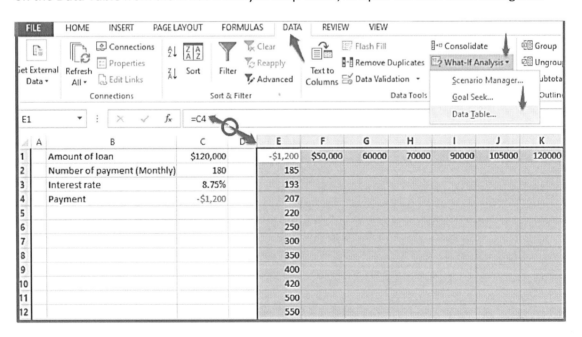

- Right inside the Data table dialog box, insert into the:
1. **Row input cell, C1**

2. Column input cell, C2

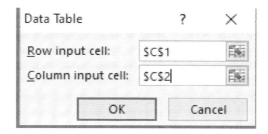

- Tap **Ok** and Excel will quickly run the check and fill the selected range which you can check carefully to select the combination of the loan amount and number of the monthly payment that best suits you.

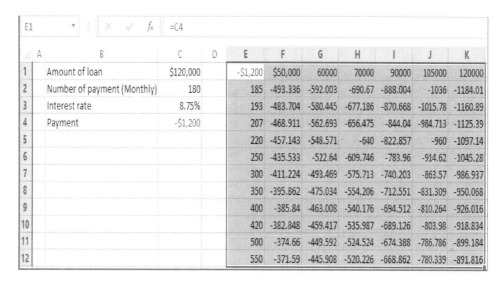

The above worksheet vividly shows how much you can borrow with respective numbers of payment from which you can extract monthly payment that is below $600.

Clear the Data table created by:

- Selecting the whole **Data Table** and tap on the **Delete** button. You cannot delete part of the table and that is why you need to select the whole table.

Using Pivot Table for Data Analysis

Pivot table is one of Excel's indispensable features that grants you the privilege of arranging a large set of data in a worksheet and rationally analyze them. The pivot table works soundly by changing the column to row and also changing the row to column.

Note: Pivot table works perfectly with a set of data that has a column heading label which Excel will use to identify each column.

USING RECOMMENDED PIVOT TABLE

Excel provides a means of generating automatic pivot table; there are many recommended pivot table options that are available for Excel users. To explore and make use of a readymade pivot table, observe the followings steps:

- Select **any cell** that contains data inside it in the worksheet.
- Move to the **Insert** tab and tap on the **Recommended Pivot Table** option

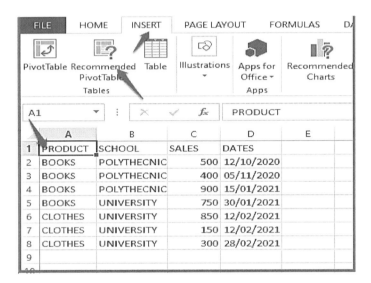

- And you will be provided with a recommended table dialog box for your worksheet data. Pick any format of the recommended pivot table that suits your needs. For this illustration, we will be choosing the **"Sum of SALES by PRODUCTS and SCHOOL.**

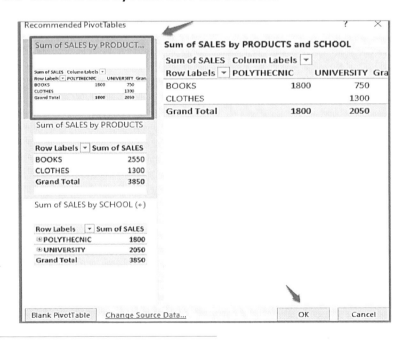

- Then tap **Ok** and you will see the generated Pivot table.

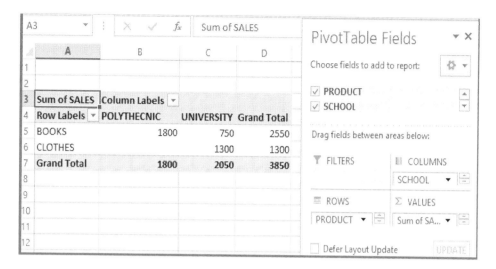

Creating A New Pivot Table

You can create your Pivot table. If the structure of the recommended Pivot table does not correlate with your information, creating a pivot table by yourself will help you to organize list around any of the command label, such as ordering by date to indicate the highest and lowest date order, arrange the price of the product to check the best and least sales and many more. Check the below guide to create a new Pivot table of your choice:

- Select **a cell** that contains data anywhere in the list.
- Go to the **Insert** tab and click on the **Pivot Table** button; Excel will select the entire list in your worksheet and use it to open a Created Pivot Table Dialog box.

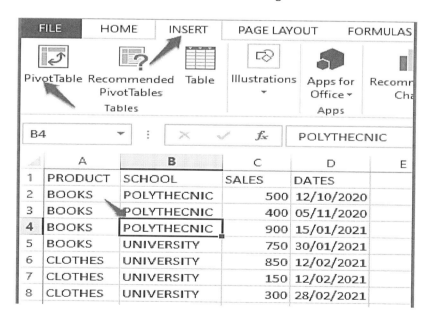

- Pick **"select a table or range"** button, while the new worksheet will be there on default mode which is the best option. You will edit in the new worksheet and later transfer it to the existing worksheet.

- Tap on **Ok** and you will be provided with a PivotTable field, select each field you want and drag them to any of the four areas of the Pivot table which are: Rows, Columns, Filters, and Values.

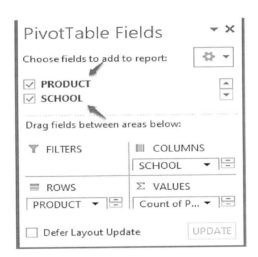

- In this case, **PRODUCT is added to Value while SCHOOL is added to Column.**

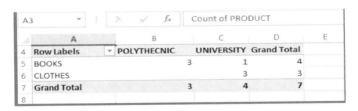

Note: you can choose the field with the mouse by placing your mouse on the field, then click and drag it to any of the four areas as you desire, immediately, the Pivot table will compute the selected field and the summation of the amount of products sold in each field.

You may as well sort and filter the Pivot table with the "Sort & Filter" button situated at the upper right side of the **Home** tab.

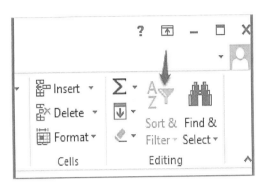

ADDING FINAL TOUCHES TO THE PIVOT TABLE

You are permitted to touch or restructure the default pattern of your Pivot table with Grand total, Report layout, and pivot table styles. Let us check this one by one.

1. **Grand total:** Grand total is the addition of total value. Excel estimates the total value of the column and row by default, but if you are not pleased with it, navigate to the **Pivot Table** design and click on **Grand Total**, and then you can choose **"Remove either column or row or both"**.

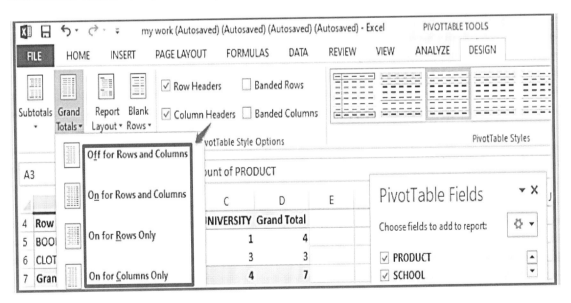

2. **Report layout:** Layout shows how your Pivot table is presented. From the **Pivot table design**, click on **Report layout** to choose diverse layout from various alternatives.

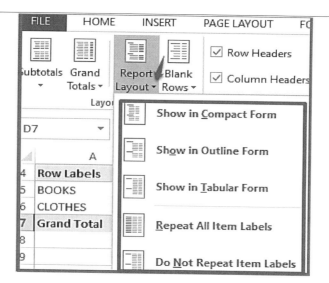

3. **Pivot table style:** Pivot table style breathes some color and design to your pivot table. Once you draw a pivot table, the pivot table style will be there by default, to change it, simply click on the drop-down arrow to see all the pivot table styles; the table style is there by default.

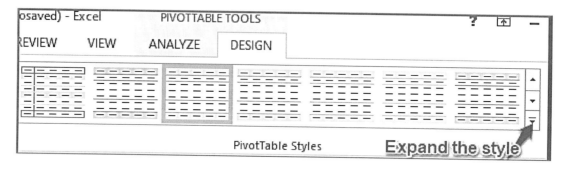

CHAPTER SEVEN

EXCEL 365 SHORTCUTS, TIPS AND TRICKS

Useful Shortcuts

When you find yourself making an exploit through keyboard shortcuts, that is the time you can gain speed in whatever you are doing in Excel. The following shortcuts are amazing shortcuts that you will find useful and necessary as you begin to use the Excel program:

Formula Shortcuts

SHORTCUTS CODE	USES
= Equal to	Start a formula.
Ctrl + '	Switch between formula and cell value.
Shift + F3	Enter a function.
Alt-=	Entering an AutoSum function.
Ctrl + `	From the cell above into the current one.
Ctrl + Shift + U	Expand or collapse the formula bar.
Alt + F8	Create, run and edit a macro.
Ctrl + shift + End	Select all texts from the cursor to the end in the formula bar
Ctrl + End	Inside the formula bar, move the cursor to the end of the text formula.

General Excel Shortcuts

SHORTCUTS CODE	USES
Ctrl + N	Open new workbook
Ctrl + O	Open exiting workbook
Ctrl + W	Close a workbook
Ctrl + F	Open the Find and Replace dialog box
Ctrl + 9	Hide the selected rows
Ctrl + O	Hide the selected columns
Ctrl + shift+ (	Unhide hidden row in a selection
Ctrl + shift +)	Unhide hidden column in a selection

Ctrl + '	Switch between displaying formula and cell value
Ctrl + shift + U	Expand or collapse the formula bar.
Ctrl + shift + %	Percentage formatting without decimal
Ctrl + shift + #	Date formatting with date, month, and year pattern.
Ctrl + shift + @	Time formatting with 12 hours pattern.
Ctrl + Q	Open the Quick analysis tools for selected cells with data.
Ctrl + 1	Open the Format cell dialog box.
Alt + `	Open the style dialog box.
Ctrl + shift + &	Apply a border-box.
Ctrl + shift + _	Remove a border from a cell or selection.
Ctrl + C	Copy cell's item into the clipboard.
Ctrl + X	Cut cell's item into the clipboard.
Ctrl + V	Paste from the clipboard into a cell.
Ctrl + Alt + V	Open paste special dialog box.
Enter	Moving to the next cell down
Shift + Enter	Moving to the next cell up
(Ctrl + A or Ctrl) + (shift + space bar)	Select the whole worksheet
Ctrl + Home	Navigating the selection to the beginning of the selected rows
Ctrl + Shift + Home	Navigating the selection to the beginning of the selected worksheet
Ctrl + space bar	Selecting a column.
Shift + spacebar	Selecting a column.
F5	Open "Go To" dialog box
Ctrl + left arrow	Move to the left end while you are still in a cell
Ctrl + right arrow	Move to the right while you are still in a cell
Esc	Erase your cell entry
Ctrl + ;	Enter the current date.

Ctrl + Shift + ;	Enter the current time.
Ctrl + T	Open the create table dialog box.
Tab	Move to the next cell to the right.
Up / down arrow key	Move the cell one up / down.
Home	Move to the beginning of a row.
Ctrl + Home	Move to the beginning of a worksheet.
Shift + tab	Move to the next cell to the left.
Ctrl + End	Move to the last cell that has contents inside.

Indispensable Tips and Trick for Quick Command

The following tricks and tips will not just help you to analyze or simplify an issue, but also save your time by simplifying things and aid you to crunch long data item. With these simple tools, do not worry, because you will move at a faster pace with Excel.

Absolute and Relative Reference

Excel references cells using an absolute or relative reference, or both. For instance,

a. = **C4*D1**, is referred to a relative referencing because it refers to a certain location by one cell to the left or three cells up the row.

D4		:	×	✓	f_x	=C4*D1	
	A	B	C	D	E	F	
1			Rate	5%			
2							
3		Detail	Price	Rate	Total		
4		chair	300	15			
5		desk	230				
6		book	400				
7		pen	150				
8		bag	1000				

b. And thus, if you decide to copy down the formula using Autofill, you will be getting an error notice, because each cell you copy will still be referring to one cell to the left and three cells up the row. In this case, it is either it will give you the wrong answer or give you an error because that D1 should apply to all formulas in that column. For instance, three cells above the row; in this case, it's a text (Rate), in the case of cell D6 =C6*D3, D3 is a text and it is because the formula is relative referencing.

D6	▾	⋮	✕	✓	*fx*	=C6*D3

◢	A	B	C	D	E
1			Rate	5%	
2					
3		Detail	Price	Rate	Total
4		chair	300	15	
5		desk	230	0	
6		book	◈ 00	#VALUE!	
7		pen	150	2250	
8		bag	1000	0	

c. In such a scenario like this, we will make use of absolute referencing by making D1 fixed to this location for all the rows, do this simply by highlighting it and press **F4** to switch between relative and absolute cell referencing.

SUM	▾	⋮	✕	✓	*fx*	=C4*D1

◢	A	B	C	D	E
1			Rate	5%	
2					
3		Detail	Price	Rate	Total
4		chair	300	=C4*D1	
5		desk	230	0	
6		book	400	#VALUE!	
7		pen	150	2250	
8		bag	1000	0	

SUM	▾	⋮	✕	✓	*fx*	=C4*D1

◢	A	B	C	D	E	F
1			Rate	5%		
2						
3		Detail	Price	Rate	Total	
4		chair	300	=C4*D1		
5		desk	230	0		
6		book	400	#VALUE!		
7		pen	150	2250		
8		bag	1000	0		

d. Then, you can lock the column, row, and both; but in this scenario, we will keep cell D1 locked, then, if you copy it down now, it will copy the right formulas for each cell.

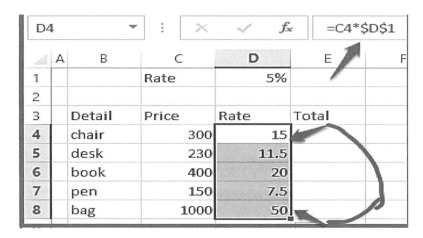

D4	▾	⋮	✕	✓	*fx*	=C4*D1

◢	A	B	C	D	E	F
1			Rate	5%		
2						
3		Detail	Price	Rate	Total	
4		chair	300	15		
5		desk	230	11.5		
6		book	400	20		
7		pen	150	7.5		
8		bag	1000	50		

Note: Anytime you copy a formula, make sure you set the relative or absolute referencing appropriately in respect of how the formula will be applied to the data.

Quick Analysis Tool

Quick analysis is used to perform numerous quick actions on the list of data in the worksheet, check this case:

- When you highlight the list of data and click on the "Quick Analysis" tool icon, it will show up a group of information.

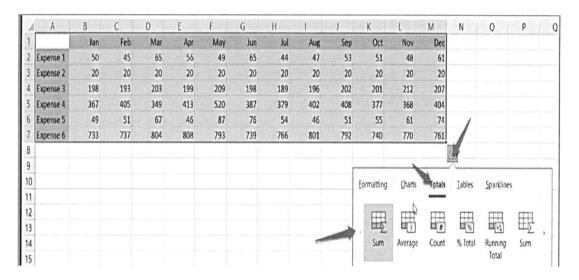

- Click on the **Total** tab where you will be able to select **SUM, AVERAGE,** and others. When you pick from SUM, there is also row sum, column sum, or Running total or percentage.

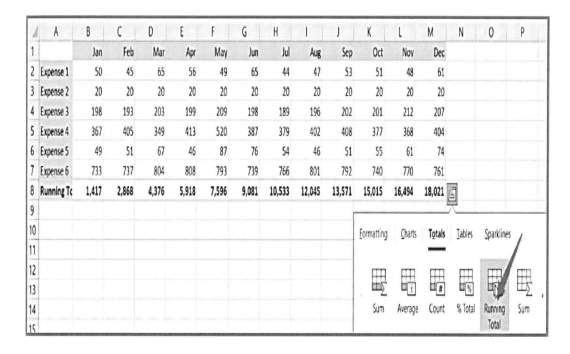

376

- Click on the **Chart** option, and you will be given a line, clustered area, and so on.

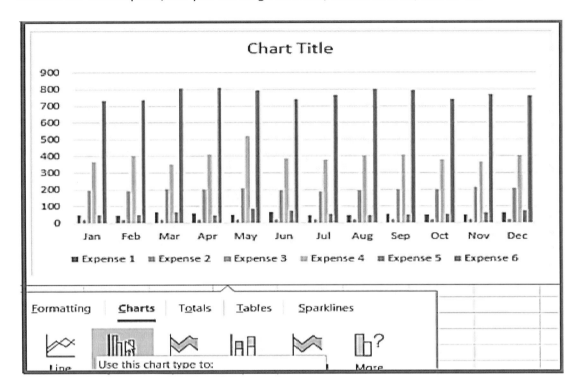

- Click on **formatting** and you will be given Data bar, color scale, icon set, mark 10%, and others. With the Data tab, all your cells will be represented with a graph in respect of the value they have inside.

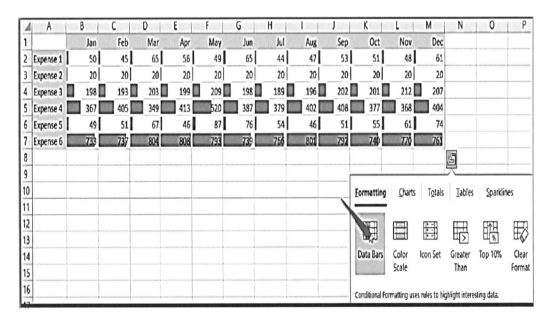

The color scale helps you to adjust the color.

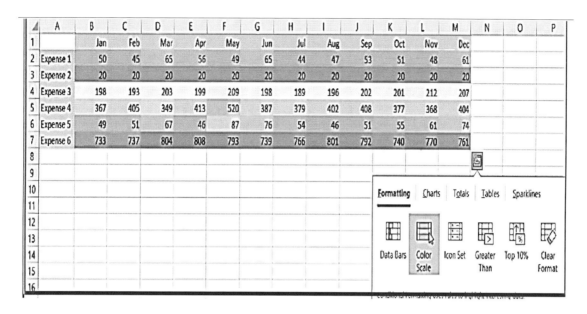

While icon set gives you a pictorial illustration of each data in the list and mark the top, 10% will mark top ten in the list. When you click on the Sparklines, it shows you the small chart of your data.

Autofit Column Width

The Autofit command is the quickest way of adjusting column, to use it;

- Move to a **boundary between any columns** until you see the cursor change to a black-headed arrow.

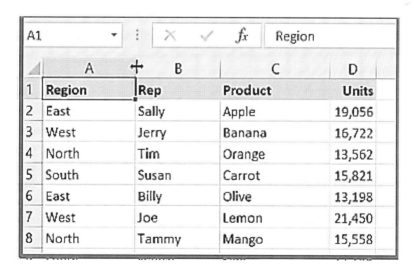

- Then double-click it, immediately it will readjust the size of the column width to fit the data inside the cell in the column selected perfectly.

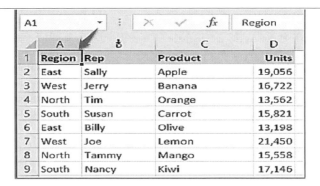

- You can as well highlight **multiple columns** and double-click any of them and all the column width in the column will be adjusted.

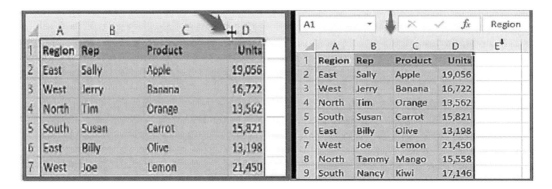

XLOOKUP Function

XLOOKUP is a powerful new function design to replace HLOOKUP and VLOOKUP. Take for instance:

- We want to look up the name of John in this table and return a value from the February column.
- You can quickly use **XLOOKUP** and the first element in this LOOKUP value is **John,** the array through which we are going to look up John's name in this area is the John row and we want to return the value from the February column.

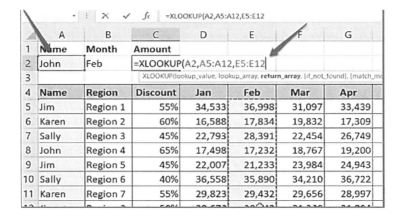

- You will see the result it returns is **17232**, which is the meeting point of **John and February.**

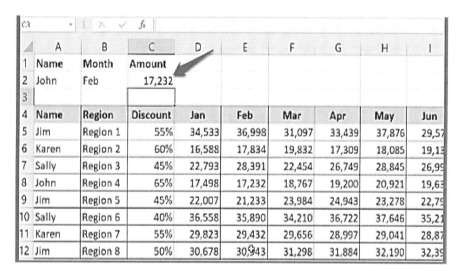

Note: XLOOKUP has one merit and that merit is that it can perform horizontal XLOOKUP as well, let's say we want to lookup February in this list, we are going to return the value from John and it will be the same number **17232**, in the February column next to John.

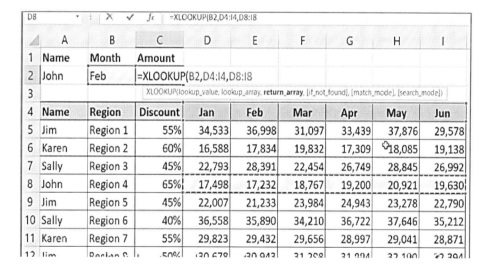

Remove BLANK

You may have multiple blank cells in a list of a given data; it will not be wise to remove them one by one. To remove multiple blank cells, kindly:

a. Highlight the **total list** of the data.
b. Navigate to the **Home** tab and select the **Find & Select** option from the home tab, then select "**Go to special**" from the drop-down list to open the "Go to special" dialog box.

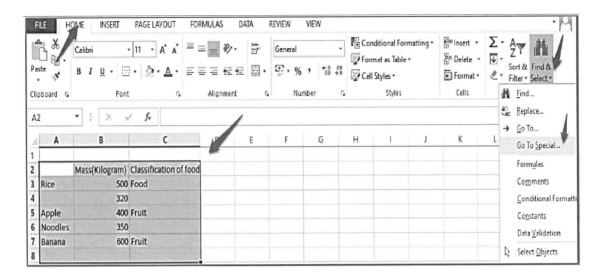

c. Pick **Blank** from the box and tap **ok,** immediately, Excel will highlight all the blank cells in the list.

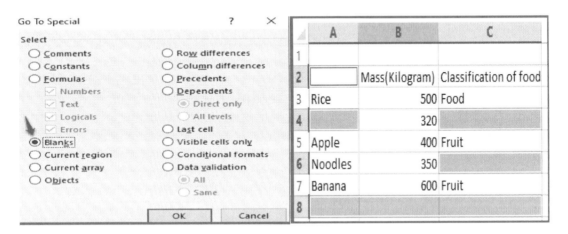

d. Simply right-click on any of the blank cells highlighted, then select **delete** from the drop-down list.

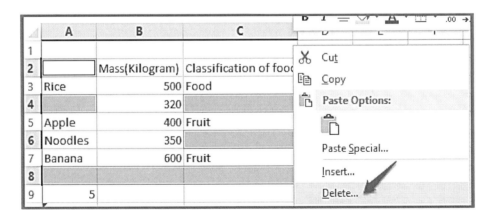

e. You can now pick the "**Shift cells left**" option from the dialog box and tap **Ok**, instantly, all the blank cells will be cleaned up.

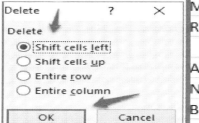

Mass(Kilo	Classification of food	
Rice	500	Food
320	6090	price
Apple	400	Fruit
Noodles	350	
Banana	600	Fruit

CONCLUSION ON EXCEL 365

Excel 365 has been the talk of the whole world, not because Excel is just a spreadsheet program employed in recording and analyzing various data, but it has also been tested to be beneficial with its new features and updates for everyday business activities.

The idea of Excel 365 is to make Excel an essential part of business enterprises, and as a result of its best techniques used in analyzing various business issues, Excel has been the most used program in every office.

At this point, you will agree with me, that the method and technique analyses used inside this user guide as Excel 365 is capable of managing and analyzing every data and brings it under control, even if it is so large.

I so much believe you must have familiarized yourself with the formulation of formulas and functions that are necessary for executing data, including the techniques for coordinating and regulating data. I hope those techniques will give you a better chance of managing your lists of data and even extract the basic and most important information from the list of data within a given shortest period.

I must confess to you, that the major aim of the user guide is to give you an overview of Excel tools and functions which has improved over time in running our day-to-day Excel operation.

I hereby, wish you the very best of luck as you journey through the era of Excel 365, an online-based version.

BOOK THREE

POWERPOINT 365

WRITER'S PRESENTATION

Hello everyone, welcome to the PowerPoint 365 training and learning through this book, my name is Felix and I'm going to be your instructor. I have been using different versions of PowerPoint for some years and I see this PowerPoint 365 software program as a simple application to create a slide show of important information, charts, and images to display during a presentation. Recent advances in PowerPoint include subtitling on slides, Presenter Coach, and other enhanced interactive features.

In this book, I'll provide you with a comprehensive overview of the different features available in PowerPoint 365, whether you are going through this book as a beginner with no prior knowledge in PowerPoint, or whether your skills are a little more intermediate or advanced. I'm giving you 100% assurance that by the end of going through this guide, you would have at least something which will increase and improve your efficiency when working with PowerPoint.

I also hope to introduce you to some of the newer features that you probably do not know existed or unsure of how to use, and also show you some cool tips and tricks that can help you increase your PowerPoint use from basic to advanced level.

CHAPTER 1

INTRODUCTION

PowerPoint is a presentation program developed by Microsoft. It is included in the standard Office suite along with Microsoft Word and Excel. The software allows users to create anything from basic slides to complex presentations.

PowerPoint is often used to create business presentations, but can also be used for educational or informal purposes. The presentations are comprised of slides, which may contain texts, images, and other media, such as audio clips and movies. Sound effects and animated transitions can also be included to make the presentation more appealing.

PowerPoint is a presentation application that is used to create a slide show of important information, charts, and images to be displayed during a presentation. Recent advances in PowerPoint include subtitling on slides, Presenter Coach, and other advanced interactive features.

The Importance of this Book

This book, PowerPoint 365 is designed for beginners and for readers who have never used this particular software application nor know the importance but are familiar with the workings of PC in general and specifically the Windows operating system. It is also designed for use as a learning and reference resource by home, work and business users of Microsoft Office programs who want to use PowerPoint to create and present slides and printed materials. Likewise, it is meant for readers who want to expand their knowledge about PowerPoint 365.

The Components in this Book

1. Steps

This book uses a step-by-step format to guide you easily through each task. Numbered steps are actions you must do; bulleted steps clarify a point, step, or optional feature; and indented steps give you the result.

2. Notes

Notes give additional information on special conditions that may occur during an operation, a situation that you want to avoid, or a cross-reference to a related area of the book.

3. Tips

Tips offer additional information, including warnings and shortcuts.

4. Bold

Boldened texts show command names, options, and texts or numbers you must type or note.

5. **Icons and Buttons**

Icons and buttons show you exactly what you need to click to perform a step.

PowerPoint Approach

This PowerPoint 365 book is divided into different parts or topics representing general PowerPoint skill sets. Each chapter and the topics are groups and are divided according to their related functions or performances.

CHAPTER 2

GETTING STARTED WITH POWERPOINT 365

Lesson objectives:

- PowerPoint basics
- Exploring the PowerPoint Start Screen
- How to Create Different Presentations
- Creating a Presentation from Backstage View
- Saving a Presentation
- Exploring Normal View
- How to Navigate Different Slides View
- Arrangement of Presentation Windows
- Using Help

PowerPoint Basics

What is PowerPoint?

PowerPoint is a presentation application that is used to create a slide show of important information, charts, and images for display during a presentation.

Most PowerPoint presentations are created from a template, which includes a background color or image, a standard font, and a choice of several slide layouts. Changes made to the template can be saved to a "master slide" which stores the main slide theme used in the presentation. When changes are made to the master slide such as choosing a new background image, the changes are propagated to all the other slides. This keeps a uniform look among all the slides in the presentation.

Things to Know about PowerPoint Approach Function

1. **Slide Theme and Layout**

The slide theme is meant to apply preset design elements such as colors,

background graphics, and text styles to a slide. A particular slide layout applied to a slide determines what type of information the slide includes. For example, a Title Slide layout has a **title** and a **subtitle**. A Title and Content layout include a title, plus a placeholder that holds a list of bullet points, a table, or other graphic elements.

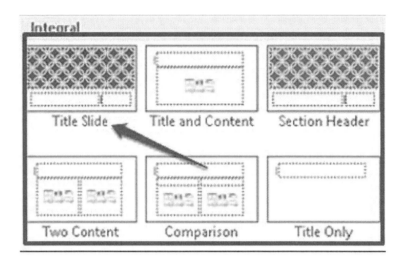

2. **Adding Contents and Media**

Adding content and media can be done after creating original texts, charts, graphs, and graphics in PowerPoint. A media file, such as a photo, logo, or video created in another app can be imported.

The Normal view displays all the elements in your slide. The Slides pane shows miniature versions of all your slides, whereas, the Outline pane displays only the text of each slide. You can insert text boxes that enable you to add text slide that does not appear in the presentation outline.

3. **How to Organize Slides**

When creating several slides, you may need to reorganize them to create the proper sequence for your presentation. You can reorder slides in **Slide Sorter** view. This view shows slide thumbnails that you can move, delete, duplicate, or hide. You can also perform these actions on the Slides pane in Normal view.

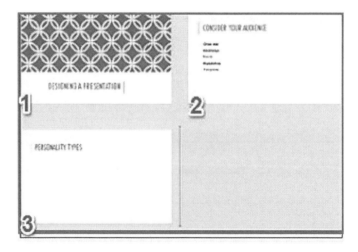

4. Building an Outline

You can type texts in outline form to build slides for your presentation. In the Outline pane in the Normal view, an icon represents each slide, and each slide contains a slide title next to the icon. Second-level lines of text on the outline appear as bullet points on the slide. These bullets convey the main points you want to make about each topic.

5. Working with Masters

A set of slide themes and layouts are combined to create a set of master slides. Masters enable you to change design elements and add content(s) that you want to appear in a particular location on all slides that have that template. This saves you from having to repeatedly add content, such as your company logo, to each slide. For example, you can set up a master so that an identical footer appears on every slide.

6. Setting Up Your Show and PowerPoint Options

You can add audio, animations, and transitions to your slides. You can record a narration that plays as you give your presentation. You can as well use animation to move an element on-screen, such as a ball bouncing onto the screen. Transitions control how a new slide appears on-screen, for example, a slide can fade in over the previous slide.

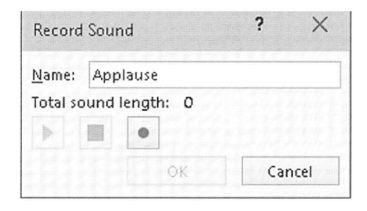

7. **Present or Share a Slide Show**

Once you add the content, choose slide designs, and add special effects, then, you are ready to run your slide show presentation. Tools appear on-screen during the slide show; they help you control your presentation and even enable you to make annotations on your slides as you present them. The Presenter view shows your notes and provides a timer to ensure that your presentation is flawless.

Hope you got the explanation above? Good!

Exploring the PowerPoint Start Screen

There are ways you can launch PowerPoint 365 and this is dependent on the operating system you are running on your computer. For example:

- In Windows 10, you can start PowerPoint from the Start menu, the All-Apps menu, the Start screen, or the taskbar search box.
- In Windows 8, you can start PowerPoint from the Apps screen or Start screen search results.
- In Windows 7, you can start PowerPoint from the Start menu, All Programs menu, or Start menu search results

Here I'm going to use Windows 10. The PowerPoint 365 program can be simply searched here and located easily. Once located, click once to open the PowerPoint.

You will be presented with the interface on the left side, there will also be a listing of presentations that you have used earlier.

You also have an option here to open prior presentations that you have saved on your computer.

Then, on the right-hand side, you have the option to start a **blank presentation** or to use one of the templates. Using one of the templates is very easy, just simply click on the one you want, and it will download from Microsoft.

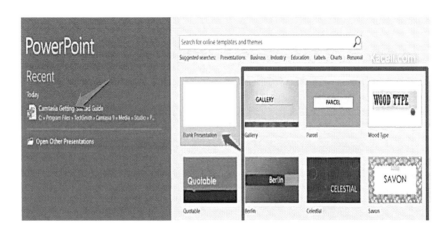

Working on PowerPoint User Interface

This PowerPoint user interface provides intuitive access to all the tools you need to develop a sophisticated presentation tailored to the needs of your audience. You can use PowerPoint 365 to do the following and much more:

1. Create, import, format, and edit slide content, including texts, pictures, tables, charts, shapes, symbols, equations, Smart Art business diagrams, audio recordings, and video recordings.
2. Capture screenshots, screen recordings, and audio recordings.
3. Organize and manage slides in sections.
4. Animate slide content and the transitions between slides; managing the form, timing, and sound associated with animations.
5. Document speaker notes for each slide.
6. Control the layout of content by creating custom masters; precisely align slide elements by using gridlines and Smart Guides.
7. Create, rehearse, present, and record custom slide shows.
8. Save, export, and send presentations in a wide variety of formats.
9. Create notes in a OneNote notebook that link to specific slide content.

When working with a presentation, it is displayed in the app Window that contains all the tools you need to add and format content.

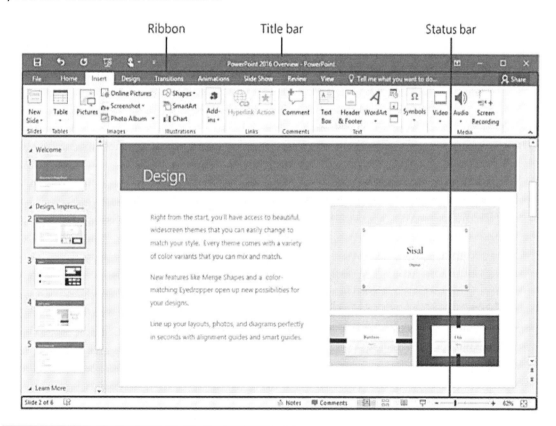

Having PowerPoint 365 from the Windows 10 Start screen will help you to begin designing a presentation. When you open PowerPoint 365, the Start screen appears automatically.

From the Start screen, you can start a new presentation or open an existing one. The Start screen list will open presentations and enable you to create a presentation from templates on your computer, or search for PowerPoint templates on the Internet.

To explore PowerPoint 365, follow the steps below:

1. The first thing you need to do is to **launch** the PowerPoint program.

   - Click or press the **Start menu** either from the PC screen or keyboard.

   - Then, select **All apps.**

   - From the list of **All apps** displayed, select the **PowerPoint** program by scrolling down.

Note: The PowerPoint can be pinned to the taskbar. If pinned to the taskbar, click on the **taskbar** icon directly to launch or open the PowerPoint program.

- You can then expand the PowerPoint Window by clicking "**maximize**" if it is minimized.

2. **PowerPoint** opens and displays the Start screen.

   A. You can click on a recently opened presentation if you wish to work on it again.
   B. You can open a file from your computer, an external drive, or a cloud service.
   C. You can create a new presentation by clicking on a **Template** of your choice.
   D. You can use the search box to look for a **Template** on the Internet.

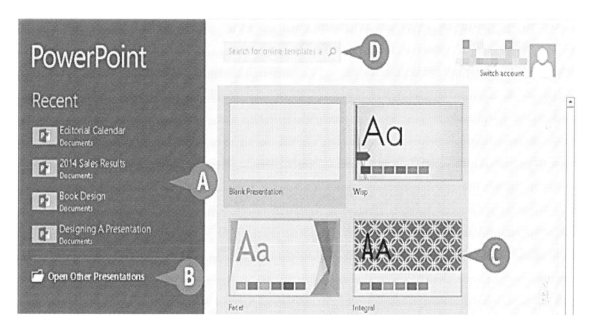

3. You can make your choice of theme by clicking one of the **themes**, it will display the theme preview dialog box.

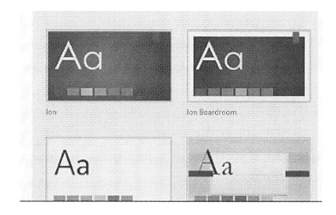

E. Click the **arrows** either on the left or right side to view the theme's layouts.
F. Click here as illustrated below to preview different theme designs.
G. Click on these **arrows** either on the left or right side to view the previous or next theme.
H. Click on **Create** to start a new presentation.
I. Click the **Close Button** to cancel the preview dialog box.

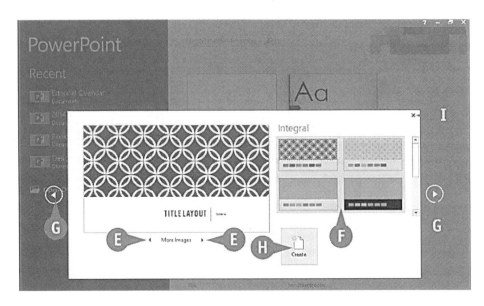

Identification of PowerPoint Window Elements

PowerPoint contains the elements described in this section. Commands for tasks you perform often are readily available, and even those you don't use frequently are also easy to find.

Title bar

At the top of the app Window, this bar displays the name of the active file, identifies the app, and provides tools for managing the app Window, ribbon, and content.

Quick Access Toolbar

The Quick Access Toolbar at the left end of the title bar can be customized to include any command that you want to have easy access to. The default Quick Access Toolbar in the PowerPoint app Window displays the Save, Undo, Redo/Repeat, and Start from Beginning buttons.

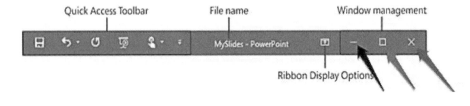

Those four buttons at the right end of the title bar serve the same functions in all Office apps. You control the display of the ribbon by clicking any command on the Ribbon Display Options menu.

In the above illustration, clicking the button where the **Black** arrow is pointed is used to Minimize the Window, the **Blue** arrow that symbolizes the "Restore Down/Maximize" button is used to adjust the size of the Window and the **Red** arrow which is the Close button closes the active presentation or exits the app.

Ribbon

The ribbon is located below the title bar. The commands you will use when working with a presentation are gathered together in this central location for efficiency.

Across the top of the ribbon is a set of tabs. Clicking a tab displays an associated set of commands arranged in groups.

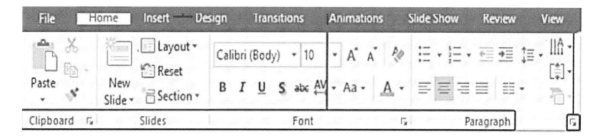

All commands related to managing PowerPoint and presentations can be seen from the **Backstage view,** which will be displayed after clicking the **File tab** located at the left end of the ribbon.

Commands available in the Backstage view are organized on named pages, which is displayed by clicking the **page tabs** in the colored left pane. You redisplay the presentation and the ribbon by clicking the **Back arrow** located above the page tabs.

How to Create Different Presentations

In this section, I'm going to discuss how to create the first slides and how to insert different types of slides in your presentation. So, let's proceed.

1. After you have launched **PowerPoint** as earlier discussed,
   - Click on **Blank Presentation**

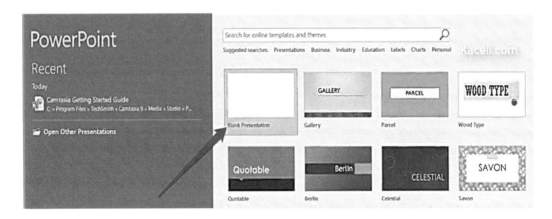

   - Go to the **Home** tab, and click on "**layout"** to display several layouts or designs, then select your choice.
   - Click on "**Title slide"** under "layout"**.
   - Click on **Add Title** to type whatever you desire e.g. "Using PowerPoint 365".
   - Click on the **Subtitle** to type whatever you desire to be there e.g. by Felix.

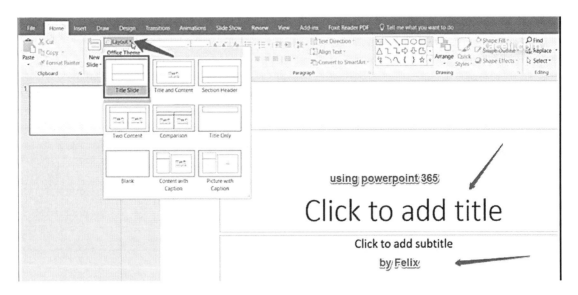

2. Now, to add another slide presentation which is the second slide; it is slightly different from the first one, this is because the first one is a **Title Slide.** If probably you wish to change the design, you can use the **Layout** option and change it to your choice.

- From the **Home** tab, click on "**New slide",** it will display another slide that is different from the first slide.
- You can click on **Layout** to select the slide layout of your choice.

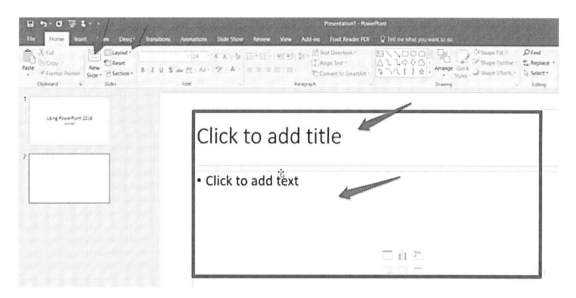

- Then click on **Add Title** to type whatever you want there e.g., you can type "Getting started with PowerPoint".
- Click on **Add Text** and type whatever you desire. As you proceed by clicking on each area you want to type, it begins to add bullets.

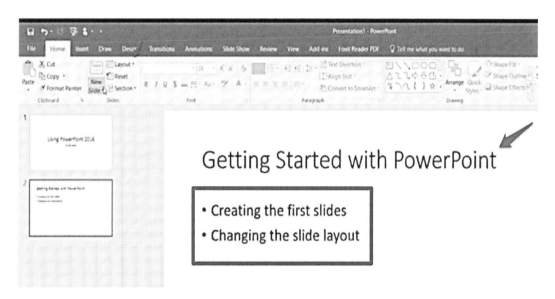

In this stage of presentation, you will keep moving by adding other slides and creating the general flow of texts for the presentation.

It is very easy to waste a lot of time messing with the colors, choosing images, and animations while you are still in the first or second slide and you have spent hours. So, it is best to do the outline first, then come back later to insert images, smart art, and other components that will cover in the later sessions.

3. To open another slide again.
   - Click on **New Slide** to add another slide. Then it is going to be by default, it's going to be a title slide with content.
   - Then click on **Add Title** to type whatever you want to be there e.g., you can type "creating your outline"
   - Click on **Add Text** and type whatever you desire to be there.

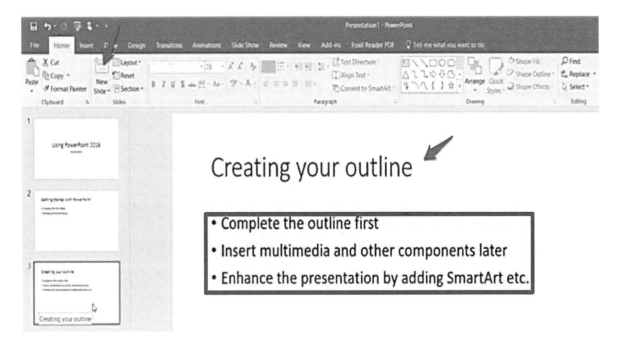

NOTE: You can also use **Ctrl + M** on your keyboard to open a New Slide.

Check out another way again to change or select a different layout of a slide presentation.

1. Right on the New slide button,

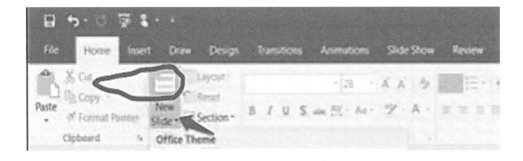

- Click on the **drop-down arrow**, this is where you can choose a different type of layout.
- Then pick the one you wish, to change the layout, either when you insert a **New slide** or you have an existing slide. Below is what it will display, it will add another Slide**.**

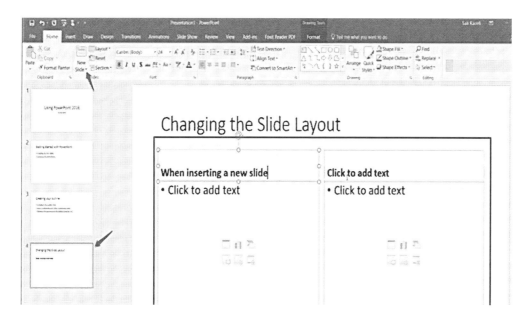

- Click on any of the **Slides** and then click on **layout**.

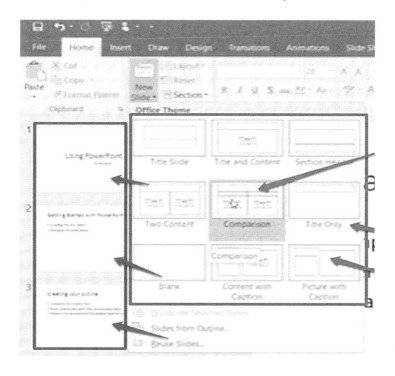

- Then adjust it accordingly if you want to undo whatever you did earlier. This is to move the Slide to where you prefer it to stay.

Creating a Presentation from Backstage View

You can create a new presentation from the PowerPoint Start screen or the File tab on the Ribbon known as Backstage view. You can create a new presentation from scratch or use templates. Creating a presentation from scratch enables you to design freely without preconceived notions, and working from a template saves time and promotes ideas by starting you off with a certain look and color scheme. You can find templates on your computer, as well as on the Internet for free or for a fee.

1. The first thing to do is just to click on the **File** tab to display the Backstage view.

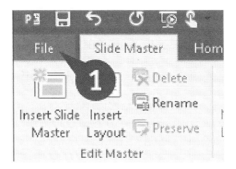

2. Then click on **New**, it will display the templates on the right side of your PC.

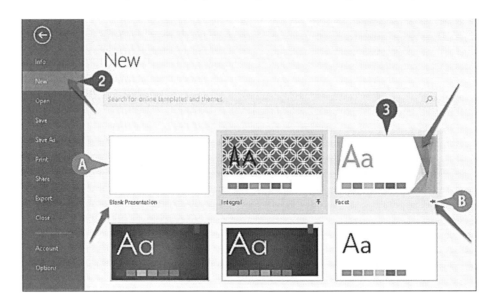

A. Next thing, click on **blank presentation**, to create a new presentation.

B. Then direct the mouse pointer over a **Template** and click the **Pushpin** button, it will pin a theme to this list and change it.

3. Click on the presentation **theme** of your choice.
4. Click the **color scheme** you prefer. After clicking, the preview changes to reflect your preferences.

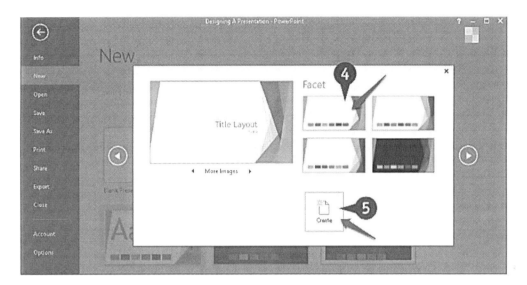

5. Click on **Create**, the PowerPoint will create a presentation from the template immediately.

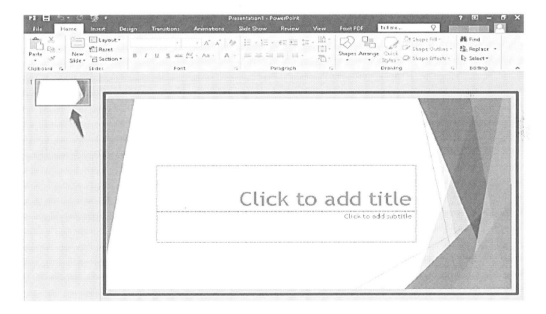

Saving a Presentation

Once you have created a presentation, you should save it for future use. Saving a PowerPoint file works much like saving any other Microsoft Office program file.

What you need to do is just specify the location to save the file and then give the file a name for easy identification. By default, PowerPoint saves your presentation every ten minutes.

If you want to save a presentation that has previously been saved, you can click on the **Save** icon in the upper left corner of the PowerPoint Window to quickly save it.

Now, to save a presentation, follow the steps below:

1. Click on the **File** tab, it will display the backstage view.

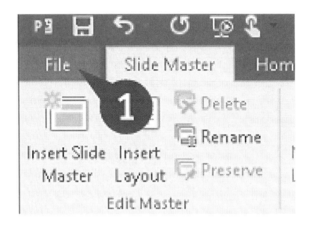

2. Locate **"Save As"**

3. Next, click on **"This PC"**,

4. Then click on **"browser"**. The Save As dialog box will be displayed.

5. Select the folder where you want to save your file. Your work presentation will be saved to the Documents folder.

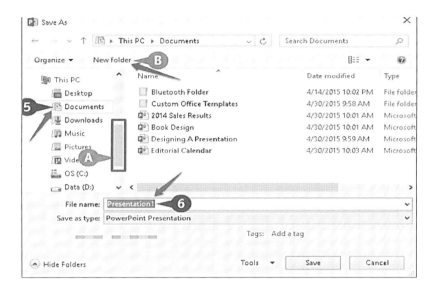

6. Double-click on the **File name** text box to select the text and then type the name you want.
    A. You can also scroll down to select any **Folder** of your choice for easy location.
    B. You can as well create a folder by clicking "**New Folder**".

7. Click on the drop-down arrow of the **Save as type** option to change the file type from default.

Is it clear? If no, you can go all over it again and take time to follow the process.

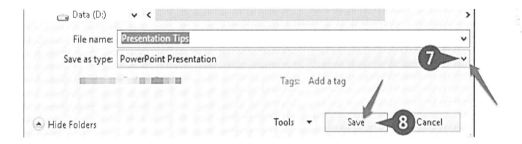

8. When you're done with that, click on the **Save** option, the PowerPoint saves the presentation, and the Save As dialog box closes.

    C. The new file name displays in the title bar.

Note: While saving, if you choose a format other than the default PowerPoint format, you may see a prompt about an issue of version compatibility, respond to the prompt to continue saving.

Quicker Way to Save your Presentation

1. From the top of the **File** tab, you will see the **Quick Access Toolbar**.

↓ Click on the **Save** icon

2. Press **Ctrl + S** on your keyboard

Exploring Normal View

The Normal view is where you will usually work; where you can create, position, and format objects on each slide. This PowerPoint software offers several views that you can use to work on different aspects of your presentation. With the different views, you have the opportunity to work on your presentation easily because certain views are for performing certain tasks. For example, arranging slides is easiest in the **Slide Sorter** view.

In the **Outline** view, you can enter presentation text in an outlined form and the text automatically appears on the slide.

In the **Slide Show** view, you can preview your presentation as your audience will see it.

A. **Navigation Buttons: How to change from one view to another**
- The views can be changed by
  - ➤ Clicking the **View** tab in the ribbon.

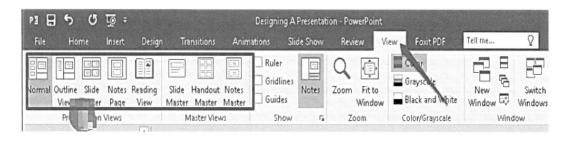

➢ Then click the command buttons for the view you want to use **OR**
➢ Click the command buttons down below on the right side in the **status bar**. These buttons include **Normal view**, **Slide Sorter view**, **Reading view**, and **Slide Show view.**

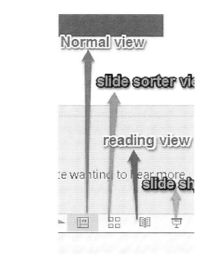

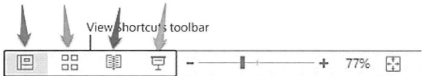

B. Slide Pane

The Slide pane is the largest in the Normal view and shows a slide and all its contents. Here, you can create and manipulate slide objects such as graphics and animations, and type text directly in the slide. Drag the scroll bar by the right up or down to move to the previous or next slide.

Navigating PowerPoint Views

You can use the Slide Sorter view to organize slides, Notes Page view to create detailed speaker notes, and Slide Show view or Reading view to display your presentation. Each view has certain tasks that are easier to perform in that particular view.

Outline View

Outline view has a pane that enables you to enter text into your slides in a familiar outline format. In this view, the Outline pane replaces the Slides Thumbnail pane. Top-level headings in the outline are slide titles, and entries at the second level appear as bulleted points, but text in text boxes does not appear. The outline is a great reference if you need to write a paper to accompany your presentation. If you double-click a slide, PowerPoint changes to Normal or Outline view whichever you last used, and displays that slide in the Slide pane.

Slide Sorter View

Slide Sorter view is the best view to change the order of slides, delete slides, or duplicate slides. In Slide Sorter view, you can click and drag a slide to move it.

Reading View

You can click Slide Show view to present your show. Slides appear one at a time at full-screen size. Reading view is very similar to Slide Show view, but gives you more navigation flexibility because the status bar remains at the bottom of the screen and the title bar remains at the top. To exit either view, press **Esc.**

Notes Page View

In the Notes Page view, you can display each slide and the associated speaker notes as one full page. You can also type notes on the page while viewing your slide. To work with this view, go to the **View** tab and click on Notes Page.

How to Navigate Different Slides View

Slide show presentations generally contain many slides. As a result, PowerPoint provides different ways to navigate the slides so that you can choose one that is most efficient and effective for what you are doing.

The way you work on your project determines the way you choose to navigate. You can use the various scroll bar buttons to navigate slides in Normal view, click a slide in the Slides Thumbnail Pane to select a slide, or view slide thumbnails in Slide Sorter view.

Navigating Using the Normal view

1. Go to the ribbon, click on the **View** tab.
2. Then go straight to the left side at the top, click on **Normal view.**
3. Next, click on the **Scroll** bar to move the slide.
4. Then click the **Next Slide** button to display the next slide.
5. You can also click on the **Preview Slide** button to display the previous slide.

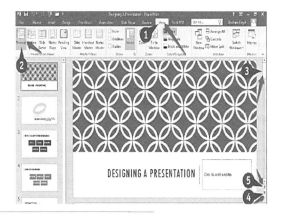

Navigating Using the Slide Thumbnail Pane

1. Here, click on the **Scroll** bar to move through the slide.
2. Proceed by clicking on the **Slide thumbnail** you want to display. After clicking, the selected slide will display in the slide pane.

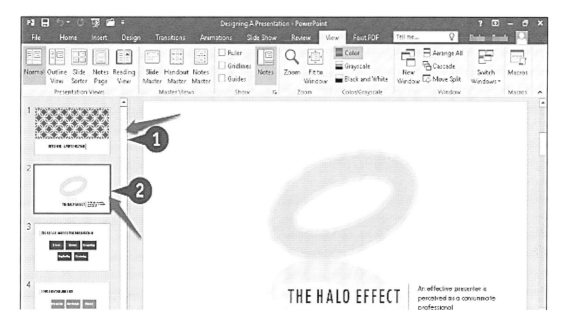

Navigating by Using the Outline View

1. Go to the ribbon, click on the **View** tab, locate **Outline view** and click on it.
2. From the left side, click and drag the scroll bar to move through the slides.
3. Following this illustration, click on the **Director** box, it will display immediately in the Slide pane.

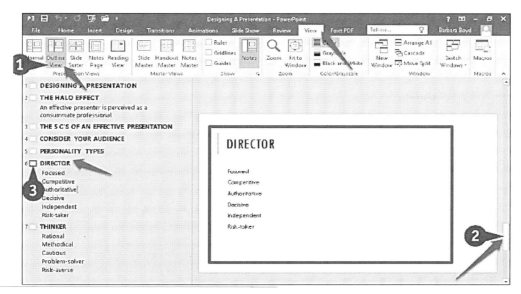

Navigating in Slide Sorter View

1. First, click on the **View** tab in the ribbon and click on **Slide Sorter view,** the Slide Sorter view will display after clicking.
2. Then click and drag the scroll bar to move through the slides.
3. You can as well click any of the **Slides** from the pane.

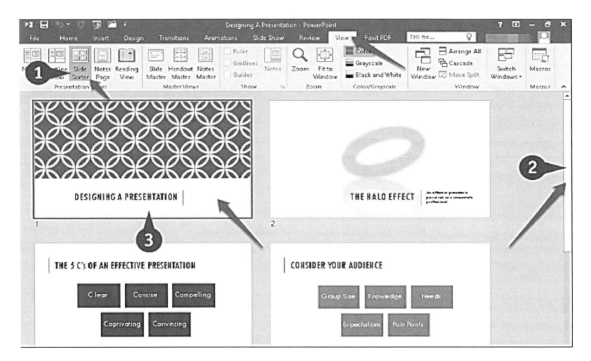

Arrangement of Presentation Windows

If probably you need to view multiple presentations on-screen at once, I mean, if you want to compare their contents or copy a slide from one presentation to another, you can arrange PowerPoint in such a way that you can see multiple open presentations Window at the same time using the Cascade feature. This feature is found on the **View** tab.

Unless you have a really big monitor, you should limit the number of opened presentations to three or four, otherwise, you won't be able to have a complete view of each presentation, thereby, making the feature less useful.

To achieve the multiple view presentation Windows, follow the steps below:

1. Open two or more presentations.
2. Click on the **View** tab.
3. Next, locate the **Cascade** icon and click on it. Immediately, overlapped presentations Windows will display.

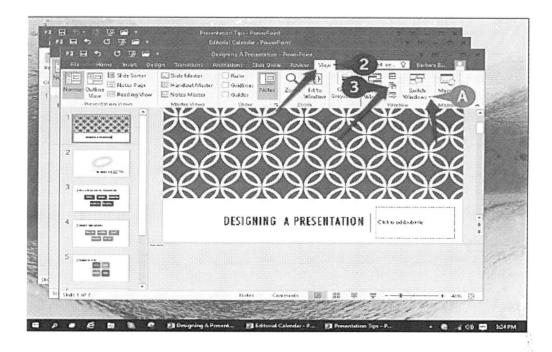

A. Click on **Switch Windows** and then pick the presentation you want to display; it will make that presentation active.

4. Then click on **Arrange All** to arrange the presentations.
   B. You can drag the Windows title bar to move the Window.

5. Click on the **Maximize** button to display the Window on full screen.
   C. If probably you do not see the Windows button on the Ribbon, click the drop-down arrow on the **Windows** tab to see the gallery of commands.

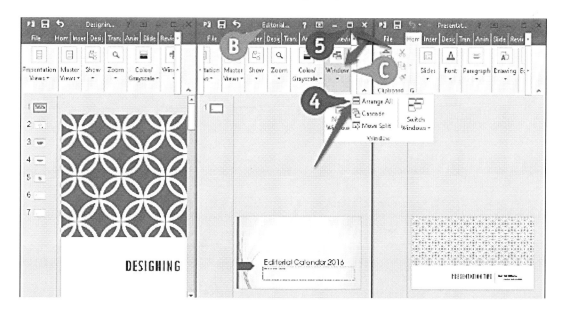

Using Help

"Help" on Microsoft Office PowerPoint program offers two ways to get help.

1. If you are connected to the Internet, it provides Help articles and videos from Microsoft Office Online. You find answers to your questions by typing keywords.
2. If an Internet connection is not available, type your keyword in the "Tell Me" field in the Ribbon, PowerPoint then displays where to find the task you seek in the Ribbon.

To achieve this, follow the steps below:

1. Click on the **Help** button symbolized with a **Question mark "?"**.

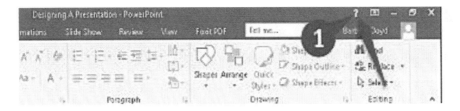

2. In the PowerPoint Help Window, type any keyword you want to know in the **Search textbox**.
3. Click on the **Search** button to show the available online articles and videos for the typed word.

    A. Clicking any **Article** here may give steps to answer your question.
4. You can click a video to view a probable answer to your question.

    B. You can click any of the buttons **Pause, Volume,** turn on **Closed captioning** as seen in the illustrations below.
5. Move the cursor to the upper right corner of the screen to reveal the button to close the **Help** Window.

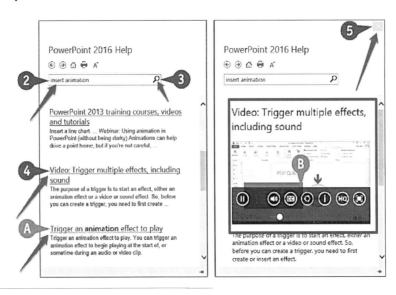

CHAPTER 3

USING THEMES AND TEMPLATES

Lesson objectives:

- Understanding Themes
- Searching for Themes and Templates Online
- Applying a Theme to Selected Slides
- Modifying Background
- Applying a Texture or Picture Background

The Microsoft PowerPoint program preset themes, templates, and layouts make it easy to create presentations with a consistent look and attractiveness. You can use built-in themes or choose from hundreds of themes online. Although you can design your slide templates by applying backgrounds and graphics as well as formatting elements on master slides manually, most people commonly use themes and templates to develop presentations.

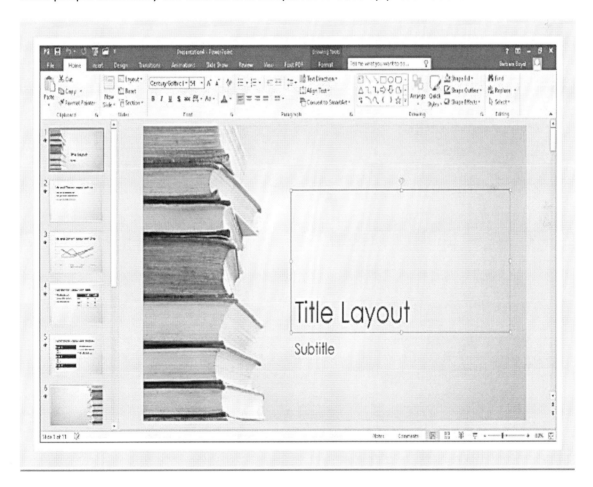

Understanding Themes

A theme is a predefined set of colors, fonts, and visual effects that can be applied to any slide for a unified and professional look. A theme gives an attractive look and color to your presentation. The colors and the style you choose supports the mood of your presentation, professional, entertaining, fun, or sober. A consistent style throughout your presentation carries your audience along, from one point to the next.

You can use a theme from the PowerPoint program, get one from Microsoft Office Online or any other online source, or use a theme from an existing presentation. You can also create a blank presentation, apply a background and graphics to create your theme and then save the theme to use again.

Theme Elements

When you create a new presentation, PowerPoint prompts you to choose a theme. When you choose a specific non-blank theme, PowerPoint applies a set of colors, fonts, and placeholders to the slides. All these elements vary from theme to theme. Themes include background color, background graphics, and effects for background graphics, and most themes offer color scheme variations.

Applying Themes

It is an easy way to apply a theme to a single or multiple slides for a section, or the entire presentation. Generally, it is better to use one theme for an entire presentation so that the slides have a consistent look. However, you can also choose to apply a different theme to a particular slide for emphasis.

Modifying Themes

Having known that PowerPoint provides professionally designed slide themes, you can also tailor existing themes to meet your specific needs. You can change the background, background color, or the color scheme of the entire theme. After you design a theme you like, you can save it to the Theme gallery to use again.

Themes and Masters

Slide masters determine where placeholders and objects appear on each slide layout. Each theme has a master slide for the Title Slide, a master slide for the Title and Content slide, and so on. After you apply a theme, you can modify the master slide. Any change you make to the master slides automatically appears in your presentation slides. You can also change the fonts on the master slides.

Searching for Themes and Templates Online

The larger your choice of PowerPoint themes and templates, the greater the chance you will find one that suits your needs. Fortunately, there are thousands of PowerPoint theme templates available online. You can search for them by using the PowerPoint search feature, or an Internet search engine.

The PowerPoint search feature enables you to search by a keyword and shows you online presentation templates associated with that keyword. The search feature shows you a preview of the template and the name of who provided it, and then downloads the template for you! Remember to download files only from websites that you trust.

To do this, follow the steps below:

1. Click on the **File** tab in the ribbon and it will lead you to the Backstage view.

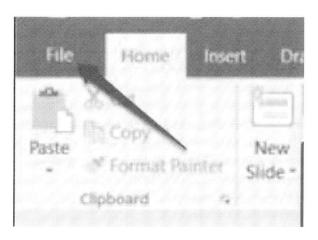

2. Click on **New,** the templates will display on your computer.

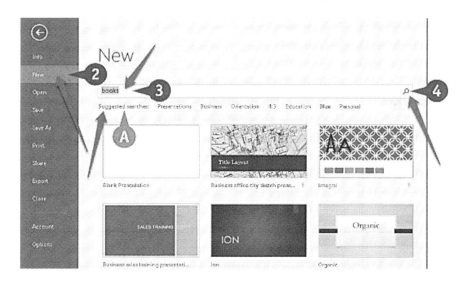

A. You can search by clicking one of the suggested searches.
3. Click inside the **Search text box, type** whatever you want to search. For example, type "Book".
4. Then click Search or press **Enter** from your keyboard, immediately PowerPoint displays online templates that match the searched text.
   B. You can click the **Pushpin** button to pin a template to your list of templates

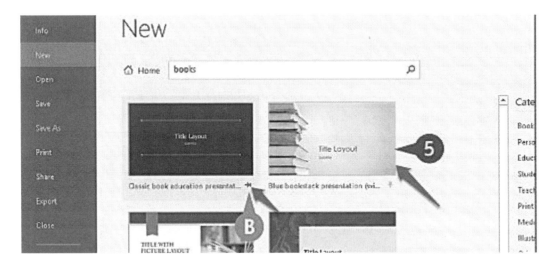

5. Click the template of your choice. The dialog box display, showing a preview of the template.
   C. You can click **Back** or **Forward** to view other slides from this template.
   D. You can also click **Back** or **Forward** to view other templates from this list.

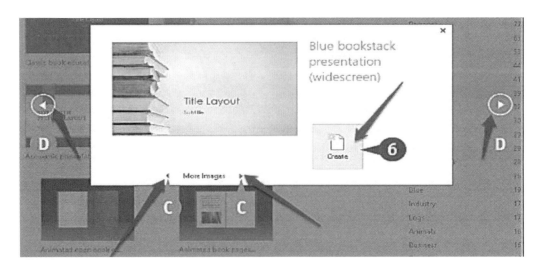

6. After clicking on the template of your choice, click on **Create.**

The Microsoft program PowerPoint creates a presentation from the template.

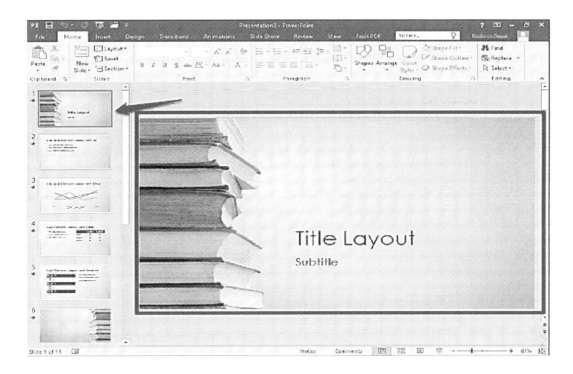

Applying a Theme to Selected Slides

A different theme can be applied to a single slide in either the Normal or Slide Sorter view. You may want to apply a different theme to one or more slides to make them stand out. If you decide to use more than one theme in the same presentation, you will normally want the designs of the themes to be complementary. Also, you can apply a theme to multiple slides you select manually or apply a new theme to all slides that use the same theme.

To apply one theme to your Slides, follow these steps below:

1. First, either click on the **View** tab in the ribbon or click this icon (⊞) down below.
   - If you click on the **View** tab, then go straight to the left side at the top, click on the **Slide Sorter** button.

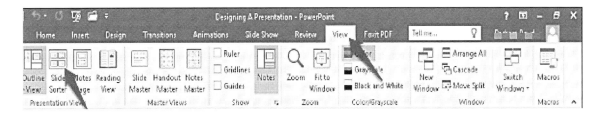

2. Next, click a **slide** or the **slides** you want to apply the theme.

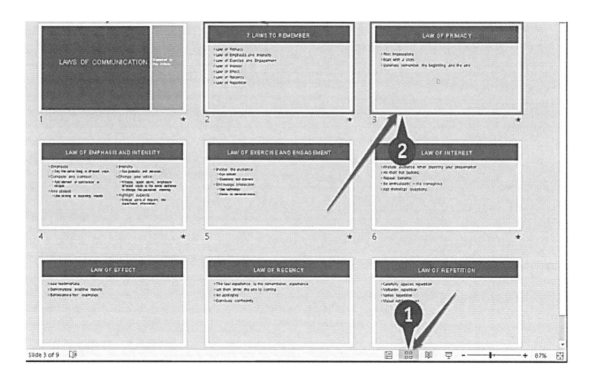

Note that to select multiple slides, click the first slide and then press the **Ctrl** key on your keyboard while you click the other slides.

3. Go to the ribbon and click the **Design** tab.
4. Next, click on the **Themes** drop-down arrow to display different themes.

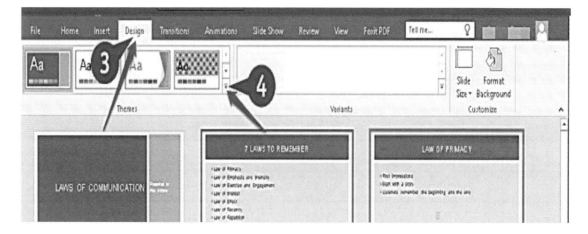

5. Then right-click a **Theme** to display the shortcut menu.

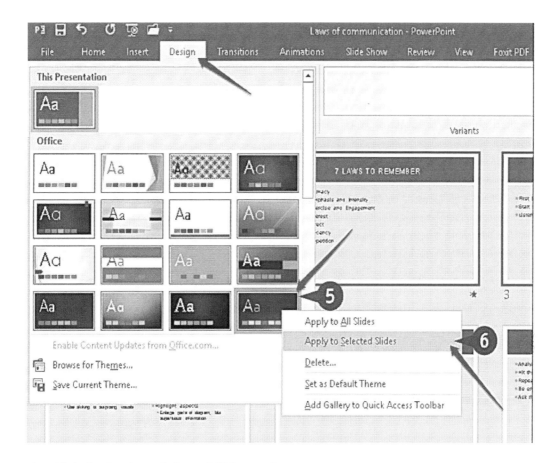

6. Click the **Apply to Selected Slides** option.
A. Microsoft PowerPoint applies the theme to the slides you selected

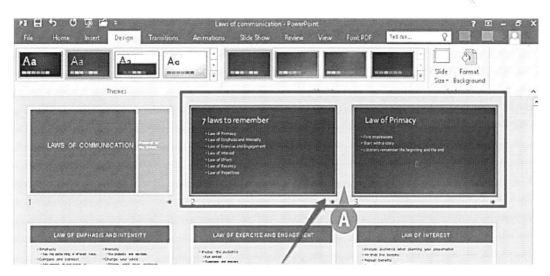

Applying a New Theme to Slides Using the Same Theme

1. The first thing to do is to go to the **Status bar** and click the **Slide Sorter** button.

2. Next, select a **slide** that uses the theme you want to change.
3. Then, go to the **Ribbon** and click the **Design** tab.
4. Click the **Themes,** it will display the gallery of themes.
5. Then right-click a **Theme** and the shortcut menu displays.
6. Click on **Apply to Matching Slides.**

Your chosen theme is applied to all slides that have the same theme as the slide you selected.

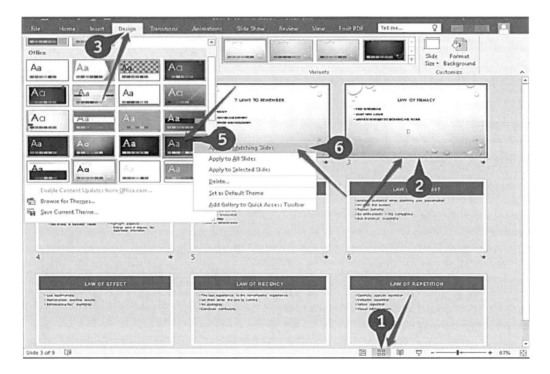

Adding a Different Theme to a Section

It is common to change topics during a presentation. For example, a person teaching a class about Microsoft Office changes the topic moving from teaching PowerPoint to Excel. If you change the topic, you might want to alter the theme to one that is more appropriate for the new topic.

You can apply themes to sections of your presentation. Doing that gives each section a unique look and consistency with others, yet, remains obvious that that particular section of your presentation is dedicated to a specific topic. You can change the theme in either the Normal or Slide Sorter view.

Follow the steps below to do that:

1. From the **Slide Sorter view** under the View bar, click the **slide** where you want to begin your section.
2. Go to the **Home** tab
3. Click on **Section.**

419

4. Then select **Add Section** in the drop-down menu.

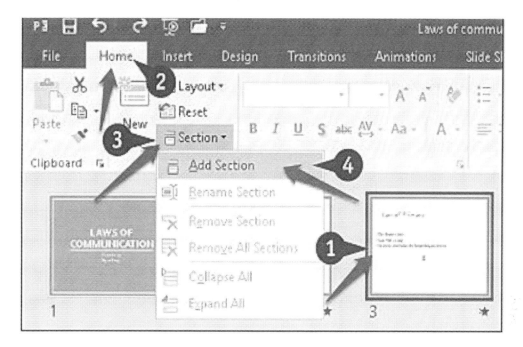

A. The slides you selected are placed in an **Untitled Section**.

Right-click on **Untitled Section** to rename the section as it suits you.

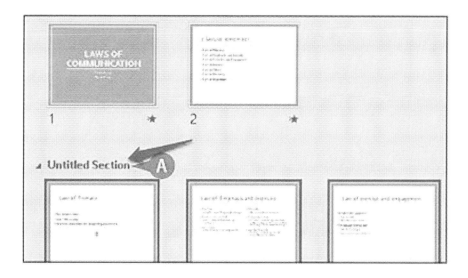

5. Go to the **Design** tab and select a theme of your choice.

B. The theme effect reflects on all slides in the section.
C. Click a **Variant** under the Design tab in the Ribbon to apply a different color scheme to the theme.

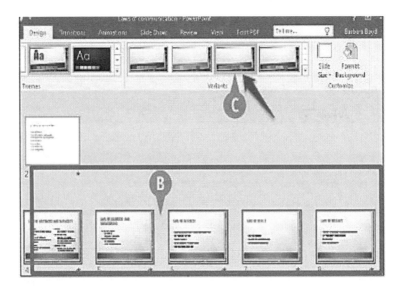

Modifying a Background

A theme applies a background on which all slide elements sit. You can make the background plain white or any color you want, or you can even use a texture or digital image as a background. For example, you can use a photo of a new product as a slide background for a presentation introducing the product. You can change the background for one slide, for a theme, or throughout the presentation and you can do this in the Normal or Slide Sorter view. Be careful with your choice of background as a complicated background can make a presentation hard to read or distracting.

To modify your slide background, do these:

1. Select the slide(s) you want to modify in the **Slide Sorter view.**

To select multiple slides, click the first slide and then press **Ctrl** while clicking the other slides you want to modify.

2. Next, click on the **Design** tab from the ribbon.
3. Then click **Format Background.** The Format Background pane will display.

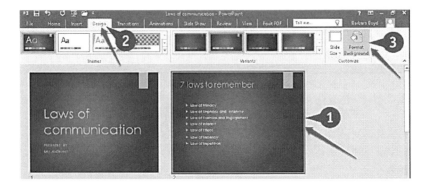

4. Click on the **Solid fill** command.
5. Click the **Color** icon.
6. Select your choice color.

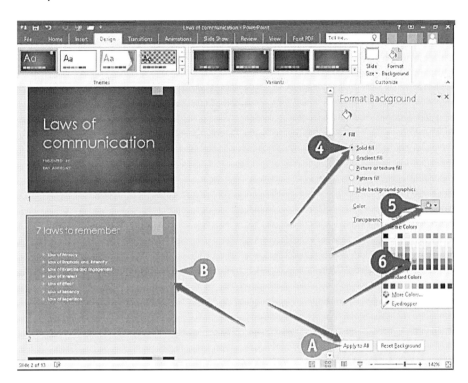

A. Clicking the **Apply to All** option, the color will be applied to all slides.
B. The selected color has taken effect on the background color of the selected slide.
7. Then click on the **Gradient fill** command to add a preset gradient to the background.

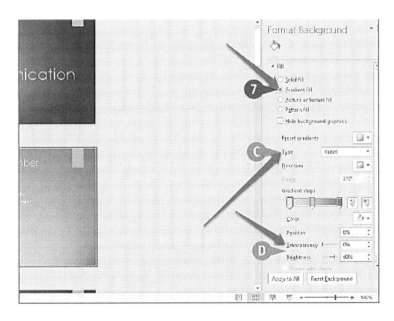

C. Here, click to adjust gradient options to change the direction and gradient type.
D. Here, click to tune the gradient by adjusting its characteristics, such as brightness and transparency.
8. Click on the **Pattern fill** command.
9. Choose a pattern from the gallery.

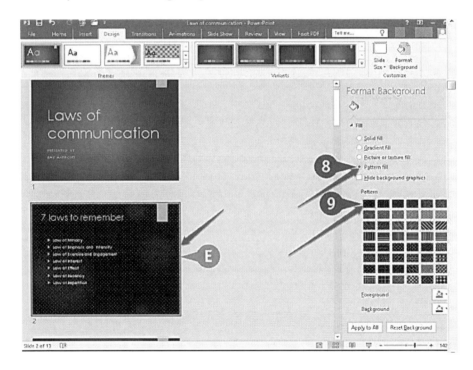

E. PowerPoint applies the background pattern to the selected slides.

Applying a Texture or Picture Background

If you want to make a slide more dramatic, you can push design limits by using either a texture or a digital picture as a background. For example, you can use a digital photo of a landscape and sunrise for a slide introducing a new idea. Typically, you would not do this for an entire set of slides because a complicated background makes a slide difficult to read and can be hard on the audience's eyes. You can add a picture to the background of a slide in either Slide Sorter or Normal view.

To apply a texture or picture background, follow the steps below:

1. Select the slide(s) you want to modify in the **Slide Sorter view.**
   - Click on the **Design** tab in the ribbon section
   - Locate **Format Background** at the right side of the pane and click on it to display the options.
   - Click on **picture** or **Texture fill.**
2. Click on the **Texture** icon, the texture gallery will open.

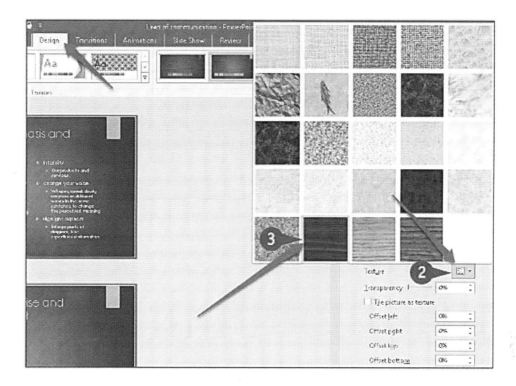

3. Choose a texture that best suits you.
A. The texture takes effect on the slide(s) you chose.

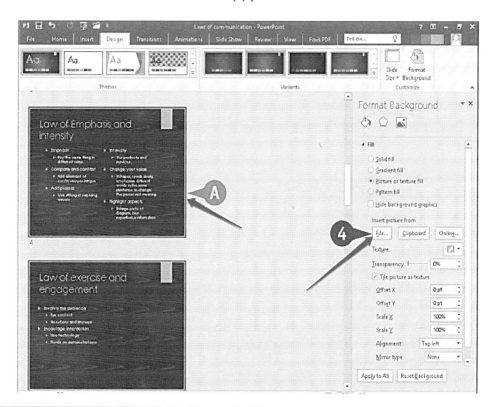

To apply a picture from your PC,

4. Click on the **File** option as seen above to apply an image from a file on your computer. The Insert Picture dialog box will display.
5. Click the **folder** that contains the picture you want to insert.
6. Select the picture.

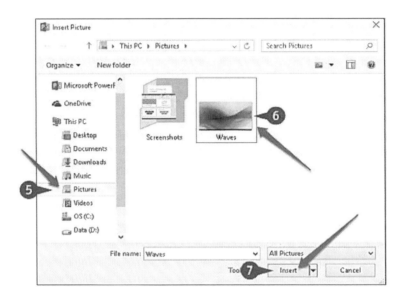

7. Then click on **Insert.**

B. The Insert Picture dialog box closes and the picture becomes the background on your selected slide.

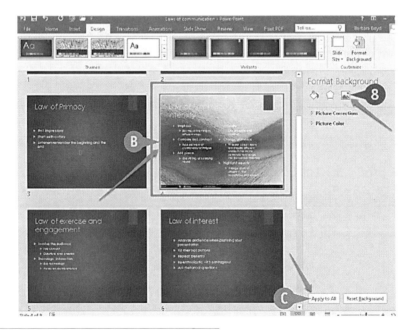

8. Click the **Picture** icon to apply color corrections to the picture.

C. If you click on **Apply to All**, the picture will be applied to all the slides in the presentation.

Is it clear up to this stage? Now let's proceed to the next chapter

CHAPTER 4

INCORPORATING MEDIA INTO PRESENTATIONS

Lesson objectives:

- Inserting a Picture
- Removing the Background from a Picture
- Creating a Photo Album
- Inserting Video and Audio Clips
- Recording an Audio Clip
- Inserting Video from the Internet
- Inserting Hyperlink
- Screen Recording
- Trimming Audio Clips

The Microsoft PowerPoint gives the ability to add visual and sound effects that enhance your presentations. You can place photographs, videos, and audio clips anywhere on your slides. You can add dramatic artistic effects to your photographs or remove the background from them. PowerPoint also lets you edit photos and videos directly. Finally, you can insert or link to media from the Internet.

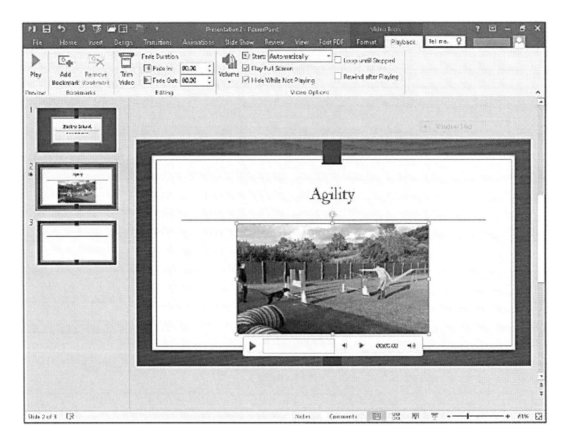

Inserting a Picture

Adding an image to any presentation gives a clear illustration of points of view and enhances your presentation. You can insert various types of images into placeholders or as independent objects, which gives you more versatility when you work with them.

Pictures include digital photos, scanned images, clip art, and bitmaps. These can come from the collection on your PC, such as your company logo or a picture of your product, or a Bing search from the Internet. After you insert an image file, it becomes an object on your slide.

To insert pictures from your computer, follow the steps below:

1. Click or Select a **slide** in the Normal view.
2. Then click the **Insert** tab.
3. The next thing is to click on **Pictures.** The Insert Picture dialog box will display.

Note: If probably you use a layout with a placeholder, click the **Pictures** icon.

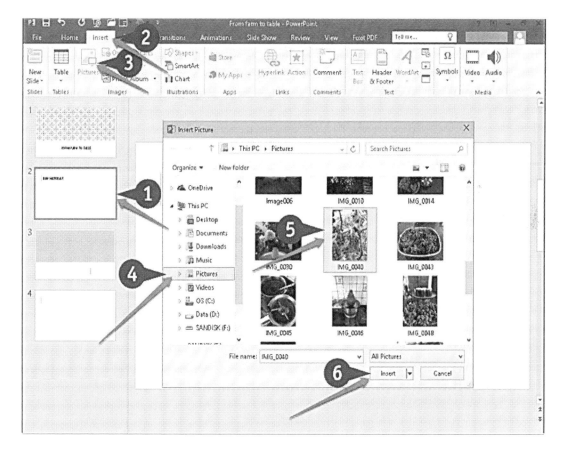

1. Click or Select the **folder** that contains the image you want to insert.
2. Pick any of the **Images.**
3. Then click the **Insert** option**.**

A. The image displays on your slide. You can resize and position the image as needed.

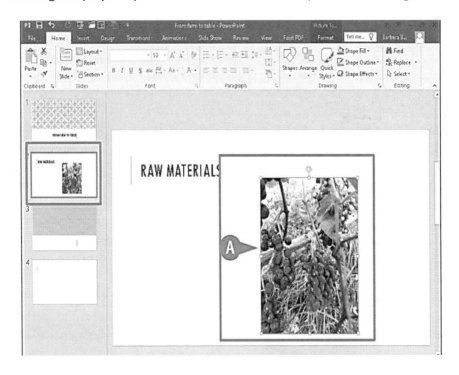

To insert pictures from an online source, follow the steps below:

1. Click or Select a **slide** in the Normal view that contains a placeholder.
2. Click the **Insert Online Picture** icon, the Insert Online Pictures dialog box will display.
3. From the **Bing Image Search** box, type the image name you need e.g. grape.

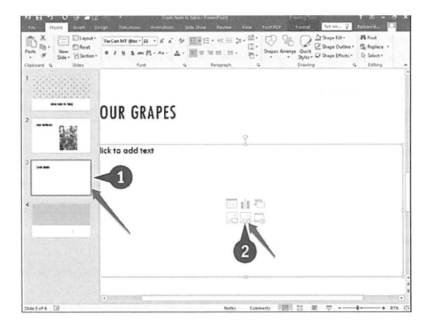

429

4. Then click the **Search** icon.
5. Pick any picture from the gallery.
6. Click on **Show all web results** for more results.

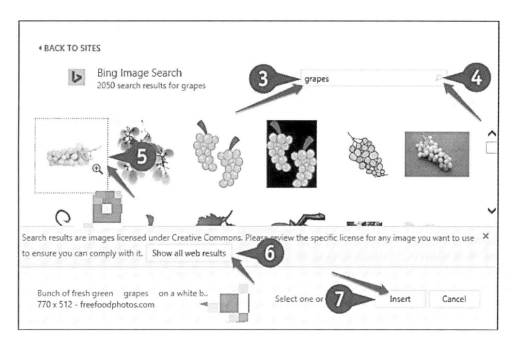

7. Then click on **Insert**. PowerPoint inserts the selected picture into the placeholder.

Note: If you want the picture to occupy most of the slide, choose a slide layout such as **Picture with Caption.**

Removing Background from a Picture

PowerPoint comes with a great feature to remove the background on images because, looking at a picture, you might want to remove the background so you can work with just the main object in the picture.

Using the Remove Background feature in PowerPoint, you can remove the background from a picture easily. This feature helps you avoid the inconvenience of importing the picture into PowerPoint after using a separate program to remove the background.

To remove background from a picture, follow these steps:

1. Select the **slide** that contains the picture.
2. From the right side at the top, click on the **Format** tab.
3. Locate the **Remove Background** option by the left side and click on it. PowerPoint automatically attempts to detect the object in the foreground, a marquee with handles appears.

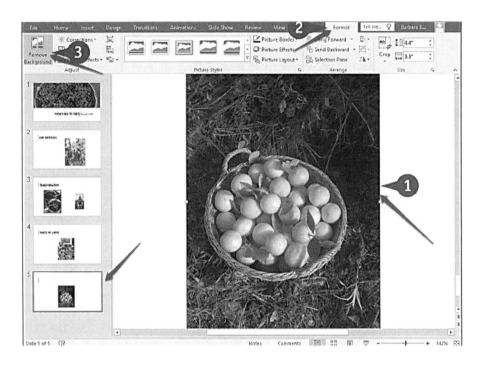

4. Then click and drag one of the handles if probably you want to resize the image.

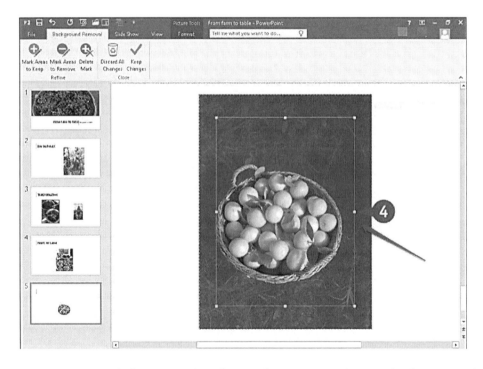

5. Repeat Step 4 with the various handles until PowerPoint detects the foreground object.
6. Click **Keep Changes.**

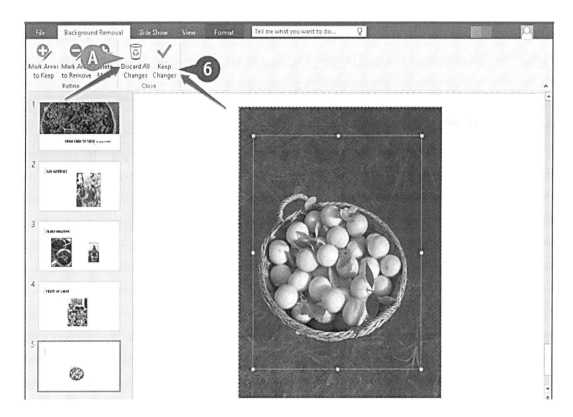

PowerPoint removes the background and only the foreground object remains.

A. To revert without saving the changes, you can click **Discard All Changes**.

You can as also follow this method:

Let's assume you insert a picture from the stock image list and you select the image of a bird

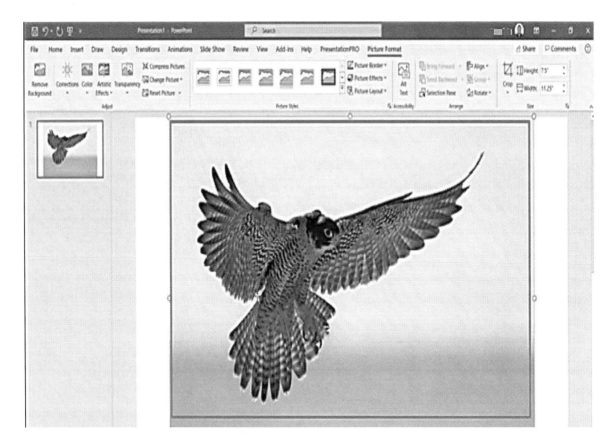

You will see that the picture has a bird in the foreground and a background. Now, to remove the background,

1. First, click on the **Picture Format** tab which becomes available anytime you click on an image

2. Locate **Remove Background** at the left side and click on it.
3. Click to highlight the entire background around that image. To avoid everything being removed, you are going to mark the areas to keep.

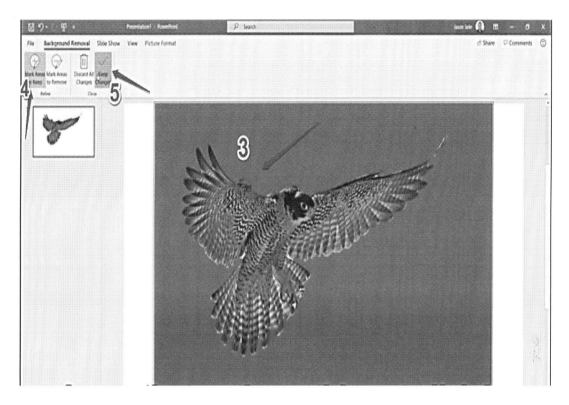

4. Click here to mark the **Areas to keep**
5. After marking the areas to keep, proceed to click on **Keep changes**. It will display the image without the background, it removes everything in that colored area and leaves only the image.

Hope the two methods are clear to you? Let's proceed then

Creating a Photo Album

You can set up slides so that they advance automatically, and you can also play an audio clip across slides and have it loop indefinitely. This is a perfect scenario to show a photo album. You can create a professional-quality photo album and show it like any other slide show or set it up to flip through the pictures automatically and then complete with background music! The procedure described here creates a new presentation.

To create a Photo Album, follow the steps below:

1. Open a new or existing PowerPoint file.
2. Click on the **Insert** tab located on the left side.

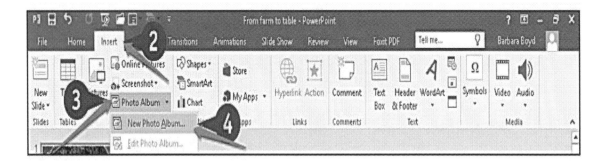

3. Then, click on the **Photo Album** drop-down arrow.
4. Click **New Photo Album** and the dialog box will appear.
5. Next thing, click on **File/Disk,** the Insert New Pictures dialog box will appear.

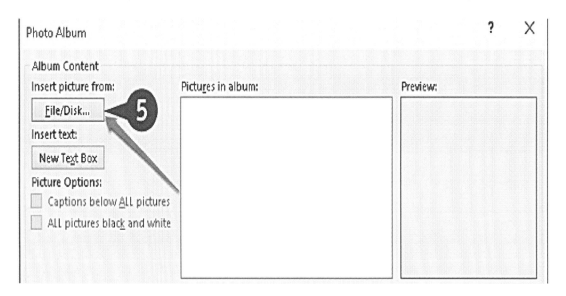

6. Then click the **folder** that has your picture files.

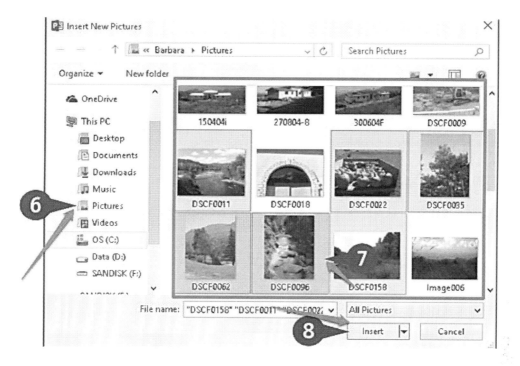

7. Click the **pictures** you want from your photo album while you simultaneously press **Ctrl** to select multiple files. All selected pictures appear in the photo album.
8. Click on the **Insert** option. The Insert New Pictures dialog box will close immediately. Then the Photo Album dialog box reappears again.
9. Click a **picture** to view it.

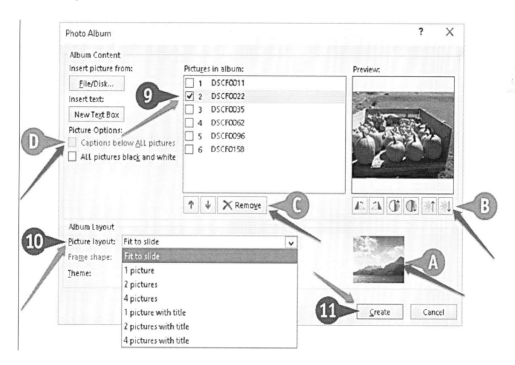

10. Click the **Picture layout** drop-down arrow and select a layout.

  A. Clicking this part will lead you to see the preview of the layout.
  B. Clicking here will lead you to use the picture correction feature if you select only one picture.
  C. You can click to select one or more pictures to move or remove them.
  D. This option is available only when the layout has multiple pictures.

11. Click on **Create.** The Microsoft PowerPoint creates the photo album.

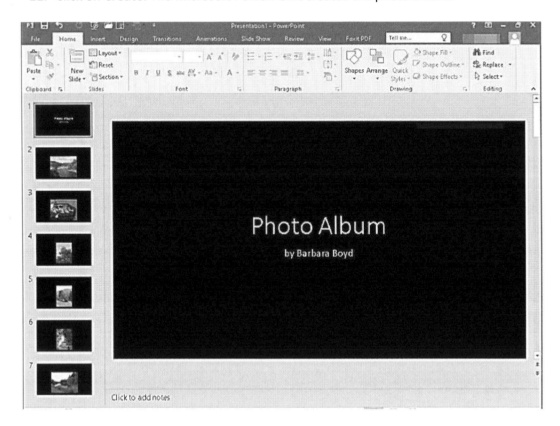

Take Note: You can design a photo album like any other presentation. What you need to do, just click on **Edit Photo Album** from the Photo Album drop-down menu on the **Insert** tab to change the pictures in the slide show.

Inserting Video and Audio Clips

You can enhance your slide show by inserting a video or audio on a slide. An instructional video can explain a complex task, and a funny video can liven up your presentation. PowerPoint recognizes videos in a variety of formats, such as Windows Media Video (WMV) files and Motion Pictures Experts Group (MPEG) files. Use an audio clip to play interesting sounds, such as applause during a slide display, or play an audio clip as background audio during several slides display or an entire slide show. Both audio and video clips use the steps in this section, except when you insert audio, a megaphone icon appears on the slide rather than a video icon.

To Insert Video and Audio Clips, follow the steps below:

1. Click or select a **slide** in the Normal view.

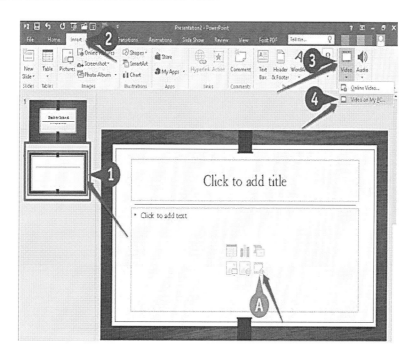

2. Go to the **Insert** tab and click on it.
3. Then from the right-side angle at the top, click on **Video** or **Audio.**
4. Click the **Video on My PC** option from the drop-down menu**.**
A. If probably you use a layout with a content placeholder, click the **Insert Video** icon and then click the **Browse** button next to the "From a File" button.
   The Insert Video or Insert Audio dialog box will appear.
5. The next thing to do is to click or select the **folder** or **external drive** that contains the file.

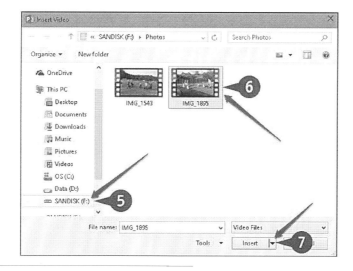

6. Click the file.
7. Then click on **Insert.** The video or audio displays on your slide immediately.

B. When you position the cursor over the clip, the Control bar appears.

8. Click on the **Play** button.
C. You can click anywhere on the scrubber bar to jump to any part of the clip.
D. You can click the **Move Forward** or **Move Back** buttons to move the clip forward or backward.

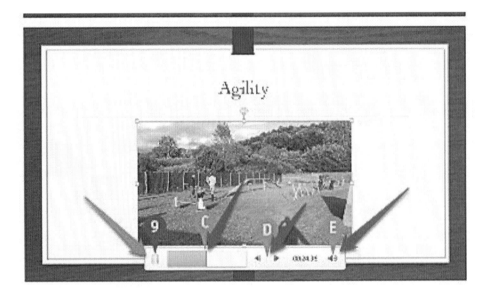

E. Clicking the Volume button lead to adjust the sound.
9. Click on **Pause** then video or audio will stop playing immediately.

Do you understand? Good!

How to play a video in full screen during a slide show

To make a video play in full screen, follow the steps below:

1. First, click the **video.**
   - Next, click the **Playback** tab from the right-side angle at the top of the Window.

   - Then tick the **Play Full Screen** option box to mark it. The video will start playing on full screen.

Recording an Audio Clip

You can captivate your audience's attention to your slide show by playing audio such as interesting sound effects, background music, or voiceovers at the right time during the show. For example, you may want applause when a slide with sales figures appears. You may also want to display your presentation where you are not present to speak in person. For example, you may have a looping presentation on display at a kiosk or on your website.

PowerPoint lets you record audio clips that link directly to slides. You can record an audio clip in PowerPoint and insert it directly into a slide without using different software to record it first.

To record an Audio Clip, follow the steps below:

1. Click or Select a **slide** in Normal view.

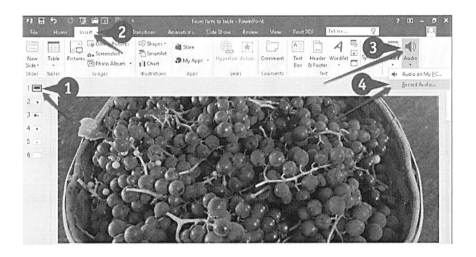

2. From the left side under the **Quick Access toolbar**, click on the **Insert** tab.
3. From the right-side angle at the top, click on **Audio.**
4. Then click on **Record Audio.** The Record Sound dialog box will appear.

Note that to carry out the recording, you need a microphone built-in or attached to your computer to perform this task.

A. Clicking on **Cancel** will abort the recording and it discontinues the insertion of the audio.

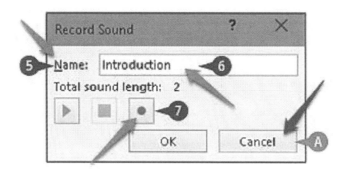

5. Click in the **Name** text box.
6. Type a name for your recording e.g. "**Introduction**."
7. Click the **Record** button.
8. Recording of your audio into the microphone starts.
9. When you are done with the record, click the **Stop** button.

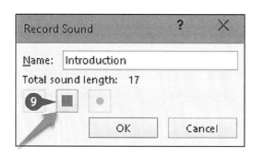

10. Click the **Play** Button to listen to your recording.

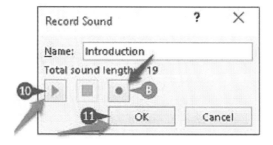

B. If probably you wish to continue the recording, click the **Record** button to continue recording your audio.

11. Then click **Ok** when you complete your recording.
12. Click on the **Audio Tools Playback** tab.

13. Click **Play** on the Ribbon or the Playback controls on the slide to play the audio.
C. You can click on **Volume** to adjust the sound.

Inserting a Video from the Internet

The Internet has unlimited numbers of clip art and pictures, which we've discussed how to access earlier in this chapter. The Internet is also a great source of video clips. Some media are royalty-free and some are licensed under Creative Commons. Make sure you have permission to use the media you want to use in the way you want to use it and give credit where credit is due. Although searching the Internet for video can be cumbersome, PowerPoint has a search feature that saves you time and effort. You can insert the perfect video directly into your presentation using keywords.

To Insert a video from the Internet, follow this procedure:

1. Click or Select a **slide** in the Normal view.
2. From the left side corner at the top, click on the **Insert** tab.

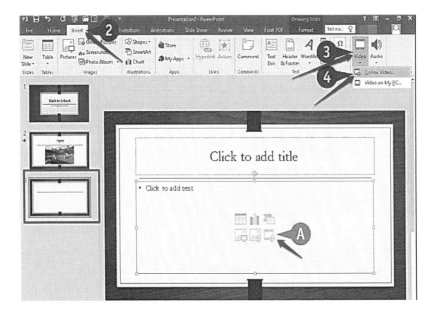

3. From the right side angle at the top, click on **Video**. The Insert Video dialog box will display.
4. Then select **Online Video.**

A. If probably you are using a layout with a placeholder, click on the **Insert Video** icon.

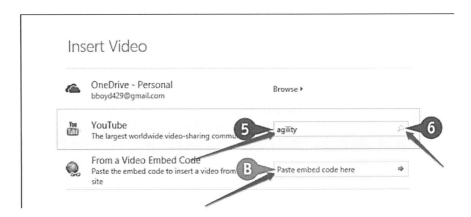

5. Click in the **YouTube Search** text box and type the name of the kind of video you want to download.
6. Then click on the **Search** icon.

B. If you have a specific YouTube video you want to use, copy the **embed code** on it and paste it in the field on the **text box** showing **"paste embed code here"**.

Note: to copy the embed code, click the **Share** button under the video, then click **Embed.**

After pasting the embed code, the YouTube results being requested will be displayed.

C. Take note of the video description below.

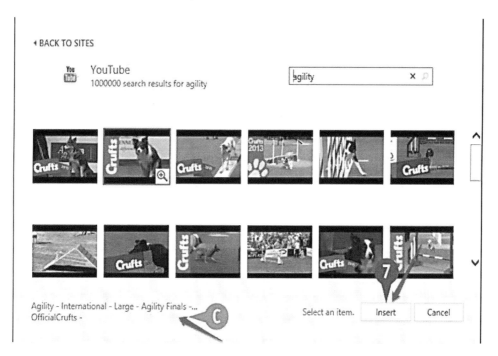

7. The next thing is to click on **Insert.** The video you selected appears on the slide.

D. Resize and move the video as you would to an object.

Inserting Hyperlink

Hyperlinks change your PowerPoint presentation from a traditional slide show to an interactive extravaganza. A hyperlink can perform a variety of actions during a PowerPoint slide show. It gives you an easy way to go to a different, non-sequential slide in your slide show. It can open another PowerPoint presentation or open a document from another Office application.

A hyperlink also provides a way to open and create an email message helpful for presentations that people watch on your website and gives you the convenience of opening a web page from your slide show. Using hyperlinks enables you to run a smooth presentation and impress your audience.

To Insert a Hyperlink, check the following steps below:

1. Select a Slide in the Current Presentation and click inside a placeholder where you want to insert the hyperlink.

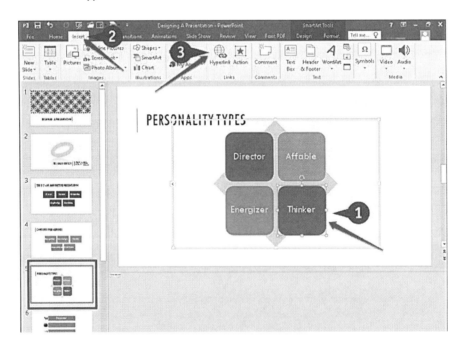

Note: To use an object as the button to the hyperlink, select it in the slide before clicking Insert.

2. From the left side corner at the top, click on the **Insert** tab.

3. Locate **Hyperlink** and click on it. The Hyperlink dialog box will appear.
4. Go to the **Text to display** text box.

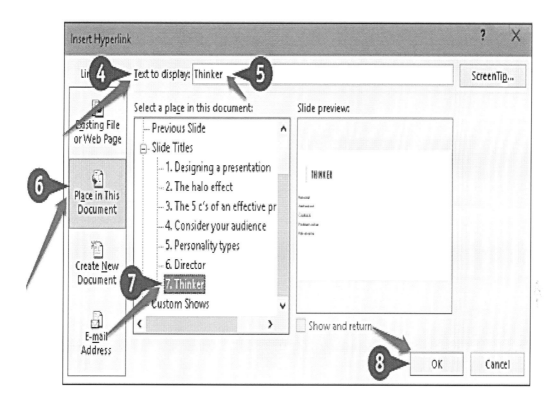

Take Note: If you select an object as the hyperlink button, this box reads "Selection in Document", you cannot edit it.

5. Type a name for your hyperlink.
6. Click on **Place in This Document**.
7. Then click on the **slide** you want to link it to.
8. Click **OK**. Immediately, PowerPoint inserts the link to the slide.

Note that you can have more than one hyperlink on the same slide. Repeat the steps to add others if you wish to do that.

Opening a File

1. Repeat steps 1 to 4 in the subsection "**Go to a Slide in the Current Presentation.**"
2. Then click on **Existing File or Web Page**.

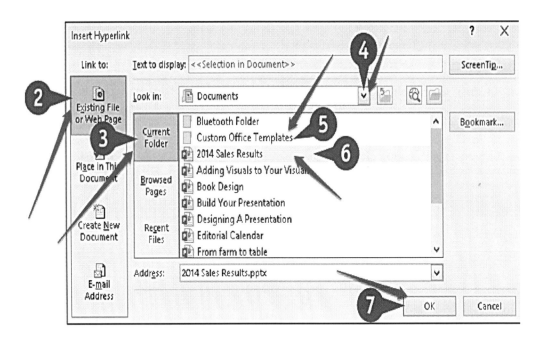

3. Next, click on **Current Folder**.
4. Click the **Look in** drop-down arrow.
5. Navigate and click the **folder** that contains the file you want to open.
6. Click the **file** to open.
7. Then click **Ok.**

Opening a Web Page

1. Repeat steps 1 to 4 in the subsection "**Go to a Slide in the Current Presentation.**"
2. Then click on **Existing File or Web Page.**

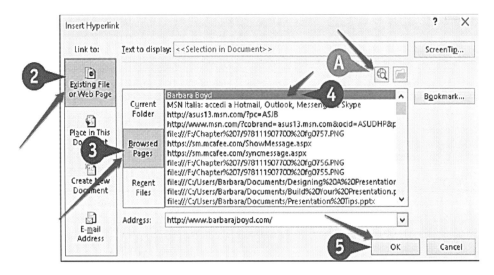

3. Click on **Browsed Pages.**

4. Scroll through the list of web pages you have visited and click the one you want to link it to.

A. Then click the **Browse Web** button to open the page you want to link it to, then return to PowerPoint; you'll find the page in the Browsed Pages list.

5. Click **Ok**.

B. PowerPoint places the link on your slide. During the slide show, click the **text** to follow the link.

How to Remove the Link from a File and Leave the Link Text

1. Right-click the **hyperlink.**

2. Then click **Edit Link** on the shortcut menu to open the Hyperlink dialog box
3. Next, click on **Remove Link.** The link is removed, but the link text remains.

Screen Recording

In this section, I will demonstrate how to record a portion of your screen, whatever you are saying and doing on that screen at that particular point in time, and have that clip automatically embedded into a slide.

So, this is how it works, let's assume we have a slide here that we want to have a concept demonstrated with narration and all types of things.

To apply screen capture recording, follow the steps below:

1. Click a **Slide** from the Normal view.

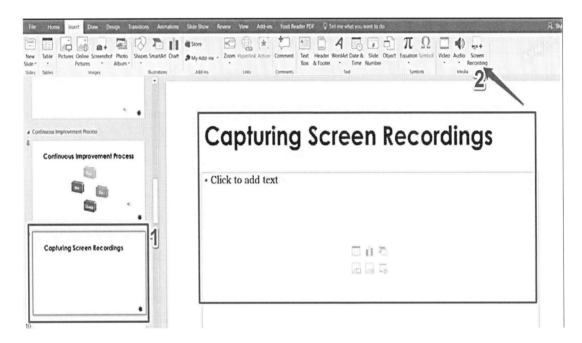

2. On the slide ribbon, click on the **Insert** tab and locate the **Screen recording** option located at the top right corner. It will open the application where you want to record.

3. Then click one **Application** icon below that you want to capture.
4. Click on **Select Area**.

Screen Capture and Embeding.

5. From the left edge side at the top, click and drag around where you want to record.
6. Then click on **Record**. It will display this, press Windows logo key + shift + Q to stop recording".

Now, there is another basic thing that you can do again when working on recording. For example, if you want to point to someone from my YouTube channel or a website. I can capture this recording along with the direction of whatever I say during the process. To do this,

7. click on the **YouTube** website.
8. Then type youtube.com for Caselin and press **Enter**.

It will direct you to another page, you can then access whatever you need there. It will capture all your audio, whatever you say at that moment with what you are doing on PowerPoint.

9. Then scroll down and click on this selection.

10. Press the Windows **Shift** key and click.
11. After clicking, return to PowerPoint.

Note that it has been placed automatically into your slide and now, this is just like another video that you covered.

12. Click and drag to resize
13. Then click on **Playback**. You can click on **Play full screen** if you want it to be full screen.

14. The next thing is to click on the **Center of the screen recording**. It will start recording both the voice and the screen immediately.

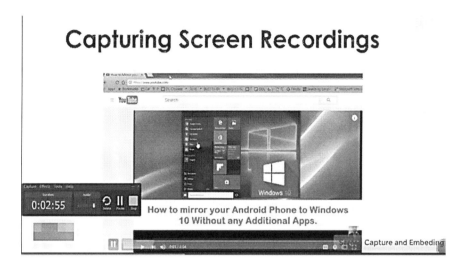

Trimming Audio Clips

A decision may come to your mind to play an interesting part of a song for your audience, or a clip from an interview to share with them, but you do not want to play an entire audio clip. You might have an audio clip that you recorded and inserted directly into a PowerPoint slide, but you want it to be shorter. In any of these cases, you can trim the audio clip directly in PowerPoint to make it the perfect length you want. This handy feature saves you the inconvenience of trimming the audio clip in a different program and then importing it to PowerPoint.

To trim Audio clips, do the following:

1. First, click the audio clip you want to trim.

2. Click the **Playback** tab in the ribbon.
3. Now, you can proceed by clicking on **Trim Audio** to display the dialog box.
4. Click any of the **slides** where you want the audio to play.

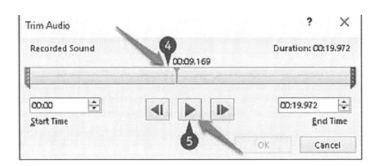

Take Note: Do not click any slide if you want to start listening from the beginning.

5. Click the **Play** button.
6. Then take your time to listen and locate where you want to trim the beginning and end of your audio.
7. You can click the **Pause** button if you wish to pause the audio.

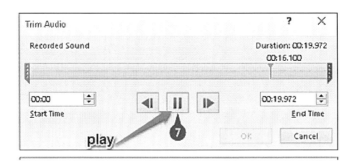

8. Then click and drag the **green marker** to the beginning of where you want to start trimming.

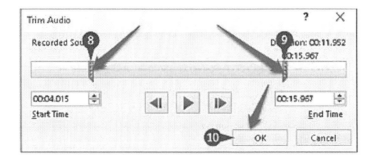

9. Click and drag the red marker where you want to end the trimming of the audio.
10. The next thing to do is to click **Ok.** The dialog box closes and the audio is trimmed to the length that you specified.
11. Click on **Play** to listen to the trimmed audio.

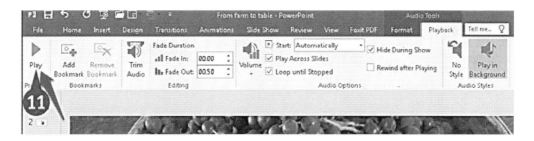

Take Note: The trimming audio clip process is reversible. You can repeat this process to reverse it if you wish to.

Trimming Video Clips

Videos are usually not the length you want for your presentation, and so you will probably want to trim them. You may want to play only a snippet of a video during a presentation to show a little information about something, or you may have a part in the video that you do not need your audience to see. PowerPoint gives you the convenience to trim the video right on the slide so you do not have to leave PowerPoint and use another software to do it.

To trim Video Clips, follow the steps below:

1. Click on the video clip you want to trim.

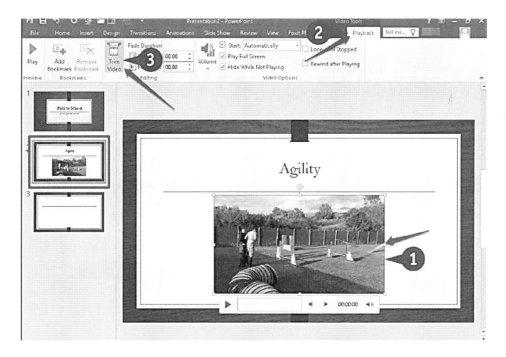

2. Then from the top right corner in the ribbon, click the **Playback** tab.
3. Next, click on the **Trim Video** option. The Trim Video dialog box will display.
4. Then click and drag the **Green marker** where you want the video to begin.

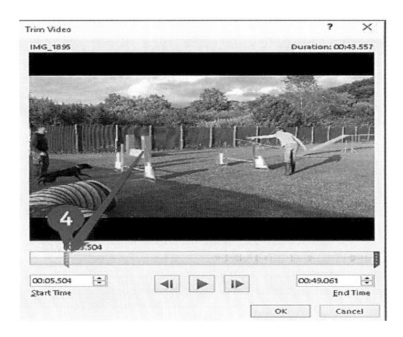

The video frame that plays at that moment will appear on the screen.

5. Click and drag the **Red sign line** to where you want the video to end. The video frame that plays at that time will be displayed.

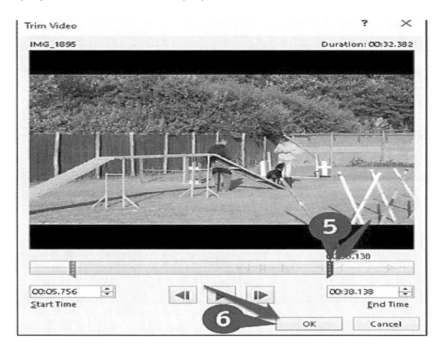

6. Then click **Ok.** The dialog box closes and PowerPoint trims the video according to your specifications.
7. Click the **Playback** tab.

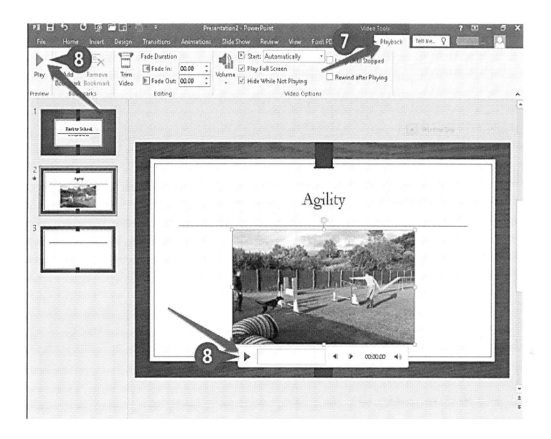

8. Click **Play** to watch the trimmed video.

Hope it's clear to you? Great!

CHAPTER 5

TIPS AND TRICKS IN POWERPOINT

How to insert stock images into your presentation

In 2020, Microsoft added stock images to PowerPoint.

1. First of all, click on the **Insert** tab from the PowerPoint ribbon.

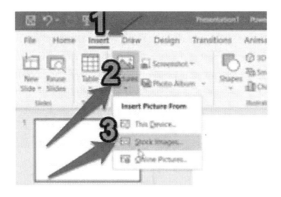

2. Then click on **Picture.**
3. Next, click on **Stock Images.** It will display stock images you can choose from to insert into your presentation.
   - To select the stock image, you can click any of the four stock image names depending on the stock image you need for your presentation.
4. Now, click or select any **stock image** you want and insert it into your presentation.

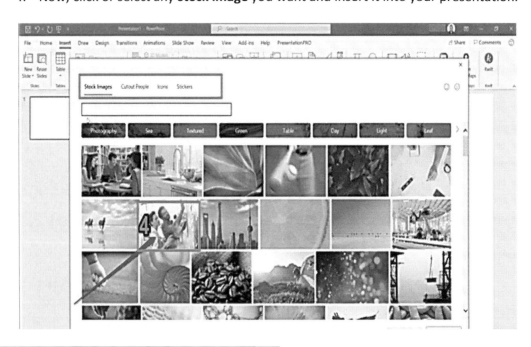

5. Then, click on the selected **Stock Image,** resize as you want, and move it to where you want it to be.

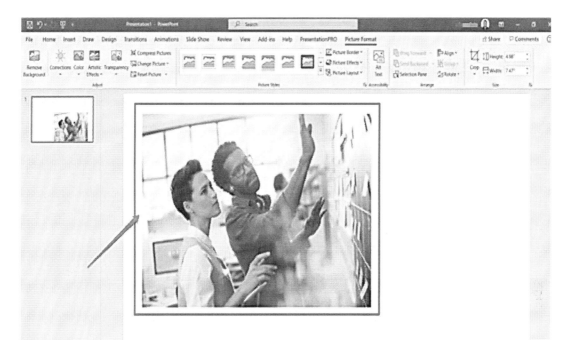

Editing Shapes

Do you know that you can customize a shape you inserted into your PowerPoint presentation? Let's try it.

First, I'll show you how to insert a shape into a presentation before discussing how to customize it.

1. First, click on the **Insert** tab in the ribbon.

2. Locate the **Shapes** command and click on it.
3. Select the **Shape** you want to use for your presentation.

How to customize a selected shape

1. On the left side, you have the option to **Edit Shape,** click on the **Edit Shape drop-down arrow,** and select **Edit points**

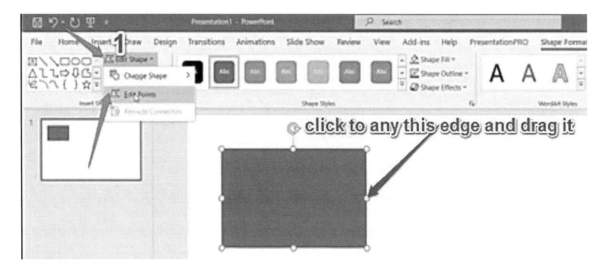

2. Go ahead to click on any of the shape points and drag to change the shape.

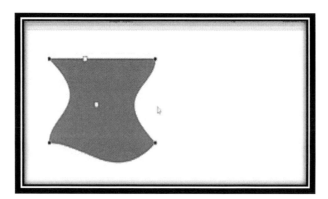

3. When done, click outside the shape and the shape is customized.

Morph Transition

Morph transition is a great tool that helps you animate movement from one slide to another.

The morph transition can be used by following the steps below:

Let's assume you have a slide for the presentation from the Window.

1. The first thing to do is to right-click on the **Slide** to duplicate the slide.

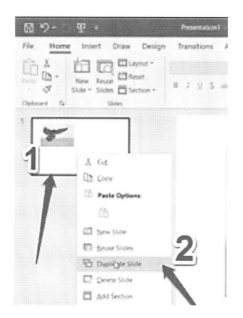

2. Click on **Duplicate Slide**
3. Then click on the second **Slide** you want to transfer the images from.

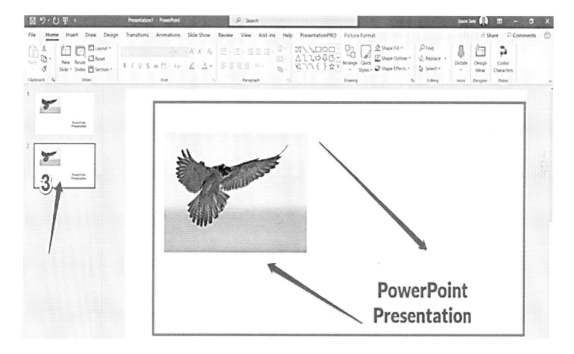

4. Next, drag the first image from the top to the down area and the second image from the down to the top area.
5. Then click on the **Transition** command.

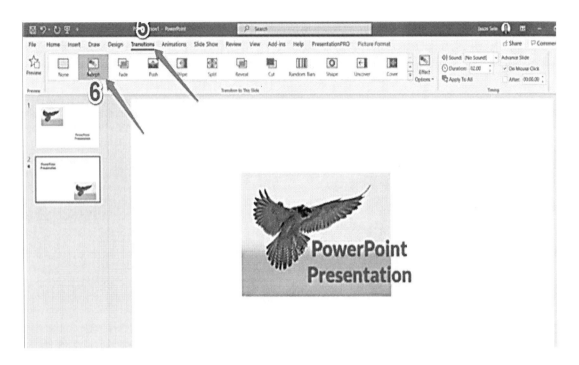

6. Click on **Morph.** After clicking, it will display the images in an interchanged position.

Filled Map

For a quick method to show a map on your PowerPoint presentation, use Filled Map You can create a map in PowerPoint using a table. This can be done by following these steps below:

1. Go to the ribbon section, click on **Insert**.

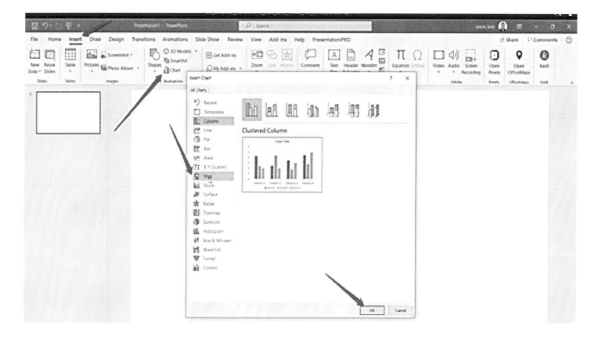

2. Locate the **Chart** icon and click on it.
3. From the menu option, select **Map.**
4. Then click on **Ok.** It will be inserted into your presentation.

Note: The table you see represents the data to be shown on the map.

5. You can click to remove some of the data from the list if you wish. Following this illustration, the table consists of the names of countries. Immediately you remove some, the map will be updated and the ones you didn't remove are the ones you will see on the map.

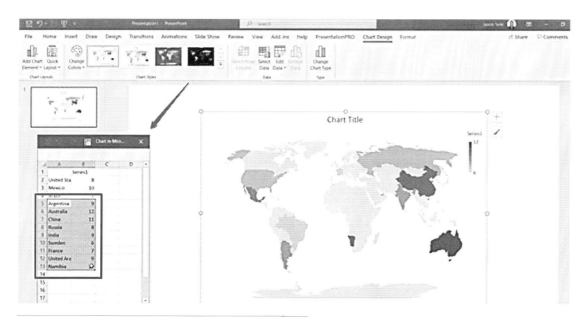

6. When you click again to remove, it will show the remaining ones on the map.

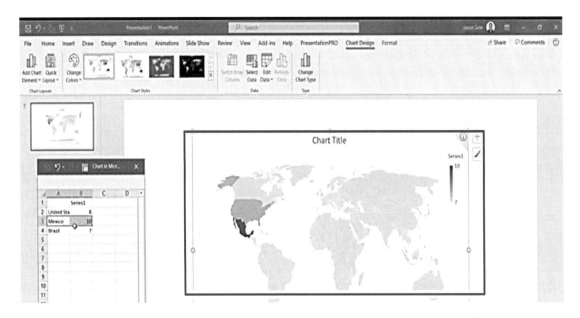

7. You can also click on the table to insert some states by typing the names of the states you want to see on the map.

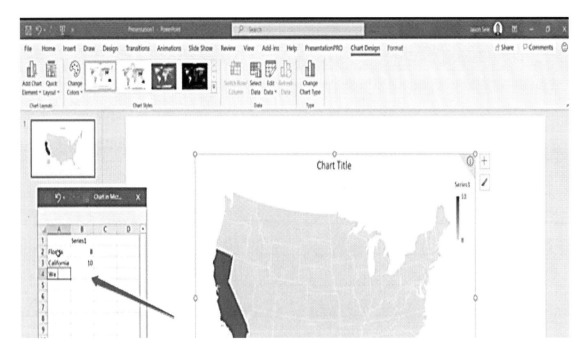

Take note: Clicking inside the table data, you can use the names, countries regions, and cities zip codes, or any other location-specific data that can be mapped.

Hope you understand the steps above? Let's proceed then

Quick Alignment

When you move objects in a slide, alignment and spacing guides will appear around the objects to help you align them. However, if you have many objects in a slide, it may be difficult and time-consuming to get them perfectly aligned. Thankfully, PowerPoint provides you with several alignment commands that allow you to easily arrange and position objects.

To align two or more objects into a slide, follow the steps below:

1. Click on the **objects area** to highlight all the objects to be aligned

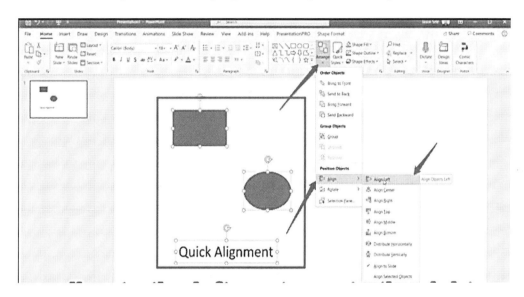

2. Go to the **Home** tab, locate the **Arrange** button and click on it.
3. Then select the **Side** you want to align the object, either left or right.

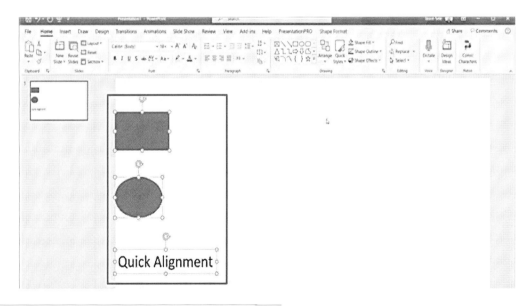

Note: you can also align the distribution vertically or horizontally. Whichever way, space will be made between them.

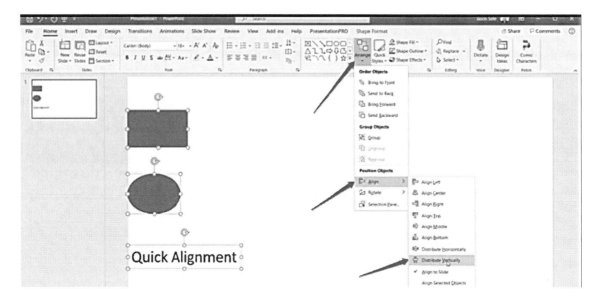

How to group multiple objects into one

Another thing you can do with the Arrange command is to group multiple objects into one.

1. Highlight the objects you want to group by dragging the cursor over them.
2. Go to the **Home** tab, click on **Arrange**.
3. Under **Group Objects**, click on **Group**.

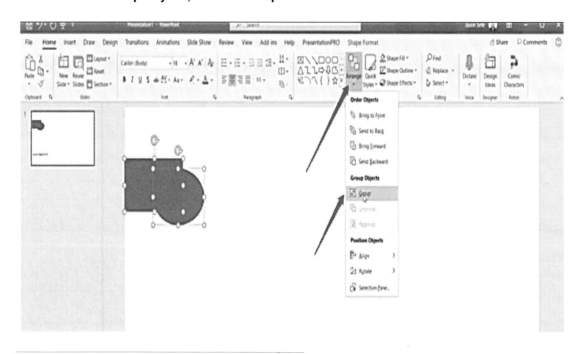

Now the objects will be grouped as one and thereby move and act as one object.

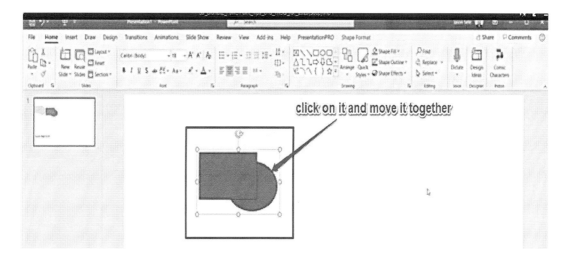

How to ungroup objects

Another option under the Arrange command that you should be aware of is the option to ungroup objects you have previously grouped. Follow these steps to do that:

1. Click on the **grouped objects** to highlight it.
2. Right-click and locate "**Group**", click on it to see the options
3. Select **Ungroup**.

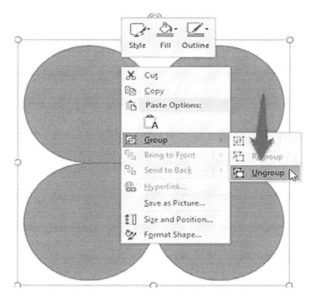

Note: you can press **Ctrl+ Shift +G** on your keyboard as the shortcut to ungroup the objects

Hope the steps are clear to you?

Ink to Text

When you are presenting, you can draw on the screen with a digital pen to emphasize a point or show connections. PowerPoint comes with a great drawing tool that you can use to convert Ink into Text or shape.

Now to apply the ink to text tool, follow the steps below carefully:

1. Click on the **Draw** tab from the ribbon.

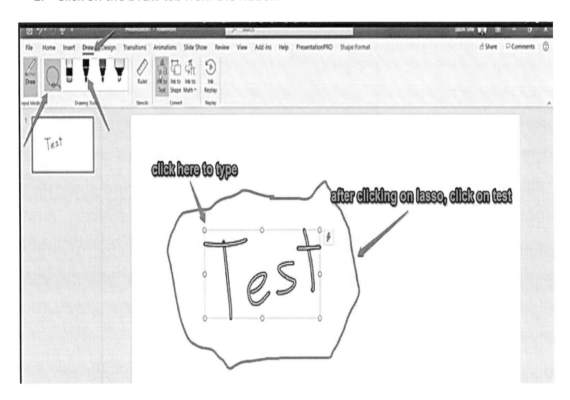

2. Click a **Pen** of your choice to pick it.
3. Then click to start writing some words on the screen, for example, write "**Test**".
4. Now click on **Lasso** and select that area.
5. Then click the **Ink to Text** button.

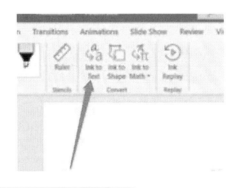

It displays the converted text.

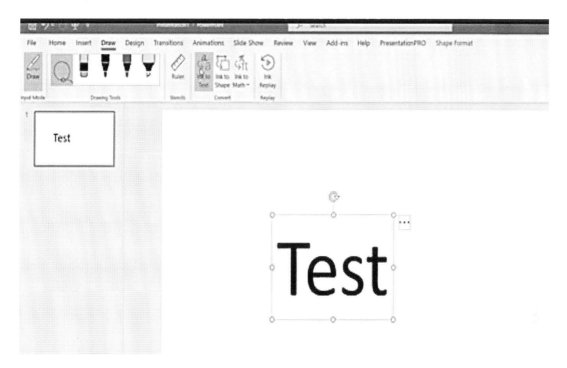

Take note: You can continue the edition of the text, just make sure you turn off the draw tool and click the text to continue to edit.

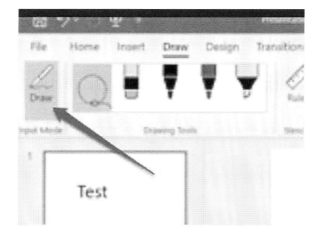

Ink to Shapes

Interestingly, you can also convert **Ink** to **Shapes**. To convert Ink to Shapes,

1. Repeat steps 1&2 above
2. Here, draw the shape(s) you want

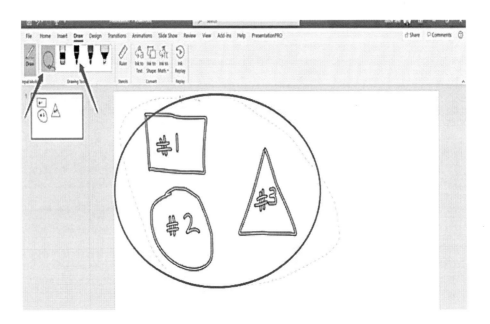

3. Click on **Lasso** and select that area.
4. Then click the **Ink to Shape** button.
   It displays the converted shape.

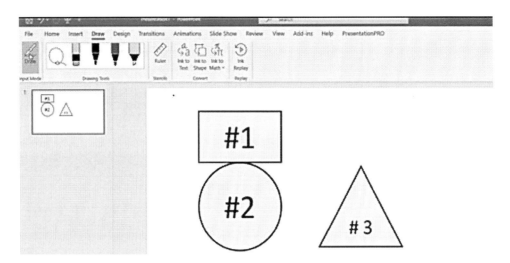

Ink to Math Equation

Do you know that you can also convert **Ink** to **Math Equation** as well?

To convert the **Ink** to **Math Equation,**

1. Repeat steps 1&2 above
2. Write the equation you want to convert and click on **Lasso** to select area.
3. Then click **Ink to Math Equation**.

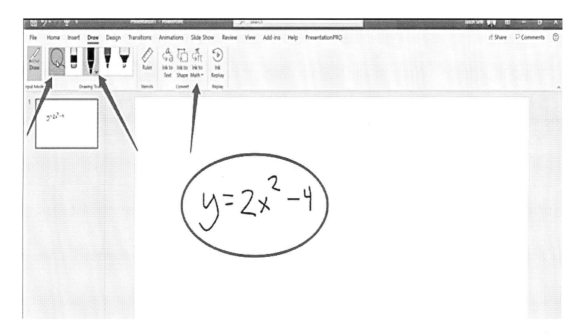

It displays the converted Math Equation.

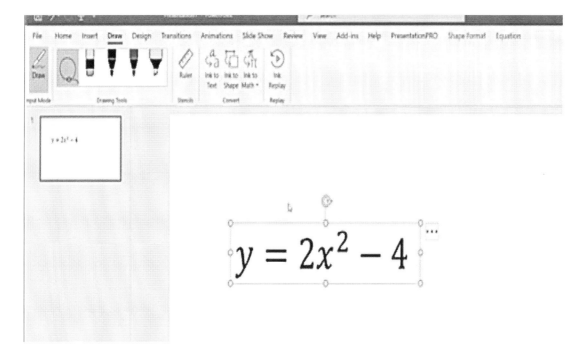

Ink Equation Editor

Under the Ink to Math Equation button, you can also click on **Ink Equation Editor** and write your formula.

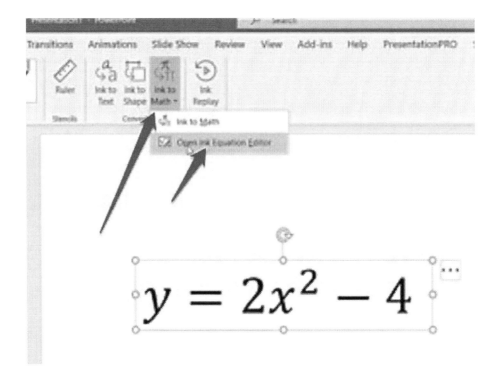

After writing your formula, click on the **Insert** option to display it on your presentation.

inside here you can type the equation

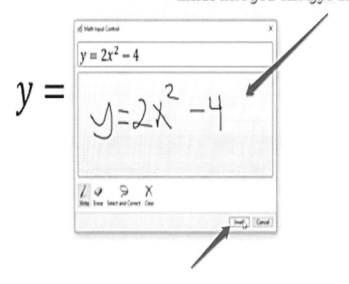

$$y =$$

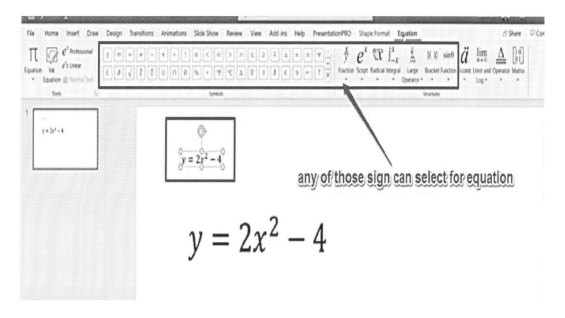

$$y = 2x^2 - 4$$

Ink Replay

Ink Replay is the final option under the Draw tab. This option can be used for animation presentations. Let's see what it is about.

1. Draw something on your screen.

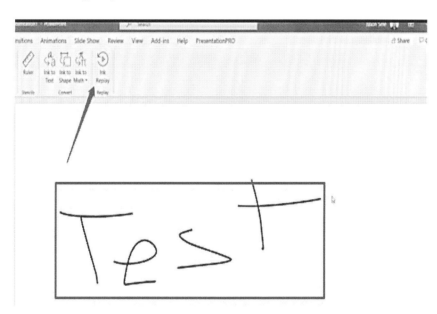

2. Then click on **Ink Replay.** It will redisplay your text created.

Do you observe all the steps above? Do you get everything right? Good

Eye Dropper

The Eyedropper tool helps you match the colors in your slides in PowerPoint. You can use this feature when you want to "pick" the color of another object on your slide.

Even more, you can extract the colors from pictures, shapes, or other elements. This allows you to apply a specific color to multiple objects on your PowerPoint presentation. Now to apply this, follow the steps below:

1. Press the **Ctrl** key from the keyboard and click on the entire object on the screen.
2. Locate "**Shape Format**" on the menu and click on it.
3. Click on **Shape fill.**
4. Then click on **Eyedropper** and place it inside the object.

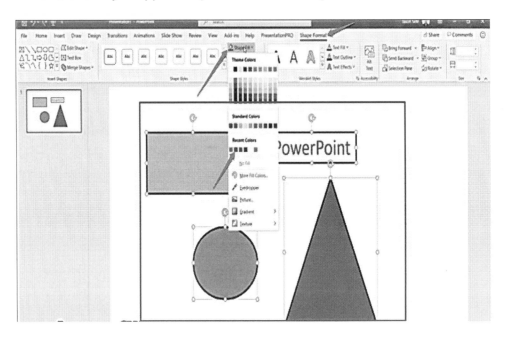

5. It will display the same color on the entire object on the screen.

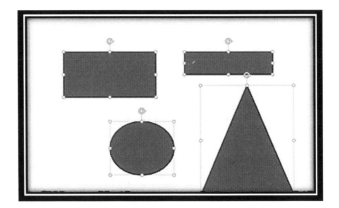

You can also do the same thing for **Shape outline** by repeating the steps above, but after clicking the **Shape format**, locate **Shape Outline** and click on it, then click on **Eyedropper**. It will take an immediate effect on the outline of all the shapes as illustrated below.

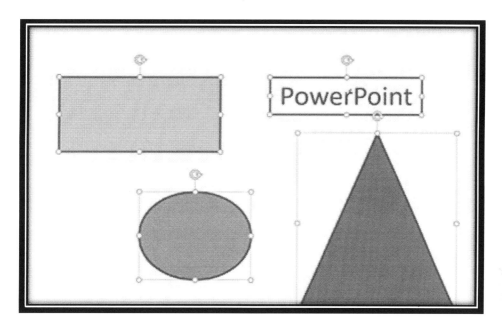

Dictation and Translation

The Dictation tool lets you use speech-to-text to author contents in Office with a microphone and a reliable internet connection. It's a quick and easy way to add content(s) into presentation placeholders and slide notes.

To apply this, just go straight to the ribbon section.

1. First, click on **Insert.**

2. Then click on the **Text box** and set it up somewhere you prefer it to be.
3. Next, click inside the **Text box.**

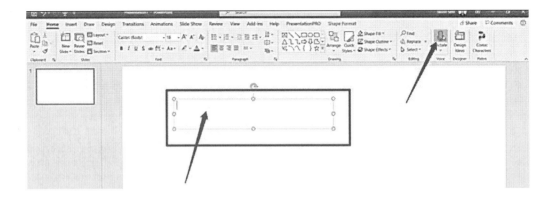

4. Now, click on **Dictate** and it will display where to record your voice.
5. You can also click here for different variety of languages to record.

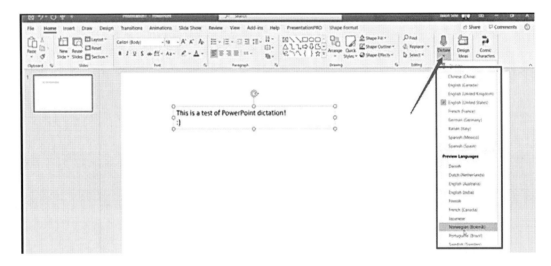

6. Then click on the **Review** tab.

7. Highlight the **text.**
8. Next, click on the **Translate** button. It will display your request on the right side by translating and converting it to any language you choose.
9. Select any language you want your record to be translated to.

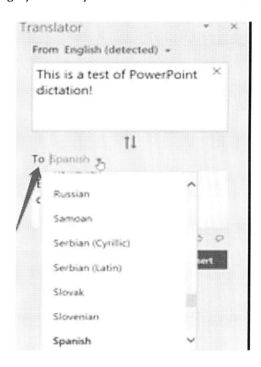

10. Then click on the **Insert** option.

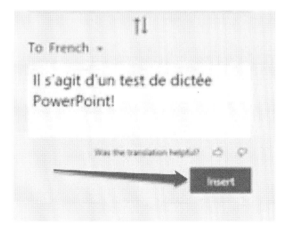

Note: The translation can also be reversed, and click on your choice of translation.

Instant Photo Album

It is really simple to create an instant photo album using some pictures. To use Instant photo album, follow these steps carefully:

1. From the PowerPoint ribbon, click on the **Insert** tab.

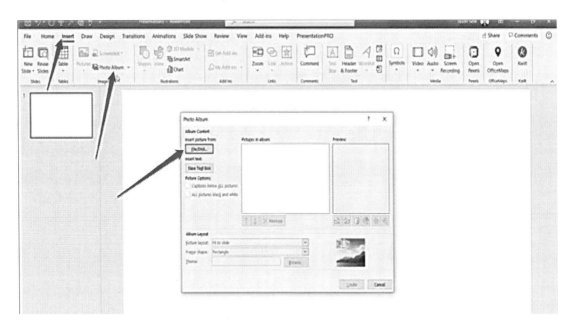

2. Then locate the **Photo album** command and click on it.
3. Next, click on the **File disk** command.
4. Then pick or select the pictures you want to insert into your photo album.

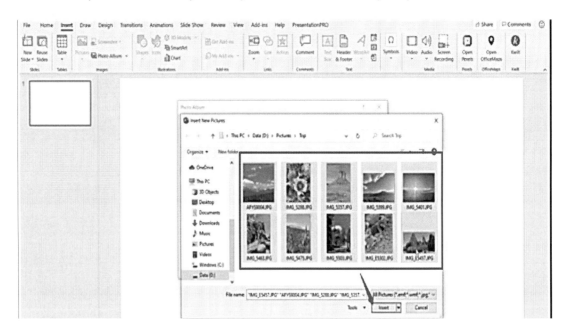

5. On this page, there are many options to perform specific tasks like turning the album into **black** and **white** or others function you may like.

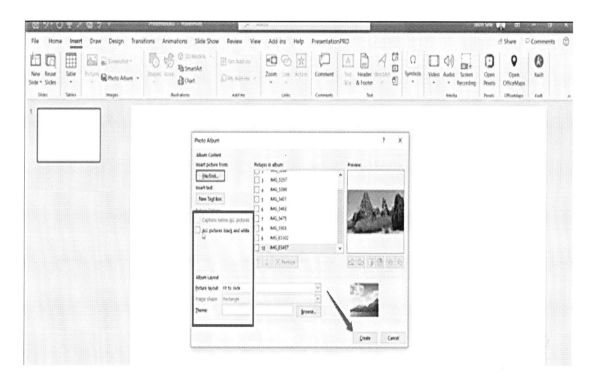

6. Proceed to click on **Create.** It will open the page where your entire album is created.

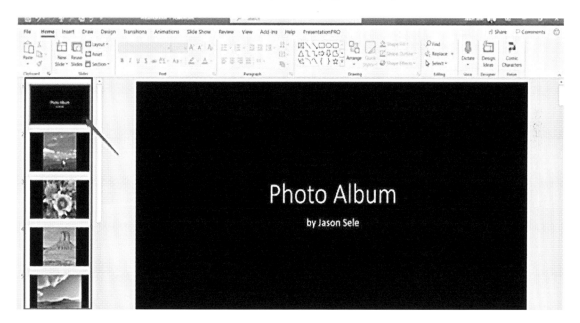

7. Then click the **Slide** to view each picture.

Note: You can also improve the look of your photo album. To achieve that go straight to **Design ideas** from the top right side.

1. Click on the **Design ideas** tab command.

2. Then select a format from the format list that makes it look nice

CHAPTER 6

SHORTCUTS IN POWERPOINT

Shortcuts and their importance

Keyboard shortcuts are a great way to improve your productivity with PowerPoint. Why? Because usually, you already have your hands on the keyboard. There is no need to disrupt your workflow by reaching for the mouse and moving the mouse cursor across the screen, thereby making your work faster.

Shortcuts to use while working with shapes and slides

- **Ctrl+D:** Duplicates the selected item (shape, slide, etc.), which is much faster than copy and paste
- **Ctrl+G:** Groups the selected shapes together
- **Ctrl+Shift+G:** Ungroups grouped shapes
- **Ctrl+Y**: Redoes a previous action
- **Ctrl+Z**: it is used to undo a previous action
- **Ctrl+Shift+C:** Copies the formatting of a shape
- **Ctrl+Shift+V:** used to paste copied shapes to another shape
- **Ctrl+Alt+V**: Opens the Paste Special dialog box

Shortcuts to use while Formatting and Editing Texts

- **Ctrl + Shift+>:** Increases the font size of a selected text (use **Ctrl+Shift+.** on a QUERTZ keyboard)
- **Ctrl+Shift+<:** Decreases the font size of a selected text (use **Ctrl+Shift+,** on a QUERTZ keyboard)
- **Ctrl+B**: Applies bold format to a selected text
- **Ctrl+I**: Applies italic format to a selected text
- **Ctrl+E:** Centers the text in a selected shape
- **Ctrl+L:** Left-aligns the text in the selected shape
- **Ctrl+R:** Right-aligns the text in the selected shape
- **Shift+Enter:** Creates a line break in the text (instead of a paragraph break that is inserted when simply pressing Enter) at the current position

Shortcuts to use while navigating

- **Ctrl+F1:** Hides/unhides the Ribbon (very useful for quickly freeing up space on small screens)
- **Ctrl+Shift+Tab:** Switches between the Thumbnail Pane and the Outline View Pane
- **Alt+F10:** Shows/hides the Selection Pane
- **Alt+F5:** Shows the presentation in Presenter View
- **Shift+F5:** Starts the presentation from the current slide

Shortcuts to use during Presentation

- **+** : Zooms into the slide (up to three zoom levels); once zoomed in, you can point the slide with the mouse cursor or the arrow keys
- **-** : Zooms out slides to provide an overview of all the slides of the presentation (including sections)
- **B** : Blackens the screen

Shortcuts that involve Mouse and Keyboard

- **Shift+tap (select) with Mouse**: Adds the selected item to the current selection (makes it easy to quickly select texts or multiple shapes on a slide)
- **Ctrl+Moving an Item with Mouse**: Duplicates the selected item
- **Shift+Moving an Item with Mouse**: Restricts movement of the item up/down or left/right
- **Alt+Moving an Item with Mouse**: Moves the item with Smart Guides and Snap to Point features turned off (can be helpful when making small position adjustments)
- **Ctrl+Resizing an Item with Mouse**: Resizes the item around its center
- **Shift+Resizing an Item with Mouse:** Keeps the original proportions of the item while resizing it
- **Alt+Resizing an Item with Mouse**: Resizes the item with Smart Guides and Snap to Point features turned off.

CONCLUSION ON POWERPOINT 365

Wow! It's such a great delight that we have come to the consummation of this book. I believe no matter the level you were before you started with this user guide, maybe a beginner, advanced beginner, or you probably didn't have any idea about how to use PowerPoint, by now your knowledge about it has stepped up, and now, you can make better use of it.

With the acquired knowledge from this book, do ensure you put to practice all you have learned over again to become familiar with the features and their specific uses, and with that, I believe you will be able to make the most of the PowerPoint Office Suite by making attractive, professional and outstanding slides for your presentation.

With your leveled up knowledge, make progress and be the best.

BOOK FOUR

MICROSOFT
ACCESS 365

INTRODUCTION

Microsoft Access is a database management system (DBMS), provided by Microsoft to analyze large amounts of information and manage data efficiently. Access 365 is a member of the Microsoft 365 suite of applications that are included in the Professional and higher editions or sold separately. The Microsoft Access stores in its format based on the Access Jet Database Engine, import or link directly to data stored in other applications and databases.

Virtually, every organization benefit from the use of Access to organize, store, and document important information. With Microsoft Access, data such as inventory and customers' information, order details, and vendors can be effectively organized, analyzed, and processed.

Here in this book, with the use of Access 365, you will be familiar with commonly used data management software and learn some basic functions associated with it.

By the end of this book, you should be able to:

- Create a table from the scratch or use the template
- Create field from the scratch or use the template
- Get conversant with the use of the Access shortcut keys etc.

To use this book, especially as a beginner, you must have the following

- A good computer system with a strong and stable internet connection
- Installed Access 365 or 2019 version on the computer system

With all these available, becoming proficient in Access 365 is much easier than you must have thought.

See you in the next stage!

CHAPTER ONE

INTRODUCING ACCESS 365

What Is Access?

Microsoft Access is a database management system (DBMS) that is used to store and manage data. This is a member of the Microsoft 365 suite of applications which is made for business and enterprise users.

Microsoft Access is also an Information Management Tool that allows you to store information for referencing, reporting, and also analyzing.

Just like Microsoft Excel, Access allows the users to view and edit data. One of the features that make Access better than Excel is that it can take in more data at a stretch.

Microsoft Access provides the users, the features of a database, and the programming proficiencies to create an easy-to-navigate screen (Forms). Not only that, Access helps to process a large bunk of information and manages them effectively and efficiently.

Microsoft Access saves data in its format based on the Access Jet Database Engine, and can also link or import directly to the data that are stored in other applications or databases.

Just like every other Microsoft application, Access also supports the use of Visual Basic for Application (VBA)

To use Microsoft Access, you will need to follow the procedures below

- **Database Creation:** The first thing to do is create a database and indicate what type of data to be stored in the database
- **Data Input:** After creating a database, the next thing to do is enter the data into the database.
- **Query:** This is a process of retrieving information from a database
- **Report:** This is where information from the database is organized in a nice and presentable manner that can be printed out in an Access report

Why Should You Use Access?

There are many benefits attached to the use of Microsoft Access and some of them will be outlined below

- **Cost Of Development**: One of the benefits of using Microsoft Access is that it is less expensive compared to the larger database systems like Oracle, SOL server, etc., which requires a huge amount of set up and high maintenance costs
- **Software Integration**: One of the notable features of Microsoft Access being a product of the Microsoft Office suite is that it can integrate well with two other apps in the MS office suite.

- **Legacy Data**: Microsoft Access can easily import many data formats, in such a way that the existing data is retained and not lost. It does not only save 100's of hours of input time but can remove potential human input errors.
- **Distribution**: Microsoft Access has its Jet Database format that contains both the application and data in one file. With the ability of having the application and data together in one place, it is convenient to distribute the applications to many users, who can, in turn, run the apps in disconnected environments.
- Microsoft Access provides a fully functional, relational database management system in a few minutes.
- Microsoft Access can function well with many of the development languages that work on Windows OS.
- With Microsoft Access, you can create tables, queries, forms, reports, and connect using the macros.
- Microsoft Access allows the users to link data from its existing location and manipulate it for viewing, updating, querying, and reporting.
- Microsoft Access allows for customizing according to personal and company needs.
- Microsoft Access executes any challenging or difficult office or industrial database tasks.
- Access in its uniqueness can function with the most popular databases that are compatible with Open Database Connectivity (ODBC) standards, including SQL Server, Oracle, and DB2.
- With Access, software developers can use Microsoft Access to develop application software
- Microsoft Access requires less code to get work done unlike SQL server and some other client-server database).
- Microsoft Access is a very good tool for creating database applications with a large array of readily available functionality.
- Another reason you need to use Access is that it is flexible i.e., it allows you to put together a custom database and later change as needs are likely changes as needs arise.
- Access can be used alongside VBA, a programming language. Developers can create a custom solution for their database using the VBA code, an effective programming language that contains codes or commands for specific programs.
- Microsoft Access allows users to choose any of the four ways to view reports:
  - Report view
  - Print view
  - Layout view
  - Design view
- Microsoft Access is a simple desktop application that does not need any particular hardware or license to function. Thus, making it more suitable and cost-effective for individual users and smaller teams who do not need larger and complicated databases for an extra price.
- Users of Access do not need to undergo any special training to get the skills needed to use this application. In a nutshell, Access is easy to master especially to users who are conversant with the use of Excel

CHAPTER TWO

MICROSOFT ACCESS OBJECTS

Here in this section, we will be learning about the basic objects in MS Access. These objects are what Access uses to help its users list and organize information and prepare specially designed reports. When a database is created, Access provides the users with objects such as tables, queries, forms, reports, macros, and modules.

What Is A Database

A database is a tool that is used for the collection and organization of information. The database can store information about people, products, orders, etc. The database stores its information in a single file and the file contains database objects, which are the components of the database. The database consists of six components which are listed below

- *Tables*
- *Queries*
- *Forms*
- *Reports*
- *Macros*
- *Modules*

Tables

This is the heart of the database where data are defined and stored in rows and columns. Here, you can create as many tables as you need to store all kinds of information. The following are what you should keep in mind when using the table

- Each field must carry a unique name and data type
- You can also define the primary key in a table.
- The table must contain fields or columns that must be able to take in different kinds of data, such as name, address, and a row that collects information about the subject, and such information can be details about the employee or customer.

Query

This is one of the objects in the database that gives a custom view of data from one or more tables. The query selects sorts and filters data based on the search criteria. Take note of the following hints when using the query

- Running a query is compared to asking an in-depth question of your database
- Building a query in Access implies that you are defining the specific search conditions to find precisely the data you need
- You can define your queries to Select, Update, Insert, or Delete data
- You can also set queries that create new tables from the data in one or more existing tables

Form

Form is also one of the databases objects that is mainly created for data input, display, or control of application executions. Forms can be used to modify the presentation of data that the application extracts from queries or data. Not only that, forms give an easy way to view or change information in a table. Note the following about forms

- Forms is a database object used for creating a user interface for database application
- Forms are used for entering, customizing, and viewing records
- Forms are used from time to time because they are easy to guide people to entering data correctly
- When you input data into a form in Access, the data goes precisely the database designer wants it to go in one or more related tables
- Forms also display live data from the table. This aimed at easing the process of entering or editing data.

Report

Report is also an object of the database that is used to format, calculate, print, and summarize selected data. The report helps to print some or all of the data in a selected data. Report allows you to choose where the information is displayed on the printed page, and how it is grouped, sorted, and formatted. Take note of the following when working with report

- You can view or display a report on your screen before printing it out
- Report is for output purposes
- Reports are very important because they permit for the displaying of the database components in an easy-to-read manner
- You can modify the report's appearance to make it more attractive
- You can create a report from the table or query

Macro

Macros are mini computer programming constructs that the users to set up commands and processes in the forms. Some of the activities in the form include searching, moving to another record, and running of formula. With macros, you can customize your data, even without being a programmer. Take note of the following tips about macro in the Microsoft Access

- The macros can be used to open and execute queries, to open tables, or to print or view reports.
- You can run other macros or Visual Basic procedures from within a macro
- Macros can attach data directly to table events such as inserting new records, editing existing records, and deleting records
- Data macros in web apps can also be stand-alone objects which can be called from other data or macro-objects.

Module

A module is an object in the database that contains the procedures which are used in the Visual Basic for Application (VBA).

With these procedures, you can do anything. The modules give a more distinct flow of actions and permit the users to trap errors. Take note of the following when using the modules to execute any operation in Access

- Whatever can be done in the macro can also be done in the modules
- Modules are most suitable when the users intend to write codes for a multi-user environment, unlike the macros which cannot do error handling
- The modules being a standalone object can be called from anywhere in the application, or they can be linked with a form or a report to react to events on the associated form or report.

Microsoft Access Data Types

The data types are the properties of each field in a table. These properties are what define the features and performance of the fields in a table. The Datatypes determine the type of values the users can store in any given field. Below is the table of the most common data types that can be used in the Microsoft Access database

TYPE OF DATA	DESCRIPTION	SIZE
Short Text	These are texts and numbers which do need calculation e.g., mobile numbers	Up to 255 characters
Long Text	This data type is used for lengthy text or combination of texts and numbers	Up to 63,999 characters
Number	These are numerical data used for storing mathematical calculations	1,2,4, 8, and 16 bytes
Date/Time	This stores data and time for the years 100 through 9999	8 bytes
Currency	This allows you to store currency values and numeric data used in mathematical calculations involving data with one to four decimal places	8 bytes
Auto Number	This assigns a unique number when a new record is created or added to a table.	Four bytes (16 bytes if it is set as a Replication ID)
Yes/No	It stores only logical values Yes and No	1 bit
Attachment	This stores file such as digital photos and multiple files can be attached per record	Up to 2 GB of data can be stored.
OLE objects	OLE objects can store audio, video, other Binary Large Objects.	Up to about 2 GB

Hyperlink	Text or combination of texts and numbers stored. The text is used as hyperlink address	The Hyperlink data type allows you to store a maximum of 2048 characters
Calculated	This creates an expression that uses data from one or more fields.	You can create an expression that uses data from one or more fields

CHAPTER THREE

CREATING A DATABASE FILE

Here in this chapter, we will be learning how to create a database. Here, we will be learning how to create a database by using a template or building a database from the scratch

Before we create a database file, we will need to open Microsoft Access and to open Microsoft Access, follow the steps below

- Click on the **Windows icon** where you will find the list of installed programs
- Search and click on **Access** to open it

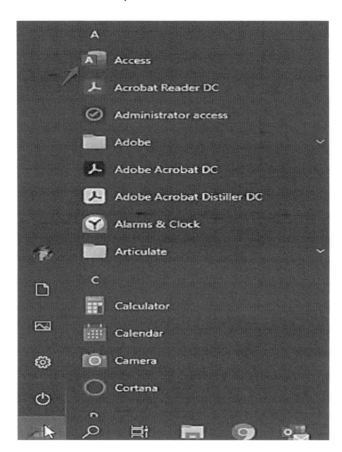

Creating A Blank Database File

To create a new blank database file

- Open the Microsoft Access
- From the right panel of the screen, click **on Blank database** and enter the name of the database.

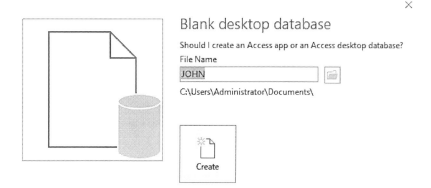

Blank desktop database

Should I create an Access app or an Access desktop database?

File Name

JOHN

C:\Users\Administrator\Documents\

Create

- Choose the folder where you want to store your data

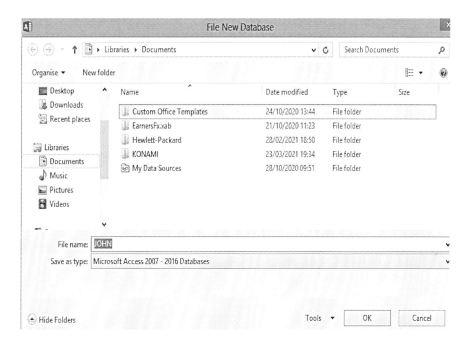

- Click on the big **Create button** under the file name box, and Access will open a blank table

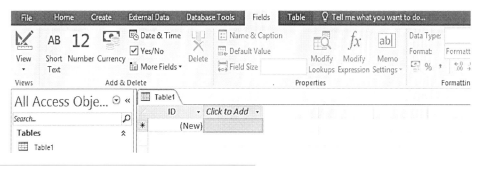

Creating Database from Template

An Access template is a ready-made file that, when opened, creates a complete database application. The template contains all the tables, forms, forms, reports, queries, and macros needed to achieve your goals.

To create a database from a database

- Go to the **File menu** and choose from the lists of templates or use the search feature to search for any template among the list of templates

- When you click on the template, a preview panel will pop up, displaying the description of the database and a preview of the database fields. If the template suits your need, click on **Create button**, and the database will launch for usage.

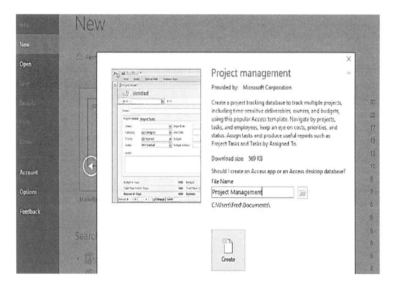

The Navigation Pane

The Navigation Pane is the center point of the database that displays or shows objects, tables, queries, forms, reports, and macros that allows you to filter, and search through these objects to locate the one you are looking for in the database. The Navigation Panel is a rectangular object located at the left session of the database.

The Navigation Panel by default appears as a rectangular box with a tile on top, a yellow down pointing button, and Shutter Bar Open/Close Button

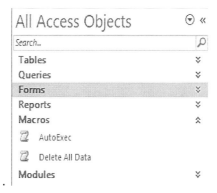

The Navigation Pane has the following features:

- Easily show and hide the Access navigation panel view
- Select a type of category including the custom-built categories
- Sorting items and groups
- Searching for objects create and modify custom group
- Copy and paste Access objects
- Hide and unhide objects.

Managing The Navigation Pane

Here are some of the operations that can be performed in the Navigation Pane

Show Or Hide The Navigation Pane

To show or hide the Navigation Pane in Access, follow the steps below:

- To show the Navigation Pane, click on the shutter bar or press F11

- To hide the Navigation Pane, click on the shutter bar or press F11

To Select A Predefined Category

When a new database is created, the category that is displayed by default is **Tables** and **Related Views** and the group is **All Tables**. But you change the categories to whichever one you desire.

- To display the **Navigate to category**, click on the title bar of the Navigation Pane
- Then select the predefined category

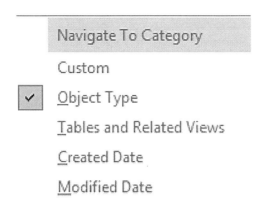

Filter By Group

While working on your database, you may want to display a particular set of database objects, to help your focus. By default, under the Filter by group are Tables, Queries, Forms, and Reports

- To display the **Filter by Group** menu, click on the title bar of the Navigation Pane
- Then select a group

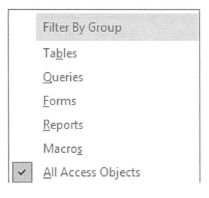

Sort Objects

By default, the objects in the Navigation Pane are sorted by object type in ascending alphabetical order. However, you can change the sorting order of the objects by following the steps below

- Right-click on the top of the Navigation Pane
- Select **Sort by** and then click on any of the sorting options

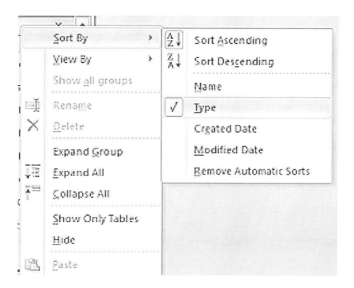

Finding Objects In Database

You can search for any object in the database using the Navigation Pane. Access allows you to search for objects in the categories and groups that are currently displayed or shown in the Navigation Pane.

To find any object in the Navigation Pane

- Click on the **Search box** in the **Navigation Pane**
- Input the name of the characters you need to find and it will be displayed for you to see.

- In case you need to carry out another search, click on the **Clear Search String**, or press **BACKSPACE** to delete the previous character, and then enter another character you wish to search for

Changing How Objects Are Displayed

Objects in the database can be displayed any way you want in the Navigation Pane. To indicate how objects should be displayed, follow the steps below

- Right-click on the top of the Navigation Pane
- Select **View By** and then click on any of the viewing options (**Details, Icon, or List**)

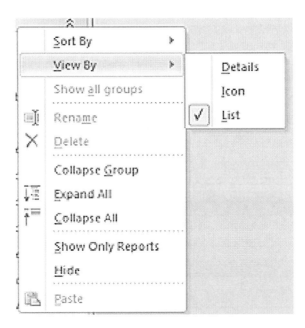

How To Hide And Unhide Objects And Groups

Rather than deleting an object or group from the database, you can hide the object or group and later unhide it.

To hide an object or group

- To hide an object, right-click on the object and then select the **Hide in this Group**

497

- To hide an entire group, right clock on the group, and then select **Hide**

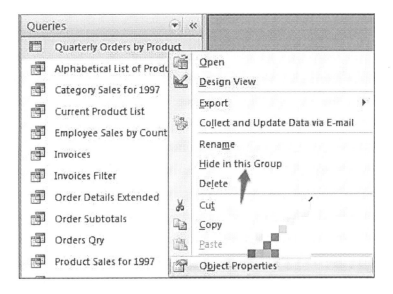

To unhide or display hidden objects or groups

To do this

- Right-click on the **Navigation Pane** and then click on the **Navigation Options**
- In the **Navigation Options** dialog box, click on the **Show Hidden Objects** check box. Then click on **OK**

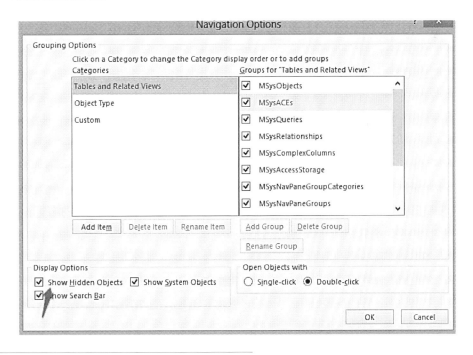

Customizing The Navigation Pane

The Navigation Pane is one of the most important features of Access. To organize the objects in the database the way you want, Then you will need to customize your Navigation Pane. Customizing your Navigation Pane involves creating custom categories and groups, renaming and deleting categories and groups, and lots more. In few minutes, we will be learning how to customize with the Navigation Pane.

Creating A Custom Category

To create a custom category in the database, follow the steps below

- Right-click on the top of the Navigation Pane and then select **Navigation Options**
- In the **Navigation Options** dialog box under the **Categories list,** click on **Add Item**
- Input the name of the new category and then press **Enter**

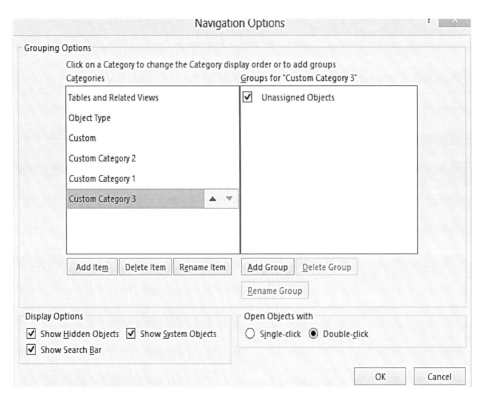

Renaming A Custom Category

To rename a custom category to whatever name you want, follow the steps below:

- Right-click on the top of the Navigation Pane and then select **Navigation Options**
- In the **Navigation Option** dialog box under the **Categories list,** select the item you want to rename, and then click on **Rename Item**

- Input the new name of the category and then press **Enter**

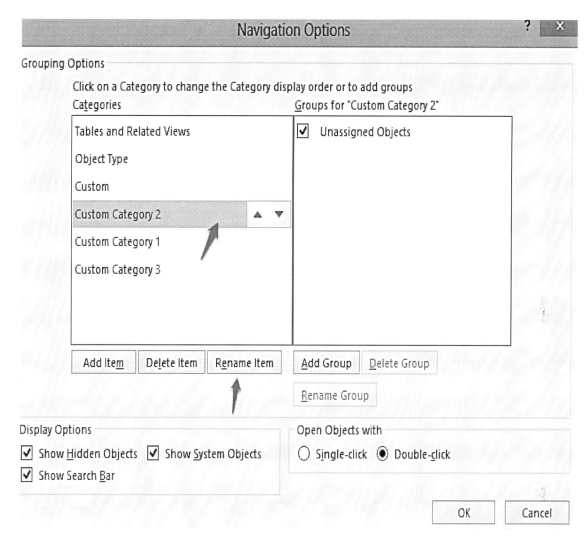

Deleting A Custom Category

- Right-click on the top of the Navigation Pane and then select **Navigation Options**
- In the **Navigation Option** dialog box under the **Categories list,** select the item you want to delete, and then click on **Delete Item**
- A dialog box will pop up, asking if you want to delete the item from the Categories, then click on **Ok** for the item to be permanently deleted

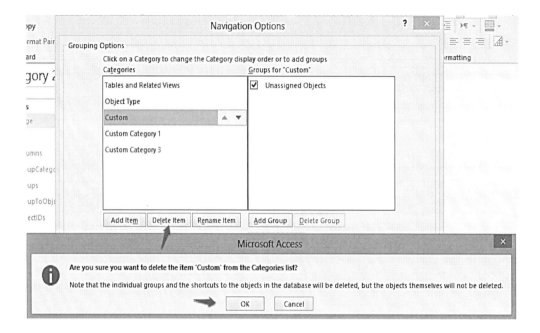

Creating A Custom Group

- Right-click on the top of the Navigation Pane and then select **Navigation Options**
- In the **Navigation Option** dialog box under the **Categories list,** select the category you wish to add the new group
- Click on **Add group** under **Groups**
- Then input the name of the new group and then press **Enter**

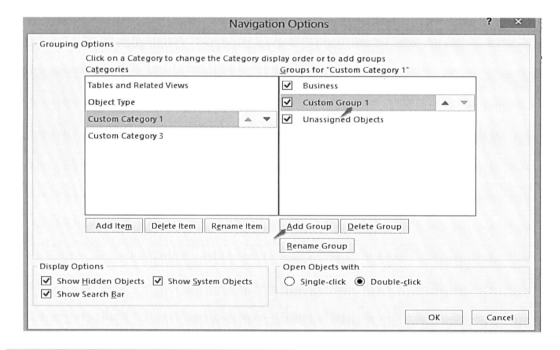

Renaming A Custom Group

- Right-click on the top of the Navigation Pane and then select **Navigation Options**
- In the **Navigation Option** dialog box under **Group for**, select the group you wish to rename
- Click on **Rename Group**, input the new name of the group, and then press **Enter**

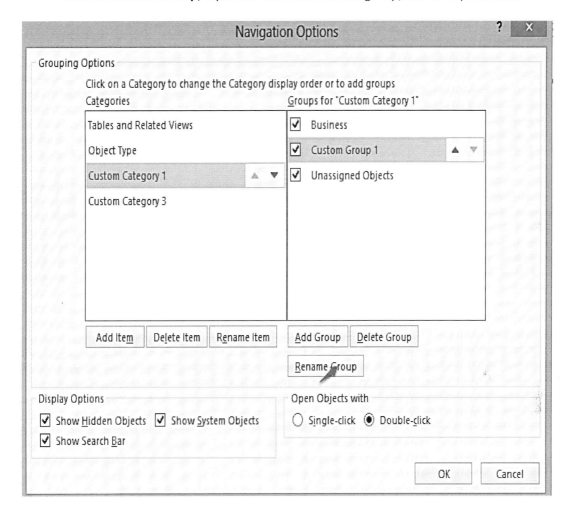

Deleting A Custom Group

- Right-click on the top of the Navigation Pane and then select **Navigation Options**
- In the **Navigation Option** dialog box under **Group for**, select the group you wish to delete
- Click on **Delete Group**, and a dialog box will be displayed asking if you want to delete the group. Click on **Ok** and the group will be deleted

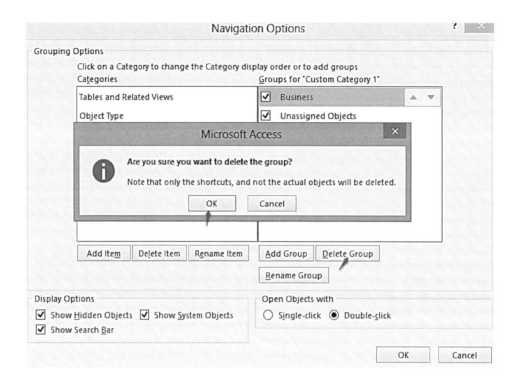

Creating A Custom Group From A Database Object

- **Right-click on the object you wish to put in a new group**
- Move to **Add to group,** and then click **New Group** (A new group will appear in the Navigation Pane)
- Then input the name of the new group and press **Enter**

Designing A Database

The main purpose of using access is to be able to create a database and not just anyhow database, but one that provides up-to-date and accurate information. Creating a good design is paramount to actualizing your goals while working with the database. With a good database, you can enter information accurately and you can also get the right information from it when needed.

Here in this section, the guidelines to be considered when designing a database. Here, you will get to learn how to decide what information you need, how to decide the information into the appropriate tables and columns, etc.

To design the database, the following guidelines must be put into consideration

Deciding What Information You Need

The first thing to put into consideration is the kind of information you want in the database. This could be customers' information or the record of the purchase orders. With this being put into consideration, you will be able to get every piece of the information required by the organization's record.

To find the kind of information required by an organization, you can start by examining or checking the previous forms used to record the information used by the organization.

While deciding on what information you need, ensure that each piece of information is broken into smallest useful parts.

Separating Information into Different Database Tables

After deciding on what information you need to put in the database, the next thing to do is to think of how to separate the information into database tables.

Deciding on the numbers of database tables, you need and how to separate data across the different tables is one of the most difficult parts of designing.

Below are the rules to apply when separating into different tables

- Limit a table to one subject only each table in the database should contain information about a single subject.
- Avoid duplicate information i.e., do not keep the same information more than once in a database or duplicate information across different.

Choosing Fields for Database Tables

For all the tables that the information is separated into, there must be at least one field. The table is the subject while the fields are the details or facts about the subject.

To create a field that will be added to the database table, follow the guidelines below:

- Ensure to break down information into smaller logical parts. For instance, create separate fields for the first and last name. With this, you can easily sort out the tables using the fields.
- Ensure to give clear and detailed descriptive names to the fields, to know exactly what they are meant for, and also avoid errors

- While separating information into different database tables, do not include calculated data. This implies that you should not store the result of calculations in tables. Rather, let the Access execute the calculation you which to see the results.
- As you begin to input the information into the table, include the field for each piece of information. Do not wait until the information is entered into the table before adding the fields, because this can be so stressful and tiring.

Deciding On A Primary Key Field For Each Database Table

For each table in the database, there must be a primary key field.

The primary key field is the unique identification number which can be ID number, serial number, etc. The primary key field prevents you from inputting or entering duplicate data into two different records by displaying a dialog box, warning you not to insert duplicate data. In the query, the primary key field is also important, this allows access to search for information and obstructs you from obtaining the information twice.

Mapping The Relationship Between Tables

When the database contains more than one table, there is a need to map how the table relates to one another. With this in place, the information from different tables is linked or brought together in a meaningful way.

The relationships are usually formed between the primary key field in the table and the corresponding field, which is known as the foreign key in another table.

CHAPTER FOUR

BUILDING YOUR DATABASE TABLES

The database tables are the foundation or building blocks of a database. These are what contain or hold the raw data that are later manipulated

Here in this chapter, you will be learning how to create database tables from scratch or the template.

Creating A Database Table

One of the most important things to learn while using the database is to learn how to create tables, and how the data are entered. In few minutes, we will be learning how to create a table using the three methods

- Creating a database table from scratch
- Creating a database table from a template

Creating a database table by importing database table from another database

Creating A Database Table from The Scratch

To create a database table from the scratch, follow the steps:

- Open **Access,** go to the **Create tab,** and click on the **Table Design button**

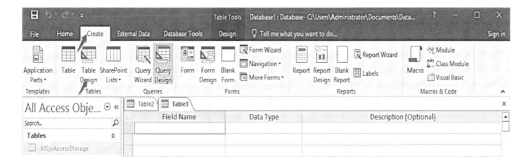

- Click on the **Save button** on the **Quick Access toolbar**
- In the **Save As** dialog box, input the descriptive name of the table and then click on **OK**

Creating A Database Table from A Template

Access provides four templates' types to create a table which are

- **Contacts:** This is used for storing contact addresses and phone numbers
- **Issues:** For prioritizing issues
- **Tasks:** This is used for tracking projects and their status
- **User:** For storing email addresses

Just like using a template for tables. Access also offers ready-made queries, forms reports.

To create a table using a template, follow the procedures below

- Open **Access,** go to the **Create tab,** and click on the Application Parts button
- In the drop-down list, under Quick Start; you can select **Contacts, Issues, Tasks, or Users**
- In the **Create Relationship** dialog box, click on **There is no relationship** and then click on **Create.**

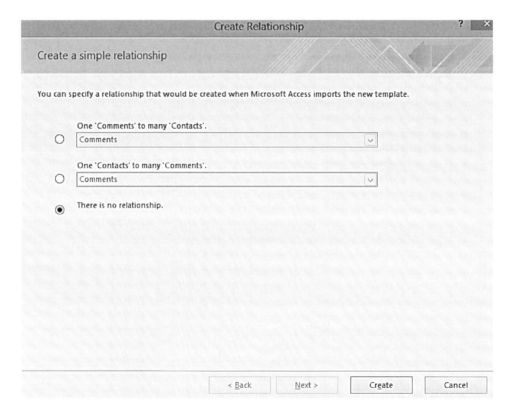

- On the Navigation pane, right-click on the name of the table you created and then select **Design View** (The Design view displays the names of the fields in the tables)

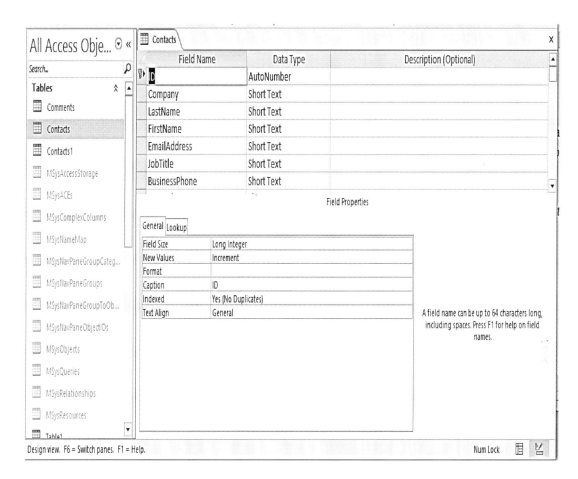

NOTE: Before you create a database table using a template, ensure that all objects that are opened are closed

Importing A Table From Another Database

Assuming the records, you need have been inputted in another table and you need to input them in a new table, follow the steps below

- Open **Access,** go to the **External tab,** and click on **Access**
- In the **Get External Data – Access Database dialog** box, click on Browse.
- In the File Open dialog box, select the Access database with the table, and then click on Open
- Select the first option button (Import, Tables, Queries, Forms Reports, Macros, and Modules) and click Ok
- Select the database table you want from **the Tables tab** and then click **on Ok**

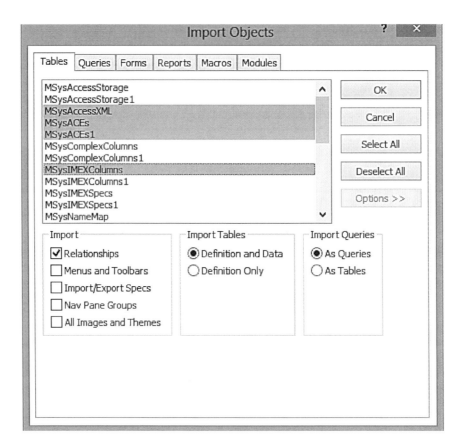

Opening And Viewing Tables

To open a table, you will need to go to the Navigation pane and to view the names of the database table you created, you will need to select the Table group.

While opening and viewing tables in the database, there are two keywords you need to know

- **Datasheet View**: This is used for entering and checking data in a table
- **Design View**: This is used for creating fields and giving details about their parameters

To open and view the tables in the database, there are several ways to go about it. Below, are the ways to open and view tables

Opening Table In Design View

To open the table in the design view

- Select the table in the **Navigation Pane** and right-click on it
- In the shortcut menu, select **Design view,** and the objects in the table open as a tab on the work surface

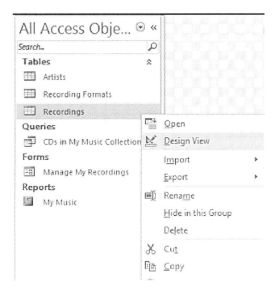

Opening Table In Datasheet View

To open the table in the Datasheet View

- Select the table in the **Navigation Pane** and right-click on it
- In the shortcut menu, select **Open** and the objects in the table opens as a tab on the work surface

Switching Between Views With The View Buttons

To switch between the view buttons

- Select the table and move to the **Home tab**
- Select **View Button** and choose **Database Sheet View** or **Design View**

Switching Between Views On The Status bar

To switch between views on the Status bar

- Select the table and move to the Status bar to either choose **Datasheet View** or **Design View**

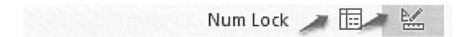

Switching Between Views By Right Clicking

To switch between views by right-clicking, all you need to do is right-click on the table's tab and either choose **Datasheet View** or **Design View**

Entering And Altering Table Fields

After you must have a created a table, the next thing to do is to input the fields. You can also allow Access to create the tables for you and manipulate the fields to your liking.

Here in this section, we will be taking a tour on how to insert fields into the database table

Creating A Field

Let's quickly learn how to create a field from the scratch or using the ready-made fields available in Access.

Creating A Field On Your Own

To create a field on your own, follow the steps below

- Open the table you need to enter a new field
- Switch the view to **Design View**
- Insert a new row to the field; to do this, right-click on the new field and then click on **Insert Row**
- Input a name in the **Field Name** column
- Click on the **Data Type** column to choose the data type from the drop-down list
- You can enter a description in the **Description column** when necessary

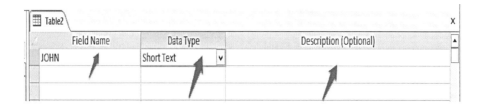

Using The Ready-Made Fields

To create a field using the ready-made field, follow the steps below

- Switch to **Datasheet View** and select the field you intend for your new field to look like
- On the **Field tab,** click on **More Field b**utton, and select the name of the field you want on the drop-down menu
- Go to the **Add & Delete in the Field button** to select the data type
- After all these have been done, switch back to **Design View** to check the field properties

The Data Types

In chapter 1 of this book, I discussed explicitly on the data types in a tabular form, in case you have forgotten what we discussed on data type, you can go back to read all over again

Designating The Primary Key Field

In the course of creating a table, the primary key field is one of the most essential parts of the table that cannot be overemphasized, and Access won't permit the closing of the table unless a primary key field is created. As earlier said about the primary key field, the primary key field does not allow duplicate and null data into the table.

To make a field in the database to be a primary key field, follow the steps below

- Go to the **Design View**, select the field you want to make the primary key
- Right-click on the field and then click on the **Primary key button** (Here, a small symbol appears on the row selector to indicate which of the fields is a primary key field.

Table2	
Field Name	Data Type
JASON	Short Text
JOHN	Short Text

To remove a primary key from a database table, click on the row selector and then select the Primary key all over again. With this being done, the primary key will be removed from the field.

Moving, Renaming, And Deleting Fields

In case you need to move, rename and delete fields in the database table, and you are wondering how to go about it, switch over to the Design View and follow the steps below

Moving A Field

To move a field, do the following

- Click in the Field's row and release the mouse button
- Click and drag the selector to the desired location

Renaming A Field

To rename a field in a table, follow the steps below

- Click in the Field Name box where the old name is
- Erase the old name and type the new name

Deleting A Field

To delete a field in a table, follow the steps below

- Click in the Field Name
- Navigate to the **(Table Tools) Design tab**
- Then click on the **Delete Rows button**

Understanding Field Properties

Every table in the Access database comprises fields and each field has its properties. The properties of the fields are what describes the characteristics and behavior of the data that are found in the field.

The properties of the field determine the type of data that can be entered into the fields.

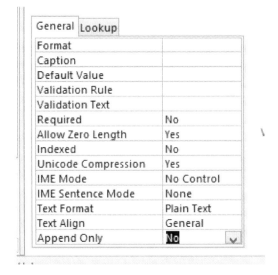

Below are the field properties:

- **Field Size**: The field size contains the text field and the number field. The text field allows for a maximum number of 255 characters that can be inputted in the field, and the default setting is 50. The Number field, just like the Text field allows for maximum numbers of 255 characters, and the numbers are stored as Byte, Integer, Long Integer, Single, Double, or Replication ID.
- **Format:** The Format property is what allows you to set the way or manner in which an Access will display or print out the data located in the table. The Format property can be displayed in form of text, numbers, dates, and times
- **Decimal Places:** This indicates the number of decimal places Access can display. The default specification is Auto, which allows Access to display two decimal places for the Currency, Fixed, Standard, and Percentage format and the number of decimal places. You can also set the number of the decimal places, ranging from 0 to 15.
- **Input Mask:** The Input Mask creates a pattern on how data must be entered into a particular field. For instance, when you enter a phone number into a field, the Input Mask by default, allows the number to take the phone number format. The Input Mask supports the following data types; Text, Number, Date and Time, and Currency.
- **Caption:** This property allows the user to give a fully descriptive detail about a field in which the Access displays in form of labels and report headings. When the caption is not entered, Access uses the field name as the caption. The field property supports all data types.
- **Default Value:** This property allows the user to specify or indicate a default value for a field that Access automatically uses for a new row if there is no value given. If a default value is not set, the field will be null when the user refuses to input a value. The Default Value supports Text, Memo, Numbers, Date and Time, Currency, and Yes/No data types
- **Validation Rule**: This is the field property that allows you to supply an expression that limits or controls the values that can be inputted in the field. To set a validation rule, enter an expression in the Validation Rule text box. The following are the instances of the validation rules
    - >100 means that the value entered must greater than 100
    - <=200 means that the value entered must be less than or equal to zero
    - >#1/2/2020# means that the date to be entered must be greater than February 1, 2020 (Each time a date is used in an expression, the date must be enclosed in a number sign (#)
- **Validation Text:** This is the message that is displayed by Access when the data entered does not follow the validation rule. You can also create your message. If the default message is not suiting for you. To do this, enter the custom message in the Validation Text dialog box.
- **Required**: This is one of the important properties of the field that helps to specify whether or not a value must be entered in the field. By default, the property is set to No. If No is selected, no entry is required to be entered, but if Yes is selected, an entry must be made otherwise, a message box will be displayed telling you to ensure that an entry is made.

- **Allow Zero Length:** This property allows the user to input zero-length strings i.e. a string containing no characters. The Zero-length text strings come in handy when you want to enter data in a field, and some data do not exist. For instance, you want to enter a person's data but he does not have an email address, and there is a space for it. All you need to do is to enter the zero-length string. To enter the zero-length text string in the cell, type **".**
- **Indexed:** This is the property that indicates if the user wants to index the field to speed up searches and sorts operations performed on the field. By default, this is set to No
- **Unicode Expression:** This is a property setting of the field that compresses data stored in Unicode when set to Yes, thus saving space in the database file.
- **Smart Tags:** This property allows you to enter a smart tag name and actions in the field, by clicking the three dots next to the Smart Tags box and selecting an option in the Action Tags dialog box.
- **Text Align:** The Text Align property determines how the texts in the column, forms, or reports are to be aligned (Left, Right, Center, or Distribute). When you select General, Access determines how the texts are aligned.
- **Text Format:** This property allows Access to set the text format to either Rich text or Plain text. The Rich text allows to make words bold, italics, underline, and change font sizes and colors. The Plain text makes words plain without formatting. The Text format is only available in the Long Text field.
- **Append Only:** This property allows Access to add data to a Long Text field to collect a history of comments. This property is only available in Long Text fields.
- **Show Date Picker:** This property displays the built-in date picker control to select a date when the field receives focus in a table datasheet or query. This property is only available in the Date/Time fields.
- **IME Mode/IME Sentence Mode:** This property is what is used in Access to convert characters and sentences from the East Asian version of Access.

Creating A Lookup Data-Entry List

The Lookup Data-entry List is one of the most important features in Access that allows one to enter data correctly in the database. With this feature, you can enter the data into the database, without having to type them. This feature saves time and avoids the entering of invalid data into the database.

There are two ways of creating a drop-down list

- Creating the lists by entering the items yourself
- Get the items from another database table

Creating A Drop-Down List On Your Own

You can create a drop-down list on your own with entries you type by following the steps below

- Go to the **Design View** and select the Field that you wish to apply the drop-down lists
- Go to the **Data Type** drop-down list and choose **Lookup Wizard**

- In the **Lookup Wizard dialog**, select the second option **I Will Type in the Value That I want**, and then click on the **Next button**

- In the next dialog box, under **Col1** and then type the item you want to appear in the drop-down list. Then click on the **Next** button

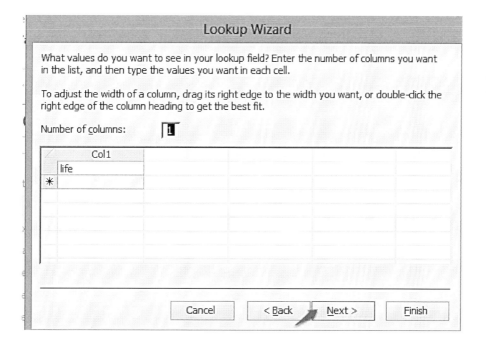

- Input the name for the field and then click on the **Finish** button

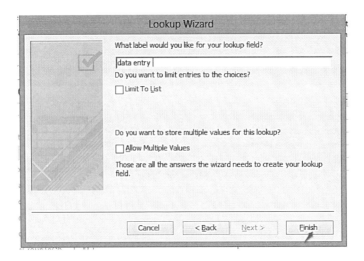

To remove the lookup list from the field;

- Select the field, go to the **lookup tab** in the **Design View** window
- Open the **Display Control** drop-down list, and choose **Text Box**

Getting List Items From A Database Table

You can get items in a drop-down list from another database table, follow the steps

- Go to the **Design View** and select the Field that you wish to apply the drop-down lists
- Go to the **Data Type** drop-down list and choose **Lookup Wizard**
- In the **Lookup Wizard dialog**, select the first option **I Want the Lookup Field to Get the Values from Another Table or Query,** and click **Next**.

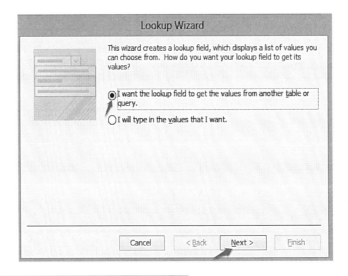

- **In the Lookup Wizard,** select the table with the data you need and click on the **Next button.**

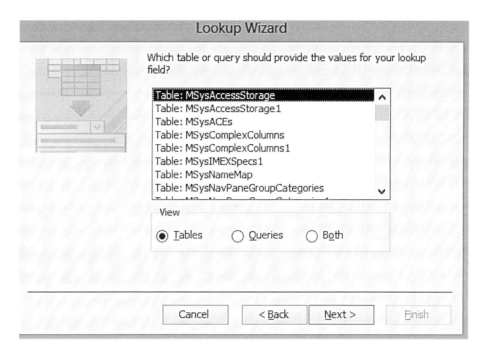

- Select the field where the data for your list is stored, select the > button, and then click on the **Next** button.

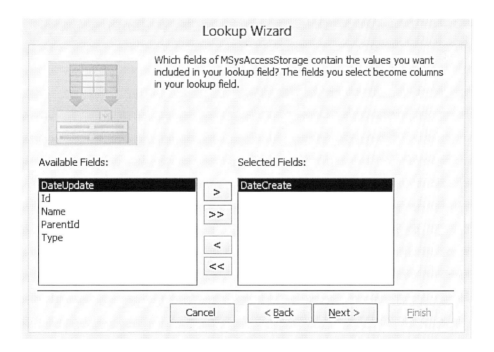

- On the next page, you will be asked, what sort of order do you want for the items in your list box (Ascending or descending order). Then click on **Next.**

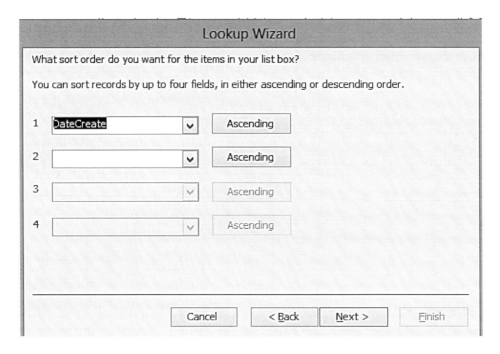

- Here on this page, you will be asked, how wide you like the columns in your lookup field; just place the cursor in between the line, until it becomes a cross sign, adjust the width of the column and then click on **Next.**

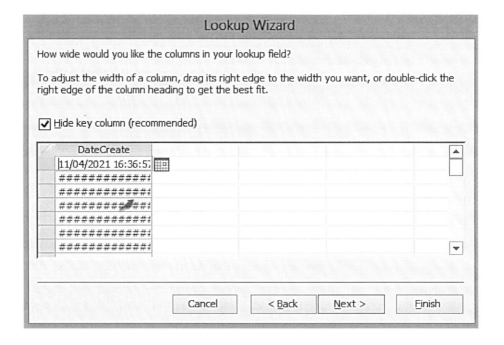

- Input the name for the field and then click on the **Finish** button.

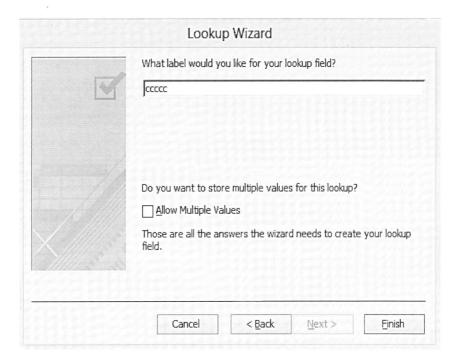

Indexing For Faster Sorts, Searches, And Queries

Indexing is a process in Access of keeping information about data in one or more fields. With indexing, Access does not have to go through the long process of searching through every record in the database table to sort data, search for data, or even run a query, rather Access checks through its data where it is stored.

Indexing data in the fields helps the Access to speed up queries and sorts especially in a large database table. In a nutshell, indexing helps Access to improve the speed of its data retrieval process.

By default, the field you select as the primary key field is indexed. If you do queries and searches very well, it is recommended to add other fields to the primary key field for indexing.

Below are some important notes about indexes:

- Since indexes speed up searching and sorting, it is recommended to index the fields that are used frequently to search and sort.
- Avoid indexing too many fields in a table. The more fields you index, the slower the searches and sort will be.
- Index supports all data types except for memo, OLE, and hyperlinks fields.
- By default, the primary key fields are indexed.
- Indexing helps prevent duplicate and invalid entries in your table.

The Indexed Property Settings

The Indexed property has three functions which are highlighted below

No: This does not allow the field to be indexed and even deleting existing indexes.

Yes (Duplicate OK): This allows the field to be indexed and allow duplicate values to be entered in the field

Yes (No Duplicate): This allows the field to be indexed but does not allow duplicate values to be entered. This works like the primary key fields.

Indexing One Field In A Table

To index a field, follow the steps below

- Switch to the **Design View**, select the field you wish to index
- Go to the **General tab** of the field property, open the **Indexed** drop-down list and choose any of the options available

Indexing Bases On More Than One Field.

To index more than one field. Follow the steps below

- Switch to the **Design View**, go to the **Table Tools (Design tab)** and click on the Indexes button where the Index windows appear
- In the Index Name column, in the first blank row, type a name for the index
- In the Field Name column, open the drop-down list and select the first field you want for the multi-field index
- In the next row, leave the **Index Name** column blank and then enter the second field for the index in the **Field Name** column until you have selected the fields to be indexed

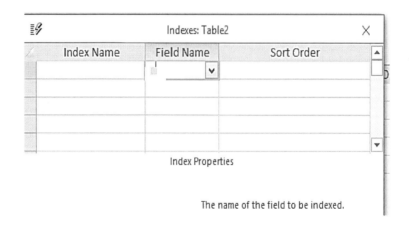

- In the **Sort Order column,** you can either choose **Descending** or **Ascending** order
- Then click on the **Close button**

Deleting An Index

To delete an index in a field

- Switch to the **Design View**, select the field you wish to delete the index
- Go to the **Table Tools (Design tab)** and click **Index**
- In the **Index** window, select the rows that contain the index you wish to delete and then press **DELETE**

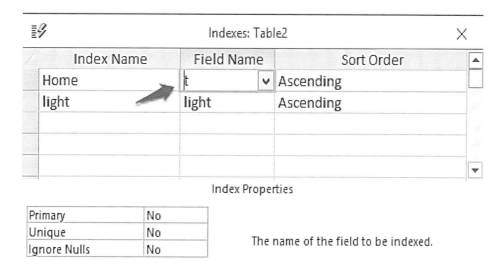

- Then close the **Index** window

Viewing And Editing Index

To view or edit indexes is the same way as following the steps involved in deleting an index. The difference here is that; you are not deleting but viewing or making changes to the indexes

To view and edit the index

- Switch to the **Design View**, select the field you wish to view, and edit the index.
- Go to the **Table Tools (Design tab)** and click **Index**
- In the **Index** window, view and edit the indexes to meet your needs
- Then close the **Indexes** window

CHAPTER FIVE

TIPS AND TRICKS ON ACCESS

In this chapter of this book, you will be learning some of the tips and tricks that will help you to get the best of Access, and at the same time utilize it for the desired goals. Below are some of the tips and tricks in Access

Every Table Should Have A Primary Key

Ensure that every table in Access has a primary key. This helps the database to locate specific records easily and faster. Also, it helps the data to be indexed by default.

Keep Your Access Database Fields As Small As Possible

While building the tables, ensure that the text fields are in the right format size. By default, the setup text for Access is Short Text which holds 255 characters. To adjust the file size, go to the **Field size** settings on the **General tab** in the **Design view**

Don't Over Index

In as much as indexing is very important, do not index the fields you don't need. Indexing all the fields may cause it to load slowly when it wants to update, delete or add records to the database

Choose The Optimal Data Types

While entering data into the fields, you should choose the best data types for your fields. Selecting the optimal data type helps to reduce the disk space used to store data, and the time it involves for Access to retrieve, manipulate, and write data.

Validating Your Access Data

Validating the data in your tables is one of the ways to prevent bad data from being entered into your table. The amazing thing about this is that you can set the validation rule to what suits the purpose of your table without compromising.

Use Simple And Direct Names In Access

Before creating a table or database, ensure to have simple and direct names to tag your database file, fields, and tables. This helps to remember what your database is all about even if you have not opened it for a long period. Also, another can quickly relate with information on the database, even without you being there

Shortcut Keys And Controls

The following are shortcut keys and their functions used in Access 365

Frequently Used Shortcuts Keys

Shortcut keys	Functions
Alt or F10	To select the active tab of the ribbons and activate keyTips
Alt + H	To open the Home tab
Alt + Q	To open the Tell me box on the ribbon
Shift + F10	To show the shortcut menu for the selected item
F6	To move the focus to a different pane of the window
Ctrl + O	To open an existing database
F11	To show or hide Navigation Pane
F4	To show or hide a property sheet
F2	To switch between Edit mode and Navigation mode in the Datasheet or Design View
F5	To switch from Design view to Form view
Shift + Tab	To move to the next or previous field in the Datasheet view
Alt + F5 (type the record number in the record number box, and then press Enter)	Navigate to a specific record in the Datasheet view
Ctrl + P	To open the Print dialog box from Print
S	To open the Page Setup dialog box
Z	To zoom in or out on s part of the page
Ctrl + F	Open the Find tab in the Find and Replace dialog box in the Datasheet view or Form view
Ctrl + Plus Sign	To add a new record in Datasheet view or Form view
F1	To open the Help window
Alt + F4	Exit Access

CONCLUSION ON ACCESS 365

Amidst the applications available in the Microsoft Office suite, Access is no doubt, one of the most resourceful and a must-learn application for every organization, which desires to have a well-planned and detailed way of gathering and analyzing data that will be of help to the organization.

In the world at large especially in the business world, there is a need to be proficient with the use of Access. With this in place, every organization out there will have the opportunity to gather, managed, and process a large bunk of data, which in no time be of great help to the organization.

Therefore, as you take your time to explore this book, ensure to have Access 365 software installed on your computer with a strong internet connection.

With all that has been said so far, I wish you all the best as you explore this user guide.

See you at the top!

BOOK FIVE

MICROSOFT SHAREPOINT 365

WRITER'S PRESENTATION

Hello dear reader, welcome to SharePoint 365. Today, we are going to talk about everything you need to know to get up and run as either a site owner or a site administrator.

In this book, I'm to provide you with a comprehensive overview of what SharePoint features are all about. SharePoint helps organizations store, retrieve, search, manage, track, archive, and report on various electronic documents and records. Because of the flexibility it offers, it makes an ideal content management system and is one that Pro Serve IT highly recommends.

Well, I don't know whether you are coming up as a beginner with no prior knowledge in this SharePoint training or whether your skills are a little bit more intermediate or advanced. This book is meant to take you from beginner to advanced stage, hence, giving you full knowledge about Microsoft SharePoint 365.

CHAPTER 1

INTRODUCTION TO SHAREPOINT 365

SharePoint is a web-based platform developed by Microsoft and first launched in the year 2001. It provides an enterprise collaboration and content management portal, which enables users to connect and share information across the organization. Since it is a content management portal, it also allows non-technical users to easily create and manage their websites.

SharePoint provides sufficient space to store and share data, information, and documents.

SharePoint is a website-based collaboration system that uses workflow applications, "list" databases, and other web parts and security features to empower business teams to work together. SharePoint also gives the company using the platform the ability to control access to information and automate workflow processes across business units.

The Microsoft Cloud version of SharePoint, SharePoint Online, has many additional integration capabilities with other cloud applications. It is paired in functionality with many of the other offerings Microsoft packages with an Office 365 or Microsoft 365 license.

SharePoint enables increased productivity and visibility for information workers across all verticals, in businesses large and small. The features of SharePoint are centered around an intranet-based cross-collaboration experience that enables secure sharing, content management, and workflow collaboration features among many others

What to expect from this book

- How information can be shared
- Understanding the SharePoint content
- Accessing content from anywhere on any device
- SharePoint site Navigation and Creation of the site collection in SharePoint
- Creation of calendar, wiki page library, survey
- Overview of SharePoint structure

SharePoint Approach

This book is divided into different parts or sections representing general SharePoint skill sets. Each chapter and topics are groups and divided into their related skills source function or performance.

SharePoint is a web-based platform in which we can build and create websites, it provides tools and services to help us manage and share information in effective ways and perhaps most importantly it helps to provide a collaborative online environment, where everybody can go to add and retrieve information.

So let us get started with the work on SharePoint.

CHAPTER 2

GET STARTED WITH SHAREPOINT 365

Lesson objectives:

- SharePoint 365 basic
- Navigate the SharePoint interface
- Access SharePoint
- Creation of site collection in SharePoint

SharePoint basic

What is SharePoint is all about? The majority find SharePoint very difficult to understand, it's a question that I hear most of the time, not just from computer users but also from savvy IT professionals. With over 24 different Microsoft Server products, it is understandable that not everyone knows what SharePoint is all about. SharePoint can be expressed in many and different ways, it has so many definitions.

What is SharePoint 365?

SharePoint is a website-based collaboration system that uses workflow applications, "list" databases, and other web parts and security features to empower business teams to work together. SharePoint also gives the company using the platform the ability to control access to information and automate workflow processes across business units.

SharePoint aims at improving team productivity by allowing staff to collaborate efficiently and providing them with the information they require.

OR

SharePoint is a cloud-based platform that provides an organization with the ability to manage their content, track processes, collaborate with other employees, manage business activities, and publish information. It is one of the collaborations tools for Office 365 and easily integrates into those Office 365 tools you are already using (Exchange Online, Skype for Business, OneDrive, etc.).

It can also be defined as a place where you go to work with others and also stay informed. What does that mean and what can you do with SharePoint? With SharePoint, you can set up an intranet site for your team, basically a web page and you can customize it without needing to know any coding. You can set up a document repository, so you can also upload a file to your SharePoint site, and then everyone on your team will have access to that file.

You can share calendars; you can create lists and everyone can contribute to that list and you can also publish news posts to keep your entire team informed.

Types of SharePoint

There are three main types and versions of SharePoint and they are:

- SharePoint Foundation
- SharePoint Server
- Office 365

1. **SharePoint Foundation**

    SharePoint Foundation is used to build a standard web-based collaboration platform, secure management, and communication solution within the organization. These are the following features of SharePoint Foundation:

    - It is used to reduce implementation and deployment resources.
    - It provides effective document and task collaboration.
    - It offers features to secure your organization's important business data.
    - It provides Power Shell support.
    - It provides basic search operations.

2. **SharePoint Server**

    SharePoint Server offers the additional features of the SharePoint Foundation. It provides a more advanced collection of features that you can use to utilize your organization's solutions. Some additional features of SharePoint Server are given below:

    - SharePoint allows you to create and publish web content without writing any complex code.
    - SharePoint uses Enterprise Services that allows you to quickly and easily build custom solutions.
    - SharePoint Server allows the more advanced features that can be implemented with the environment.
    - SharePoint Server allows you to connect with external data sources and display business data via Web portals, SharePoint lists, or user profiles.
    - It provides enterprise search.

3. **Office 365**

    Office 365 is a cloud-based multiplatform designed to help your business grow. It provides various apps like Word, Excel, PowerPoint, and more. The key features of Office 365 are:

    - Office 365 allows you to communicate and collaborate with co-workers, anywhere, anytime.
    - It provides better security.
    - It provides a simple way of creating workflows for projects.
    - Using office 365, you can insert links to stored files instead of sending entire files to co-workers, business partners, and friends.

Sharing of Information

Information sharing describes the exchange of data between various organizations, people, and technologies. There are several types of information sharing:

- Information shared by individuals (such as a video shared on Facebook or YouTube)
- Information shared by organizations (such as the RSS feed of an online weather report)
- Information shared between firmware/software (such as the IP addresses of available network nodes or the availability of disk space).

Check Out How Information is Shared

As it's stated earlier above, information can be shared in diverse ways depending on its usefulness on what to share and where to share. The image below shows that to share and where the information can be shared.

Site Collection in SharePoint

SharePoint Site is a website that contains different SharePoint Web Parts like Document Library, Calendar, Task List, etc. SharePoint sites can have 1 or more pages to display content to the user.

SharePoint Site Collection, just as the name implies, is a collection of SharePoint Sites. Each site collection contains a single top-level site and sub-sites below it. SharePoint sites are the most versatile options for collecting a large number of files or directories. It works as a hub where team members can access content, organize content, or collaborate on content.

Types of SharePoint site

In SharePoint, there are two different types of SharePoint sites and they are known as:

- Team site
- Communication site

Create a site
Choose the type of site you'd like to create.

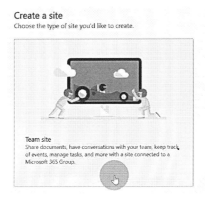

Team site
Share documents, have conversations with your team, keep track of events, manage tasks, and more with a site connected to a Microsoft 365 Group.

Communication site
Publish dynamic, beautiful content to people in your organization to keep them informed and engaged on topics, events, or projects.

- **Team site**
  A SharePoint team site is designed to connect you and your company to store and collaborate on files or creating and managing lists of information. A team site includes web pages, a default document library for files, lists for data management, and web parts.
- **Communication site**
  SharePoint communication site is designed to create a site collection that is mobile-friendly and adapted to display information dynamically. It means communication sites can be viewed from anywhere on any device. It provides a great place to share news, reports, status, and other information.

We will walk through what some of those differences are. Alright, before we can start the practical aspect, let us get started by having the understanding from the beginning of SharePoint 365.

Have Understanding of SharePoint Task

- The majority of people don't understand how SharePoint works and how it can be a useful Microsoft tool in their environment and organization. Using SharePoint, you can manage your colleagues and your documents, social activities, data, and information. Also;
- It allows groups to set up a centralized, password-protected space for document sharing.
- Documents can be stored, downloaded, and edited, then uploaded for continued sharing.
- SharePoint offers such a wide array of features that it is very challenging for any one person to be an expert across all the workloads.

Officially, Microsoft represents SharePoint 2019 as a "business collaboration platform for the enterprise and web. SharePoint is a platform from Microsoft that allows businesses to meet their diverse needs in the following domains:

- **Collaboration:** Use SharePoint's collaboration sites for activities, such as managing projects or coordinating a request for proposal.

- **Social networking:** If you work in a large company, you can use SharePoint as a social network for the Enterprise experience to help you track coworkers and locate people in expertise networks.
- **Information portals and internal websites:** With SharePoint's web content management features, you can create useful self-service internal portals and intranets.
- **Enterprise content management:** SharePoint offers excellent document and record-management capabilities, including extensive support for metadata and customized search experiences.
- **Business intelligence:** SharePoint is an ideal platform for providing entrée into your organization's business analysis assets. You can use insightful dashboards that allow users to get the big picture at a glance and then drill down to get more detail.

The SharePoint is divided into three separate areas such as:

1. **Collaboration**
   The term collaboration contains a very strong theme for SharePoint. It means bringing people together through different types of collaboration, such as enterprise content management, web content management, social computing, discoverability of people and their skills.
   - In SharePoint 2019, collaboration is managed through Apps.
   - Developers can extend, customize, or build their Apps for SharePoint as well manage collaboration on SharePoint.

2. **Interoperability**
   SharePoint is also about bringing this collaboration together through interoperability such as:
   - Office and web-based document integration.
   - Capability to build and deploy secure and custom solutions that integrate line-of-business data with SharePoint and Office.
   - Integrating with wider web technologies, or deploying applications to the cloud.

3. **Platform**
   SharePoint is also a platform that supports not only interoperability and collaboration but also extensibility, through a rich object model, a solid set of developer tools, and a growing developer community.
- One of the key paradigm shifts is the notion of the cloud in SharePoint.
- The cloud introduces new App models such as:

   o New ways of developing, deploying, and hosting SharePoint applications.
   o New forms of authentication through OAuth.

o   New ways of data interoperability using OData and REST.

Navigate the SharePoint Interface

A SharePoint site provides a structured environment for building specific websites. SharePoint 365 and above version provides the functionality to communicate, share documents, and data with your team members using a single SharePoint site.

SharePoint provides various types of SharePoint site with its different unique structure. These sites include team sites, project sites, community sites, and blog sites. Every site's home page brings the site component together and provides capabilities for navigating them.

Navigate the Team site Home Page in SharePoint

A home page is the main page of every SharePoint website. It provides a structure that links the site components together. SharePoint team site contains two main types of navigation:

- Quick launch navigation and
- Site collection navigation

Quick launch navigation is also known as the current navigation. In SharePoint 365, quick launch navigation is located at the left corner of the home page. It displays a list of all links that are used in your SharePoint site. Using SharePoint, you can add, remove, or change the order of links. Quick launch navigation contains the following links:

a.   **Home:** It points to the home page of the current site. It brings you to the Home Page where you most likely started.
b.   **Conversation:** In SharePoint, the conversation is possible with yammer. It allows you to create a general team with all employees as members of the main channel.
c.   **Documents:** The document link opens the built-in document library. It shows the main document library that you can also see inside your Home Page (+ new document). You can directly upload a new document there.
d.   **Notebook:** The notebook link allows you to open the online version of OneNote, which is Microsoft's note-taking tool and a part of the Microsoft office package.
e.   **Pages:** Using the SharePoint page link, you can add the web part, images, and links to the site to make the site more attractive and can be easily managed by the users.
f.   **Site contents:** Site contents open the Site content page, which contains all libraries, lists, surveys, and other apps on your site. It also provides links to the subsites. This is like your Site Map where you can see all the content you already have on your site. Even if you haven't created anything in it yet, every list or library you will create next will appear there automatically.
g.   **Recent:** If you haven't done anything yet, you're not supposed to see any link there. However, when you'll create a new List or Library, the link to this new app will appear under "Recent" in the menu and you'll be able to access it quickly.
h.   **Recycle bin:** Recycle bin allows you to restore the items that are deleted from the site.

Site collection navigation

The site collection is also known as Top Navigation. It contains links to the subsites that are present on your site. It is located above the page title.
Site collection navigation mainly includes the following two links.

a. Current Site Title

The current site title is the link to the home page of the current site. It is displayed on the first tab at the left end of the top link bar.

b. Links to sub-sites

Site collection navigation contains tabs with links to the subsites of the current site. For example, the site collection of team sites displays the team site's link such as the home page and other links related to your websites.

Finally, you can edit the links available in your quick launch menu and add or remove any link very easily.

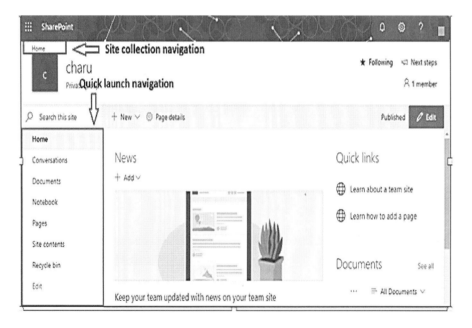

Accessing the SharePoint 365 from the Beginning

First off let us look at how we can get SharePoint. You don't need to install any software to use SharePoint on your computer because SharePoint 2019 provides a web-based platform that can be easily accessed using the web browser.

So instead of trouble your mind, just connect through your web browser and sign to your work or school account **office.com**. The Office 365 account designated for business use or the school Microsoft 365 account will give you access to SharePoint. Make sure you are set up with the right user privileges.

The following steps below will help you to access SharePoint (Enterprise level SharePoint and Office 365) on your computer:

- Go to **Internet Explorer**, **Chrome,** or any other browser and copy-paste the following link given below or you can simply click on the following link: *https://www.microsoft.com/en-in/microsoft-365/business/office-365-enterprise-e3-business-software?rtc=1&activetab=pivot%3aoverviewtab*
- Down below click on the **Free trial** after the following window will appear or display.

- Once you click on **Free trial**, the following page will appear.
  - Then click the box to **Enter your email address**

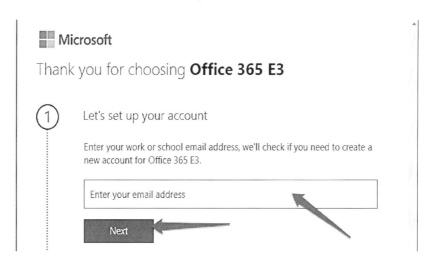

- Click on the **Next** after your email address is being entered.
- Now, verify your **email address**, if it is correct before proceeding.

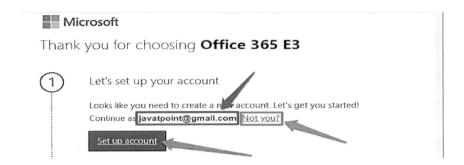

- If it is correct, then click on the **Setup account**. But if it is otherwise, click on the **Not you**? And re-enter your **email address.**
- After clicking on the **Setup account**, it will appear on another page, fill in the required information display on that page.

- Click on the **Next** after the required information is filled in.
- To prove that you are not a robot, select either **text me** or **call me** to receive the **OTP**.

- Enter your phone contact in the box.
- Then click on the **Send verification code.**
- Enter the generated **OTP** sent to you and click on **Next.**
- Now, **create your business identity** by providing the **name for your domain,** followed by **onmicrosoft.com**

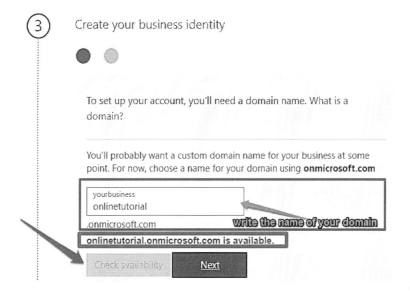

- Click on **Check availability,** If the name is available, then you will see the message "**your domain name onmicrosoft.com is available**"
- Click on the **Next.**

If it is Otherwise, an error message will appear.
- Create your **user ID** and **password** to sign in to your account, then:
  - Click to fill in the required instructions.

- Click on the **Sign up** after you are done with the instruction above.

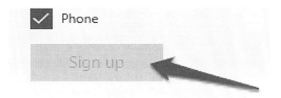

- The screenshot below shows your Sign-in page and your user ID.

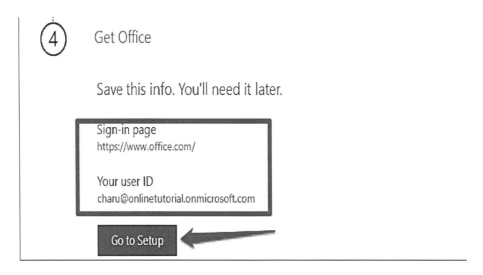

- Click on the **Go to Setup**.
- Open the Internet Explorer, Chrome, or any other browser.
- Type the link *https://www.office.com* to enter in **Sign-in page.**
- Enter your **password** then click on the **Sign in.**

- Once you **Sign in** successfully, you will be present at the Office 365 Home page.

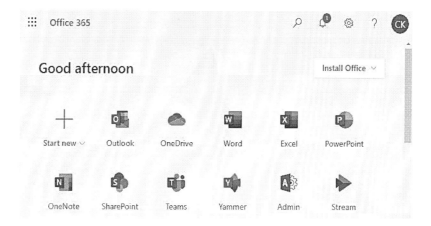

Creation of Site Collection in SharePoint

As is being mentioned above, SharePoint sites are the most versatile options for collecting a large number of files or directories. It works as a hub where team members can access content, organize content, or collaborate on content.

- Team site
- Communication site

Difference between Team site and Communication site

Team site	Communication site
It is designed for a group of people to collaborate and work together.	It is designed for a few people to create
It contains many editors (likely all members).	It contains few editors.
It has a selected audience	It has a wide audience.
It automatically creates an Office 365 group, mailbox, Planner task area, and OneNote.	It just contains a communication site.
Example: HR colleagues - everybody who works in HR. Project team collaborating to complete and manage the task.	**Example:** Travel group publishing rules about corporate travel. Assets for the sales team for a service or product.

Team site creation

- First login to your Microsoft office account to get access to SharePoint.

- From your left-hand side click on **SharePoint,** it will lead you to the SharePoint page where you can start any of your activities.

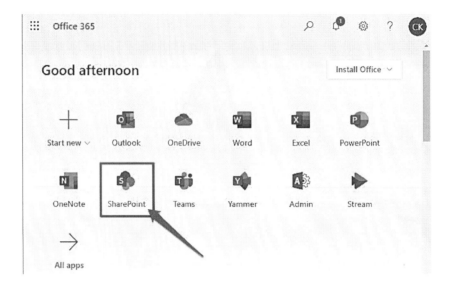

You can also find the SharePoint by clicking the **icon box** apps at the top corner

- Then click on **SharePoint,** which will lead you to the SharePoint page where you can start any of your activities.

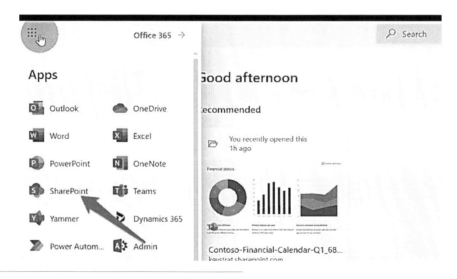

- At the top from the angle, click on **Create site.** It will display two types of sites.

- Then click on **Team site.** A site creation wizard will appear on the right side of the screen where required instruction needs to be filled.

Create a site

Choose the type of site you'd like to create.

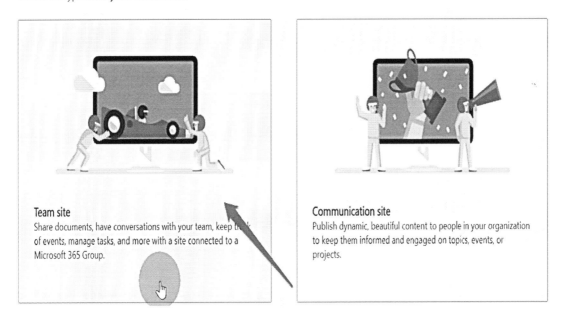

Team site
Share documents, have conversations with your team, keep track of events, manage tasks, and more with a site connected to a Microsoft 365 Group.

Communication site
Publish dynamic, beautiful content to people in your organization to keep them informed and engaged on topics, events, or projects.

- Under **Site name** click inside the boxes to fill in the required instruction:

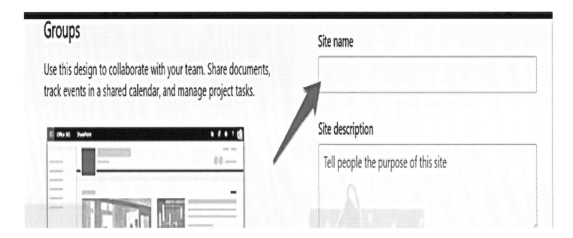

- o Type the name of the team site you want to use, for example, "**Honesty is the key team**"
- o Click on the next box and type the group email address you want to use.
- o Fill the remaining box according to their instructions.
- o Under **Privacy settings**, click inside the box to select or choose a different option.
- o Then click on "**Public- anyone in the organization can access this site**".

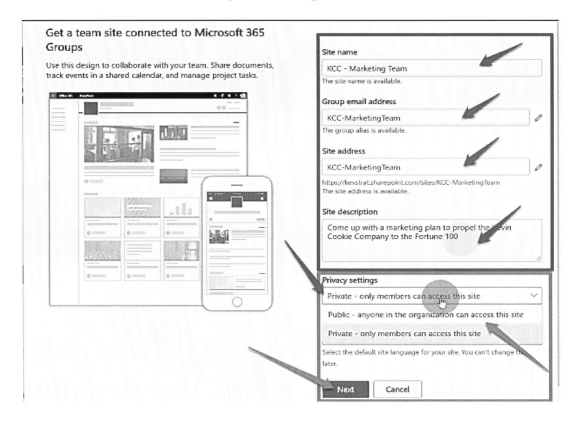

- • When you are done with everything, click on **Next.** It will take you to another page.

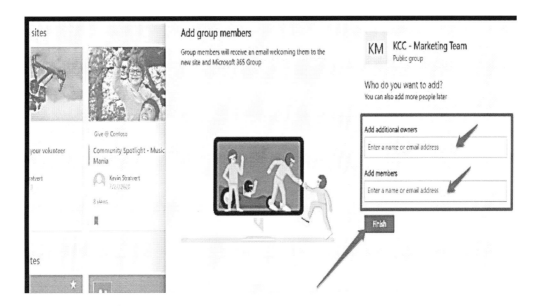

- Click here to **add additional owners** if probably you want to add another person.
- Click on **Finish** when you are done. It will display your **home page Team site** creation. Now, you can see the layout of your site. You are now set to start your work team.

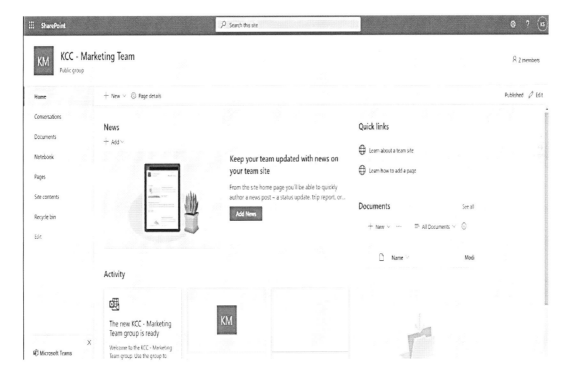

Add Component in Quick Launch Navigation

To add the component in quick launch, the following given steps should be observed:

1. Go to the Home page of your current site.

- Click on the **+New**, a drop-down menu opens.

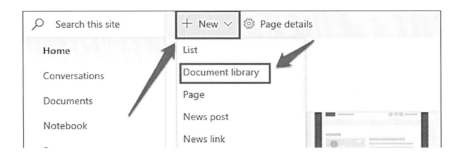

- Click or select components according to your requirement e.g., **document library**.

2. Now, on the right side of the screen, a window opens.

- Click inside the box and enter the name of the component that you want to create e.g., **University.**

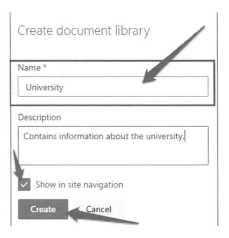

- Then click on the **Show in site navigation**.
- Next click on the **Create**. The screenshot image below shows that a new component named "**University**" is added in the Quick Launch navigation.

Removal of the component from the Quick launch navigation

In Quick launch navigation, you can also delete the component that is no longer used in the SharePoint site.

At the bottom of the Quick launch navigation:

- Click on the **Edit**.

- Click on the ellipses **(...)** associated with the link that you want to remove.

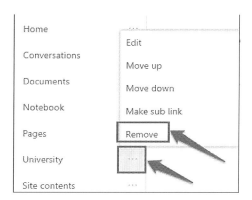

- Click on the **Remove**.
- Click on the **Save**.

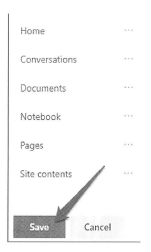

Now, the image below shows that component "University" is removed from the Quick launch navigation.

Home

Conversations

Documents

Notebook

Pages

Site contents

Recycle Bin

Edit

Create Site collection navigation

To create site collection navigation, the following steps should be observed:

- Go to the home page of your site
  - Click on the **Settings** at the top of the screen.

- Click or Select **Site information** from the drop-down menu.

Settings

SharePoint

Add a page

Add an app

Site contents

Site information

Site permissions

Site usage

Change the look

Site designs

Keep yo
your te

- From the Edit site information window page, scroll down the window.
  - Click on the **View all site setting**.

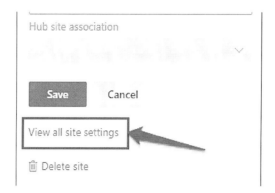

- At the top of the Site Settings page, click on the **EDIT LINKS**.

- Then click on the **+ link**.

- Enter the **name of the link (**e.g. **about)** that you want to display and the **Address** of the site.

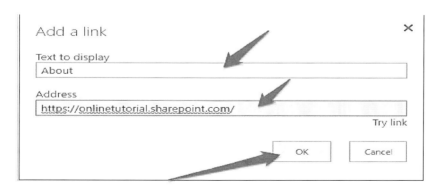

- Next click on **OK**.
- Click on **Save.**

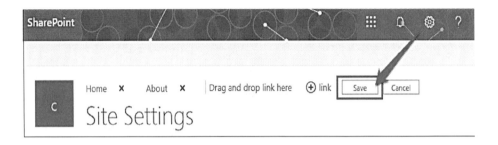

Now, you can see that a new link **"About"** is created in the site collection navigation bar.

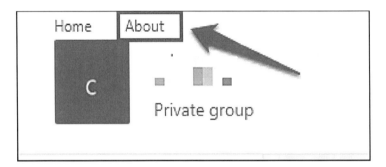

SharePoint Components

In this SharePoint component, to successfully operate within a SharePoint environment, it's important to note all the different tools and components that plug into the overarching hierarchy that is SharePoint. There is a different SharePoint component, so we will be talking about a few of those components here in this book.

These are the following component we are going to start and observe below:

- **Site:** A site is a Web site that SharePoint manages in ways that are compatible with its content-management features. SharePoint sites can contain many user-facing SharePoint features such as Document Libraries, Lists, Wikis, Blogs, and Discussion Boards.
- **Webpage:** The web page displays stored content the site threads all of these web pages together into a single platform and single box. So, web pages are the user-facing portion of a SharePoint site. Whenever you visit a SharePoint site the very first thing you see is a page.
- **Lists:** A list of data, made available on a SharePoint site, which stores data in columns and rows. Almost all of the user-facing SharePoint features stem from Lists. For example, a Calendar is a specialized list under the covers.

- **Library:** A mechanism for storing content within SharePoint. A Document Library provides content management (which includes document check-in and check-out, versioning, security, and workflow).
- **Web part:** This allows us to take data either within a SharePoint site or outside of s SharePoint site and display it on a SharePoint web page. So, it's important to note that the web part can pull both within and outside of a SharePoint site.
- **App part:** The app part can only pull data from within a SharePoint app. A SharePoint app refers to either lists, libraries, or another third-party plugging that can be integrated with a SharePoint site.

Getting Familiar with SharePoint Building Blocks

To obtain a perspective on SharePoint, it is important to understand how SharePoint is put together. As mentioned previously, SharePoint is a web-based platform. Many technologies are required to make the platform available. Each technology builds on the one below it. In this manner, it is common to call the whole ball of wax a technology stack.

The SharePoint technology stack begins with server computers running the Microsoft Windows Server operating system. On top of Windows Server are some additional technologies required by SharePoint. In particular, SharePoint needs a database and a web server Microsoft SQL Server and Microsoft Internet Information Services (IIS), respectively. In addition, SharePoint also needs Active Directory, which manages the servers in the domain.

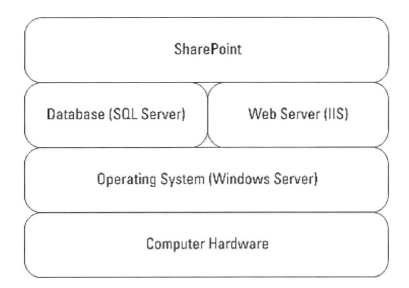

Have a Peek at a SharePoint Site

The primary purpose of SharePoint is to provide websites. When you create a website, you select which type of template you want to use to create the site. The dialogue box shows the different templates available.

The templates you have available depend on where you are creating your SharePoint site and what features have been activated for your SharePoint environment. For example, in SharePoint Online, a tab for Duet Enterprise and Publishing only shows up if the feature is activated.

The template tells SharePoint which features and functionality should be included on the site. Keep in mind that you can always add more features and add and remove features as you decide to make your site more specific for your needs.

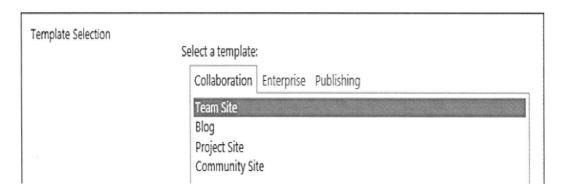

One of the most common SharePoint site templates is called the Team Site template. The Team Site website template includes features such as a discussion board, a library to store documents, and a calendar. Many books simply talk about the Team Site template and call that SharePoint. As you will learn in this book, the Team Site is very important, but it is just another SharePoint website template. Part 2 explores building a site based on the Team Site template. A SharePoint website was created using the Team Site template. This team site has been customized a bit to show the latest team morale event for Portal Integrators along with some additional navigational items.

CHAPTERS 3

GETTING TO KNOW THE COMMUNICATION SITE

Lesson objective:

- Exploring Communication Sites
- SharePoint Permissions
- SharePoint Templates
- Create Survey in SharePoint

Exploring Communication Sites

After understanding the differences between communication sites and team sites, it's time to explore SharePoint communication sites independently. A SharePoint online communication site is a place to share information such as news, report, statuses, and events in a visually captivating format with a large audience that's part of your organization.

SharePoint communication sites are ideal for internal collaboration during campaigns, news and insights, business highlight, year-end leaders review and new customer wins. The sites are accessible across various devices. Users can consume information using mobile devices available through SharePoint apps.

You can create a beautiful Communication site in seconds using the SharePoint home available in Office 365. Then you can improve your methods of communicating and collaborating with large audiences, integrate your existing collaboration channels into a SharePoint Communication site, and plenty more. Communication sites allow people to create and share periodic updates beyond email.

Steps to Create SharePoint Communication Sites

To begin with communication site creation, you can follow the steps above from the **Team site** or better still follow the steps below:

- Login to your Microsoft office account to get access to SharePoint.
- From your left-hand side click on **SharePoint,** it will lead you to the SharePoint page where you can start any of your activities.

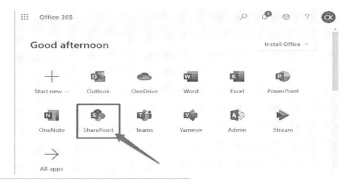

You can also find SharePoint by clicking the **icon box** apps at the top corner.

- Then click on **SharePoint,** which will lead you to the SharePoint page where you can start any of your activities.

- At the top from the angle, click on **Create site.** It will display two types of sites.

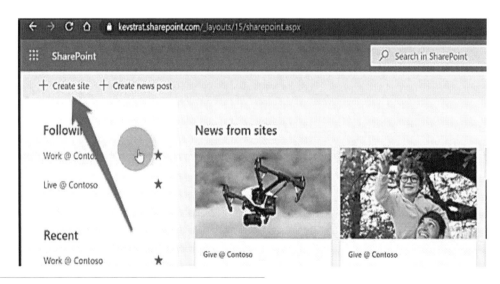

- Then click on the **communication site.** A site creation wizard will appear on the right side of the screen where required instructions need to be filled.

Create a site
Choose the type of site you'd like to create.

Team site
Share documents, have conversations with your team, keep track of events, manage tasks, and more with a site connected to an Office 365 group.

Communication site
Publish dynamic, beautiful content to people in your organization to keep them informed and engaged on topics, events, or projects.

- Under **Site name** click inside the boxes to fill in the required instruction:
    - Type the name of your communication site you want to use, for example, "**Honesty is the key team**".

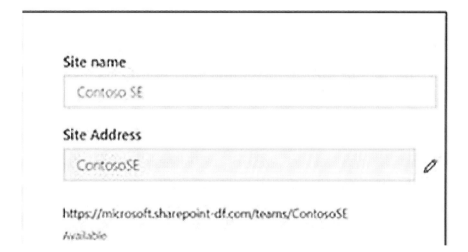

- Click on the next box and type the **site address** you want to use.
- Fill the remaining box according to their instruction.
- Under **site classification settings**, click inside the box to select or choose a different option.
- Then click on **"confidential".**

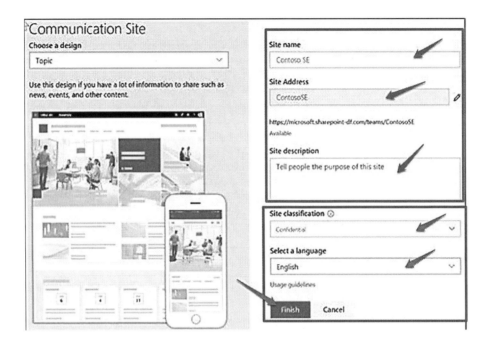

- Click on **Finish** when you are done. It will display your **home page Communication site** creation. Now, you can see the layout of your site. You are now set to start your work team.

What Do Communication Sites Include?

You can create a blank **Communication site** from SharePoint Online and use the following design options, which come with a set of default web parts to design your communication site. You can **add, remove,** or **re-order** web parts whenever you want. Here are three design options:

1. **Topic:** To publish information such as news, events, and announcements.
2. **Showcase:** To display photos or images taken during events, conferences, or customer visits.
3. **Blank:** To create your design.

At the top of the Communication sites, there is a link to add a list, a Document Library, a page, a new post, and a web app to the site, as shown in the image below.

To design your communication site, let us look in detail at the different options available to design sites. When you select an option (Topic, Showcase, or Blank), you see several web parts available for you to design your site.

1. **Topic:** Under Topic, you have the Hero, News, Events, and Highlighted Content web parts.
    - **Hero**: Generate focus and visual interest on your page. A maximum of five items can be added to a Hero web part. You can also add images. The Hero web part is included by default in all Communication sites. Once you click the Hero web part, it will appear pre-populated with images, text, and links, and you can modify them or add your own. This web part has a tiled layout with five tiles and you can modify them from one to five. For example, the image below gives an illustration of what the hero is talking about.

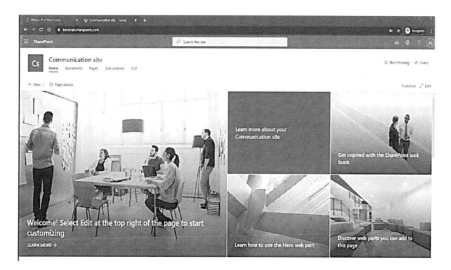

    - **News:** It keeps your team in the loop and continues to engage with them with success stories using the News web part. Using this web part, you can create eye-catching posts like new customer wins, companywide announcements, and project status updates with enriched graphical information.

- **Events:** It displays upcoming events using the Events web part, as shown from the image below.

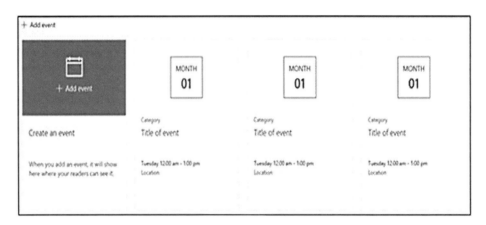

- **Highlighted Content:** This web part displays content from the Document Library or from certain sites to highlight the relevance of content. You can use this feature to highlight your company employee policy document or code of conduct.

2. **Showcase:** The Showcase design option is available in communication sites, and it has its own set of default web parts.
   - **Image Gallery:** To share a variety of images.

3. **Blank:** When you start with a blank Communication site, there is no need to remove web parts that you do not need. You just choose your page layout and add the web parts you want.

Note: The images shown here are **demo images** and do not link to any production SharePoint site. They are simply used to describe the Communication site features.

SharePoint Permissions

Permissions are one of the important elements of any organization and should be managed with care. SharePoint permissions allow you to manage your business websites by assigning the permissions that who can access your website and who cannot.

Default Permission

Default permission allows you to quickly and easily provide a common level of permission for one user or group of users.

The following default shows the list of permissions in SharePoint:

- **Full Control:** By default, it contains all available SharePoint Permissions. These permissions are assigned to the group owner. It can't be deleted and customized.
- **Design:** It allows users to view, update, delete, add, and customize items or pages on the website.

- **Edit:** It enables users to manage lists.
- **Contribute:** It enables users to manage personal views, edit items, and user information. It enables users to manage personal views, edit items, and user information.
- **Read:** It enables users to view pages and list items.
- **Limited Access:** It enables users to access shared resources, specific lists, document libraries, folders, list items, or documents. It cannot be edited or deleted.
- **Approve:** It is used to edit and approve pages, list items, and documents.
- **Manage Hierarchy:** It creates sites, edit pages, list items, documents, and change site permissions for publishing sites only.
- **Restricted Read:** It enables users to view pages and documents for publishing sites only.
- **View Only:** It enables users to view application pages. It is mainly used for the Excel Services Viewers group.

Default Permission level

Default Permission level is associated with the following three standard groups:

Group	Permission Level
Visitor	**Read:** This level includes the following permissions: • Open • View items, pages, versions, and application pages. • Create Alerts • Use Remote Interface • Use Client Integration Features • Browse User information.
Members	**Edit:** This level includes some additional permission that are: • View, add, update, and delete items • Add, update, and delete lists • Browse Directories • Manage Personal Views • Edit Personal User Information • Delete Versions
Owners	**Full Control:** It includes all available SharePoint permissions.

User Permissions

These are the following User Permissions in SharePoint:

i. List Permission
ii. Site Permission
iii. Personal Permissions

List Permission

The table below shows the Permissions that are applied on the lists and libraries:

Manage Lists	It allows users to create and delete lists, add or delete columns in a list, and add or delete views of a list.
Add Items	It helps users to add items to lists, and add files to the document library.
Edit Items	It is used to edit items in lists, edit files in a document library, and edit web part pages in document libraries.
Delete Items	Using delete items users delete items from a list, and files from a document library.
View Items	It is used to view items in lists and files in a document library
Approve items	Approve version of list items or documents.
Open Items	View the source of files with server-side file handlers.
View Versions	It views past versions of list items or files.
Delete Versions	Delete the past versions of list items or files.
Create Alerts	Create alerts to notify users, when any changes are performed on a site
View application page	View forms, views, and application pages.

Site Permission

The following table shows the permissions that are applied on the sites

Permission	Description
Manage Permission	Create and change permission on the website and assign permissions to users.
View Web Analytics Data	It allows users to view reports on the website.
Create Sub-sites	It allows users to easily create subsites such as team sites and communication sites.
Manage Web sites	It provides an ability to perform all administration tasks for the website and also manage content on the website.
Add and customize pages	Add, edit, or delete HTML pages or webpage, and also edit the websites.
Apply Themes and borders	Apply themes and borders on the websites.
Create Groups	Groups can be accessed anywhere within the site collection.
Apply Style Sheet	Apply style sheets such as a file to the website.
View Pages	Users can view pages on the website.
Enumerated Permissions	Enumerated permissions on the websites.
Browse User information	View information about users on the website.
Manage Alerts	Manage alerts for all users on the website.
Use Remote Interface	Use SOAP (Simple Object Access Protocol1), Client Object Model, or SharePoint 2013 interface to access the website.
Open	Enables users to open a website, list, or folder to access items.

Use client integration Features	It allows users to work on documents locally and then upload their changes.
Edit Personal User Information	It enables users to change their user information, such as adding alerts, deleting pictures, edit text, etc.

Personal Permissions

The table below shows the list of permissions that are applied to views and web parts.

Permission	Description
Manage Personal Views	Create, update, and delete personal views of lists.
Add/Delete Personal Web parts	Add or delete personal web parts on a web part page.
Update personal web parts	Update web parts to display personalized information.

Managing Permissions in SharePoint

As a site owner, you can manage permissions that can access your SharePoint site.

These are the following operations that you perform to manage SharePoint permissions:

- View permissions for users and groups associated with a list or library
- Add user to a library or list
- Remove user from a library or list
- Create a new permission group
- Create unique permissions for a library or list

View Permissions for Users and Group Associated with a List or Library

In SharePoint, you can view permissions for users and groups associated with a list or library by using the steps below:

1. Go to the **list** or **library** where you want to view **users** and **groups**.
   - Click on the **Setting icon** at the top right corner of the screen.

   - Select **the Library setting** or **list setting** from the drop-down menu.

2. The library setting window will appear, **select permissions for this document library** from the right-side pane.

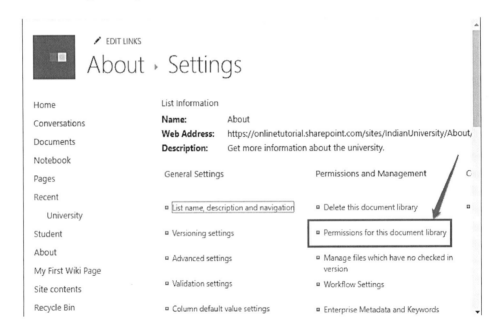

3. Now, SharePoint automatically created three groups that are: **Indian University Members, Indian University Owners, and Indian University Visitors.**

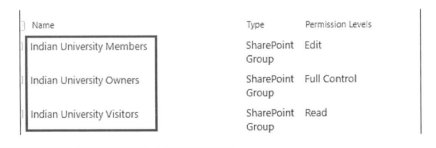

Add user to a Library or List

In SharePoint, you can add and assign user permission to a particular library or list. To add a user to the library or list, follow this step below:

1. From the **list** or **library** where you want to add the user.
   - Click on the **Setting icon** at the top right-side angle of the screen.

   - Select **Library setting** or **list setting** from the drop-down menu.

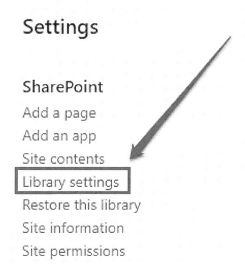

2. A library setting window opens, select **permissions** for this document library or **Permissions** for this list from the right-side pane.
3. Click on the **University Members**.

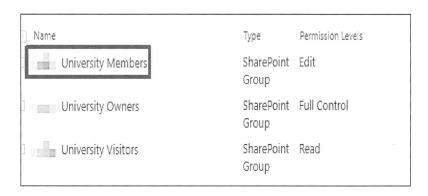

4. The following window will appear, click on the **New**.

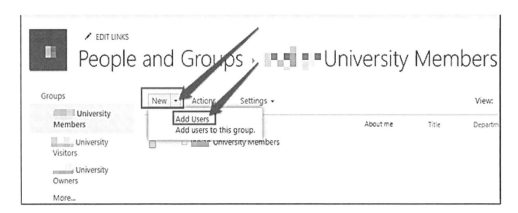

- Select **Add Users** from the drop-down menu.

5. Enter the **name** or **email address** of the person that you want to **add**.

- Fill the next box by adding a message (optional).
- Click on the **Show options**. Once you click on the Show Options, you will see that a check-box with the message "send an email invitation."

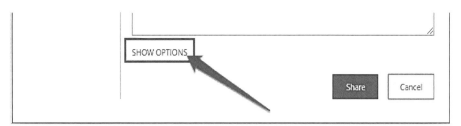

- Tick on the **check-box** and
- Click on the **Share**.

Now, the user is added to the University members group. And the user also receives an email in the outlook.

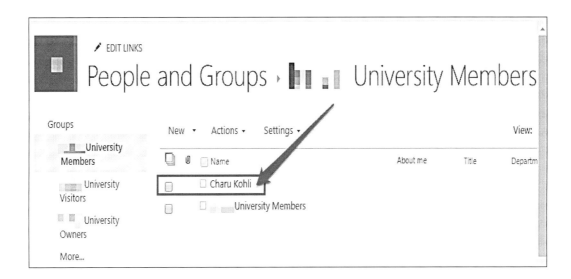

Remove User from a Library or List

To remove a user from a list or library, follow the steps below:

- Click on the **user** that you want to remove.

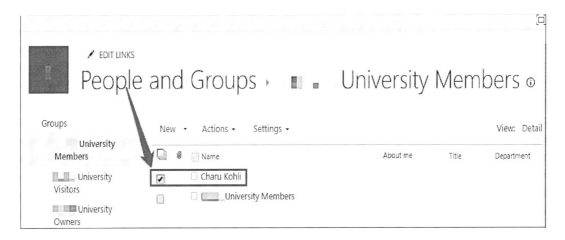

- Click on **Actions.**

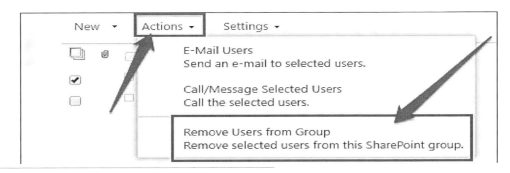

- Select **Remove Users from Group, Remove selected users from this SharePoint group.**
- A window will open with the message asking, **"Do you want to remove these members?"** click on **OK**.

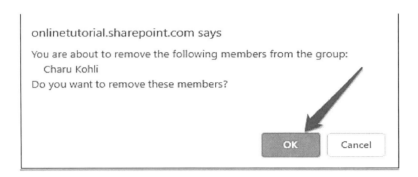

The page below shows that the user is removed from the library.

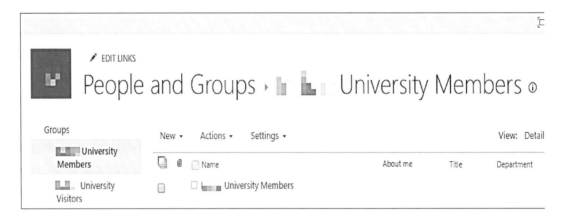

Create a New Permission Group

SharePoint default groups are created automatically when you create a site. But in SharePoint, the administrator can also create a permission group according to his needs.

The following steps below will help you create a new permission group:

1. Click on the **setting icon** at the top right-side angle of the screen.

- Click on **Site permissions**.

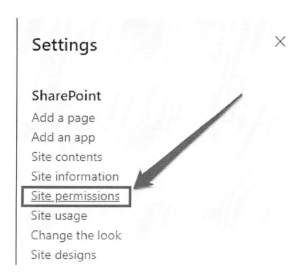

2. Below the screen, click on the **Advanced permissions setting**.

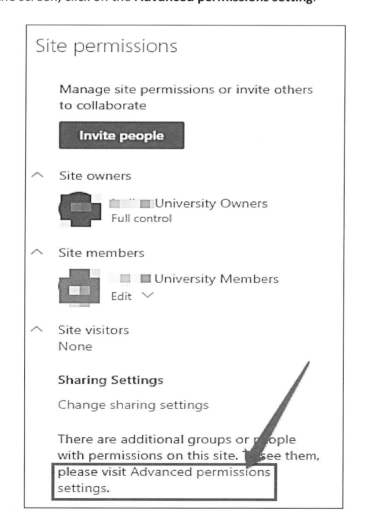

3. Click on **create a group** at the left side angle.

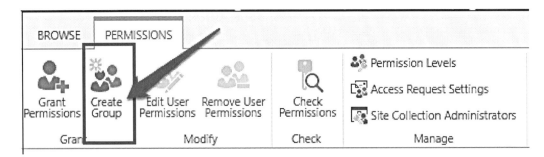

4. Enter the **Name** and **description** for the group e.g., **Faculty**

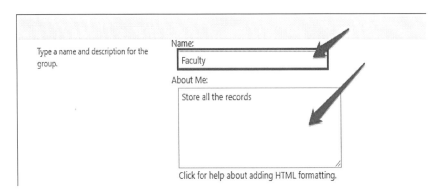

- Click on the remaining option permissions according to your wish e.g., **Owner, Group setting, Membership requests and Give group permission to this site**.

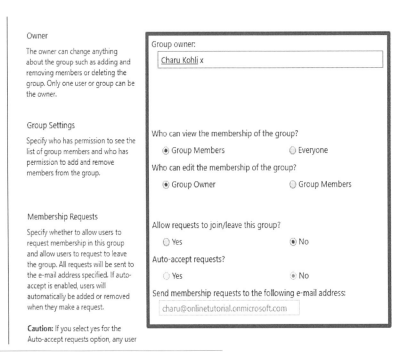

567

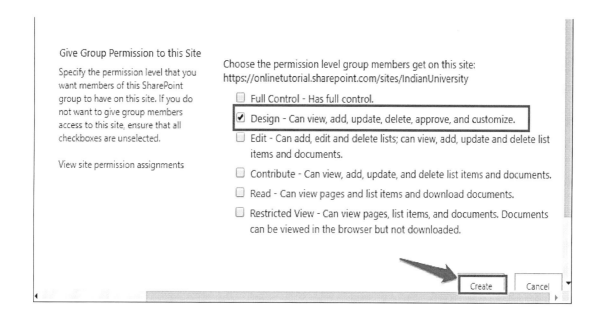

Give Group Permission to this Site

Specify the permission level that you want members of this SharePoint group to have on this site. If you do not want to give group members access to this site, ensure that all checkboxes are unselected.

View site permission assignments

Choose the permission level group members get on this site:
https://onlinetutorial.sharepoint.com/sites/IndianUniversity

☐ Full Control - Has full control.

☑ Design - Can view, add, update, delete, approve, and customize.

☐ Edit - Can add, edit and delete lists; can view, add, update and delete list items and documents.

☐ Contribute - Can view, add, update, and delete list items and documents.

☐ Read - Can view pages and list items and download documents.

☐ Restricted View - Can view pages, list items, and documents. Documents can be viewed in the browser but not downloaded.

Create   Cancel

- Click on the **Create.** The new group **Faculty** created will display on the left side of your group page.

Create Unique Permission for a Library or List

In SharePoint, the administrator or owner of the library can assign unique permission to authorized users. They can also restrict unauthorized users to access the same data. By default, all sites, lists, and libraries in a site inherit permissions from the above site hierarchy. This means a site inherits permission from the root site collection, and a subsite inherits permissions from its parent site.

To assign unique permissions to a library or list, you have to first break permission inheritance and then assign unique permissions.

These are the following steps to create unique permission on a library:

1. From the Home page of your site.
   - Click on the **New**.

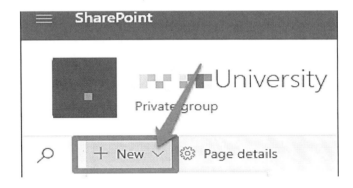

   - Then click on the **document library**.

2. A window opens at the right-hand corner, enter the **library name**
   - Click on the **Create**.
3. Once your library is created, click on the **setting icon**.

   - Select **Library settings**.

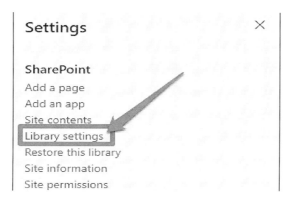

4. Click or select **Permission for this document library.**

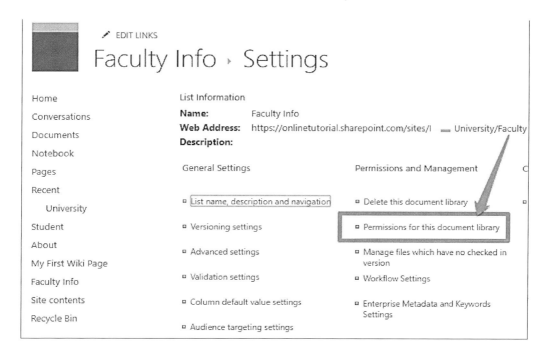

5. On the next page, click on **Stop inheriting Permissions** from the left corner of the ribbon.

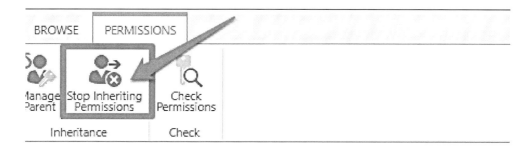

6. A small window will open, click on **OK** to the message.

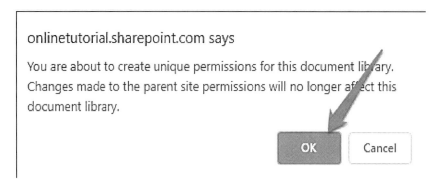

onlinetutorial.sharepoint.com says

You are about to create unique permissions for this document library. Changes made to the parent site permissions will no longer affect this document library.

OK Cancel

7. Click on **Manage parent.**

8. Select the groups in which you want to **assign** or **remove** the permission.

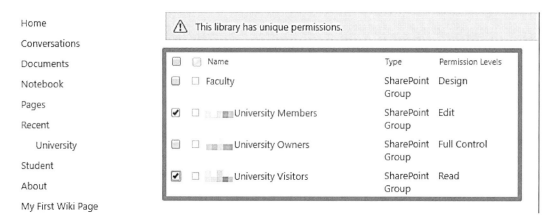

• Click on the **Edit User Permissions**.

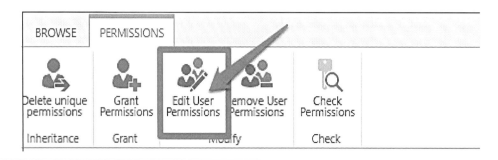

9. The following screenshot shows the Edit Permissions page.
   - Click on the permission that you want to assign for a particular group.

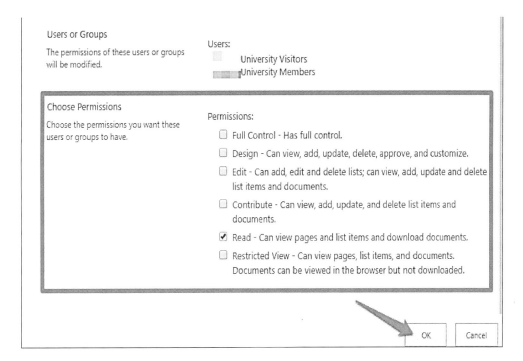

   - Click on the **OK** at the bottom of the page.

The screenshot below shows that permissions have been changed. Now, faculty has permission to **design**, the owner has **full control**, and both members and visitors have permission to **Read**.

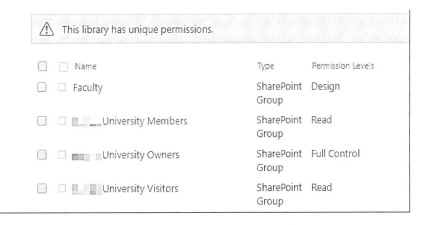

SharePoint Templates

SharePoint allows you to create templates according to your requirements. Creating templates helps the user to easily access the page according to their need.

Page Template

SharePoint page templates allow you to create a great page and make it available for other websites to use as the same page template. Once you create the page template, other users can select it from the template gallery and use it for their website. You can also make changes in the template without affecting the template that you have created earlier.

Creating a Page Template

To create a page template these are the following steps to observe below:

- From the **Home page** of your site, click on the **+ New**.

- Click on the **Page** from the drop-down menu.
- The following Pages window will appear on the screen. Click on **Blank**.

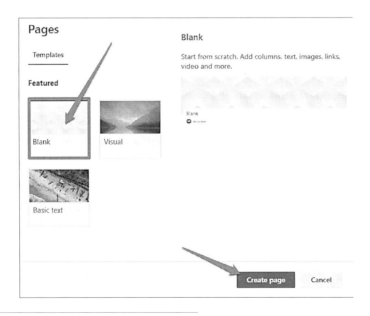

- Click on the **Create page.**

Once your page is created, you can add and remove **web parts, images, contents,** and so on according to your needs and requirement.

- After creating the template, click on **Save as a draft.**

- Select **Save as template** from the drop-down menu.

- Click on the **Save page template** at the top right-side corner of the screen.

View, Edit, and Delete page Template

How to View Template

To find the page template, go to the **home page** of your site.

1. Click on the **+New**, and click on **page**.

The screenshot below shows the recently created template (**Company's template**) is viewed on the **template page**.

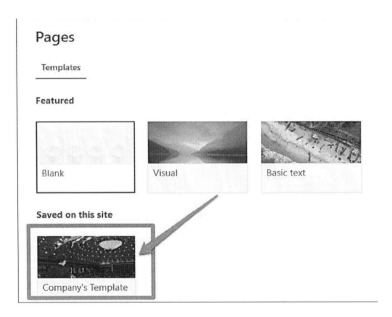

Edit template

To edit the template;

- click on the **template** that you want to **edit**.
- Click on the **edit** at the right top of the screen.

- Click on the area that you want to **edit**. And start your editing template.

If probably you want to delete:

- Click on the **web part** that you want to delete and

- Click on the **delete.**

If probably you want to add the web part:

- Click on the small **circled +** below.

- Select the **web part** that you want to add.
- Once you edit your page, click on the **Republish** at the right top corner of the screen.

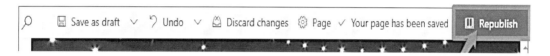

Delete a Template

To delete a template;

- At your left hand below click on **Site content**, then:
    - Click on **Site pages.**
    - Click on the **Templates** folder.

- Right-click on the **template.**
    - Click on **Delete.**

Create Survey in SharePoint

The survey provides an efficient way to collect valuable feedback to the organizations such as user's opinions on a specific product or service.

These are the operations that you can perform on the survey:

- Create a survey
- Add Questions to the survey
- Respond to the survey
- Manage results of a Survey
- Export response to a spreadsheet

Create a survey

To create a survey in SharePoint, the following steps will help you:

- Go to the **Home page** of your site and click on **+New.**

- Click on the **App** from the drop-down menu.

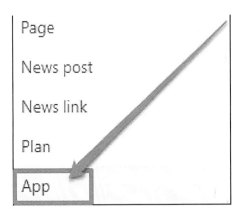

- A list of app windows will appear on the screen. Scroll down the window, and click on the **Survey.**

- A pop-up window will appear on the screen. Click inside the **box** and enter the **name** for the survey.

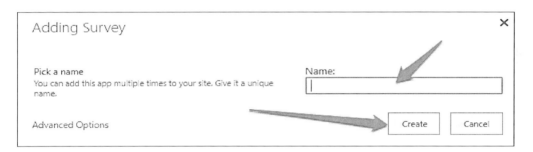

- Click on the **Create.**

The screenshot below shows that the survey list is created.

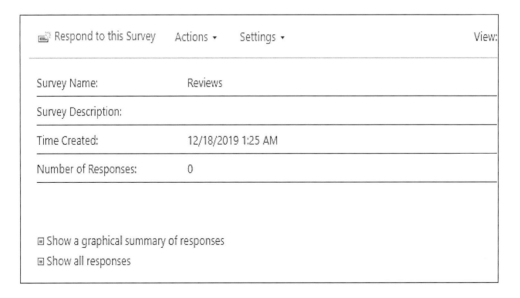

Add Questions on Survey

Once your survey list is created, you can add questions to it. To add questions to the survey;

- Click on the **Settings** at the top.

- Select **Add Questions**.

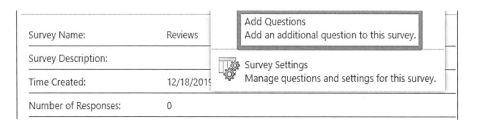

- A New Question window will appear on the screen. Inside the box, enter the **question** that you want to add to the survey.

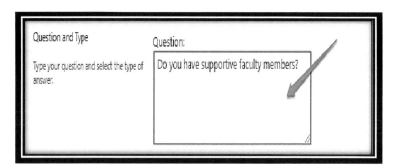

- Click the type of answer for the question.

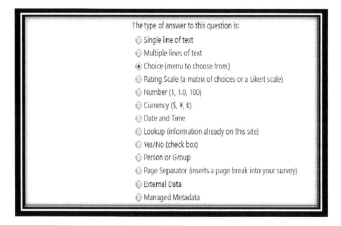

In the **Additional Question Settings** section, specify the settings options according to your wish.

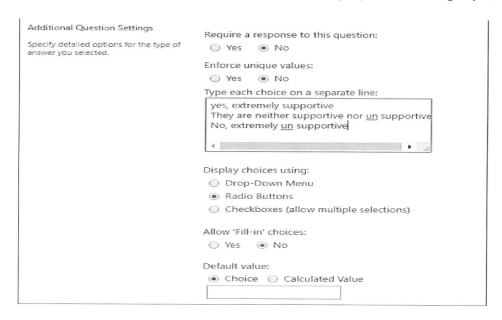

- To add additional questions, scroll down the window:
  - ✓ Click on the Next Question, and then enter the next question.
  - ✓ Repeat the process until you add all the questions to the survey.
  - ✓ After adding the questions to the survey, click on **Finish**.

Add a Link

- To add a link, click on the **edit link** at the top of the screen.
- Click on the **circled + link**. A window will appear.
  - Enter the **Name** of text to display,

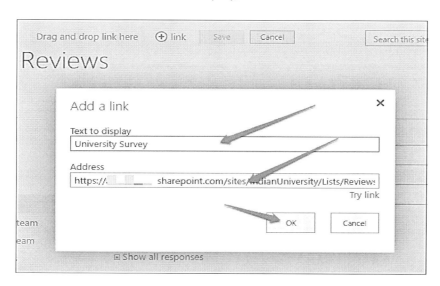

- Copy the page URL
  e.g., *https://sharepoint.com/site/University/List/Review*
- Paste it into the Address, and click on the **Ok**.
- Click on the **Save** at the top of the screen.

Respond to the Survey

To respond to the survey, you must have permission to access the survey. It allows you to respond to the survey only once.

Follow the steps below to respond to the survey:

- Go to your survey page, click on the **Respond to this Survey**.

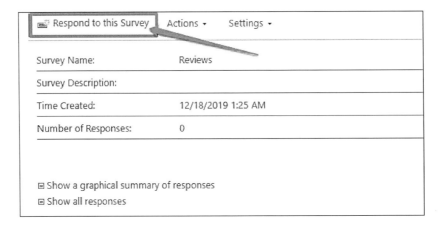

- Answer the questions in the survey and

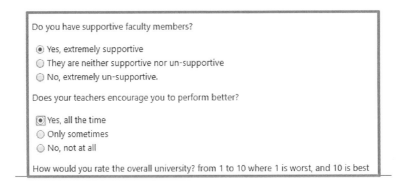

- Click on **Finish**.

Manage Results of a Survey

Once you create the SharePoint survey, you can view and manage the results of surveys.

To View a graphical summary of all responses:

- Click on the **survey name** on Quick Launch.

The following window will appear, click on the **Show a graphical summary of response.**

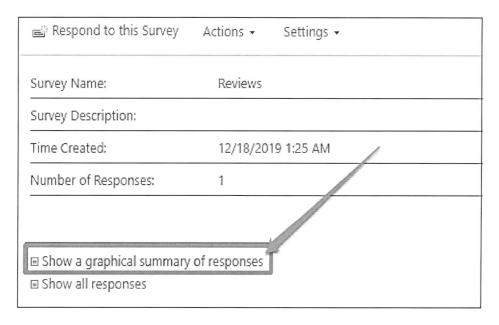

The page below shows the graphical summary of responses.

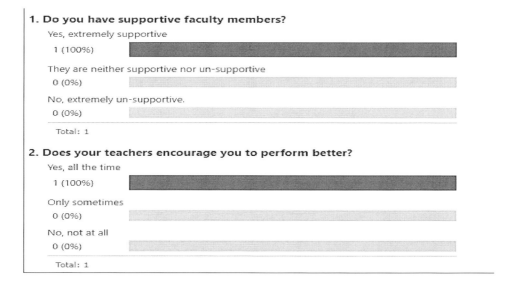

View Survey Response

- Click on the survey name on the Quick Launch. The following window will appear
  - Click on the **Show all responses**.

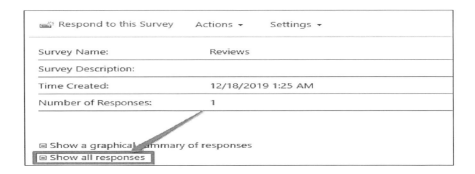

The screenshot below shows the result of all users.

Export Response to a Spreadsheet

To export responses, you must need a spreadsheet that is compatible with Windows SharePoint Services.

To export the response, first, go to the survey page.

- Click on the **Actions** menu.

- Click on **Export to Spreadsheet** from the small menu.

- A window will appear with the message, click on **Ok**.

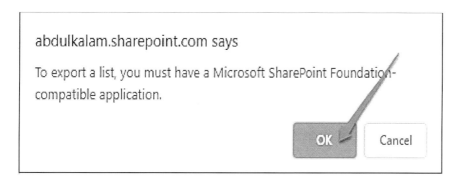

The image below shows that the response is exported in the spreadsheet.

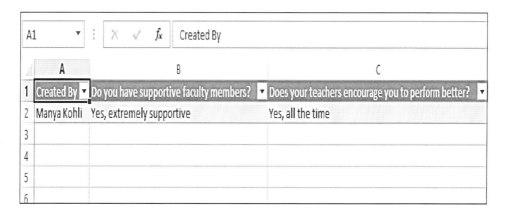

CHAPTER 4

WORKING WITH WEB PAGES

Lesson objectives:

- Choosing between wiki pages and Web Part pages
- Creating new wiki pages
- Adding media to your wiki pages
- Creating new Web Part pages

Choosing Between Wiki Pages and Web Part Pages

How many times have you been hearing this statement: "**We need the team to get on the same page**"? Well, there is no problem if you are using SharePoint. If you are a facilitator, communicator, or have a creative streak, this chapter will be a help to you.

Although SharePoint gives you a lot of helpful tools to work with content and the ability to communicate effectively with your team, starting with a customizable home page that pulls everything together.

Web pages and Web Parts let you arrange and present information on a collaboration site. Pages can display freeform text, tables, hyperlinks, and images, as well as Web Parts showing app content from your site (or other sites) arranged as you want.

Web Parts can be closed temporarily or moved. You can modify the Web Parts to show only the data you want from an app. You can inform, organize, and focus your team with your pages, something that otherwise would take a lot of effort with emails and network shares. In this chapter, we are going to show you how to work with web pages.

Introducing the Ribbon

To edit the contents of a SharePoint 2016 page, you need to access the Ribbon. The Ribbon is tucked away in the header of the SharePoint 2016 team site and is accessed by clicking the Page tab. When you click the Page tab, the header automatically switches to the Ribbon, and you can begin editing your SharePoint page. To flip back to the standard header, click the Browse tab. The Ribbon was introduced in Microsoft Office and is a convenient way to display many menu items in a small amount of screen space.

The Ribbon in SharePoint 2016 features menu items that are relevant to the kind of page you're viewing, arranged in tabs. For example, the home page of a team site displays two tabs: Browse and Page. You find most of the menu commands you need to use on the Ribbon, and some Ribbon buttons contain drop-down lists.

An app display commands on the Ribbon that provides additional configuration options. These commands are contextual because the commands that appear depend on the context of where you are on the site. For example, the Document Library app adds a Files and Library tab to the Ribbon, in addition to the standard Browse tab.

In past versions of SharePoint, all data containers were a list or library. The list and library are still there, but in SharePoint 2019 they are called apps.

Understanding SharePoint Web Pages

Your team site is really just a collection of web pages. There are two different types of web pages for displaying your content; **Wiki Content pages** and **Web Part pages**. There is also an advanced type of page known as a publishing page.

If you are already familiar with SharePoint team sites, you have probably worked with Web Part pages. In SharePoint 2019, Wiki Content pages are now the default web page type. They are stored in a wiki page library called **Site Pages**.

Choosing Wiki Page

A wiki page is designed to be intuitive and easy to run with SharePoint pages. A wiki page is similar to an Office Word document. You place the page in Edit mode and start adding content. Just like a Word document, you have the Ribbon at the top to format text and insert items. And when you want to get advanced and modify the HTML, all you need to do is click a button to edit the source code. Only members of your team site's default Members group have permission to modify wiki pages. If you want some people to be able to read your wiki pages but not edit them, add those users to your site's default Visitors group.

A Wiki Content page consists of a very editable region where you place your content. In this editable region, you can place almost any kind of content imaginable freeform text, tables, hyperlinks, images, even Web Parts. A Wiki Content page combines the best aspects of a typical wiki page with a Web Part page.

You can create new Wiki Content pages for your site by clicking the Settings gear icon and choosing Add a Page. (The Settings gear icon is found in the upper-right corner of the page.) These new Wiki Content pages are also stored in the Site Pages library.

As with most things in SharePoint, there are multiple ways to achieve the same outcome. For example, you can also create a wiki page by opening the New Document drop-down menu and selecting Wiki Page. You can create additional wiki page libraries if you want to manage a specific wiki topic on your site.

Choosing Web Part Page

A Web Part page contains various Web Part zones in which you can place Web Parts; it doesn't have the same editing experience as the Wiki Content page. The Web Part page, however, provides for a consistent layout of Web Parts to create ordered pages with Web Part functionality. For example, you can drag and drop Web Parts between zones without reconfiguring the Web Parts. A Wiki Content page, on the other hand, is more freeform. You could insert a table on a Wiki Content page and then insert Web Parts into different cells of the table, but that's a lot of work.

With a Web Part page, you choose the Web Part zone layout when you create the page and add Web Parts to the available zones.

Web Part pages live in a library just like a Wiki Content page. You can create a new Web Part page in your Site Pages library by clicking the Files tab in the Ribbon and then selecting Web Part Page from the New Document drop-down list.

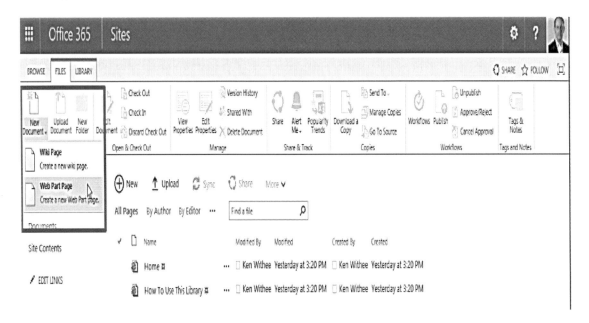

Preferring Wiki Content Page Over Web Part Page Vice versa

Several people have lived through different versions of SharePoint over the years and their familiarity with SharePoint kept them using a Web Part page. Converting previous sites to the new version may be a factor as well.

However, the need for creating rich content pages in a collaboration site is now better served by the Wiki Content page. The following list helps you decide which type of page to create, based on your needs:

- Web Part page: Use when you need mostly Web Parts with little text content. Examples include pages with multiple List View Web Parts, Office application Web Parts, custom search and site directories, and pages that use connected Web Parts.
  Web Part pages are simple to create without the editor needing skills in rich content editing. Although versioning may be turned on in the library you store your Web Part pages in, the Web Parts themselves don't retain history.

- **Wiki Content page:** Use when you have mostly a need for rich text content, for example, text, tables, links, and images. You can still insert Web Parts or use no Web Parts at all. The HTML content in wiki pages is also subject to versioning if versioning is turned on in the library.

There is also a special type of site called a publishing site. Publishing sites contain a special type of page called a publishing page. You can lock down a publishing page and allow people to enter or edit content but not change the look and feel or the location of the content. This is important for broadly consumed websites to maintain a consistent look and feel of content throughout the site. Publishing sites are a very advanced topic and require significant resources to implement and manage and are beyond the scope of this book. However, if you are a large organization and want to control at a very granular level how content is published to your SharePoint website pages, then dig further with publishing sites.

Creating New Wiki Content Page

If probably you want additional pages on your site that look and function like the home page, create a new Wiki Content page. Creating a new page of this type is slightly different from creating other content.

You can create a new page in multiple ways, including clicking the Settings gear icon and choosing to Add a Page, creating a Forward link in a wiki page, and selecting the New Document command in the wiki library.

To create a new Wiki Content page, the following steps below will be a help for you:

1. Click the **Settings gear icon.**

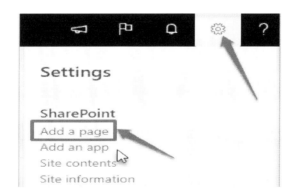

- Click or select **Add a Page.**
- From your Apps page, type **Wiki** into the search field.

- Click on the **Search icon** or hit enter on your keyboard.
- Then click the **wiki page library.**

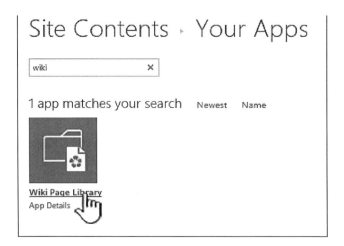

2. In the **Name box**, type a name for the new wiki page library for example **My first Wiki Pages.**

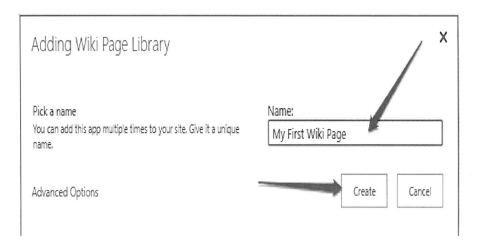

3. Then click on the **Create button.**

I suggest typing a single word that's a meaningful name and use the text editors to type any title or other text on the page to communicate its purpose. As you type the name of the page, you see how the URL will look as the location preview is automatically updated.

Your new page is created and placed in Edit mode. You see other recently modified pages in this wiki library via links on the lower-left corner of the **Quick Launch pane**.

By default, the page is a single column, but you can change the page's layout to include more columns by clicking the **Text Layout** button on the Format Text tab of the Ribbon.

Adding Media

Of course, you can add much more to a wiki page than just text. The Insert tab of the Ribbon provides menus for adding tables, media, links, reusable content, App Parts, and Web Parts. One advantage to using wiki pages over Web Part pages is that you can upload your media file and display it on your page without leaving the page. You don't have to upload your media files first and then link to them.

Video Inserting or Embedding YouTube Video

To display media on your wiki page such as YouTube video, follow these steps:

1. Create a **new wiki page** or browse to an existing page.
2. On the Page tab of the Ribbon, click the **Edit button** to place the page in Edit mode.

3. Click inside the layout area where you want to display the media, for example, a YouTube video.
4. On the Ribbon, click on the **Insert** tab.
5. Click the **Video** and **Audio** drop-down list.
   - Select **From Computer**. The Upload Media dialogue box will appear.
6. Click on **Browse** and choose the media you want to upload.
   - You can also embed YouTube or other video sites.
   - On YouTube, find the video you want to place on your **page.**
   - Click the **Share link**.
   - Click the **Embed link**, and copy the code.
   - To insert this code in your wiki page, click the **Embed Code button** on the Ribbon.
   - Then paste the code into the page. Your YouTube video will display right on your SharePoint wiki page.
7. Accept the default setting to upload the file into the Site Assets library and click **OK**. SharePoint upload the file to the Images document library.
8. Click the **Web Part.**

- Then click **Edit Web Part.** A property window will appear so you can enter metadata about the video file.
- Enter any **metadata** you want and click on **Save.**

Note: If you wish to include a preview image, you can upload one to the images folder and then provide the link in the metadata field called **Preview Image URL.** You don't need a preview image, but it makes your page look more polished.

9. Move over the **Media Web Part** and click the **Play button.** The video will then start to play.

Inserting a Note Board

To insert **Note Board Web Part** to capture social comments, the following steps need to be considered:

c. Create a **new wiki page** or browse to an existing page.
d. On the Page tab of the Ribbon, click the **Edit button** to place the page in Edit mode.
e. Click inside the **layout** area where you want to display the media, for example, a Note Board Web Part.
f. On the Ribbon, click on the **Insert** tab.
g. Click on **Web Part** to display the Web Part gallery.
h. In the Categories list, click on **Social Collaboration.**
i. In the Parts list, click on **Note Board.**
j. Click on **Add** to add the Note Board Web Part to the page. The web part is added to the page.

Creating a Wiki Page Library in SharePoint

A wiki page is designed for the group of people to quickly capture and share ideas by creating simple pages and linking them together.

To create a wiki page, follow the Steps given below:

1. Go to the Home page of your site.

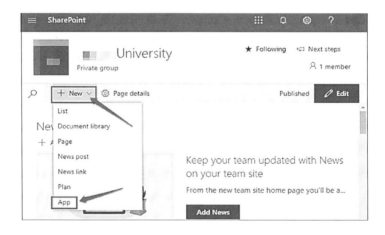

- Click on the **+New** at the top of the screen
- Click or select **App** from the drop-down menu.
2. Search for the **wiki Page Library** by scrolling down.

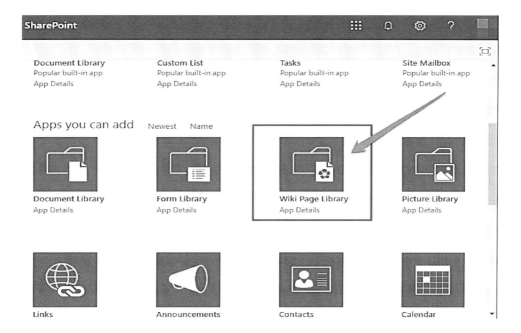

- Click on the **wiki page library app.**
3. A small pop-up window will open, click inside the box.

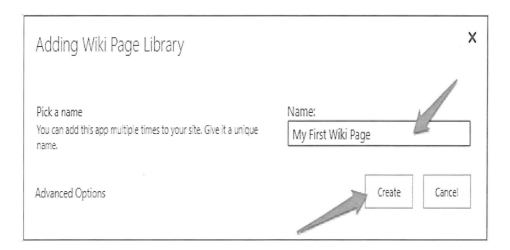

- Enter the library name e.g. **"My first wiki page"**
- Click on **create.**

When the wiki page library gets created, you will see it on the site content.

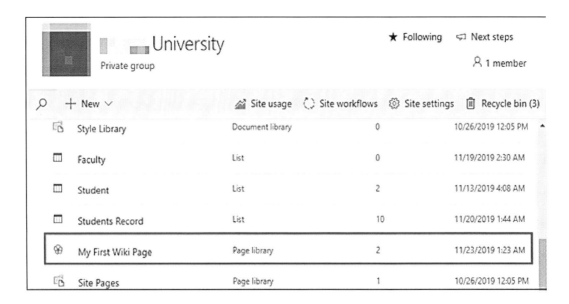

4. Drag cursor over the **My First Wiki Page**, you will see three dots.
   - Click on the **three dots (...)**, a drop-down will open.

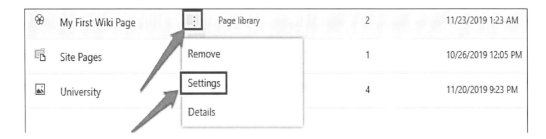

   - Click on **Settings**.
5. Once you click on the Settings, the following window opens then select **List name, description**, and **navigation**.

6. Now, it will ask for Display this document library on the Quick Launch?
   - Click on **Yes**.
   - Click on the **Save**.

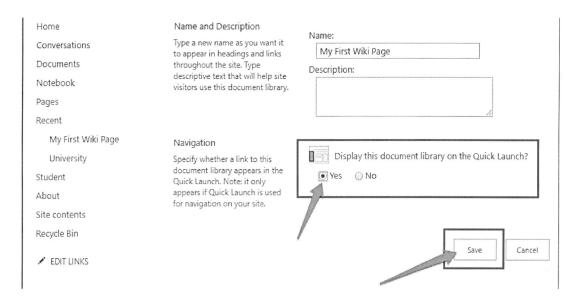

7. The following page will open, then click on the "**My first wiki page.**

8. The image below shows that the wiki library automatically created two files i.e. **How to use this library** and **Home.**

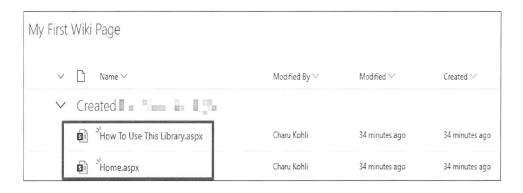

Create a New Wiki Page

To create a new wiki page, follow the steps below:

1. Click on the **+New** at the left top of the screen.

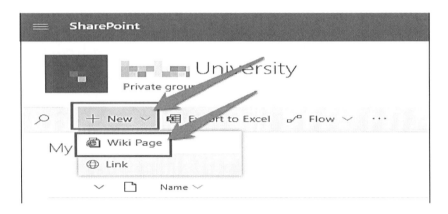

2. Click or select the **wiki page** from the drop-down menu.
3. **3.** A new item window will open, click the **box field** and enter the **page name** that you want to create e.g., **placement records.**
4. Click on the **Create.**
5. Now, the new wiki page "**Placement Records**" is created. You can enter content according to your requirement on the window page.
   c. Click on the **save** at the top left corner of the screen.

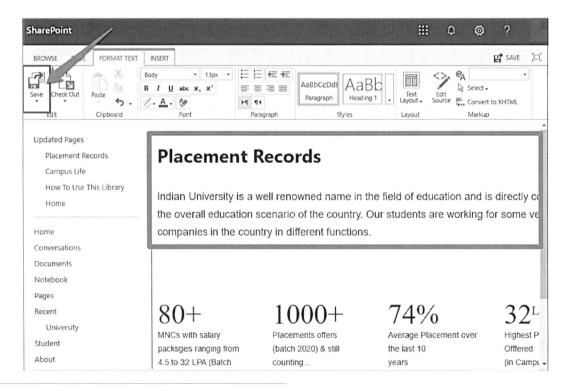

Create Link in Wiki Page

1. Go to the Home page of the wiki library, Click on the **Edit** at the top right corner of the screen.

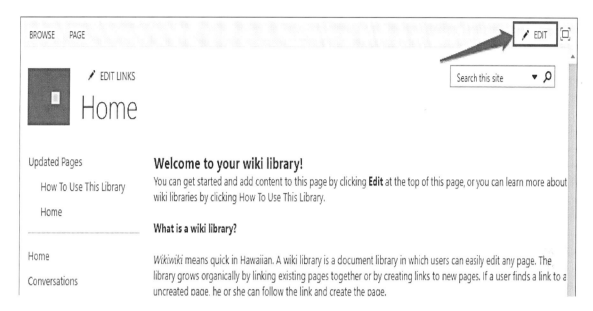

2. Once you click on the **Edit**, the wiki page will open in the word format for editing.

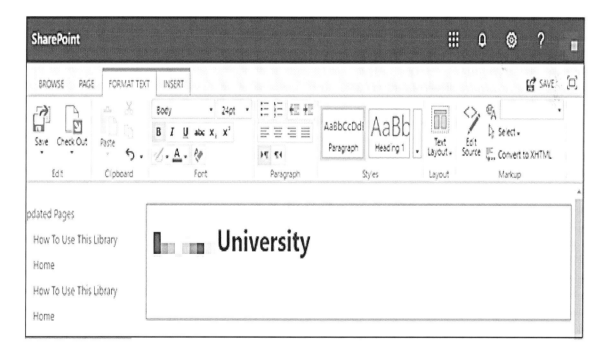

3. Now, place the cursor where you want to create the link and type double square brackets ([[), it will automatically load the file.

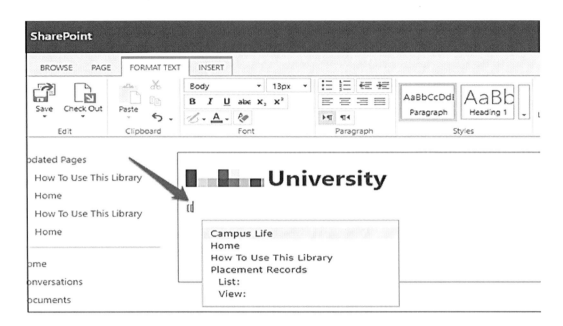

4. If you want to create a new link then type **file name** between the double square brackets [[ ]] e.g. **campus life, home** etc.

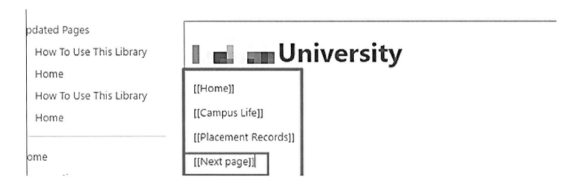

- Once you enter all links that you want to create,
- Click on the **save** at the top left corner of the screen.

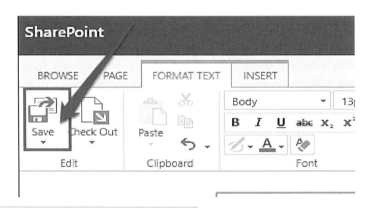

The link will be inserted now into the wiki page library.

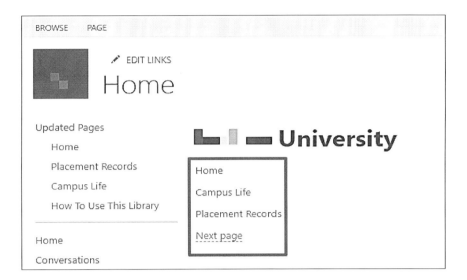

- When you click on the particular link, it will open a **new window.**
- When you click on the link that is not created, it will open a new pop-up window, if probably you want to create a page, click on the **Create** otherwise, click on the **Cancel**.

5. Once you click on **Create**, you will see that a new link has been created successfully.

Creating a New Web Part Page

The outline reasons earlier in this chapter on why you may need a Web Part or multiple Web Part pages in your collaboration site. A Web Part page can also be set as the home page. You can use links to connect your Wiki Content pages and Web Part pages.

To create a new Web Part page, observe the steps below:

- Click on the **Settings gear icon** and click or select **Site Contents.**

3. Click on the **Site Pages library** or whatever library you wish to hold your new Web Part page.
4. Click the **Files** tab of the Ribbon.
5. Click the **New Document** drop-down list on the left of the Ribbon.
   - Click or select **Web Part Page.**
6. Enter a name for the new page in the **Name text box.**
   - Then select a Layout by clicking on the **layout** in the **Choose a Layout Template box.**
   You can click different options in the **list box** to see a thumbnail of the layout options.
7. Select the document library that will contain this page by selecting an option from the **Document Library** drop-down list.
   Web Part pages are stored in libraries, so a default library, such as the **Site Assets Library** is selected for you. You can also choose a different library, such as Site Pages, or even create a new library to store your Web Part pages if you want to be different.
8. Click on the **Create** button.
   Your new Web Part page will open in **Edit mode**, ready for you to start adding Web Parts.

Tip: You can change the home page of your site to any Wiki Content page or Web Part page. Simply click the Make Homepage button in the Page Actions area of the Edit tab on the Ribbon while editing the preferred page.

SharePoint List Apps

What is list apps?

A SharePoint list is a container for information, similar to a very simple database or spreadsheet. Using a list is the most common way to manage information in a SharePoint site.

In a list, data is gathered in rows, and each row is known as a list item. A list can have multiple columns also known as properties, fields, or metadata. So, a list item is a row with data in those columns.

For example, a list of contact may have the following columns:

- First Name
- Last Name
- Company
- Phone

These columns may have the following list items:

- First Name: John
- Last Name: Doe
- Company: Intelligent Design
- Phone: 1800-000-000

Lists can be used in many cases. For example, you might use lists for links, tasks, discussions, announcements, or events. In SharePoint, users can create lists and columns. Lists can be used for almost anything that can be described by a group of columns.

The information in lists can be displayed on pages of a SharePoint site. For example, if the site manager wants to display a list of links on the site, that manager can add a web part.

These are the following List Apps used in the SharePoint:

- Announcements
- Contacts
- Custom List
- Discussion Board

1. Announcements

In SharePoint, an announcement list is used to share news and status. It also provides reminders to complete specific tasks on time.

How to Create an Announcement List

The following steps below will serve as a guideline to create an Announcement list:

1. From your **Home page** site.
   - Click on the **+New**.
   - Select **App** from the drop-down.

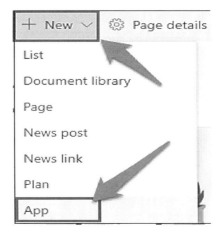

2. A list of apps will appear on the screen.
   - Scroll down the window and click on the **Announcements.**

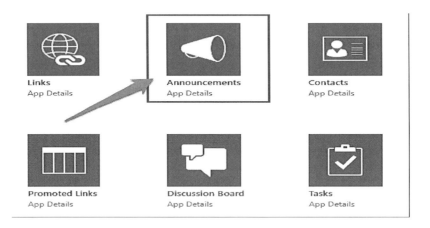

3. A pop-up window will appear on the screen.

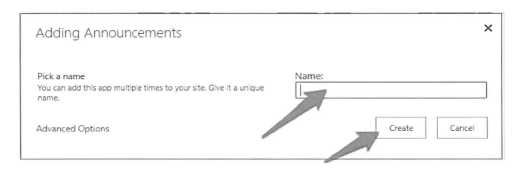

   - Click inside the box type the **name for the announcements** for example "**Exam dates**".
   - Click on the **Create** button.
4. In the site content, you will see that a new announcement of Exam dates is created. Click on this **list.**

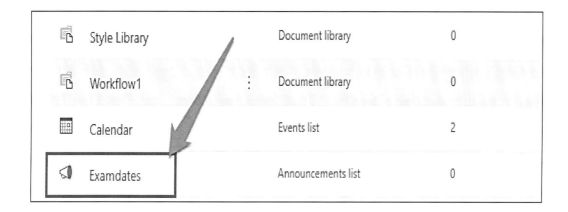

Style Library		Document library	0
Workflow1	⋮	Document library	0
Calendar		Events list	2
Examdates		Announcements list	0

5. Once the Announcement list is created.
   - Click on the **+ New**, a new item window will appear at the right corner of the screen.
   - Enter the details and click on the **Create** button.

CHAPTER 5

GETTING FAMILIAR WITH APPS

Lesson objectives:

- Understanding the concept of a SharePoint app
- Adding apps to your site
- Configuring a List app
- SharePoint Pages and Web Part
- Create Microsoft FORMS in SharePoint

Understanding the Concept of a SharePoint App

The concept of an app is relatively new in SharePoint. An app is Microsoft's attempt to help stem confusion because getting your head around lists and libraries is difficult, especially when you start customizing them. For example, you start with a custom list and then add columns to make it specific to customers. Is it still just a custom list or is it a customer's list? Microsoft posed this question to many focus groups and found that people were more comfortable with the concept of an app than a list or library. The result is that every list and library is now called an app.

Web developers can create apps that do all sorts of things. Because SharePoint 2019 is built using HTML standards, a web developer can take any web functionality and roll it into a SharePoint app. Third parties can put up their apps for sale on the online SharePoint App Store, which you access from within SharePoint.

Introduction to SharePoint Apps

The concept of an app in general is nothing new. If you use a Smartphone, you're surely familiar with apps. Each type of Smartphone has thousands and thousands of apps available. SharePoint has jumped on the app bandwagon and embraced the concept of an app. An app can be simple or complex. For example, you might create an app by customizing the Custom List app. On the other hand, you might hire a web developer to build a complete accounting system as a SharePoint app.

An app display commands on the Ribbon that provides additional configuration options. These commands are contextual because the commands that appear depend on the context of where you are on the site. For example, the Document Library app contains a Files and Library tab in addition to the Browse tab.

Add Apps to Your Site

When you create a new SharePoint site you choose a template. Depending on the template you choose, your site already has some apps by default. You can add more apps to your site. However, you might want to add a Survey app to your site.

You can add the Survey app to your site by following these steps:

1. Click the **Settings gear icon** and choose **Add an App.** Your Apps page will appear, showing all the apps you can add to your site.

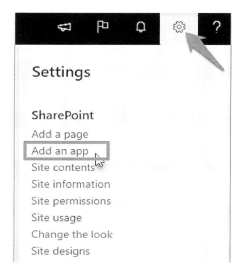

2. Scroll down and click the **Survey app.** Or
   Click on the search field box and type "**Survey app** to find the app. After Adding the Survey dialogue box will appear.

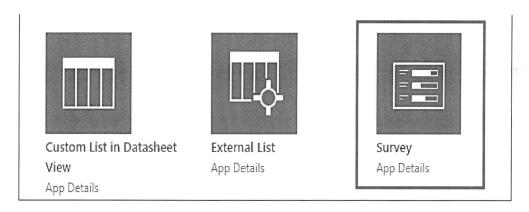

3. Provide a name for your **Survey app**. You can also click **Advanced Options** to set app-specific options. In this case, you can choose to show usernames in the survey and also choose whether you want the Survey app to allow multiple responses.
4. Click on **Create** to create the app.
   - Add it to your site. The Site Contents page will display, which shows all of the apps on your site. A green **New label** is displayed next to the **new apps created.**

You can access an app by clicking on it on the Site Contents page. If you click an app you just created, it will display on the screen. The apps that are available on Your Apps page depends on which SharePoint features are activated.

Accessing App Settings

Most apps are based on a list or library. A list or library has a settings page where you can configure your app. To view or change the configuration settings of your Library or List app, use the Library Settings or List Settings page. This page is the hub where you can find all the options for configuring and customizing your List or Library app to meet your business requirements. You can find shortcuts to many of these options on the Ribbon.

Follow these steps to access the Library Settings or List Settings page:

1. Navigate to your **library** or **list** by clicking the name of the **library** or **list** on the Site Contents page.
   You can also access it by the **Site Contents page** from the Settings gear icon.

605

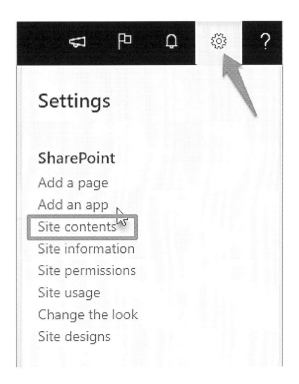

2. On the Ribbon, click the **Library** or **List** tab. Then locate the Settings section, which is on the far right.

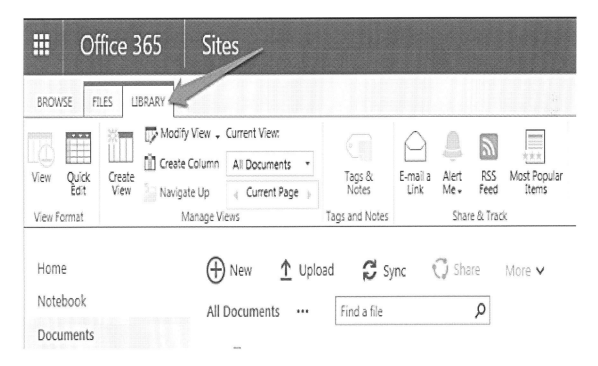

3. Click the **Library** or **List Settings** button.

Library Settings

Go to the Library Settings page to manage settings such as permissions, columns, views and policy.

The Library Settings or List Settings page will appear and it will be divided into several sections. Each section contains many configuration choices.

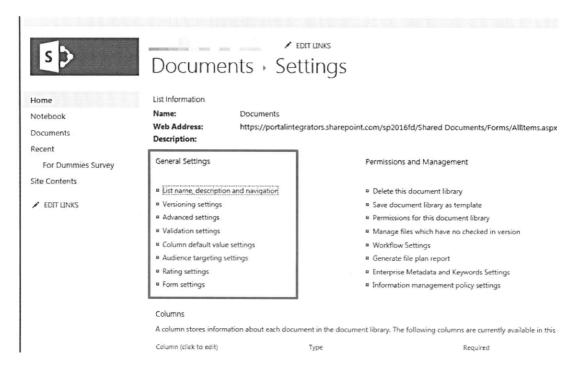

I suggest you spend some time browsing this page. Some of the sections you see include:

- **List Information:** Displays the library or list name, web address, and description. You can change the list's name and description by clicking the **List Name, Description**, and **Navigation link** in the General Settings column.

  The web address is set to the list's default view. Change the default view by scrolling down to the Views section of the Library or List Settings page.

  When you link to a list or library, use the root of the web address. That way, you can change the default view any time you want without needing to change any links that target the list. For example, to create a link to the Shared Documents library, you would use the following: **http://intranet.portalintegrators.com/shared Document**

607

- **General Settings:** Includes list name and description as well as settings for Versioning, Advanced, Validation, Column Default Value, Rating, Audience Targeting, and Form.
- **Permissions and Management:** Includes saving the library or list as a template as well as settings for Permissions, File Management, Workflow, Information Management Policy, and Enterprise Metadata and Keywords. You can also generate a file plan report from this section.
- **Communications:** Configure RSS and incoming email settings for the library or list.
- **Content Types:** If you have configured your library or list to allow for content types, a Content Types section will appear. Use this section to associate content types with your list or library. With content types, you can reuse columns across sites, as well as across lists and libraries.
- **Columns:** Create, view, add, and modify columns for the library or list. You can create your column for this list only, add a site column from the preconfigured SharePoint site columns, or create a new site column of your choosing that can be added to multiple lists.
- **Views:** Display and modify the library or list views. You can also create new views.

Many site owners never change the default settings options; some simply change the List name or delete the list. For others, this level of optional setting detail is what they want to know first! Microsoft supplies descriptions on the how and/or why to use the settings on each of the individual settings pages;

Configuring the General Settings

The General Settings area of the Library or List app has recently been expanded to include multiple new settings, including **Validation, Column Default Value** (for libraries), **Rating, Audience Targeting,** and **Form**.

General Settings Configuration Options

Setting Name	What You Can Accomplish
List Name, Description, and Navigation	Just like it sounds! this section is meant for "Changing the title, description, and navigation"
Versioning	Configure item approval, versioning (major and minor), and require check-out.
Advanced	A plethora of options, including allowing for the management of content types, search visibility, allowing for folders or datasheet view.
Validation	Allows you to create formulas that compare two or more columns in your Library or list.
Column Default Value	Add or edit default values for columns indicated in the library or list Validation settings.
Rating	A Yes or No option that allows items in the library or list to be rated.
Audience Targeting	A Yes or No option that allows the library or list to use audience targeting. Enabling audience targeting creates a Targeting column for this list. Some Web Parts can use this data to filter list contents based on whether the user is in the audience.

Form	Available for lists only. You need Info Path to utilize these settings. However, because Microsoft stopped shipping InfoPath in Office 2016, your only option is to use an older version of InfoPath. Because InfoPath is on its way out, be prepared for this option to disappear in future versions of SharePoint.

Versioning Settings

The Versioning Settings area contains some of the most sought-after settings in any app. Versioning settings cover most of the document management or content management choices. So, your new document/content management mantra is approval, versioning, and check out. By default, Approval, Versioning, or Check out Requirement settings are not turned on in a team site.

The reason versioning is turned off by default is that it takes up a large amount of space in the database. Each time a new version is created, the database grows. However, versioning is important for any real work, so we recommend you turn it on. If you want to have these options enabled when your sites are configured, consider using a publishing site instead.

Before selecting these options, make sure you know the business processes of your team. If documents are thoroughly vetted and approved outside the SharePoint process, you may not want or need Approval settings or Check Out enforced. If your documents are images, you may or may not want to apply to the version if the versions don't matter to you and you would not need to revert to an older version.

Consider using multiple Document Library apps and apply different settings based on need. For example, if you have 100 documents in a Library app and really only need versioning and approval on 5 of those documents, perhaps they can be placed in a Library app with extra configuration.

Versioning can be one of the most misunderstood features of SharePoint document management. Versioning is a helpful protection mechanism because you can revert to a previous version of the document if necessary. Versions in SharePoint are copies of the same document at different intervals during editing.

Follow these steps to apply or modify Versioning settings:

1. Click the **Versioning Settings link** in the Library Settings or List Settings page.
   The sections of the Versioning Settings page include Content Approval, Document Version History, Draft Item Security, and Requires to Check Out (Library apps only).

2. Next, you need to choose whether you want to require content approval for submitted items. You make this selection by choosing the **Yes** or **No** radio button on the Versioning Settings page (accessed in Step 1).

   If you select **Yes** in answer to Require Content Approval for Submitted Items? Individuals with the Approve Items permissions can always see draft Items. Items that aren't approved yet (meaning they are draft versions) aren't visible to site members or visitors. You can designate who you want to view drafts with within the Draft Item Security section.

3. In the Document Version History section, select a **radio** button to indicate whether to use **No Versioning**, Create Major Versions, Create Major and Minor (Draft) Versions, or (optional) specify the Number of Versions to keep by entering a number.

   The default for a List or Library app is No Versioning. You can select Major Versions; 1.0, 2.0, 3.0, and so on or Major and Minor Versions; 1.0, 1.2, 1.3, 2.0, and so on. Selecting either of the last two options enables you to designate a limit for the number of versions of each type by entering a number up to 10,000.

4. Choose who can see draft items by selecting a **Draft Item** Security radio button in the Draft Item Security section
   This section is disabled unless you allow for minor (draft) versions or require content approval of your documents or list items. Here are the three options for who can see draft items: **Any User Who Can Read Items**, **Only Users Who Can Edit Items** or **Only Users Who Can Approve** (and **the Author**).
5. Determine whether you want to require a check out for users editing documents by selecting the **Yes** or **No** radio button.
   Although it can sometimes be difficult requiring to check out is another good safety mechanism that makes sure the other users don't see a document in mid-modification or have multiple users editing at the same time (last save wins). Consider adding the Checked Out To column to your views so that users can quickly see who has an item checked out.
6. Click **OK** or **Cancel**.
   If you click OK, your Versioning settings are applied.

When viewing documents in a Library app, you can click the ellipsis to see a contextual menu. This menu allows a document's editor to check out/check in the document, approve, set off a workflow, and so forth. Because the menu is contextual, if approval isn't set on the library or list, for example, approve doesn't appear on the menu. If a document is checked out, the option to Discard Check Out will appear.

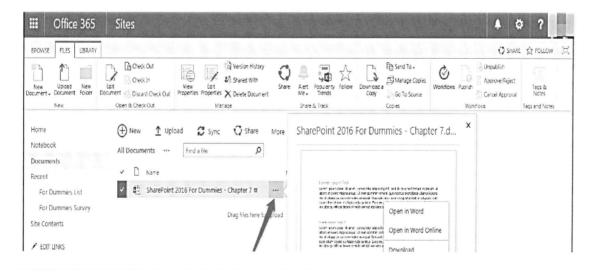

In most cases, team members navigate to the site using a browser to work with list apps. However, think about how your team interacts with documents, they may be navigating to an app using the browser, but they may also be linking from a bookmark or opening the document directly from the editing application (such as Word, Excel, or PowerPoint). Although current versions of Office support and interact with SharePoint Library app settings, users may not know where to find these commands.

Advanced settings

Advanced settings include many powerful configuration options for Library and List apps:

- **Content Types:** This allows you to add and remove content types associated with the app.
- **Document Template (Library app only):** This allows you to specify the default template, such as a Word, Excel, or PowerPoint template that is used when someone clicks the **New** button to create a new document.

You can also associate document templates with content types, so you can use multiple content types with a library to associate multiple document templates. It might sound confusing, but in a nutshell, having multiple document types and templates enables you to have multiple options for creating a document when you click the New button. For example, you might have a Word template for expenses and a Word template for vacation requests. These can both show up in the New drop-down list (located in the Ribbon on the Files tab) using content types.

- **Opening Documents in the Browser (Library app only):** Enables you to determine the behavior of the browser when someone clicks on a document to open it. If you don't want to use the Office Web apps, disable the opening of documents in the browser. This also allows users to send direct links to the documents if necessary.
- **Custom Send to Destination (Library app only):** This is a great option that lets you add your web address to the **Send To** menu on a document's Edit menu. Your SharePoint administrator can also add global addresses that appear in the Send To menu in every document library. The Send To command sends a copy of your file to another location, such as another team site where you want to share the document.
- **Folders:** Indicates whether users can create new folders in the Library app. We like to turn off this option so people don't go folder crazy. You can always turn on the option so you can create folders when necessary and then turn it back off.
- **Search:** Specifies whether items in the app should appear in search results.
- **Indexing:** Options for indexing non-default views and re-indexing the document library. Indexing provides extra data for searches so that searching the library is faster. There is some overhead with indexing, though, so SharePoint makes available some options to control it.
- **Offline Client Availability:** This allows you to specify whether users of desktop client software, such as Outlook, can download content for offline viewing Sites.
- **Assets Library (Library app only):** This allows you to designate the Library app as a Site Assets library, which makes it easier for users to browse the Library app to find multimedia files.
- **Quick Edit:** Lets you specify whether Quick Edit can be used on this library. Quick Edit lets users open the view in a grid and make edits to metadata on the fly. This is much

611

like editing the metadata (data about the documents in the library) on the fly in an Excel type interface.

- **Dialogues:** By default, list and library forms launch in a dialogue box. This option lets you specify that forms should open in the browser window as a page instead of a dialogue box.

In addition, List app advanced settings include item-level permissions and attachments.

Follow these steps to apply or modify Advanced settings:

- Click on the **Advanced Settings link** in the Library Settings or List Settings page. The Advanced Settings page will appear.

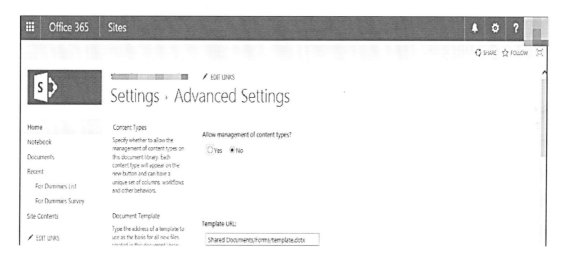

- Choose whether to enable **allow management** of content types by selecting the **Yes** or **No** radio button.
- Change the **document template** (Library app only) by specifying a template URL in the Template URL text box.
- Choose when to open documents in the browser (Library app only) the client application, or as the server default by selecting a radio button option in the Opening Documents in the Browser section.
  If the client application is unavailable, the document opens in the browser.
- Add a **Custom Send to** Destination (Library app only) by entering the name that should display on the **Send To** menu and the URL destination.
  Similar to Windows commands (for example, Send to Desktop), you can create an option to appear on the Edit menu for documents in this Library app to be sent to another SharePoint destination. Supply a short name to appear on the contextual menu and a URL for the destination in the Destination Name and URL text boxes.
- Select whether folders can be created in this app by selecting the Yes or No button in the Folders section. Selecting **Yes** or **No** determines whether the New Folder command is available on the New menu. The default is **Yes**.
  We usually disable folders unless we have a good reason to use them. In our opinion, the only good reason to use folders is when you have a set of documents that require unique permissions but must remain in the same app.

If you leave folders enabled, people will use them.

- Determine the search visibility for this app by selecting the Yes or No button in the Search section.
  Selecting No for the Search option can keep the items in the app from being presented in search results, even if the site or app is included in Search settings. The default is **Yes**.

- Enable offline client availability by selecting the Yes or No button in the Offline Client Availability section.
  The Offline Client Availability option determines whether items in the app can be downloaded to offline client applications, such as Outlook. The default is **Yes**.

- Add app location to the Site Assets Library (Library app only) by selecting the **Yes** or **No** button in the Site Assets Library section.
  This new Site Assets Library option specifies whether this Library app will appear as a default location when uploading images or other files to a wiki page. This can be especially beneficial for Document Library apps that contain images or a Picture Library app. This keeps wiki editors from searching all over for the images they should be using. The default is **No.**

- Determine whether the app can be edited using Quick Edit by selecting the Yes or No radio button in the Quick Edit section.
  This option determines whether Quick Edit can be used to bulk-edit data on this app. The default is **Yes**.

- Indicate whether forms should launch in a modal dialogue box by selecting the **Yes** or **No** button in the Dialogs section.
  Modal dialogue boxes get old pretty quickly, so we suggest you select the No option on this section quite often.

- Click **OK** or **Cancel.**

SharePoint Versioning

SharePoint versioning provides an excellent way to store, track, and restore files in a list or library whenever changes are made. SharePoint versioning is also used to track the history of a version, restore a previous version, and view the previous version of an item or file.

Versioning is available for list items such as calendars, issue tracking lists, custom lists, and libraries, including web part pages.

Note: By default, in SharePoint, versioning is on for SharePoint libraries, and versioning is off for SharePoint lists.

In SharePoint versioning, you can perform the following operations:

- View history of a file
- View previous version file content
- Restore previous version file
- Delete version from version history

How to View History of a File

These are the following steps that will enable you to view the history of a file:

- From your home page of the site, click on **About** at the left side corner to select the **file** which you want to view history.

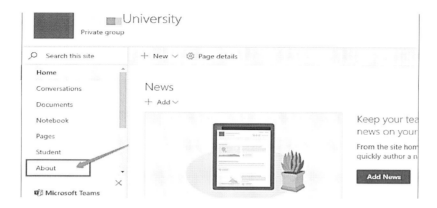

- A document library page opens, select document according to your requirement.
  - Double click the **document file** to open.

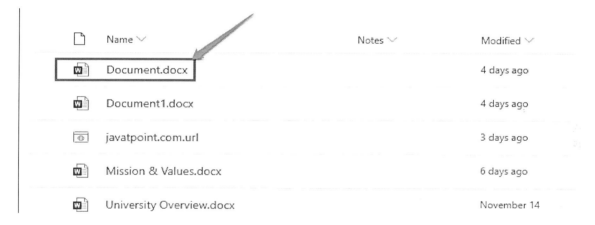

- Now after the document file is opened, **Edit** the content to the required instruction. It automatically saves the file.

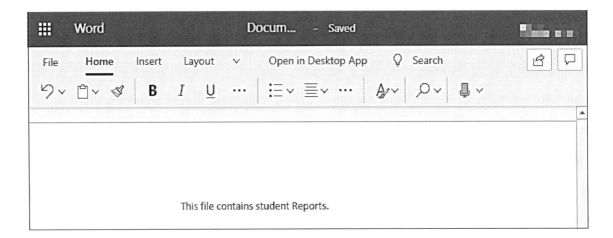

- Once the file is saved, go back to the previous page.

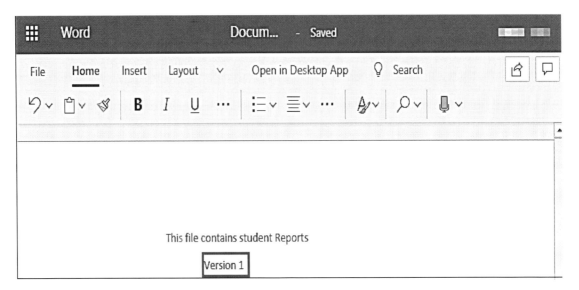

- Click on the **Document file** to mark it.

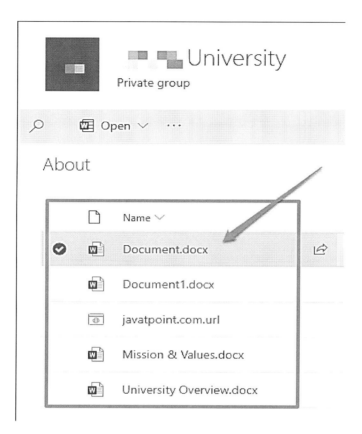

- Click on the **show action (three dots)**, a list of actions opens on the screen.
- Select **Version history** from the list.

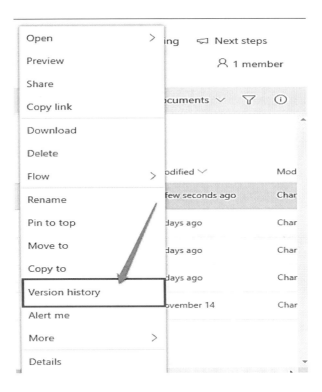

- Now, when versioning is enabled on your site, you can see when the document is modified, who modified the document, and what is the size of the document.

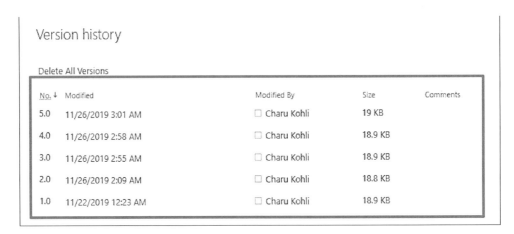

View Previous Version File Content

SharePoint versioning allows you to view previous version file content after changing the document.

To see previous version file content, follow the steps below:

1. Click on any **modified date & time file** that you want to see.

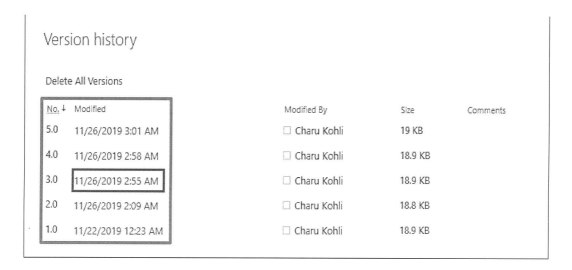

2. Click on **Open Office (desktop)**.

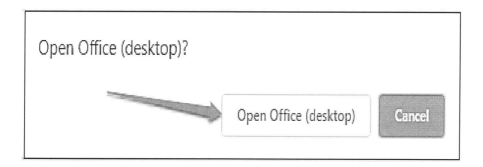

3. After clicking on the Open Office (desktop), your previous version file opens with two options: **Compare** and **Restore.**

4. If you want to compare your previous file with the original file.

- Then click on the **Compare** at the top of the window.

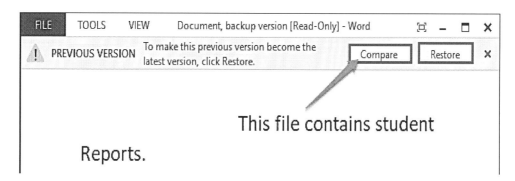

- After clicking on the compare, the image below shows your previous version files and original file.

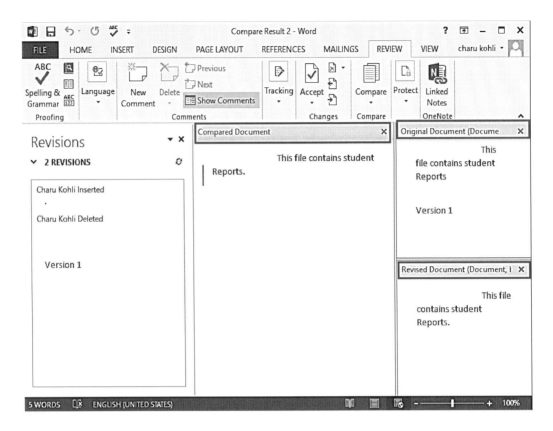

Restore Previous Version File

SharePoint versioning allows you to make your previous version file as a current version file:

1. From the **Version history page:**

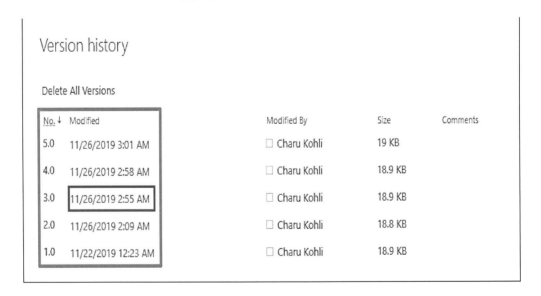

- Select the version that you want to restore.
- Click on the **drop-down icon** associated with the selected version.
- Click on the **Restore.**

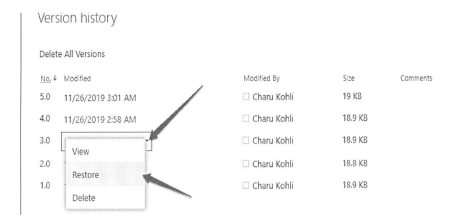

2. Once you click on the Restore, a pop-up opens with the message "**You are about to replace the current version with the selected version**".
    - Click on the **OK**, otherwise click on the **Cancel**.

3. Now, you can see that **version number 8** becomes your current version, which was previously **version number 3**

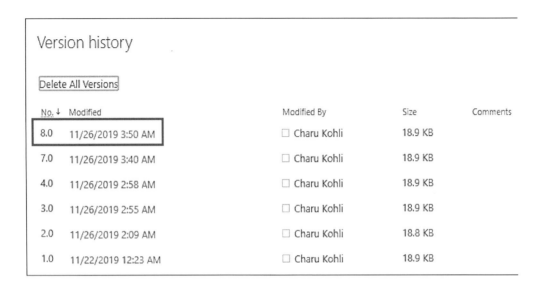

Delete Version from the Version History

1. From the Version history page, select the version that you want to delete:
   - Click on the drop-down icon associated with the selected version, it opens a drop-down menu.

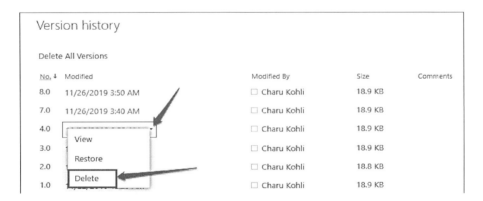

   - Click on the **Delete**.
2. After clicking on the Delete, a pop up comes up with the message, "**Are you sure want to send this version to the site Recycle Bin**?" if you want to delete a version, click on the **OK.**

3. The image below shows that the version has been deleted from the version history.

Version history

Delete All Versions				
No. ↓ Modified		Modified By	Size	Comments
8.0	11/26/2019 3:50 AM	☐ Charu Kohli	18.9 KB	
7.0	11/26/2019 3:40 AM	☐ Charu Kohli	18.9 KB	
3.0	11/26/2019 2:55 AM	☐ Charu Kohli	18.9 KB	
2.0	11/26/2019 2:09 AM	☐ Charu Kohli	18.8 KB	
1.0	11/22/2019 12:23 AM	☐ Charu Kohli	18.9 KB	

SharePoint Pages and Web Part

SharePoint Pages

SharePoint pages provide the best way to share ideas using images, Excel sheets, Word, PowerPoint documents, videos, and more. SharePoint 2019 allows you to create and publish pages quickly and easily.

On this page, we will discuss the following topics:

- Types of SharePoint pages
- Create a Page
- Upload image on the page
- Introduction to a web part
- Add web parts to a page
- Add HERO Web part on page
- How to display a page as a home page

Types of SharePoint Pages

1. **Application pages:** Application page in an ASP.NET web page designed to build the SharePoint web sites.
2. **Site pages:** SharePoint site pages allow you to add the page to the SharePoint library, enables you to customize the page.
3. **Master pages:** Master pages provide the interface and layout of the pages on a SharePoint site. It is mainly used to store the structure, elements, and design of the site.
4. **Page layouts:** SharePoint page layouts allow you to create a template for a page.

How to Create a page

To create a page, the steps below need to be followed carefully:

1. Go to the home page of your project.
   - Click on the **+ New**, a drop-down menu opens.

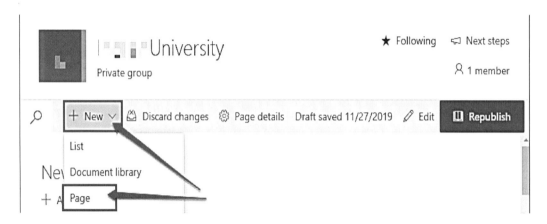

   - Click on the **Page**. A Page Templates window will open, click the **page**

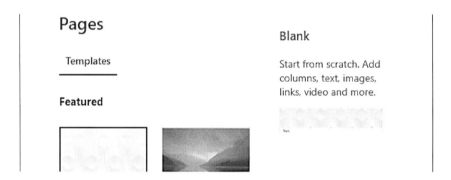

   - Click on the **Create page**.
2. The new page will be created, enter the **name** of your page according to your requirement.

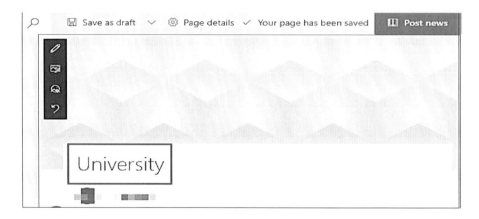

How to Upload Image on the Page

1. On the new page created, click on the **Image icon** at the left corner of the screen.

2. Once you click on the image icon, a small menu will appear, click on the **Upload.**

3. Browse the location where the file is present and select the **image.**
    *   Click on the Open after selecting the **image** you want to upload.

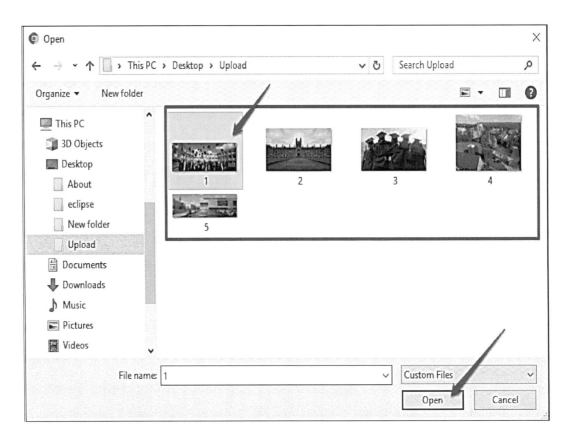

4. Click on the **Add image**.

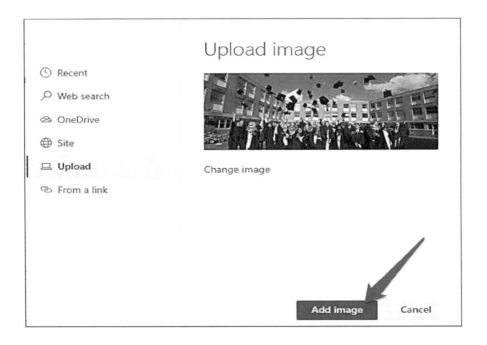

Now, the selected image will be uploaded on the page successfully.

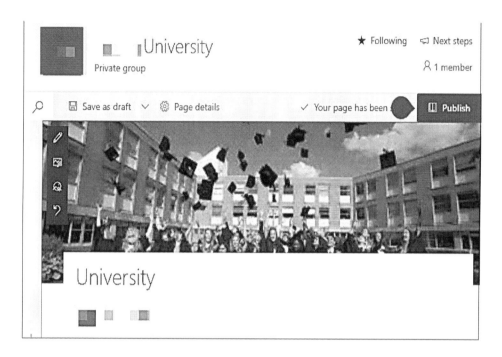

Introduction to a Web Part

SharePoint web part is a small block of user interface that allows you to modify the content, appearance, and behavior of the pages in a SharePoint site by using the browser.

How to Add Web Part to a Site

Once your page is created, move the mouse on the existing web page:

- At your right-hand side top, click on **Edit**.

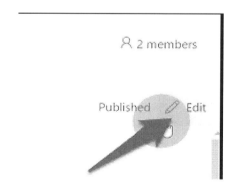

- You will see a line with a circled **+ sign**, click on the circled **+ sign**, a small featured window pop-up.

- Select web part according to your requirement. To easily find the web part, you can also start typing the name of the web part in the search box.

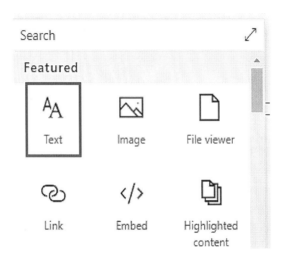

- You can also click on the line at the right angle beside search, to open all the features.

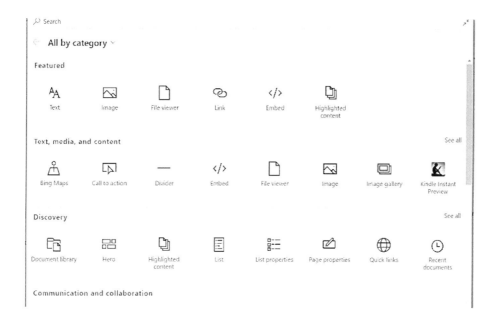

- We want to add the text, so click on the **Text** in the Featured window.

- Enter text according to your requirements. You can also perform operations on the text like **bold, italic, underline, change the font size:**
  - To see more functionality, click on the three dots **(…)**.

- Once you click on the more (…), the following window will appear, which provides you with a way to add more functionality to your text like you can change the **font colour**, **highlight colour**, **add paragraphs**, **inset link**, and **add** a **table**.

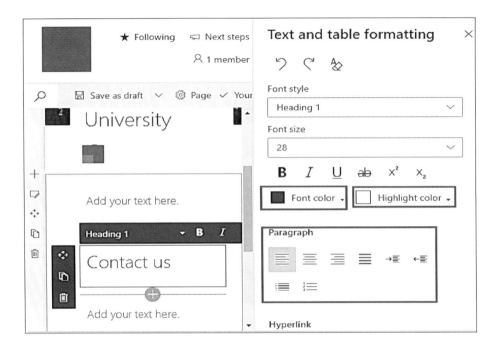

- Once you add web parts according to your requirement:
  - Click on **Publish** at the top right corner of the screen.

Add Hero Web Part in Page

Hero web parts allow you to add images, text, and links to the pages and make the page more attractive.

These are the following steps to observe to add Hero web part to the page:

1. Go to the created page where you want to add the Hero web part:
   - Click on the **Edit** at the top right corner of the page.

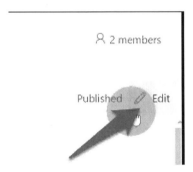

- Move your mouse on the existing page and you will see a straight line with a circled **+ sign**.
- Click on the **+ sign.**

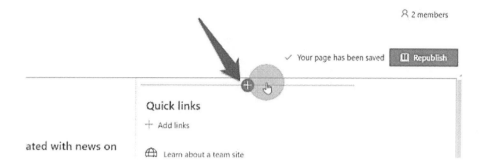

2. A small window will appear with the list of web parts:

- Scroll down and search for the **Hero**, or you can directly type **Hero** at the **search box**. Once you find the Hero web part click on it.

3. The Hero web part will appear on the page:
   - Click on the **Edit** at the top left corner of the screen.

4. Hero layout options will appear on the screen. Click on **Tiles** and

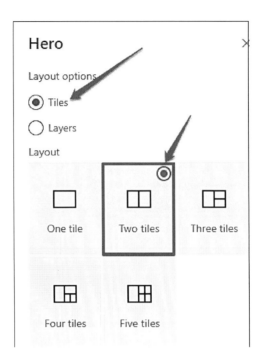

- Select the **Layout** of your choice e.g. two tiles.

5. This is what it will display below in the image; the two tiles window will appear on the screen.

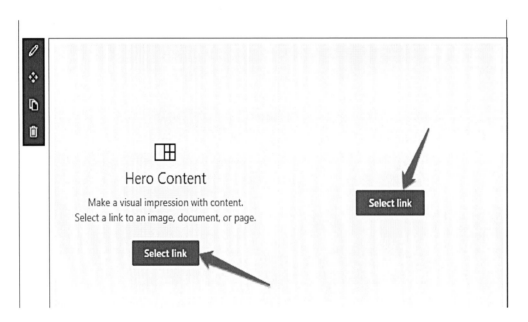

6. Click on the **Select link**, a small pop up will appear at the left corner:
   - Click on **Upload**.

7. Browse the location where the file is present:
   - Select the **file** (image) that you want to upload and

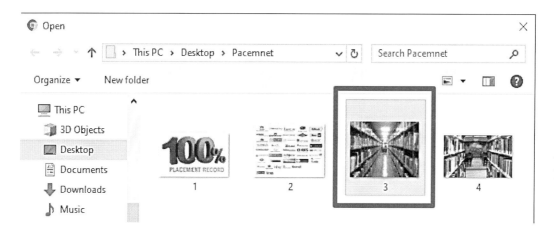

   - Click on **Open**.

8. Once the image is uploaded, click on the **Add item** at the bottom of the screen.

9. The image will be added in the Hero web part.

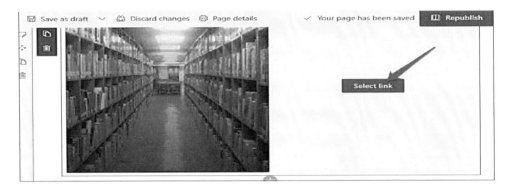

10. Similarly, you can add more images in the Hero web part:
  - Click on the **select link** beside the uploaded image shown above.
  - Follow the same procedure as the first image uploaded.

The screenshot below shows that using the Hero web part, two images are added to the page.

Move or Remove Web Parts

You can also move or remove the SharePoint Web Parts. To move the web part;

- Click on the **Edit** at the top right corner of the screen.

- Select the **web part** that you want to move and click on the **move icon** at the left corner of the screen.

- Drag the web part and drop it to the place where you want to move it and then click on **Republish** at the top right corner of the screen.

To delete the web part, select the web part that you want to delete;

- Click on the **delete icon** at the left corner of the screen

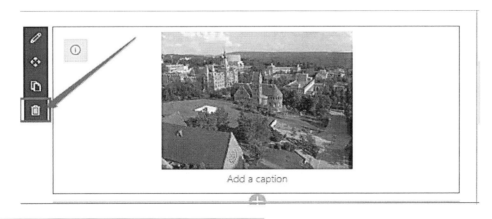

- Once you click on the delete, a small Delete Confirmation window will pop up with the message "Are you sure you want to delete this web part?", if you want to delete.
- Click on the **Yes**, otherwise click on **No.**

- Once you click on the yes, the selected web part will be deleted from the page.
- To show the page, click on the **republish** at the top right corner of the screen.

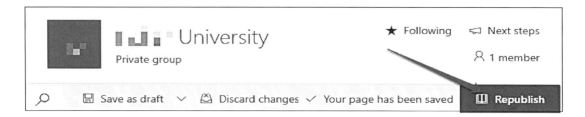

Take Note: Using web parts, you can also add more web parts to the page like, maps, highlighted text, etc.

How to Display Page as a Home Page

You can display your page as a home page, to do this:

a. Go to the Home and click on **Site content:**
   - Click on **site pages**.
b. A site page will appear on the screen, select the page that you want to display as a home page:
   - Click on the ellipse (three dots ...), a list of options will appear on the screen.

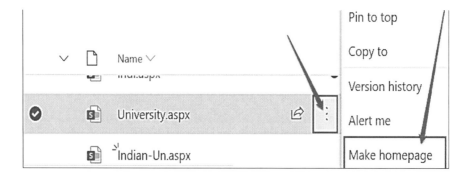

- Select "**Make homepage**.
c. The University has become the home page of your site.

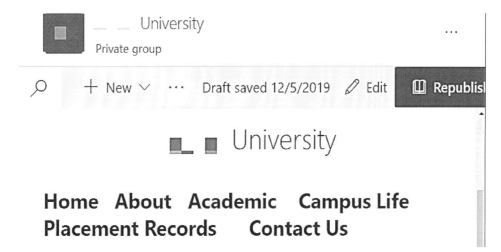

Create Microsoft FORMS in SharePoint

Microsoft forms allow you to create, add, and view forms result in your SharePoint Online page. It is mainly used to provide the best way to store ideas and feedback.

There are two methods to create the Microsoft FORMS in SharePoint and this can process by following the method below:

- Using the Web Part
- Using the Microsoft Form

Method 1: Using the Web part

- From the Home page of your site, click on the **+New** and
  - Select **page** from the small menu.
  - From the box enter the **name** of the page that you want to create.
- Move the mouse on the existing page, click on the **circled +** to see the list of web parts.

- Click on the **Microsoft Forms**, or you can directly type **Microsoft Forms in the search box.**

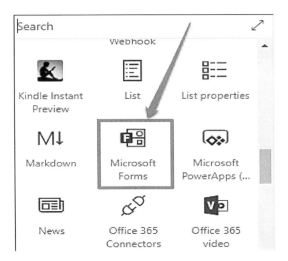

- The following window will appear on the screen. To create a new form, click on the **New form**.

- You will see a Microsoft Forms window at the right pane:
  - Enter the name for the **New** form.

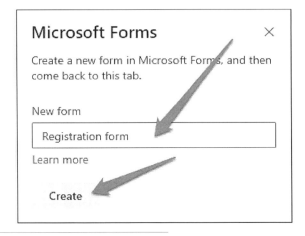

- Click on the **Create**.
▪ The screenshot below shows that a registration form's layout is created.

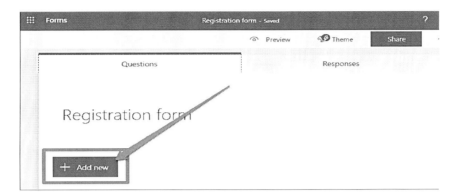

- Click on the **+ Add new.**
▪ Once you click on the **+ Add new**, some Recommended from Microsoft Forms templates appear on the screen:
  - Click on the **Add selected**.

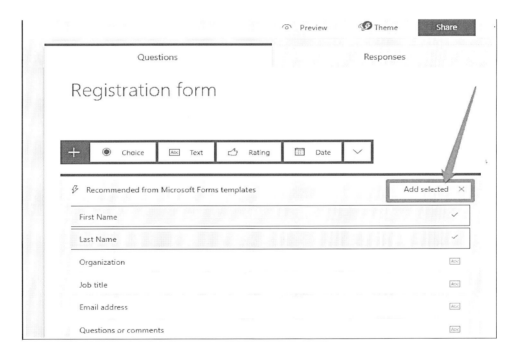

▪ To add a template according to the instruction, click on the **+ Add new:**
  - The following tab will appear, click on the **Text.**

- Enter the text, according to your requirements and
  - Once your form is completed, click on the **Preview** at the top of the screen.

Add Theme to Forms

SharePoint form theme is used to make your form more attractive. To change the theme;

- Click on **Theme** on the right side at the top of the screen. A list of themes will appear on the screen:

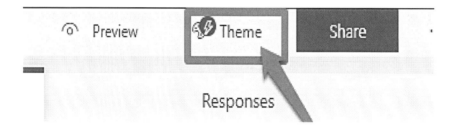

- Select the **theme** and
- Click on the **Preview**.

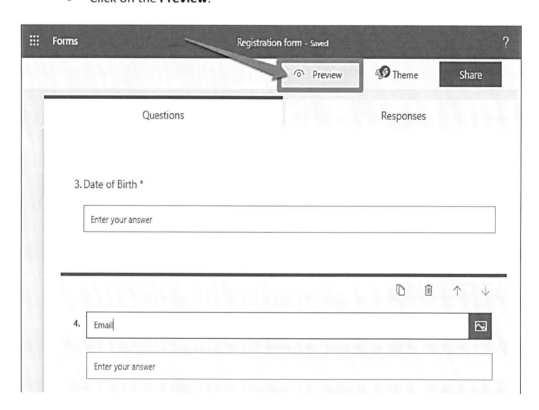

Method 2 - Using Microsoft Forms

The following are the steps to creating a form using Office 365:

1. Type **www.offfice.com** in any browser. A home page of Office 365 will appear on the screen:
   - Click on the **All apps**.

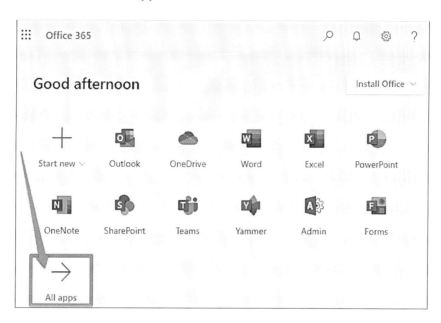

2. All Apps window will appear on the screen, then click on the **Forms.**

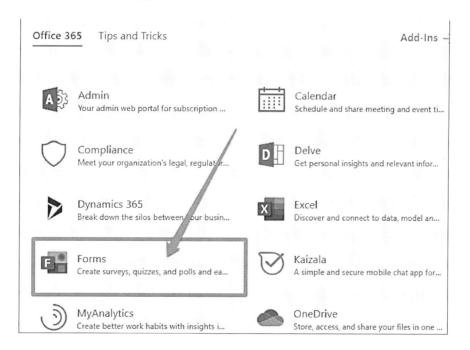

3. My forms window will appear with the two options: **New Form** and **New Quiz**
   - Click on the option that you want to work on. But we are working on **New Quiz.**
   - Click on **New Quiz.**

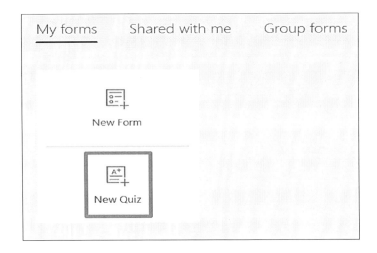

4. The following page will appear, enter the **title** and **description** for your quiz:
   - Click on the **+ Add new.**

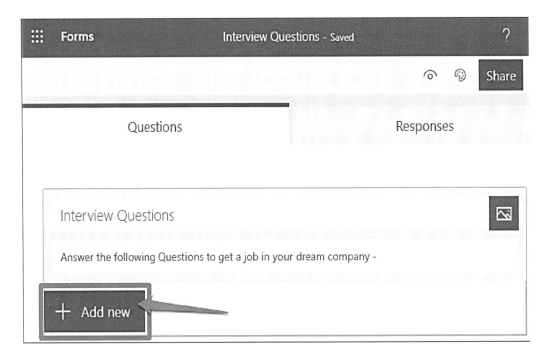

5. Once you click on the **+Add new**, the following tab will appear, to create the quiz:
   - Then click on the **Choice.**

6. Enter the question with the required options.

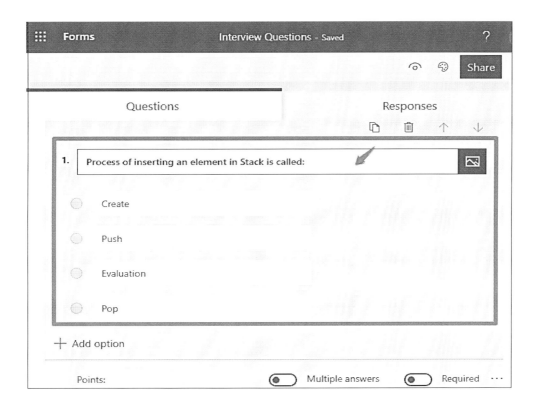

For the correct answer: Place the cursor on the correct answer. Three icons will appear on the screen:

- Click on the **correct answer icon**.

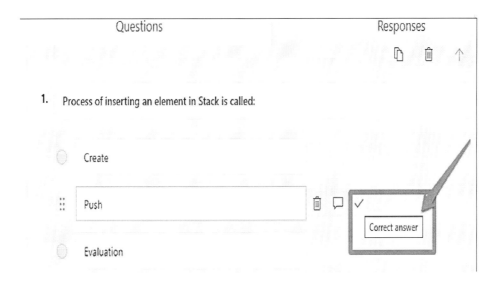

For the incorrect answer: Place the cursor on the incorrect answer. Three icons will appear on the screen, click on the **Display a message to respondents who select this answer icon.**

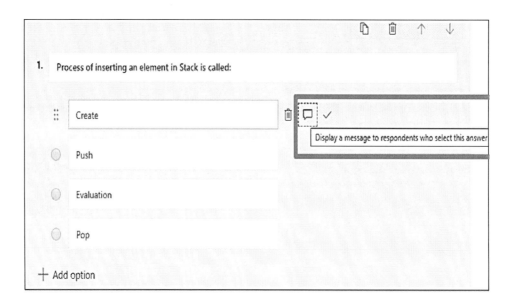

7. Add the message into this box-like **"Correct answer is Push."** Similarly, add this text to all incorrect answers.

8. Once you add all questions to the quiz, click on the **Preview** on the right side from the top of the screen.

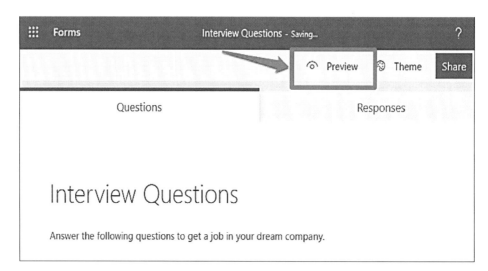

9. Now, you can start solving the quiz question. After completing the quiz question, click on **submit** at the bottom of the screen.

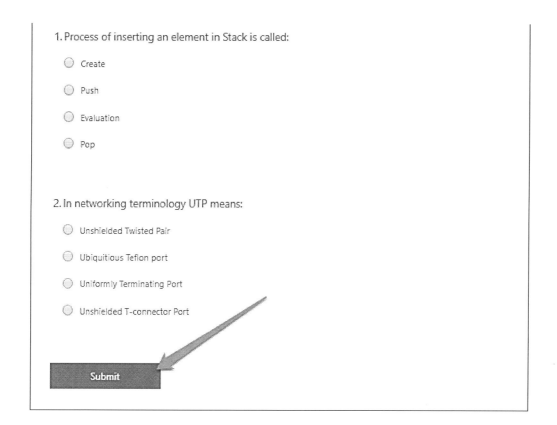

1. Process of inserting an element in Stack is called:
   - ○ Create
   - ○ Push
   - ○ Evaluation
   - ○ Pop

2. In networking terminology UTP means:
   - ○ Unshielded Twisted Pair
   - ○ Ubiquitous Teflon port
   - ○ Uniformly Terminating Port
   - ○ Unshielded T-connector Port

   Submit

10. After clicking on the Submit, it will display the **Thanks page** on the screen.

- Then click on the **View result** to check the result.

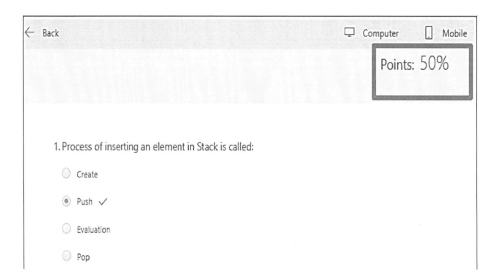

If probably you want to see how the quiz looks like in a mobile interface, click on the **Mobile icon** at the top of the screen.

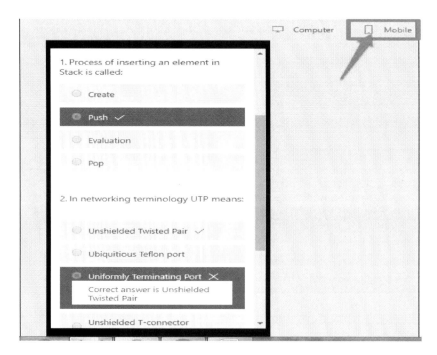

Change the Theme of the Quiz

1. To change the theme, go to the quiz page and click on the **Theme** at the top right corner. A list of pre-defined themes will appear on the screen.

- Click on the **+icon** to add the new Theme.

2. The following window will appear on the screen, type the **name** of the image in the **search box**

- Click on the **Search icon**. A list of images will appear on the screen.
- Select the **image**, and

- Click on **Add.**

How to Share the Quiz/Form

The following are the ways to share the quiz:

Using a link

If you do not have the email address of the people to whom you want to send the form or quiz, then the link is the best way to send the quiz/form:

1. Open the **form** or **quiz** that you want to share.
2. Click on the **Share** at the right corner of the screen.

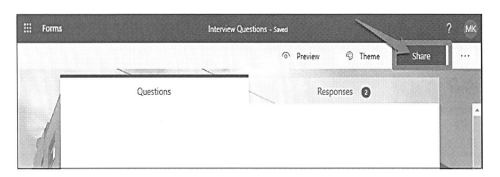

By default, only people within the organization can submit their responses to the form or quiz. If probably you want to allow everyone to submit their responses.

3. Click on the **Anyone with the link can respond**.

4. Click on the **link** and then click on **Copy**,

Now, you can copy and paste the link where you want to access it.

Using QR code

To send the form or quiz using a QR code:

- Click on the **QR button** to view a QR code.

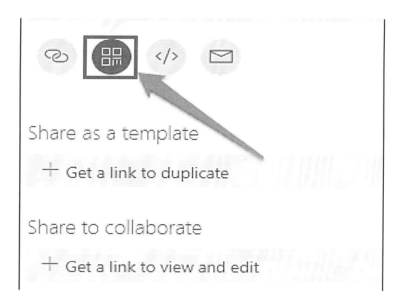

- Click on the **Download** and paste the link where you can access it with a QR code scanner, such as a mobile device.

Using Embed in a webpage:

- Click on the **Embed button.**

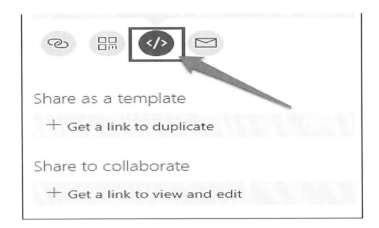

- Click on the **Copy**.

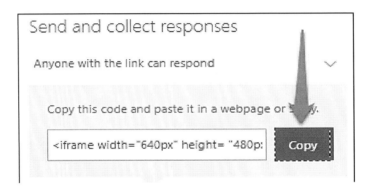

- Type or paste the code into the **web page** to embed your form within the document.
- Click on **add a web part** where you want to add it.
- Click on the **Microsoft Forms**, the following window will appear on the screen.

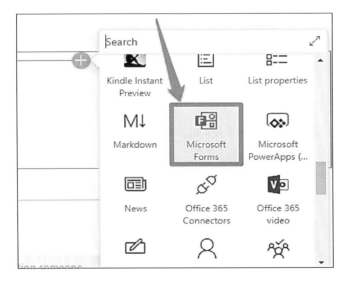

- Click on the **Add existing form**.

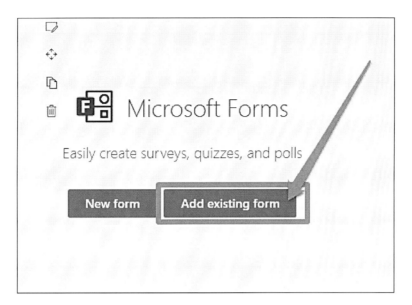

- Paste the **page URL** in the right pane.

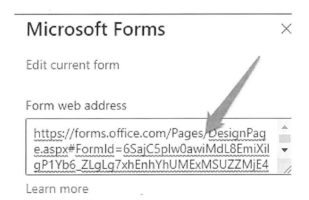

- Select **collect responses** and
- Click on the **OK**.

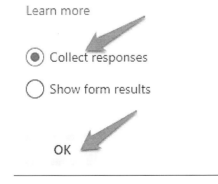

The screenshot below shows that the quiz has been added to the web page.

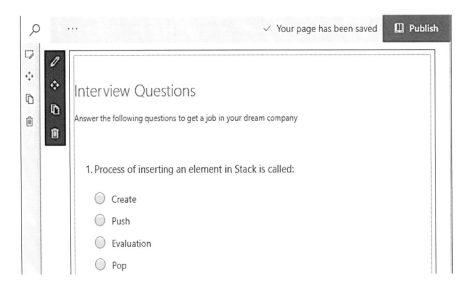

Using email:

- Click on the **email** button.

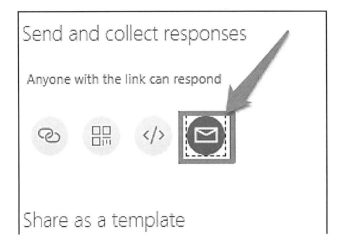

- The default email editing will appear, enter the **email address** of the people who viewed your form and
- Click on **Send.**

How to View Responses

After sharing the quiz, you can also view the responses. To view the responses, go to the quiz page:

- Click on the **response** at the top of the screen.

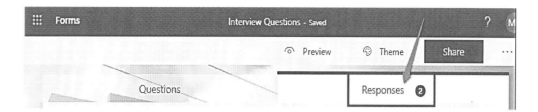

Analyse Quiz Results in Excel

To analyze quiz results in Excel, click on the **Open in Excel** option.

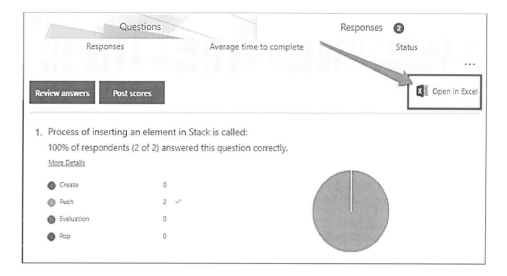

The image below shows that the quiz result is analyzed in excels form.

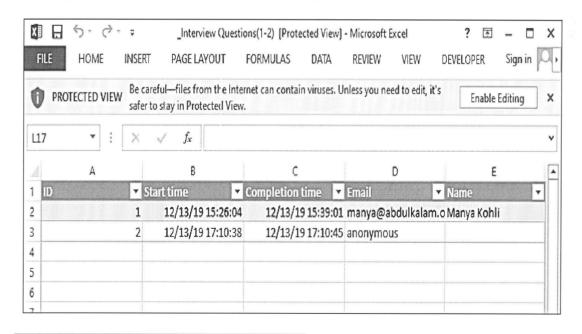

CHAPTERS 6

CREATING A CUSTOM APP

Course objectives:

- Planning and creating a custom app
- Adding new columns to a list app
- Discovering apps in the SharePoint Store
- Creating calendar and library in SharePoint
- 5 Tips Key Things to Know

Planning and creating a custom app

SharePoint ships with some very useful apps, including apps for calendars, tasks, pictures, links, announcements, contacts, discussions, issues, surveys, assets, and even reports, just to name a few. These apps are useful but there comes a time when you need to create your app for very specific data. To create a custom app based on a list, use the Custom List app.

Creating your very own SharePoint app may sound a little daunting. The good news is that creating and customizing an app couldn't be easier. The easiest way to create your app is to start with a Custom List app and then customize it for your particular need.

In this chapter, you will find out how to create your app. You will see how to add columns to store data, create views into the data, validate data, and import data into your app. Finally, you will explore the SharePoint Store, where you can search for and purchase third-party apps, and discover that your organization can even have its own private SharePoint Store.

Planning Your Custom App

Capturing information is nothing new. Ancient civilizations (millennia ago) used stone or clay tablets, pre-computer organizations (decades ago) used typewriters, and many organizations still use Excel. Often, the problem with data is not in collecting it but in sharing and aggregating it. Excel does a great job with data aggregation but not such a great job with sharing. SharePoint is all about sharing (hence the name). A SharePoint app is a centralized container of data that is easy to manage and maintain. In addition, by the very nature of a centralized web portal, the data is easily shared and viewed by anyone in the organization with access.

Creating an app specifically for your data needs is important. You need to determine the columns of data you will capture and how the data will relate to each other. In addition, you need to determine which data will be valid and which should be rejected.

Planning a custom list is similar to starting a new spreadsheet in Excel or a table in Access. In all cases, a little up-front planning saves time in the long run. Plan ahead so you know what order you want the columns to be in and what options you want in drop-down lists.

Creating a Custom App

You create a custom app using the **Custom List app**. The **Custom List app** creates a very basic list app that you can then customize for your particular scenario (example).

The following steps to create a **custom app** below will help you to achieve that:

1. Click the **Settings gear icon** and select **Add an App**. It will display **Your Apps page.**

2. Click the **Custom List app** on the Your Apps page. Adding Custom List dialogue box will appear.

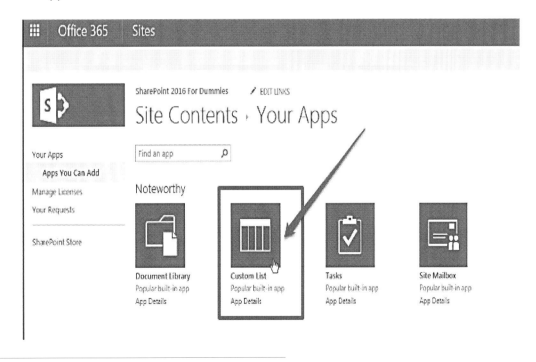

3. Provide a name for the app in the **Name text box.**
   To make things simple, you only need to give your new app a name:
   - Click the **Advanced Options link** to provide a description.
   The name you type here is used in the app's web address. Avoid using spaces in the name when you create the app. You can change the app's name to a friendlier name after you create it.
4. Click the **Create** button.
   SharePoint creates your new app and takes you automatically to the Site Contents page. Your new app has a **Green New** tag beside the app to let you know it is a new app.

Adding Columns to Your App

A new custom app displays a single text Title column. The list also contains several behind the scenes columns that you can't see, such as ID and Version. To make the custom app your own, you have to add columns to the app.

Columns are like fields in a database table. When you add a column to your app, a data entry field will appear in the app's New Form to give you a place to enter data into that column.

Follow these steps to add columns to your custom app:

a. From your app open in the browser,
   - Click on the **List** tab on the Ribbon. and

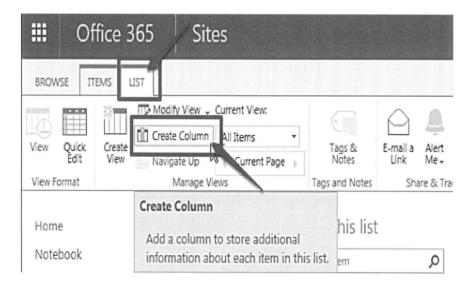

   - Then click the **Create Column** button. The Create Column window will appear.
b. Type a **name** for your new column in the **Column Name field**.
c. Select the **type of information** you want to store in the column.
   The options given here are fairly intuitive: Single Line of Text, Number, Date and Time, and so on.
d. In the Additional Column Settings section, select the **options** that further define your column's type.

The column type you select in Step 3 determines what options you have available for configuring the column.

    e. (Optional) If you want SharePoint to test the values entered into your column, use the Column **Validation section** to enter your formula,

    f. Click **OK.** SharePoint adds the column to your custom app.

You can change the column properties later and rearrange the order of the columns by using the List Settings page.

After you first create a custom app, use the List or Library Settings page to modify your app, where you have all the commands at your fingertips to power through the column creation, you can pick site columns, create your columns, and rearrange them. After your app has been created and you need to add more columns, the Create Column button on the List tab of the Ribbon is a handy way to add one or two columns without leaving the main page.

Getting to Know Column Types

Columns are used to store data, and unlike a spreadsheet, you need to define the type of column as you create it, as shown in the diagram below. For those who work with databases, this is a familiar concept. By defining the type of column, you gain extra functionality based on that type and will help to control the type of information that can be entered into the column and how that information is presented on screen. For example, users can enter only a number in a Number column; they can't add mixed text.

SharePoint provides several built-in column types that you can select for your apps, such as columns that know how to handle dates and URLs. Third-party companies and developers in your organization can also create custom column types that can be added to SharePoint. For example, if your company needs a column that handles a full zip code (the zip code plus four numbers), a developer could create it for you.

Validating Data Entry

Column validation options allow you to define additional limits and constraints for your data. For example, you may want to ensure that a value in one Date column occurs after another Date column. For example, column validation can ensure that the date in the Date Finished column can't be earlier than the date in the Date Started column you can't finish a project before it's begun.

To use column validation on your app, the following steps should be observed below:

- In your app where you want to validate data entry and
    - Click the **List Settings** button on the List tab of the Ribbon.
- Under General Settings, click the **Validation Settings link.**
- Type a formula in the **Formula text box**.

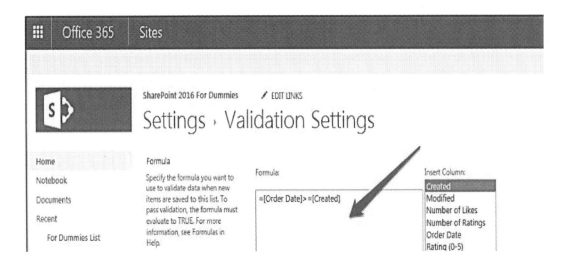

- Enter a user message that you want to appear if the validation Formula fails.

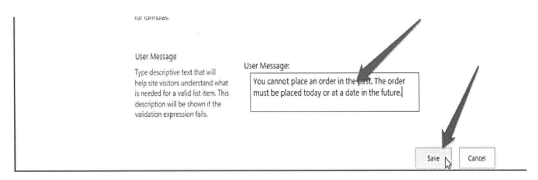

- Click the **Save** button.

When users enter data into your form, the validation formula is evaluated. If the formula evaluates to FALSE, your user message will appear on the form, as shown in the diagram below.

You can add column validation to columns created at the app or site level. Validation created for site-level columns applies everywhere that column is used, although the formula can be overriding at the app where the site-level column is used.

Working with the Title Column

Unlike SharePoint's predefined apps, your custom app has only one column when you first create it (the Title column). Unfortunately, you can't delete the Title column or change its data type, but you can rename it, hide it, or make it not required.

To rename the Title column, follow the steps below:

- Click the **List Settings** button on the List tab of the Ribbon.
- Under the Columns heading, click the **Title hyperlink**.
- Replace the title with your title and make modifications to the other properties as desired.

The Title column is used by the list as a means to access the data entry forms to view and edit the list item. You can opt to hide the Title column so that it doesn't appear on any of the app forms. The hidden column will still appear in views unless you remove it from the view.

To hide the Title column:

1. In your list, click the **List Settings** button on the List tab.
2. If the Content Types section isn't visible, enable management of content types by following these steps:
   a. Click the **Advanced Settings link** on the List Settings page.
   b. Select the **Yes** button under Allow Management of Content Types, and then click **OK**. The Content Types section becomes visible on the List Settings page.
3. In the Content Types section of the List Settings page, click the **Item content** type. The List Content-Type information will appear.
   If you want to change the Title column in a document library, you click the Document content type. The Item content type applies to custom apps only. In a predefined app, such as a Tasks app, you click the Task content type.
4. Click the **Title column.** The Title column's properties appear.
5. Under Column Settings, select the **Hidden** (Will Not Appear in Forms) radio button, as shown in the diagram below and
   - Click **OK**. The Title column doesn't appear on forms.

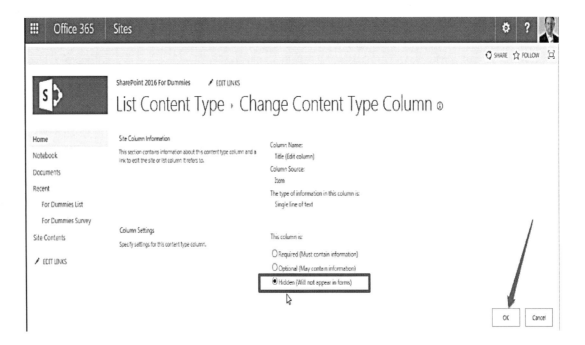

Downloading Apps from the SharePoint Store

In addition to the apps that come with SharePoint, you can also add apps from third parties. These third-party apps appear in the SharePoint Store. If you're using SharePoint Online, then you have access to the full store. If you're using SharePoint On-Premises, then your local IT administrators may have locked down the apps that you can add for security reasons.

The SharePoint Store can be found on the Your Apps page.

1. You access the Your Apps page by clicking the **Settings gear icon** and
2. Then selecting **Add an App**. Take a look and see what SharePoint apps you have available in the store.

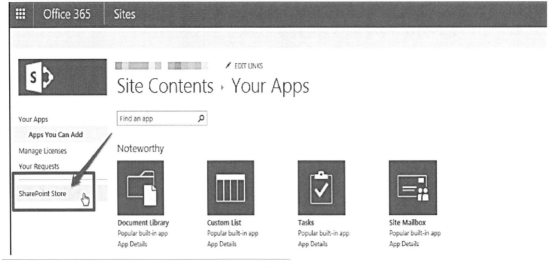

You can choose to view all apps or only those that are free by selecting the Price refiner on the left side of the page. You can also sort apps by clicking a category link. If you want to purchase an app, click it and then click the Buy It button. After you click the Buy It button, you have to log in with your Microsoft account. If you already have a credit card on file with your Office 365 subscription, then you can purchase and download the app. Otherwise, you are prompted to enter your credit card information.

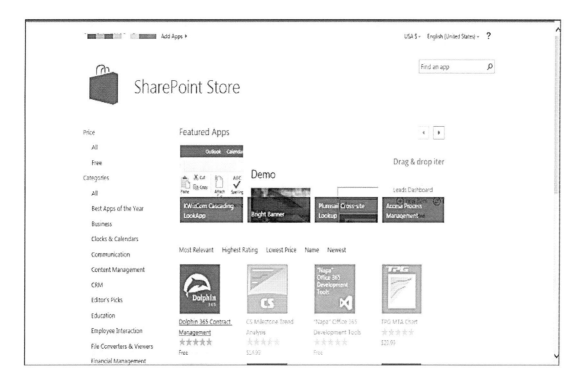

Creating Calendar in SharePoint

SharePoint calendars allow us to easily access personal events, holidays, team events, and company schedules. It also allows managers to inform co-workers about meetings.

How to Create Calendar app

To create a calendar app, these are the following steps that will guide:

1. On the **Home page** of your site:
    - Click on the **+ New**, and

- Click on **App** from the small menu.

2. Your apps window will appear, scroll down the window:
   - Click on the **calendar app**. You can also type calendar from the **search bar** at the top and click on it.

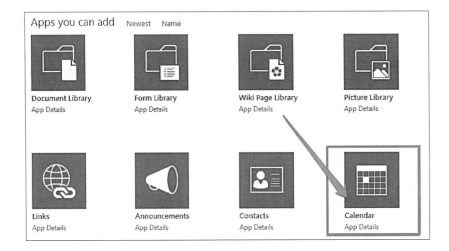

3. Once you click on the **calendar app.** Inside the box enter the **calendar name** that you want to create:

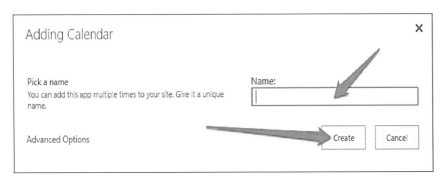

- Click on the **Create** button.
4. Now, from the site content page, the new **app calendar** is created.
5. Click on the **calendar**.

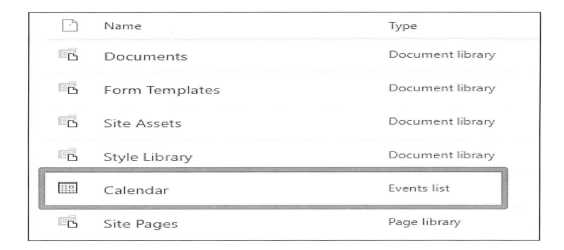

The screenshot below shows that a calendar is created.

How to Enable Versioning

1. At the top left side angle of the ribbon window:
   - Click on the **Calendar** tab.

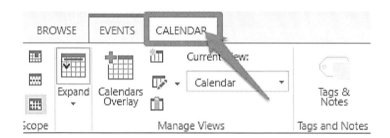

   - Click on **List Settings** at the right angle on the top.

2. A Setting page will appear on the screen, click on the **Versioning setting.**

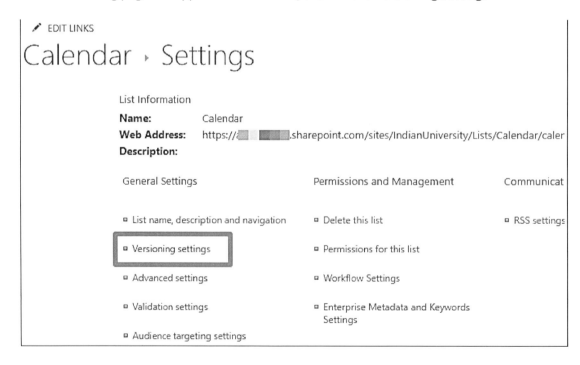

3. In the Versioning setting window, click on the **Yes** radio button for Create a version each time you edit an item in this list?

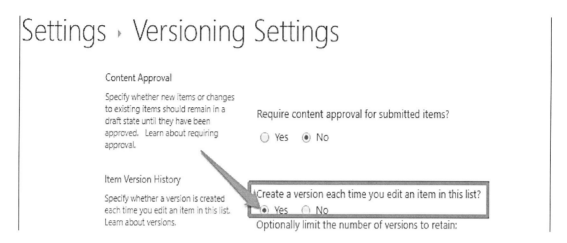

- Click on the **OK** at the bottom of the screen.

Add New Event in the Calendar

Add events in the calendar allows you to maintain and manage a list of events within the site.

To add events to the calendar, follow the process below:

1. Move the mouse on the **date** or double click on the **date** to which you want to add the event.

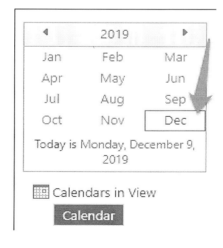

2. A link with **+Add** will appear on the date that you selected:
   - Click on the **+Add.**

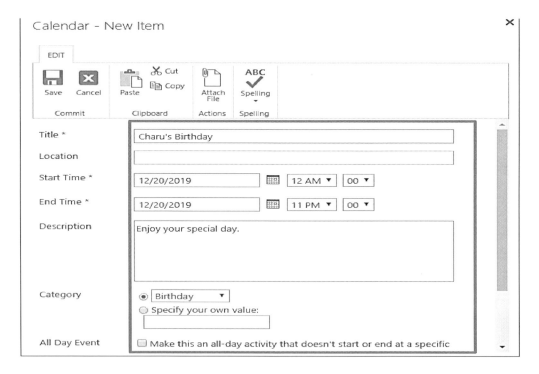

3. A page window will appear on the screen. Fill in the information required and

   - Click on the **Save** at the bottom of the screen.

The following screenshot will show that events have been added to the calendar.

SUNDAY	MONDAY	TUESDAY	WEDNESDAY	THURSDAY	FRIDAY	SATURDAY
1	2	3	4 + Add	5	6	7
8	9	10	11	12	13	14
15	16	17	18	19	20 12:00 am - 11:00 Charu's Birthday	21
22	23	24	25 12:00 am - 11:00 Christmas Day	26	27	28
29	30	31	1	2	3	4

SharePoint Libraries

SharePoint library is quite similar to a list. It provides a place on the site where you can create, update, upload, and share files with team members. SharePoint library is mainly used to display a list of files and information about the files, such as who created the file, and who last modified a file. Example: A document library is used to organize and share documents with your team members.

Performance Task in Library

These are the following tasks that you can perform in the library:

- Creating a document library
- Upload files to a document library
- Add column and edit view in the document library
- Edit a file in a document library
- Add a link in a document Library
- Creating a Picture library
- Upload files to a picture library
- Search and Filter in a document library
- Collaboration in the document library
- SharePoint Alerts
- Delete file from a document library

666

Creating Document Library

A document library provides a secure place to store files, so that you and your team members can find those files easily, and can access them from any device at any time.

The following steps will help you to create a document library:

1. From the home page of your site, click on the **+ New** then

 - Select **Document Library** from the drop-down menu.
2. Enter a name for the document library that you want to create e.g. "**About**":

 - Enter the **Description** of the library (Description is optional).
 - Click on **Show in site navigation** to mark the box.

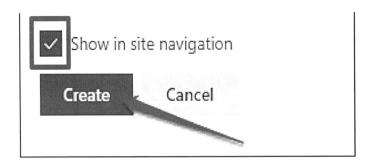

 - Then click on **Create.**

The created document library "**About**" can be seen at the left side angle.

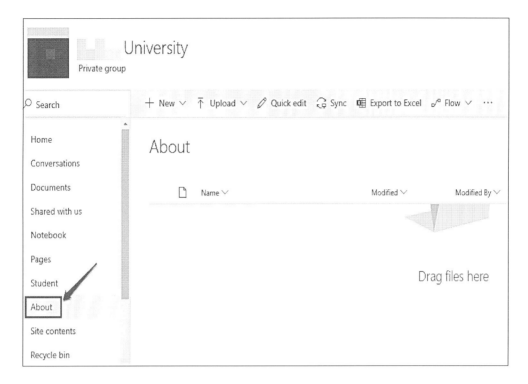

Uploading Files to Document Library

Once you create the library, you can upload your files, folders, and Templates to it.

There are two methods of uploading files to the document library.

The first method can be done by using the **Upload button.** From the home page of your site, click on the **Upload** and

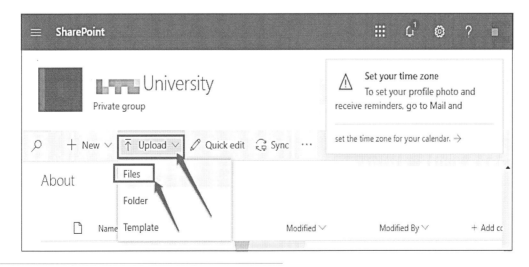

668

- Select **files** from the drop-down menu.
- Click on **desktop**.

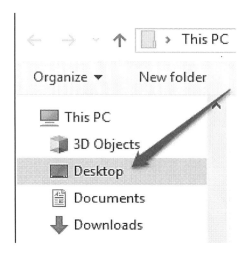

- Then click the **document file** you want to upload.

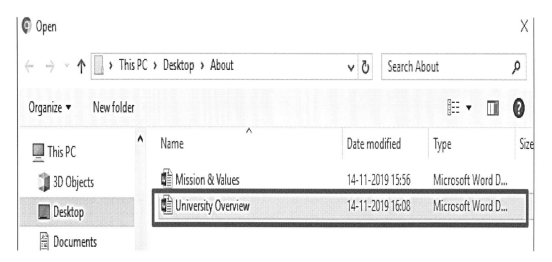

- Click on the **Open.**

You can check out the file **University Overview** is uploaded in the library.

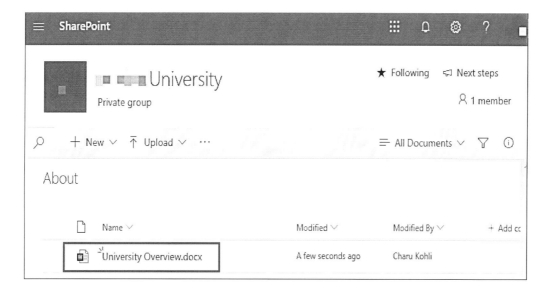

Alternatively, to upload files, you can as well use the Drag and Drop option

Drag and Drop is the easiest way to upload files in the library.

1. Click on the **document file** you want to upload:

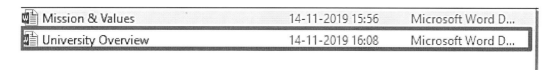

- Drag the **document file** and drop it to the **SharePoint library.**

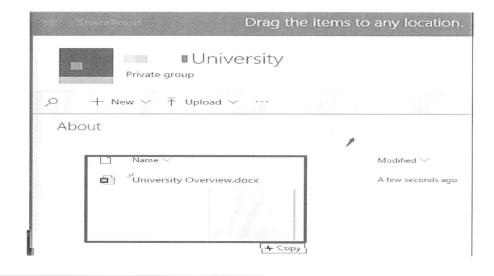

The image below shows that the file has been uploaded to the library.

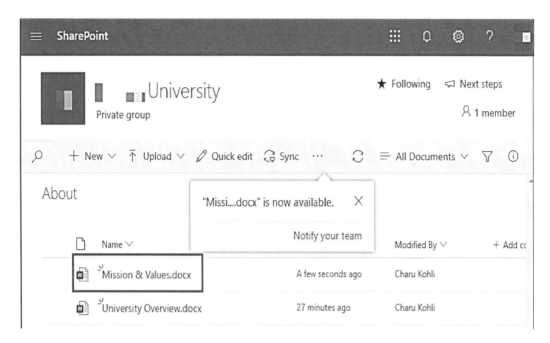

Adding Column and Edit View in the Document Library

How to Add Column

1. Go to your working library. In our case, the working library is **About**:
   - Click on the **file** in which you want to add a column, a drop-down menu opens.

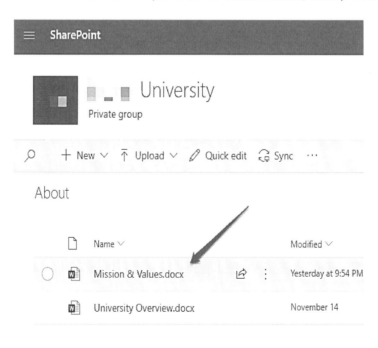

- Select a **single line of text.**

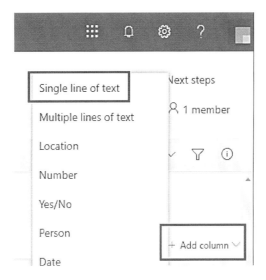

- Then click on the **+Add column.**

2. The following window will appear, enter the **Column name** and **Description** (Description is optional).

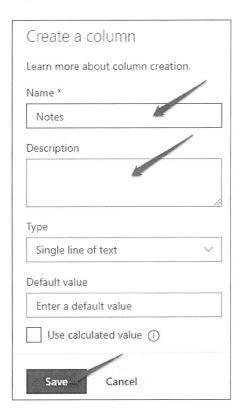

- `Click on the **Save**.

The following screenshot shows that a new column Notes is created.

How to Edit View

Edit view is one of the most important operations in the document library, to edit the view.

- First, click on the **All Documents**, a drop-down menu will appear.

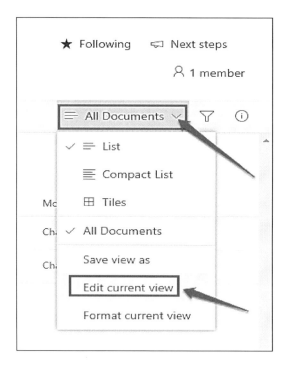

- Click on the **Edit current view**.
- The Edit view window will appear with the Column Name and Position from the left:
  - Click on the drop-down **arrow** to change the position of the column to your wish.

- Once you set the Position, click on **OK** at the top of the screen.

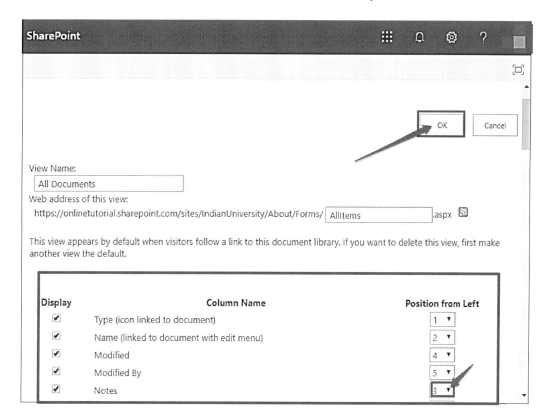

- Now, the **Notes** are in the third position, which was previously in the fourth position.

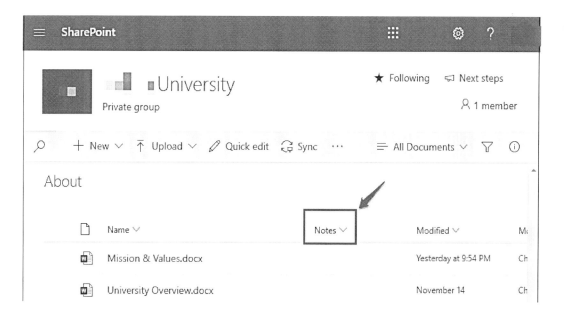

Edit File in Document Library

To edit the file in the document, follow the steps below:

- From the Home page of your site.
  - At the left side corner, click on **Site content.**

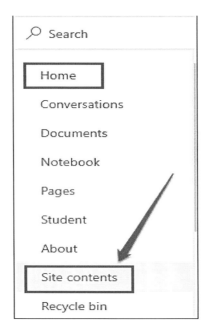

- Click or Select the **file** that you want to edit.

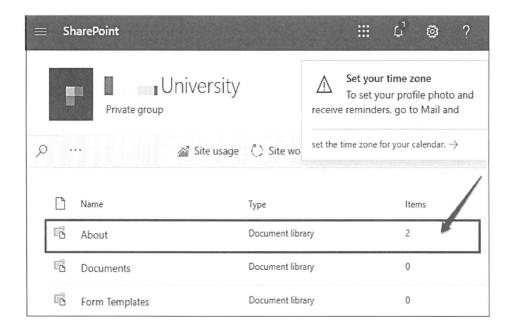

Note: If the selected file type is supported for previewing, it will open in online mode. If not, then you will get a download prompt. Once the file is opened or downloaded in an online app, you can edit and save the file.

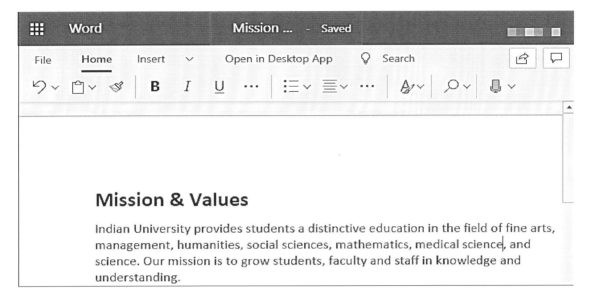

Note: When you edit the file in Office 365, your file is saved automatically. If you edit a file offline, you will need to upload it back to the library.

Add a Link in the Library

To add a link in the document library, use the following steps:

1. Go to the library where you want to add the link.
2. Click on the **+New**.

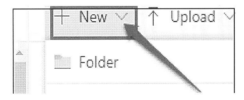

- Click or Select **"Link"** from the drop-down menu.

3. Once clicking the link, a "**Create a link to**" window will appear.
   - Inside the box, enter the **link** and enter the name in "**Filename**" option that you want to add.

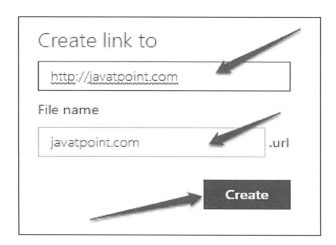

   - Click on **Create**.
4. The link is successfully added to the document library.

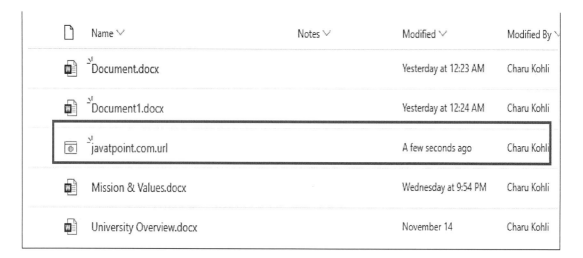

	Name ⌄	Notes ⌄	Modified ⌄	Modified By ⌄
📄	Document.docx		Yesterday at 12:23 AM	Charu Kohli
📄	Document1.docx		Yesterday at 12:24 AM	Charu Kohli
⊕	javatpoint.com.url		A few seconds ago	Charu Kohli
📄	Mission & Values.docx		Wednesday at 9:54 PM	Charu Kohli
📄	University Overview.docx		November 14	Charu Kohli

Creating Picture Library

SharePoint picture library allows you to store and upload pictures that can be used on your site or shared with others.

The following steps below will help you to create a picture library:

1. From the left side of the Home page of your site:
   - Click on the **+New**.

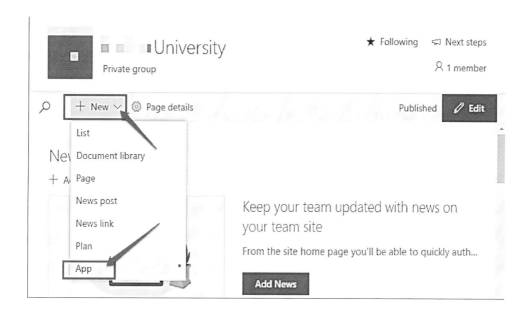

- Click or Select App from the drop-down menu.
2. Search for **picture library**, once you find the picture library, click on it.

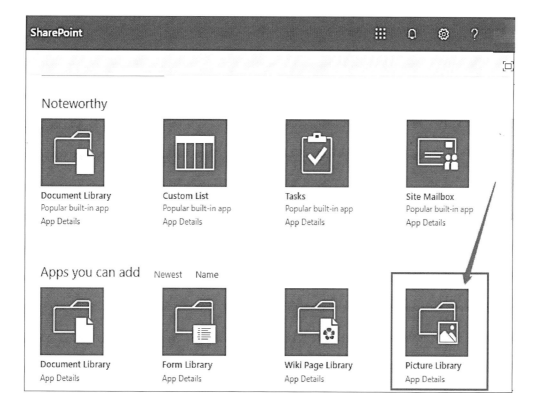

3. Provide the name of the **picture library** then,
   - Click on the **Create**.

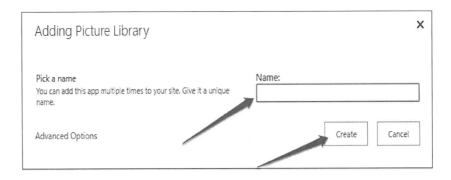

4. Now, the picture library "University" is created.

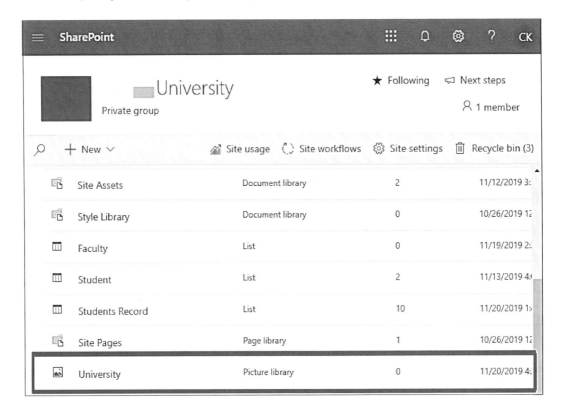

Upload Files to Picture Library

Once the picture library is created, you need to upload the documents to it.

There are two methods to upload files in the picture library.

1. Go to your stored files and click on the **file** you want to upload:
   - Drag and drop it into the SharePoint **picture library**.

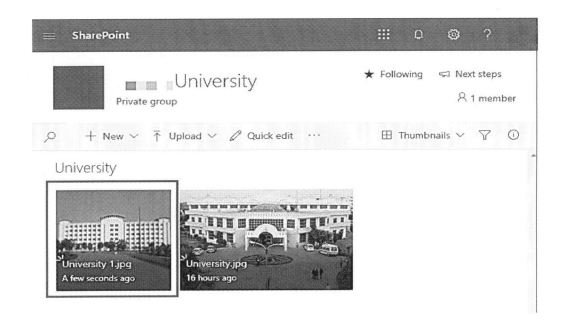

The file is uploaded to the picture library.

Alternatively, you can use the upload button

The upload button is the most frequently used method to upload multiple files and documents in the picture library.

1. Click on the **Upload** at the top of the screen.

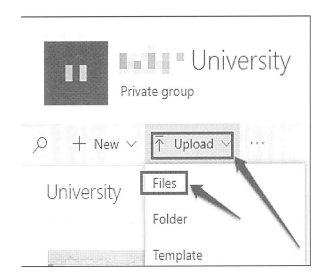

2. Select **Files** from the drop-down menu.
3. Browse the location where the file is stored, click on the **desktop** and

- Select the **file** that you want to upload.

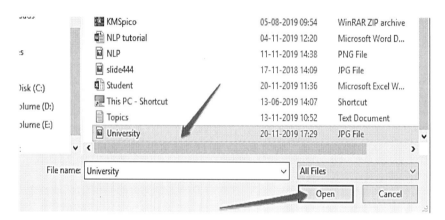

- Click on the **Open**. After clicking open the file will upload to the picture library.

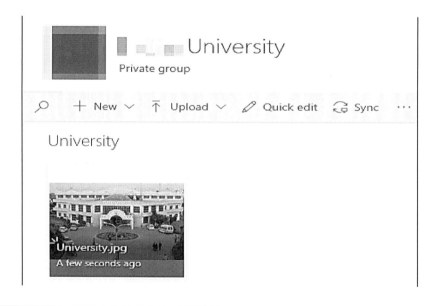

Search and Filter Files in Document Library

How to Search Files

A library may contain many different items, and there may be a chance that you cannot see all these items in the library on one screen. SharePoint searching tools allow you to easily search the files according to their name, modified time, and name of the person who has modified the files.

1. In the document library of the home page, click on the **search bar** located in the upper left corner of the screen:
   - Type the name of the file that you want to search in the **search box**.
   - Press the **enter key** on the keyboard to search or click on the **search icon** on the screen.

How to Filter Files

To filter the file, observe the steps below:

- First, go to the document library:
  - Select the **column** that you want to filter.
  - Click on the **file** name that you want to sort, a drop-down open
  - Select the order in which you want to sort the files.

- After selecting the order, this is what it will display below that files are filtered into Z to A order.

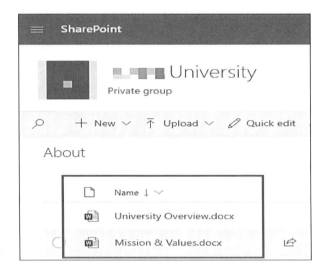

Collaboration in the Document Library

As you know, SharePoint is designed to make collaboration easy. It allows your team members to create, edit, and share documents with others.

Sharing a File

SharePoint allows you to share the file with someone who is **not** a member of the SharePoint site.

- Go to the document library or on the document library of your page site:
  - Select the **file** that you want to share.

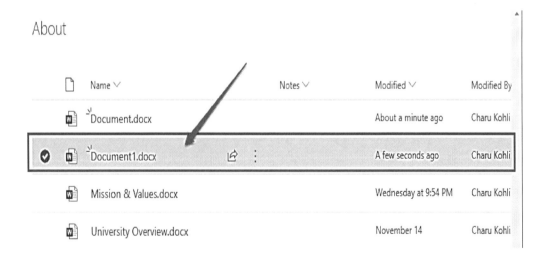

o Click on the **Share** at the top of the screen.

- Once you click on the Share, a small pop-up window will appear:
  o Then click on this **arrow "(>)"**.

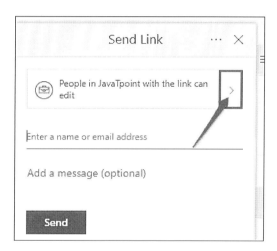

- After you click on this **arrow (>)** the following options open on the screen.

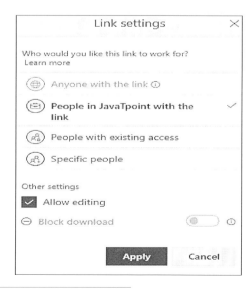

- o **Anyone with this link**: Anyone can access this link with or without logging into office 356.
- o **People in Java point with this link**: Only people who worked at java point can access this link.
- o **People with existing access**: Send link to someone who already has access.
- o **Specific people:** Enter the email address of specific people to whom you want to permit accessing the files.
- Select an option from the drop-down menu of your choice e.g. **People in Java point with this link.**

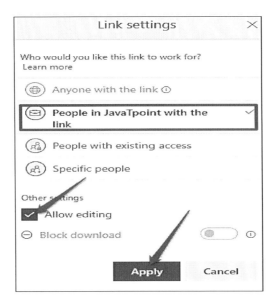

- o Tick on the **Allow editing box**.
- o Then click on the **Apply button**.
- Enter the **email address**.

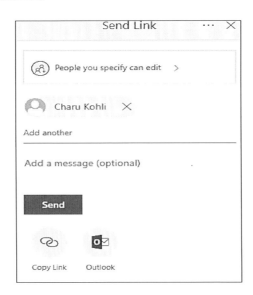

- Click on the **send**.

The link is shared successfully.

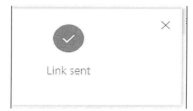

SharePoint Alerts

SharePoint alerts are the notifications that allow you to monitor changes that are made on a site.

Setting an alert on a file will send you an email message or text message to your mobile phone when changes are made in a specific file.

There are three steps to set up alerts on a file:

1. On the toolbar, click on the ellipsis **(...)** button.

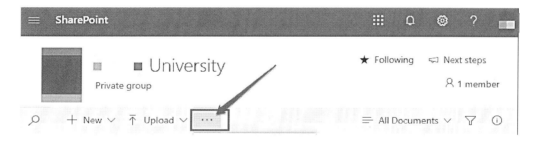

- Click or select **Alert me**.

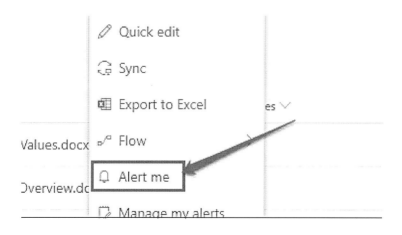

2. After clicking on Alert me, the items change window will appear on the screen. Click the following information according to your desire below:
   - **Alert Title**: Enter the title for the alert.

- **Send Alert to:** Enter the user name or e-mail address of the person to whom you want to send the alert.

- **Delivery Method:** Specify which method is used to deliver the alert.
- **Change Type**: Specify the type of changes for that you want to be alerted.

- **Send alert for these changes:** Specify whether to filter alerts based on specified criteria.

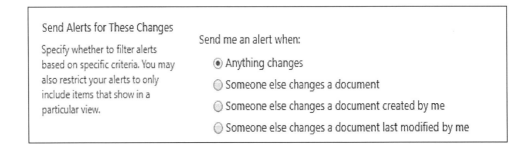

- **When to send an alert:** It shows how frequently you want to send an alert.

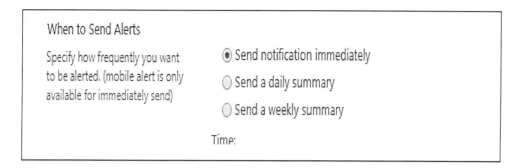

3. Now click on each of the items according to your requirement:
    - Click on **OK** at the bottom of the screen.
4. You are good to receive an alert after you have created a new file or make any changes, an alert e-mail will be sent to your outlook.

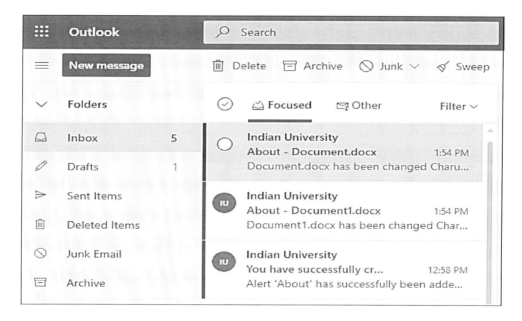

5 Key Things to Know

Organizations use SharePoint in a variety of different ways, and SharePoint itself can encompass a great number of capabilities, making it highly customizable to fit your organization's needs. However, at its most basic level, here are 5 key things you need to know to start using SharePoint.

Tip 1: How to Upload Files

Do you know that it is very easy to drag and drop files from your computer into your SharePoint document library, and there are two ways you can upload files?

The first way, this is known as the "**simple way**"

1. Open the SharePoint folder where you want to upload a document.
2. Click to **open File Explorer** on your computer.
3. Then click to **Drag** and **drop** the file from File Explorer over to SharePoint with your mouse.

The second way, it's also known as the "**Alternative Way**"

1. Click on "**Upload**" from the SharePoint folder where you want to upload the document.

2. In the box that pops up, click "**File**".
3. Select the file(s) you want to upload.
4. Click on "**Open**".

Tip 2: Opening Documents for Editing

When you open a document with SharePoint 365:

- Just simply click on the document name. It will open in Office Online.
- From there, you have the option of editing online (simply start editing) or
- Click "**EDIT IN WORD**" to open the document in Microsoft Word and edit in the application.

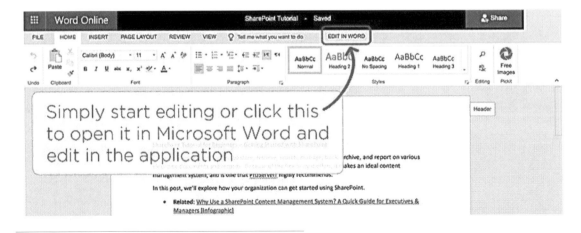

Tip 3: Collaborating with Others on a Document

SharePoint makes it extremely easy to collaborate on a document with your colleagues. When you open a document, you'll be able to see the number of people, who are currently working on the document with you, in the top right-hand corner of your screen.

When multiple people are making changes to the document simultaneously, you will see the changes being made in real-time, along with the author who is making the changes.

If you would like to invite someone to edit the document:

- Click the "**Share**" button located at the right corner and you will be able to easily share the document.

- After clicking on the share button, a small menu will pop up, enter the **name** or **email address** to who you want to share the file.

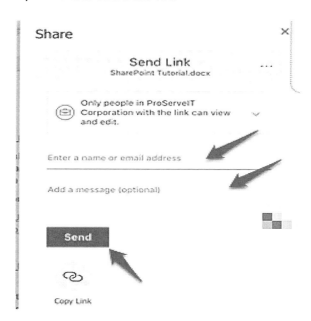

- Fill in the next option.
- Then click on **send**.

Tip 4: Searching for a Document

Just as you might search for an email in Outlook, or a file on your computer, the search function in SharePoint Online is easy-to-use and makes searching for your documents effortless.

You can search for something in SharePoint using two different methods:

1. Using the "**Search this site**" search box in the upper right-hand corner of your SharePoint site, or
2. Using the "**Find a file**" search box above your list of folders/documents.
    - **Search this Site:** This option searches your entire SharePoint site for the keyword(s) you have typed, and it pulls the search results from file names, metadata, and the text inside Office and readable PDF files.
    - **Find a File:** This option searches for the keywords you have typed in file names, metadata, and text inside Office and readable PDF files, but since the box falls under a specific document library, it's only going to search that document library for the results.

Tip 5: Copying and Moving Files and Folders

Depending on your version of SharePoint, there are different ways you can move or copy files.

Copying Files:

1. Click the **items** that you want to copy.

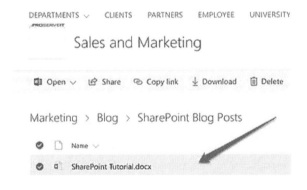

691

2. Click on the three dots at the top beside the delete command (**...**).

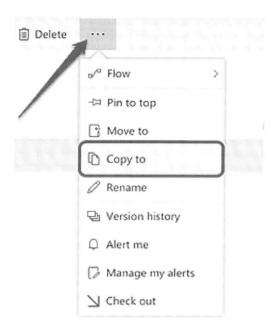

3. Click **Copy to.**
4. Under "**Choose a destination**" you can select the folder that you want to copy the information into. If probably you don't see the destination you want, click on "**Browse sites**" to see the full list of sites that you can copy to.
5. Click "**copy here**" to complete the copy.

CONCLUSION ON SHAREPOINT 365

So far, so good, I've been able to successfully show you how SharePoint can connect you with the whole world without you leaving the confines of your room. Also, you've been shown how companies can use the platform to control access to information and automate workflow processes across business units.

If you have ever tried and given up on using SharePoint or you're even a novice, at the end of this user guide, you would have become a pro in the use of SharePoint. With the compendium of information provided in this user guide, you can be nothing but the best in the use of Microsoft SharePoint. I wish you all the best!

BOOK SIX

MICROSOFT ONEDRIVE

INTRODUCTION TO MICROSOFT ONEDRIVE

Microsoft OneDrive is simply a web-based storage and sharing platform. It is very similar to Microsoft SharePoint, its advantage over the counterpart is that it provides a more personal experience for end-users to store private files or to collaborate with others both inside and outside the organization.

Whilst SharePoint is very much an organization-wide storage and collaboration solution, OneDrive provides a cut-down, more individual experience and is often likened to being the 'My Documents' replacement, whereas SharePoint typically replaces file servers.

Microsoft OneDrive is stored in form of a cloud which can be accessed with any device that contains it. It enhances the easy storage of files, documents without much stress. Microsoft OneDrive assists you to keep the proper arrangement of files, and the ability to access your relevant documents, photos, and any other related files from a different device. It also does much work on how to share those documents or photos with friends, family, and co-operators. Microsoft OneDrive can be opened on your PC, website, and your mobile phone. It also assists in the proper updating of every file on your PC. Any documents that are being edited or added in OneDrive will be synced through the cloud to people or devices you have shared with previously.

Microsoft OneDrive has become a very interesting storage folder because of its easy accessibility. One of the most interesting things about OneDrive is the ability to open it with a mobile phone which makes it easy for everyone to use because not everybody can afford to get a PC. Even if you don't have the folder on your PC or the app on your mobile phone, you can access it through direct internet by typing **OneDrive.com** and it also performs the same action as the one on your PC and mobile app.

Another thing that is very relevant here is to know how you can add the file into OneDrive. And it is very simple, this is done when you have already installed the app, then you find the OneDrive folder on your PC, after then you drag and drop the file in the folder. In the case of a mobile phone, you can add files using the OneDrive app. You will turn on camera upload for you to save every photo and video taken, and it will facilitate quick and easy views of the files on other devices.

One important thing you will understand is how to share files and create documents on Microsoft OneDrive without stress. Sharing of files via OneDrive solves the problems of sending massive files through emails. When you share with OneDrive, they will receive the link to the folder or files. You should also bear in mind that everything you put on Microsoft OneDrive is only seen by you, except you, share it with family and friends. With OneDrive, you can also create Word documents like OneNote notebooks, PowerPoint presentations, and Excel spreadsheets from any device via OneDrive websites. You just sign in and select "**New**" the word document you want to create will show up, then you click on it. There are many more things you will learn about Microsoft OneDrive as we proceed to the following chapters.

CHAPTER ONE

THE BASICS OF MICROSOFT ONEDRIVE

Definition Of OneDrive

OneDrive is an online Microsoft cloud that stores files and documents on its platform. OneDrive was first known as **SkyDrive**, but it was later rebranded earlier in 2014 due to a trademark problem brought up by a United Kingdom local broadcaster. OneDrive assimilated into Windows 10 and also as an application on Android phones, Windows phones, iOS, and on the internet through any web browser. On this platform, operators can store their photos, videos, music, and other relevant documents.

Microsoft OneDrive (formerly SkyDrive) is a file hosting service and synchronization service operated by Microsoft as part of its web version of Office. First launched in August 2007, OneDrive allows users to store files and personal data like Windows settings or BitLocker recovery keys in the cloud, share files, and sync files across Android, Windows Phone, and iOS mobile devices, Windows and macOS computers, and the Xbox 360, Xbox One, and Xbox Series X and S consoles. Users can upload Microsoft Office documents to OneDrive.

OneDrive offers 5 GB of storage space free of charge, with 100 GB, 1 TB, and 6 TB storage options available either separately or with Office 365 subscriptions. OneDrive is included in Microsoft 365 and Office 365 plans, in SharePoint plans, and can also be purchased as a standalone plan.

Benefits of Microsoft OneDrive

Undoubtedly the simplest benefit, is having a secure private cloud–based folder, to store everything you need, which you can access from any device. But more than that, you can set sharing and editing rights at either folder or document level, meaning you can start collaborating with colleagues either inside or outside your organization. In a GDPR (General Data Protection Regulation) world, you can also stop attaching documents to emails with every risk that entails, and simply work on cloud shared files instead.

The main benefits of OneDrive include:

- Unlimited file access anytime and anywhere
- Renders files available from anywhere for collaboration
- Organizational platform for files
- Free-up device storage
- Sharable content across teams, large or small
- Customizable sync experience (for admin)
- Securely store files and information
- Supports multimedia

- Tightly integrate with other Microsoft products (including 365)

Comparison Between OneDrive and SharePoint

OneDrive might appear, on the surface, to be the same as another Microsoft tool, SharePoint. But, on closer inspection, there are key differences.

In particular, these apps have different ways of achieving similar goals; file sharing, project management and collaboration are all features, but they can be experienced very differently. The project management market, when it comes to software options, is often overly competitive and it becomes harder to narrow down the better tools for your work.

OneDrive

OneDrive, as a storage solution, is typically used by those wanting to centralize their content storage. It's more intelligent than a filing cabinet with its dynamic storage settings and features and can be flexible for businesses of all sizes, from smaller parties, to larger enterprises.

SharePoint

SharePoint is a collaborative tool and a means of creating internal websites (or infrastructures known as intranets). This app goes beyond being a traditional shared team drive, with enough rich features that it's not simply just for file storage.

The similarities between the two often creates confusion, but OneDrive and SharePoint are different tools. In essence, OneDrive is a simple, effective file storage that's immediately ready (with minimal setup). To get the most out of SharePoint, however, you may require professional IT support as it can be finessed for more complex internal storage structures.

Difference Between OneDrive and SharePoint

In Microsoft 365, there are 2 main places to share your documents and they are OneDrive and SharePoint, these two apps are based on the same technology, they look and feel the same and have many of the same features. If you know how to use one, you can use the other. OneDrive is mostly used to share your files, only you have access to it, you can work on your document there privately, and if you want to share, you can do that, but its default setting is **private**. SharePoint, on the other hand, is used to share your team files, everyone in your team has access to it, teamwork can be done there and its default setting is on **shared.**

In OneDrive you can just store your document, it is optimized to make it really easy to work on your file. In SharePoint, you can also store the document in the same way, you can create pages and work with a list of dates as well, although it is more flexible, it is more complex compared to OneDrive. If you only want to work with documents and would prefer simplicity, then choose OneDrive. OneDrive has a library to share all your documents and it is called **My Files.**

In My Files, you can create and upload documents, files and have different folders to store them in. in SharePoint site, the default site is called **documents** and it works in the same way, however in the SharePoint site, you can have access to lots of libraries, and anyone who has access to the site can create them and you might end up with lots and lots of document. If you need the flexibility to create lots of libraries to be able to store all your documents, choose SharePoint. In OneDrive nothing is shared unless you change the settings and allow it to be. The default setting is private unless you share it and it is very easy to see what is being shared, and you can as well stop sharing anytime you want to. In SharePoint, everything is shared with your team unless you don't want it to be. Everything you create will be seen by all your teammates.

If you preferred to work privately on your document and maybe share it when you're done, it is advisable to use OneDrive. If you however want to share the document as soon as you're working on it, you want to collaborate, wants people to review it, then store it in SharePoint.

Comparison Between Google Drive and OneDrive

Google drive is a file storage and synchronization service created by Google. It allows users to store files in the cloud, synchronize files across devices and share files. Each Gmail account comes with a google drive, where you will get 15 GB of storage with each account.

While Google drive is associated with all google devices, OneDrive comes with Microsoft Offices. Google Drive has a cloud only model but OneDrive has one leg in the cloud and the other on the desktop. There are some certain similarities between the two, but they are quite different and have features which differs from each one.

Difference Between Google Drive and OneDrive

Google Drive is your personal photos and video backup storage unit, it works with your indoor devices, Google photos help you to bring your entire pictures store in the cloud. Google Drive offers **15 GB of data** which includes all your videos, photos Gmail data. Although you can change the setting in Google help which can give you unlimited storage space. However, it will compress your images. OneDrive on the other hand works with all your Microsoft Office apps and you can share and save your files anytime you want. OneDrive give you **5 GB free storage** and on the phone application, you have the option to upload pictures instantly but the 5GB might not be enough.

Furthermore, Google Drive has a consumer-first focus approach, OneDrive's customer base is focused on enterprises. Using OneDrive, you can host Microsoft Office apps, it has a web version and a desktop version but Google Drive doesn't.

Additionally, for video storage and playing, it is advisable to use Google drive because Google drive's video player can speed up the touch, it is fast and responsive unlike OneDrive's which is slow and takes up a lot of time to stream the videos before playing but it allows you to view different types of files like zip, photos, videos etc. but both applications cannot support the **rar** files.

In OneDrive, you can have the privacy to lock some files because this app comes with a folder called **personal vault** where you can save all your personal files. It can only exist with two-step verification and automatically unlocks after ten minutes.

If you want to upload heavy files to the cloud, then Google drive should be your choice, it supports files upload up to five terabytes, unlike OneDrive which only supports the maximum of 100 GB.

On the platform note, both apps are available on mobile devices, OneDrive is also available on Windows and macOS. Google drive is not official software for windows or mac but it can be installed on each, you can easily download it on chrome or Microsoft Edge. Both apps offer the recycle bin, search etc. their monthly plans are quite cheap and reasonable, there are many benefits of using both apps but the features differ and your usage will determine which of the app you need for each function.

How To Download OneDrive on Your Computer

The device you are using determines how you will get OneDrive on your system. In the case of a personal computer, the windows you are using will be put into consideration, for example, if you are using **Windows 7** you need to Download OneDrive, my computer is **window 10** and it already contains OneDrive. Just click on OneDrive and follow the instruction to install the app.

Set up OneDrive

Put your files in OneDrive to get them from any device.

```
Enter your email address
```

```
Create account     |     Sign in
```

1. Open and follow the instruction to "install" the app. Click on **get started** and follow the commands.

Clicking "Get started" means you agree to the Microsoft service agreement and privacy statement. OneDrive may also download and install its updates automatically.

Get started

2. When you have successfully installed the OneDrive on your computer, the OneDrive folder will be added automatically to Windows Explorer.

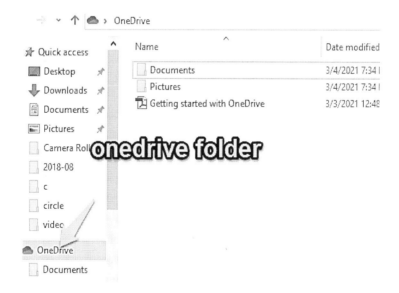

Setting Up Your Microsoft OneDrive Account

Setting up Microsoft OneDrive is very simple for those using **Windows 10** it is easier because there is no need for you to download the app for installation. All you need to do is to check the app and continue the other set-up procedures. For you to know how easy Microsoft OneDrive is with Window 10, during the Window 10 setup you will be asked whether you will like to use OneDrive if you were unable to accept OneDrive it will still be obtainable for you on the system.

In a situation where the icon refuses to come up, then you will need to prompt from the OneDrive EXE file. But for those of us using a less upgraded Windows, you will be required to download the app from the app store.

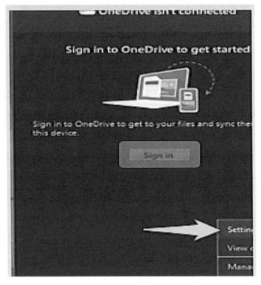

In the folder, double-click on the OneDrive.exe file, and the portrait will show in the PC tray. Then you have to right-click on the portrait and choose Settings. You have to click on the **Settings tab** and you should ensure that the box to **Start OneDrive automatically when you start signing in to Windows** is crisscross.

In the Settings screen, click the **Account tab** and choose the **Add an account** control. On the **Set-up OneDrive** display, type the email address for your Microsoft Account and after that, click on **Sign in**. You have to select your type of Microsoft OneDrive account, whether is for Work, School, or Personal use, then input your password and click on **Sign in**.

You will be required to authorize the position that Microsoft has already set on your OneDrive folder. You may decide to alternate the position or you leave it as the default and click on **Next**.

Signing Up for Microsoft OneDrive

There are procedures you follow when signing up for Microsoft OneDrive.

Step one: Enter the website **ONEDRIVE.LIVE.COM** THE INTERFACE BELOW WILL BE DISPLAYED AND YOU SELECT "SIGN UP FOR FREE"

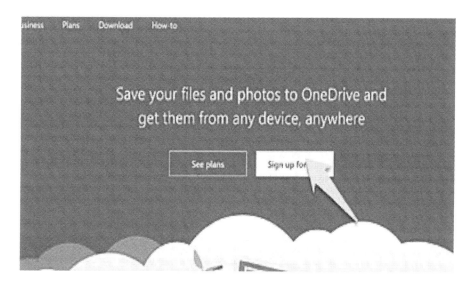

STEP TWO: CHOOSE THE ACCOUNT TYPE

IN THIS CASE, YOU WILL DECIDE WHETHER TO CREATE A PERSONAL ACCOUNT OR A BUSINESS ACCOUNT. FOR BUSINESS ACCOUNTS, THE FEATURES THERE ARE NOT FREE, YOU HAVE TO PAY TO BE ABLE TO ACCESS THEM.

Step three: Key in your **email address**

There is space provided to enter your email address, and if you don't have an email address you can also create a new one for yourself.

Step four: Enter a fresh **password**

After you key in your password, you click on **"next"**.

Step five: Other details

At this stage, you are required to indicate your country and your date of birth.

Create account

We need just a little more info to set up your account.

Country/region

Nigeria

Date of birth

Day   Month   Year

Next

Step six: Verification of your email address.

After all these processes a code will be sent to your phone number or email for proper confirmation to ensure you are the owner of the email or phone number. Then you will type in the code for it to be confirmed.

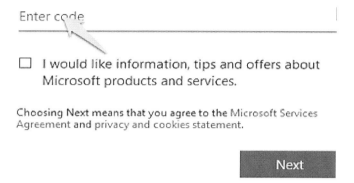

Step seven: Final confirmation and account creation

Here, you have to indicate that you are human by entering the captcha code correctly, after then your account will be created and you can now upload your files and documents to your account.

Create account

Before proceeding, we need to make sure that a real person is creating this account.

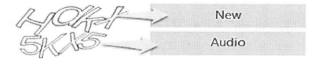

Enter the characters you see

enter code here

Signing In To Microsoft OneDrive

There are two ways you can sign in to OneDrive, either through the web page or with the application. If you already have the app on your system, then you will **sign in** with the following procedures below. But in a situation where you don't have the app on your system, then you will either install the app or log in through the web page (OneDrive.live.com).

1. You will click on the Start search case and type "**OneDrive**." Then you will see OneDrive showing in the search outcomes, and click on it.

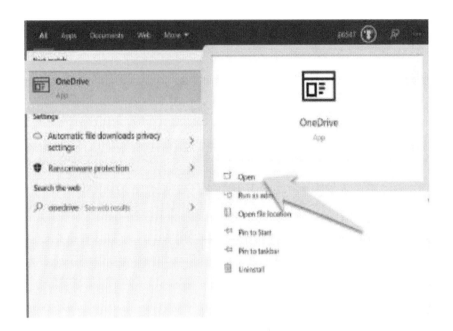

2. When you already have an account with OneDrive, you will just enter the email address you used in signing up for the account, then you will click on "**sign in**."

Put your files in OneDrive to get them from any device.

Enter your email address

3. After that, enter your password on the next page. If you have formerly set up some other form of authentication for your Microsoft account, you will be required to enter an additional code sent to your email or phone number for proper confirmation of account ownership.

4. You have **to** trail the directives to select the OneDrive folder you want. If you have signed in before on this system, you may have already had the OneDrive folder. You can click to **use this folder** or you will select **choose a new folder**.

How To Sign in To Microsoft OneDrive (For Windows 10)

For you to use OneDrive on your computer, you have to sign in to your account. Follow the procedure below to sign in your OneDrive accounts.

Step 1: Double click on the Microsoft **OneDrive icon** on your PC taskbar.

Step 2: The screen below will be displayed, then you click on sign in to access your account.

Step 3: The system will request you to key in your details for your Microsoft or OneDrive account. After then, you will click on the sign-in button.

Step 4: After then, you will be shown the succeeding screen, click the **Next** option to use the defaulting location so that the OneDrive folder will be saved, alternatively you can also choose a location for your OneDrive folder by just clicking on **Change location** connect and a fresh location is choosing.

Your OneDrive folder is here: C:\Users\Office\OneDrive

Change location

Next

Step 5: This is the last step to take, on your computer, you are required to choose the **folder** that you wish to sync your OneDrive folder. After you have chosen the one you want, click on the **next** button to proceed to setup. Then you can now click on the button.

☑ Sync all files and folders in my OneDrive

Sync only these folders
☑ ☐ Files not in a folder (182.9 KB)
> ☑ Air Doc (36.0 KB)
> ☑ Documents (0.1 KB)
> ☑ Favorites (0.0 KB)
> ☑ New folder (0.0 KB)
> ☑ Pictures (0.0 KB)
> ☑ Public (0.0 KB)
> ☑ Screenshots (770.0 KB)

Selected: 989.0 KB
Remaining space on C: 366.9 GB

Next

Signing Out from OneDrive (For Windows 10)

To delete OneDrive, all you need do is just to sign out of your Microsoft OneDrive account, and the OneDrive folder will be deleted automatically from your PC. Follow the steps/procedure below to sign out your OneDrive account

Step 1: Right-click on the Microsoft OneDrive icon that will be positioned in your computer region of the taskbar, and you will be required to click Settings for you to access Microsoft OneDrive settings.

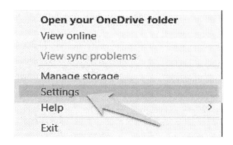

Open your OneDrive folder
View online
View sync problems
Manage storage
Settings
Help   >
Exit

Step 2: Also, you need to shift to the Accounts tab by tapping or clicking on the Accounts tag.

Step 3: Then you will be required to tap the button branded as "**Unlink OneDrive**" control.

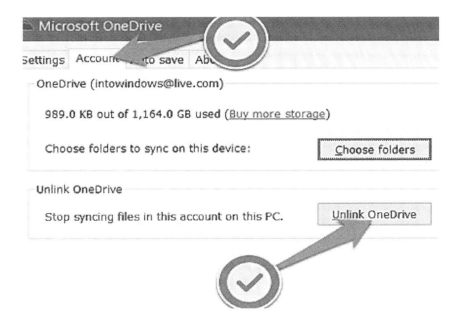

Step 4: When the account has been effectively unlinked, you will then see the "**Welcome to OneDrive**" display with the "**Sign in**" control.

CHAPTER TWO

BASIC OPERATIONS ON ONEDRIVE

The Cloud Storage

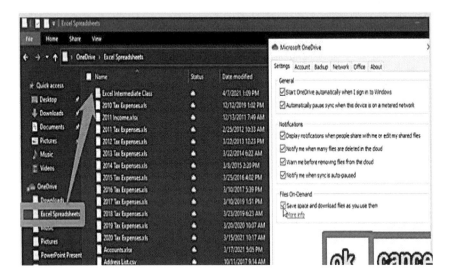

Firstly, you need to select and save your synced files or you will also be given an alternative to downloading your synced files when you need them. Just click on the **Settings tab** and you just need to search on the setting and select **Files-On-Demand**, which you will enable by default. With the help of this setting when you turned on, your Microsoft OneDrive will be saved online rather than on your PC.

The relations to your files which are online always show in your file explorer. If you click a file twice to open it, the file is already downloaded as it moves from OneDrive to your PC. The good thing about **Files-On-Demand** is the fact that more space is available for you on your hard drive. The one big disadvantage is that you are required to always open your file only when you are online.

You can choose not to go the above route if peradventure you have enough space on your hard drive. But you can activate it when you have minimal storage space. In some situations, you can just on your own decide to store some files and folders online and the rest both manually and online. You need to click on the **checkbox** if you want to turn off this alternative.

Getting Additional Space in Microsoft OneDrive

OneDrive offers 5GB of free space for storage. Consequently, if you have been using OneDrive for a very long time you can claim 15 or 25GB of free space for storage. Concerning the reports, there are limited means by which you can add extra free space on your OneDrive account for storage. For example, if you share this service with most of your friends, you can gain additional 10GB of free storage space. You can save files or documents of any type, so far they are not larger than 10GB per file. But if you still need more space, OneDrive will offer you some storage plans which can be affordable for you.

How to create folder and other documents in OneDrive

OneDrive has made it easy for you to access any of your documents or files irrespective of where you are. We will first outline the steps to create a folder in OneDrive.

The following are steps and procedures to create a folder in OneDrive.

1. Click on "**new**" then you choose "**folder**" from the down-drop menu.

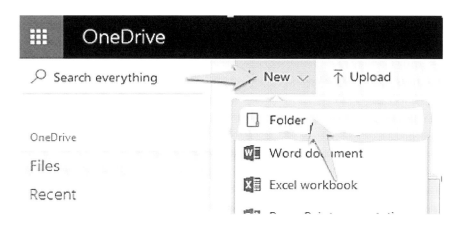

2. Type the name of the folder and click on **Create** to proceed.

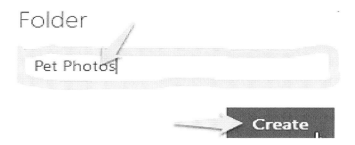

3. After the above procedure, your folder will be created, then you will click on the folder to access it. The screen below will be displayed.

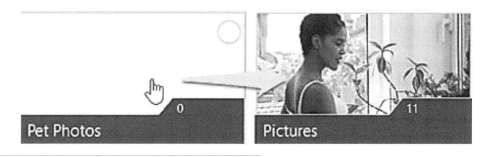

How To Create A Document

Also, follow the same procedure used in creating a folder.

1. Click on the **new** option, and then you enter the desired document you want to create from the drop-down menu.

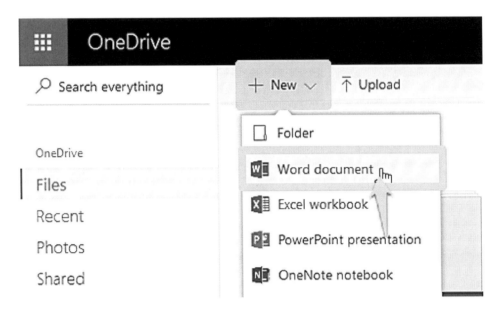

2. Your document will be created and at the same time opened at once. Below is a typical example of a word document interface display in Microsoft OneDrive.

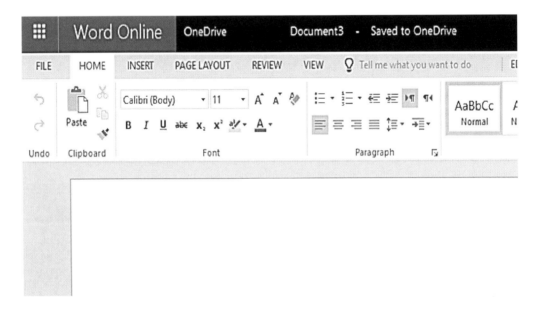

How To Add File To The Microsoft OneDrive

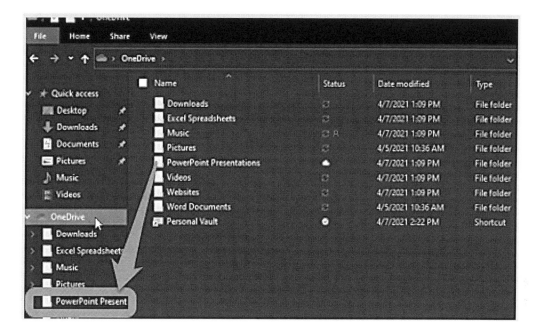

What you are required to do next is to choose the folders and files you want to add and synchronize to the OneDrive stowing. From your File Explorer, you can decide to move files and folders of your choice to sync them into where your OneDrive is found. For instance, if you decide to use a folder like PowerPoint Present for your Microsoft files, you will move the whole folder into Microsoft OneDrive (the array procedure would be in the following formats: *C:\Users\[username]\OneDrive\ PowerPoint present).*

How To Search for Files Saved in OneDrive Cloud

If you check in your **OneDrive** locker on the web it contains a **search everything box** located at the top right flank. Click on the box, then you enter the name of the file you are searching for, and available suggestions will be made for you to see whether that is what you are searching for. You can click on any of the suggested results if you found what you were searching for or you click on the **see more results** to view the complete list.

OneDrive has some other advantages when searching for files and documents. OneDrive also searches on filenames and inside the document, like PDFs, Word files, and PowerPoint presentation files. At this point, you can also limit the suggested result that will be shown by searching through the files **type** and **date** drop-down menu at the top. This helps in reducing stress when searching for a particular file or document in Microsoft OneDrive. For example, I want to see photos of the last two weeks, using the type and date drop-down menu will be of good help to you.

Another important thing is to save what you search for, so you can access it next time without much stress. The screenshot displayed below indicates a **saved search** menu where you've saved your documents. There is also a close search which will help you to end your search for any files or documents.

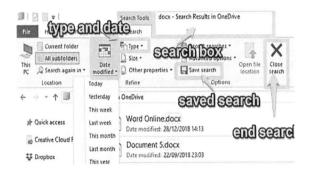

How To Upload Files in OneDrive

People think that OneDrive is only for storing files or documents, but it is not so, Microsoft OneDrive can also be used to upload files like **photos, music, videos, etc.** Under this sub-heading, we will explain in detail how to use your personal computer to upload files or documents in OneDrive without stress. Follow the procedure below to get it done.

1. First, locate the **file** you wish to upload on your computer. From the screenshot below, I indicated the file I want to upload.

2. Then click on the **file** you want to upload and drag it to the OneDrive's folder.

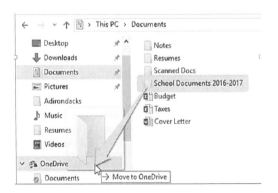

3. Next, you will see your document showing in the OneDrive.

How To Upload Files on The Web in OneDrive

In a situation where you do not have access to the OneDrive PC app, uploading through the web will be an alternative. With a **web uploader,** you can upload your files on the net without much struggle. But comparing to the PC app it is a bit slow and time-consuming and is also an easy procedure to upload your files or documents anywhere you find yourself. These are the steps to follow in file uploading on the web are stated below.

1. Move to **OneDrive.** Then you locate and choose the **upload** button.

2. You have to locate and choose the file you want to **upload**. You can upload numerous files as you wish just simply select and hold down the **Ctrl** key, then click on open.

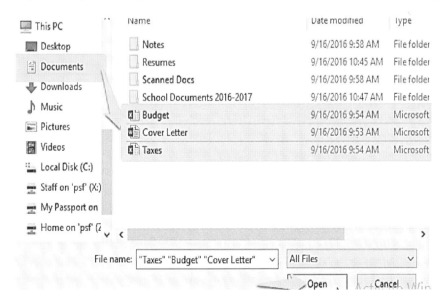

3. After few processes, your file will be sent to your OneDrive.

How To Embed Folders/Files

The simplest undertaking on OneDrive is to create a File or Folder. Follow the procedures below to share a OneDrive file or Folder. Access the web, right-click on a file to get a link you will use to share the file. Then send the link via your email account, or share straight to Facebook (this can be possible if your social media network is linked to your Microsoft OneDrive account).

Embedding could be defined as the process of showing something in detail, for instance, the screenshot above is a typical example of an embedded image. Some processes can be used in embedding a YouTube video on an internet page. For this to be done in an easy and simple form you have to apply the embedded command, this embed command will help in generating an HTML code, which can be used on a blog or internet page.

How To Save All Office Files to OneDrive

The OneDrive and Microsoft Office programs are extremely connected. For you to use OneDrive as your default, you have to save location, then follow the steps given to you below.

The first thing you have to do is to sign in to your OneDrive account. The reason we are using MS Office is that you can quickly network whether you are signed in or not by any simple method.

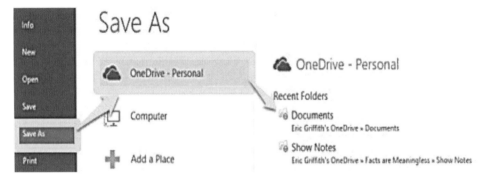

After you sign in, when trying to save a fresh document, the major alternative that will be noticeable is **OneDrive**. When you click Browse and you will acquire a list that will display the local OneDrive folders on your hard drive. You are required to tap the **Pin icon** next to any folder and it will always be saved as the evasion location assisting in saving every Office document.

How To Create A Photo Album In OneDrive

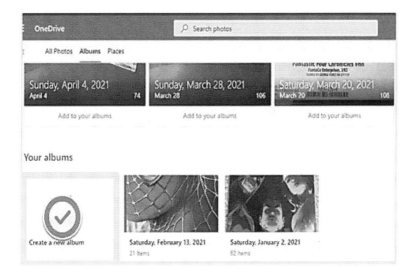

I believe you already know that albums are a collection of files or documents like pictures, music, videos, and so on in bulk. You can create your photo or video albums simply by choosing those photos or videos that have been saved in your OneDrive account. In your OneDrive site where your account is log in, you will click the Entry for those pictures at the left panel. You have to click on the caption for Albums, then click on **Create a new album** button at the first thumbnail. Give the appropriate title you like to your album, choose those pictures you prefer to add, after that you click on **Add Album** and you will have successfully created an Album.

How To Back Up Files with OneDrive

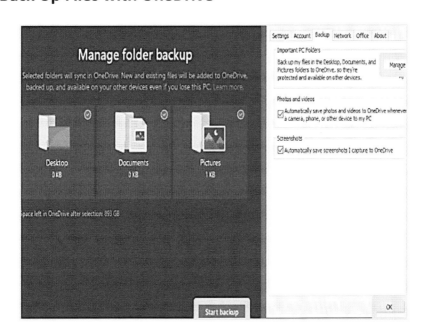

Now, that you are familiar with the workings of OneDrive, you've done so many things using OneDrive, another thing you need to know is that it can also be used to recover very relevant files or folders. First of all, you will enter the OneDrive program window, click on a tab that indicates **backup,** then choose Manage backup. You can decide to back up the desktop, pictures, and documents folder. You have to select the items you want a backup, after which you then click on a tab label **Start backup**.

How To Turn Off Automatic Sync in OneDrive

Probably you have disconnected your computer from your OneDrive account, then the first thing you have to do is to make sure that all the files you want have been synced to that particular computer. This can be done via accessing the OneDrive tray icons. Go to **Settings > Account > select folders**. You have to check the box to Sync every file and folder in OneDrive, in a situation where you had unchecked any files or folders before.

The action we have taken so far will automatically download several files from the OneDrive account which has not been in existence on your computer. The procedure will take quite some time, but we can also examine the success via right-clicking the **OneDrive System tray icon** to view how far gone and the time left on it.

So far every one of your files is backed up already to your computer, you will right-click on the **OneDrive System tray icon** and choose Settings. On that Settings tab, you can uncheck the box to Start OneDrive automatically when you sign in to Windows. Then you have to click the **Account tab** and click the **Unlink the PC** connection. On very quick notice, you click on the **Unlink account** button, and after this, your system will no more sync with your OneDrive account.

CHAPTER 3

MANAGING YOUR ONEDRIVE FOLDERS

There are numerous activities that you can perform on a particular file or folder in your **Microsoft *OneDrive*** account with the aid of the *"Manage"* alternative. First of all, you have to choose a folder or file and after that action, you will click on the *"Manage"* alternative displayed at the top, and the obtainable alternative is shown to you at the down-drop menus which contain *"Rename"*, *"Delete"*, *"Move to"*, **"Copy to"**, **"Version History"** and **"Properties"**. The alternative of seeing the folder or file is that you made a recent change before is made possible through the version history and also the property section gives you detailed information concerning the item you have chosen. The details will be stated below and some of the icons will be highlighted in bold form.

How To Sort Out Your Files

If you move to the OneDrive key page, you will view every file and folder on the main page. You will then decide the files you want to see just by choosing several alternatives in the **left triangulation panel**.

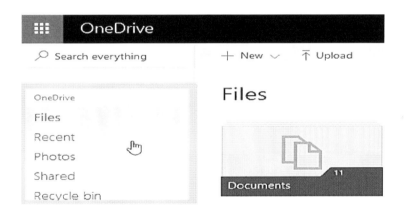

You can also alternate how your file should be displayed via clicking the **Outlook Alternative's** icon at the top right corner.

There are several methods you can use in viewing files on Microsoft OneDrive. Below are ways you can view files on OneDrive with illustrative examples.

1. **Photo Outlook**: This is one of the best ways to view your file or folder especially when you have a particular folder of photos that you do go through intermittently. It gives you an overview of thumbnails of your photos climbed down in the grid.

2. **List Outlook:** this permits you to view your files with the names associated with them and other necessary information, that you may be conversant with if you normally work with those folders and files on your personal computer.

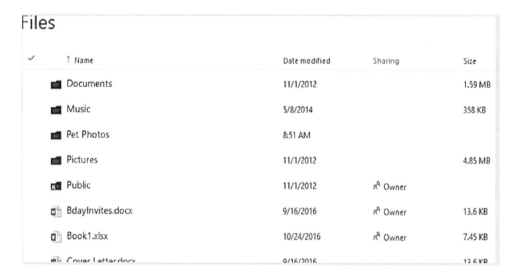

3. **Tiles Outlook:** the tiles outlook allows you to view your files and folders in a grid of icons. This type of view is an evasion view for your folders and files.

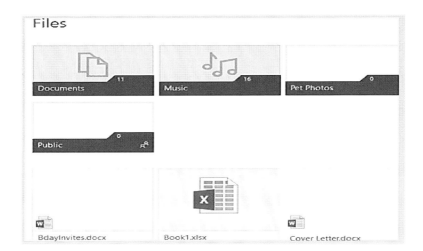

Searching For Your Files

You can search for documents via the **search** button. Searching for your documents allows you to look for a precise document using words that are confined inside the document and its label.

- If you want to search for a file, click on the **search bar**. Enter the words or title you wish to search for then click **Enter**. What you are searching for will show as long as it is saved on your drive.

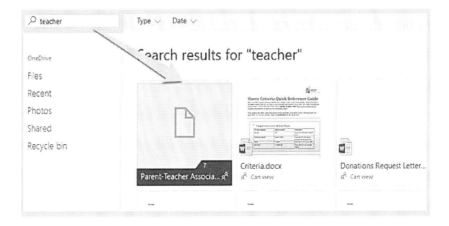

Working With Your Folders

Your folder can be used in organizing your files. You can store your documents in a folder and you can also move a document from one folder to the other without stress. The aspect of moving documents between different folders is very suitable because the document can be shared just by moving the document to a **Shared Folder**. For instance, let's assume you are operating on a certain project with some set of individuals, you may decide to share your folder with them. After that, you will decide on the file you wish to share with the set of the individual to the shared folder.

How You Can Move a File to A Folder

1. Move the mouse over any file, then click on the **checked box** at the top-right flank. You can decide to choose **numerous files** simply by clicking extra checked boxes.

2. Tap on the **Move to** control in the menu at the top-right flank.

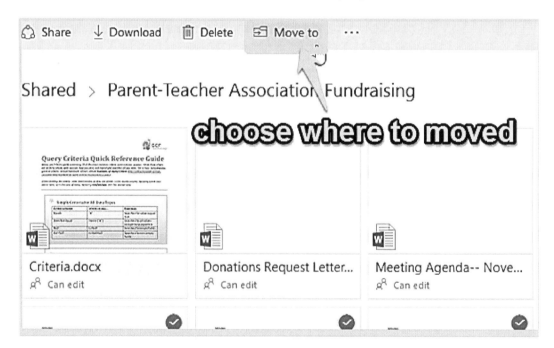

3. The **Move objects to** the panel will show on the right flank of the monitor. Choose the **folder** where you will like to transfer the file after you click on **Move**.

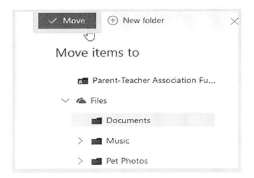

4. Your file will move as you instruct it. If you prefer your file to move to the **shared folder,** it will do so and will also be shared with a group and friends.

Other File Alternatives

If you want to get extra file managing alternatives, you will be required to **right-click** on that file. The screenshot below is an example of more options given to you.

Most of these alternatives include the following:

- **Version history**: Open and re-establish previously stored versions of the files.
- **Download**: this is a way of saving a copy of the file to your PC. The document which you download before will not be upgraded when changes are been made to them in Microsoft OneDrive.
- **Rename**: in this option, you can rename your files.
- **Delete**: when you delete any file it will be moved to the **Recycle Bin** automatically. For all the files to be finally deleted you are required to **empty** the recycle bin.

How To Explore Other Alternatives On OneDrive Website

Microsoft establishment has been able to propel its brand which was previously known as **SkyDrive.** But presently, the name of the new brand has been changed to **OneDrive**. In comparison to another cloud service, Microsoft's **OneDrive**

offers their operators a free **7GB** storage space and you will also be given an extra storing space when you decide to create a **Microsoft account.** It will be explained below to you in detail the many features and tools which will be seen on the **OneDrive** website just register for OneDrive and get your Account equipped, then track the procedure that will be shown to you below.

How You Can Access OneDrive Website

For you to open the **OneDrive** website, this can happen normally as often as you access many other websites. All you need to do is to access your preferred browser and once it is accessible, you will simply enter **"OneDrive.live.com"** into the web address search box and click **"Enter"** on your system keyboard. When you have successfully accessed the **OneDrive** website, an interface will display where you will be required to key in your **email** and **password** you used in creating your Microsoft account into the spaces provided for that information and you will be directed to the main page of your **OneDrive** account. There are numerous procedures to follow to access the **OneDrive** website.

If you look at the main page of the **OneDrive** account, you will be shown dark blue thumbnails at the top of the screen which represents several folders that you can store uploaded files into. If you place your mouse pointer on any of those folders, you will view a small square box at the top right-flank of the thumbnail. If you decide to click inside the small square box, you will view a marked sign that will show in that box. This mark shown on the square box indicates that those items have been chosen. At the top section of the screen below, all other alternatives for the chosen item will be displayed

How To Create Dissimilar Files Using Office Online

If you check on the *OneDrive* website's main page, there is room for you to create dissimilar types of files or documents like **Excel, PowerPoint,** and **Word,** all these can be done in the absence of **Microsoft Office Suite** on your PC desktop screen. Additionally, it is very easy for you to work on files of any kind very smartly while you are using any **Microsoft's** online services like **OneDrive** and this can be very simple with the aid of *"Office Online"* apps. For you to perform this action explained to you, click on the *"Create"* button at the top flank of the screen. After that, the apps that will assist you in creating the file will be shown to you at the drop-down menu, click on it to get a fresh file.

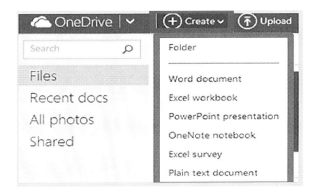

How To Open A File In Desktop Or Online Office App

If you already have some files stored in your **OneDrive** account you can then explore the options of how to open any of them. The most beautiful part of **OneDrive** is the fact that it can be assimilated with your **Windows** system irrespective of the web browser you always use in signing in to your OneDrive account.

Procedures To Adopt to Access a File

There are two methods you can use to perform this action. You can either access and edit your file on several **Online Office** apps or perform a similar job on every app's desktop corresponding to the portion of the **Microsoft Office** collection. Just choose a file adopting the procedures that we have given to you previously and when you are done selecting the one you prefer, then you can view an alternative at the top flank indicated *"Open"*. When you are done clicking on this alternative, you will be authorized to view two obtainable selections when accessing the file.

The "Open" alternatives on the screen above indicate both **"PowerPoint"** and **"PowerPoint Online"** but we have chosen a **"PowerPoint" file** from our **"Microsoft OneDrive"** account.

How To Download A File Or Folder To Your Computer Or Mobile Device

One main option which will normally show at the top section of the Microsoft OneDrive main page when you click on any file is the "**Download''** option. This option can also be used to get anything you have produced before with your mobile phone and saved it in **OneDrive**, you can decide to copy those things to a PC hard drive. For you to access any content in OneDrive, you are required to choose the file or any other document that has been saved on your PC's hard drive, after then just click on the **Download** option at the top section of the page.

How To Share A File Or Folder, Other People

One other interesting option is how to share my file with other people without stress. And this particular alternative is only obtainable on the **OneDrive** web page which is indicated **share.** The purpose of the command has already been indicated with the name, it permits you to share any folder or file with anyone on your list of contact so they will be able to download or view the file.   This is an exceptional method to share with your friends on your social media like Facebook, Twitter, Instagram, etc. The **"Share"** alternative warrants you to be connected towards a particular file that you have highlighted and send the file to any of your friends either by emailing or as a message through chat. You will be allowed to attach a quick short note to the file you want to send. Also, you can choose to allow the recipients to edit the file you are sending or not.

725

If you view the screenshot above you will see a link that indicated **"Recipients can edit"** when you click on it, it will show to you two drop-down alternatives that will enable you to select whether the file receiver should be able to edit or just view the file only and also indicate whether the file receiver will have to sign in his or her **Microsoft account** before they can be granted the permit to see the file. When you are through with all this file preparation, type in the receiver name then click on the **Share** button located at the bottom left flank of the screen.

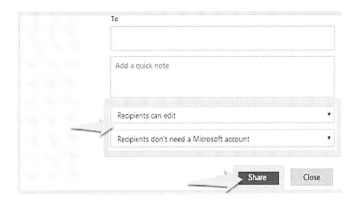

How To Embed A File To Your Blog Or Web Page

In some situations, you might have to upload your files to a website or a blog If you want this to happen you have to produce an **HTML code** with ease for any file using this alternative which indicates **"Embed"** which is located at the top section when you access your **OneDrive** via the web. The first thing you will need to do is click on the button which says **Embed,** on your ribbon. After clicking on the button, a mail will be sent to you as a screen intersection that will give you details of what to leave or enter, all you need to do is to click on *the "Generate"* button for you to get the **HTML code** which will be send to you for you to put folder or file into any of your blog or web page and you will be able to share to numerous persons visiting your page at a time.

Tools That Are Used for Sharing in Microsoft OneDrive

After you have succeeded in sharing files or documents with other people, the document or file you have shared with them will have access to the document at any time they wish. In some cases, if you grant them the right to alter any change in the file or document, they will have the ability to do so with the office online without much stress. One important thing about it is that several people can edit a particular shared document or file at the same time with ease. If there is any need for you to view someone editing the same shared document with you, you will be able to view the person at the top right flank of the page. From the screenshot display to you below, the name of the person that is currently editing the same shared document is **JULIA FILLORY**.

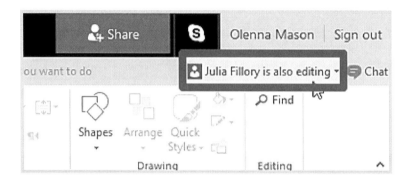

In as much as someone **alternate** a certain document you have access to before, you will have the ability to view the position of their various cursor, another you should know is that you will not have the access to view their edited work until they save their corrections or edited work. The alternation that has been done so far will apply to every edition of the documents.

The truth about it is that you cannot predict this method of sharing the document. In a situation where several you are editing simultaneously with other people, the alternation made on the document will not show instantaneously. There is a need for you to refresh or reopen the document before you will be able to view its current edits.

You also have to talk about the shared documents simply by adding what we called **document comments**. If you comment on any document you have shared before with different people, it will be very easy for them to view and reply to any comment you have made on the document.

Additionally, for you to be able to add or comment on the document, you have to visit OneDrive, then ensure that the **information panel** is also detectible, and choose the particular document you want to comment on. The last thing you should do is to key in your comment in the **comments box** located at the bottom flank of the information panel. After you are done typing your comment in the comment box, then you click on **add** to make it successfully. Below is a typical example of what I am talking about.

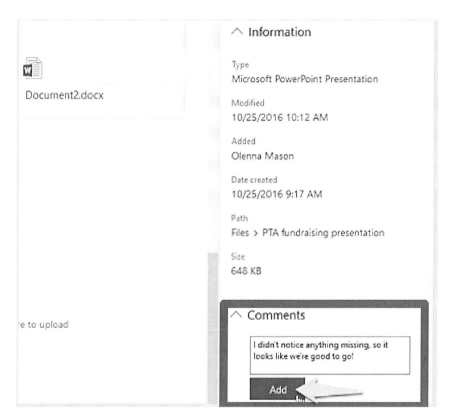

CHAPTER FOUR

NAVIGATING DOCUMENTS WITH OFFICE ONLINE

A lot of work can be done on your documents via an internet browser with the help of an **online office**. One of the big advantages that makes Office Online relevant is that it assists those who do not have the office app on their desktop to access it via the internet. You can access and edit all the documents you have in any internet browser with **Office Online**. But in a situation where you have already installed Microsoft Office on your system, you can just go ahead to access the app and edit the documents with the **desktop Office series**. Another important thing when you edit your documents with Office Online is the editing tools, it has more features and editing tools when compared to the Office desktop app.

How To Open A Document With Office Online

1. The first thing you have to do is to click on the particular document you want to gain access to. In the illustration given below, we choose a PowerPoint file to exemplify what is being discussed.

2. When you preview your file, it will access a fresh tag. At the top of the toolbar, you are required to click **Edit Presentation**, then choose **Edit in Browser** from the down-drop menu display below.

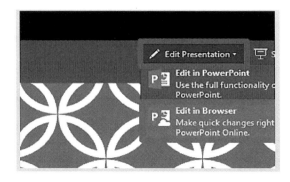

3. Automatically, your document will show on the screen. You can go on to do your editing with the office online easily.

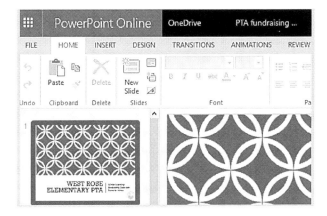

For you to **close** the document and go back to OneDrive, you will click on the **OneDrive** connection at the top of the screen below.

How To Turn Off, Disable, Or Uninstalled OneDrive

When you have decided not to use OneDrive anymore, all you need to do is to disconnect it from your system. There are procedures you will follow for it to be done smoothly.

Another thing is that, if you feel like stopping syncing files to OneDrive for some time, all you need to do is to pause OneDrive for some minutes and continue syncing afterwards.

Note:

- You should bear in mind that you will not lose any files or data in the process of disabling OneDrive on your PC. The only way to open your files is via signing in to the website > OneDrive.com.

In Windows 10, OneDrive is the evasion save a destination for all your files and documents. What this implies is that fresh files or documents are automatically stored to OneDrive, except you decide to save to a different destination on your computer.

HOW TO UNLINK ONEDRIVE

1. The first thing you will do is to choose the **OneDrive** cloud icon sited at the notification section, at the bottom right corner of your desktop.

Footnote: some time you may be required to click on the **Show Hidden Icon** indicated by arrow ^ which is towards the notification section before you can be able to view the **OneDrive** icon. In a situation where the OneDrive icon is not showing in the notification section, then you should know that OneDrive will not be running. You have to choose **Start**, then you type **OneDrive** in the search area, from the results shown to you choose **OneDrive**.

2. Choose **More** > **Settings**

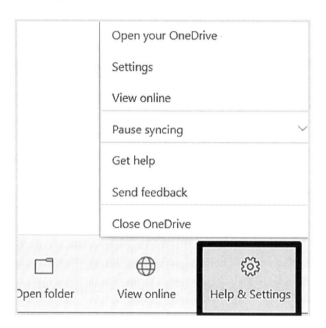

How to Hide OneDrive

OneDrive is being made into selected kinds of Windows and you cannot uninstall it. The only thing you can do to it is to hide the icon and pause the sync procedure and it will stay hidden. For this to be done successfully, you will turn off every OneDrive setting and get rid of the OneDrive folder from the file explorer.

For Windows 10

For you to be able to hide your OneDrive icon, follow the steps below. The same procedure we follow to unlink the OneDrive is also the same as hiding OneDrive on Windows 10.

1. In the **Settings** tab, you will uncheck every box which is under the **General** menu.
2. In the **AutoSave** tag, set the **Documents and Pictures** option to **The PC alone**, and then you will uncheck the other boxes from it.

In the **Account** tag, you will click on the **folders** you have chosen.

3. You will then **Sync your Microsoft OneDrive files to your computer** box, you should check and uncheck the box at **Sync for every file and folder on your OneDrive**. Then click the **OK** button to end the box and it will go back to settings.
4. You have to click **OK** to save any alterations you have made in the **Settings** menu.
5. At the **Account** tag, click on **Unlink OneDrive**. Then you close the **Welcome to OneDrive** menu that will pop up.
6. Then, go to your File Explorer and right-click on **OneDrive**, and then you click on **Properties** from the drop-down menu.
7. Lastly, choose **More** and select **Quit OneDrive**. It will get rid of the OneDrive icon from the notifications section.

For Windows 8.1

1. When you access your PC start window, click and hold the **OneDrive** icon, and after then you will handpick **Unpin from Start**.
2. Go to **Computer Settings**, making use of the **Computer Settings** icon at the **Start-up** menu, click on **Settings**, and then select **Alternate PC settings**.
3. You can check beneath the **Computer settings**, and look for **OneDrive**.
4. When you check on the **File Storage** tag, you will turn off the control at **Save documents to the OneDrive** via defaulting.
5. Looking at the **Camera roll** tag, you have to choose **don't upload photos** and then you crack off the control at Auto **upload videos** to the **OneDrive**.
6. Taking a look at the **Sync settings** tag, beneath **Sync settings** with the **OneDrive**, you crack off the control at **Sync settings** on your **Computer**.
7. When you view from the **Meter connections** tag, you can crack off all the necessary controls.
8. For you to hide OneDrive successfully from the File Explorer, you need to access the File Explorer and looking from the folder list on the left, you will right-click on the **OneDrive** and after then you click on **Properties**.

Looking at the **General** tag, at the **properties**, you will mark the **Hidden** icon. When you check the **Account** tag, you have to click on **Unlink the Computer** and after then you **Unlink account**.

How To Uninstall OneDrive

Some Windows automatically have OneDrive in them. The OneDrive application comes with Windows 8.1 and Windows RT 8.1, you cannot uninstall them from your computer, but as for the likes of Windows 7, Windows Vista, Windows XP, and other editions of Window 10 you can easily uninstall OneDrive from them. You cannot uninstall OneDrive from Windows 10 mobile Phone.

When you have successfully uninstalled OneDrive it will stop syncing immediately, but any **file or data** that you have in **OneDrive** can be obtainable if you log in to your account > OneDrive.com.

How To Unlink for Windows 10

1. Just click the **Start** menu, type the Programs in the search box, and after then you click on **Add or remove programs** from the results shown to you.
2. If you look beneath the **Apps and features**, look for and select **Microsoft OneDrive**, and after then click on **Uninstall**. When you are asked for a password, then you will type the password for validation

WINDOWS 7 OR WINDOWS VISTA

1. Select the **Start** menu, looking from the search box, you will then type in Add Programs, and then, from the list of results shown to you, select **Programs** and **Features**.
2. Select **Microsoft OneDrive**, and you click on **Uninstall**. When you are asked for a password, then you will type the password for validation.

ANDROID DEVICES

1. You just go to **Settings** and choose **Storage/ Memory**.
2. Select **OneDrive** and **Uninstall**.

iOS devices

1. Go to the **Home Screen**, tap and hold on to the **OneDrive** app icon
2. You just tap **X** that shows in the upper left flank of the app icon on your device.

macOS

All you need to do here is to drag the OneDrive app to the Garbage, simple.

CHAPTER FIVE

ONEDRIVE FOR BUSINESS

OneDrive for business enables users to securely share information and control certain levels of security through direct access or links for editing or viewing files. This OneDrive is managed by your organization and it allows you to share and collaborate work on documents with your coworkers, classmate, colleagues etc.

Benefits Of Microsoft OneDrive for Business

Microsoft OneDrive has so many positive impacts on business. Under this sub-heading, we are going to be discussing some of the importance of OneDrive concerning business:

- It will assist you in storing and arranging your work files in a very safe position in the storage cloud that you can access at any time.
- It also assists you on how to share files or documents with your colleague, so that they can also go through or edit the content of the files. This process of sharing files or documents is very easy and unique compared to the process of sending through email.
- Microsoft OneDrive assists you in synchronizing files or documents stored in the storage cloud to your PC or mobile device, this will help you to open your files or documents on OneDrive offline easily.

Note: Microsoft endorses that all operators store their business files on their OneDrive for Business purposes, it is not their private OneDrive. Microsoft OneDrive for Business deals with greater efficiency and partnership/sharing features designed for the workstation to be effective.

How To Use OneDrive for Small Scale Businesses

We know that Microsoft OneDrive is vigorous but this is merely to use storage cloud podium in setting a standard for small-scale businesses, enterprises, and other things within them. About most storage cloud suppliers, when you look at many of the innovative enterprises, the main features of OneDrive are always obtainable for all subscription types, which aid the establishment when using OneDrive in any aspect that profits them. If you notice, you will observe that this sub-heading deal more on the arrangement and placement alternatives which brings more ideas in terms of small-scale businesses which wants to involve the use of OneDrive. At this point, the establishment can choose any other managing skills needed.

Microsoft OneDrive has made it easier and secure to stockpile and open your files from every one of your devices. You can also work with others irrespective of whether they are in or out of your association and dismiss the sharing of anything you wish. Microsoft OneDrive aids in defending your work via innovative encryption meanwhile the data is in shipment and at rest in data centers. OneDrive can assist to make sure that operators follow your most demanding acquiescence standards by permitting them to make choices where their data subsists and giving a comprehensive report of how that data has been alternated and accessed. Microsoft OneDrive links you to your shared files in Microsoft 365, improving partnership competence inside Microsoft 365 apps. On OneDrive on the web, desktop, or mobile, you can open every one of your files including the files shared with you from other teams, including files from Microsoft Teams and SharePoint.

Installing And Setting Up Microsoft OneDrive for Businesses

Here, you can upload, download, and collaborate with your Microsoft OneDrive files from any internet browser, but the OneDrive knowledge originates from the Windows and Mac sync apps and the iOS and Android mobile apps. With these customers and apps, saving files to Microsoft OneDrive and collaborating with them, makes working very easier than when you visit a website any time you want anything. Via this knowledge, you can effortlessly integrate OneDrive into your prevailing file communication involvements.

There is also a need for you to install Microsoft OneDrive on some sustained devices. In the case of small-scale businesses, the physical connections make the greatest intellect. In the case of other devices, the process of the installation could be very easy just like when you download an application from the play store. But in the case of others, there is a need for you to eliminate the old editions of Microsoft OneDrive. At this point, you should be able to understand the installation and configuration of Microsoft OneDrive on Android mobile, iOS, Windows devices, and PC running macOS. There is no need for you to install on every platform depending on the devices used in your association

How To Get Started with OneDrive for Business

OneDrive is very relevant even when it comes to large-scale business, but it is not very easy to implement a policy that small-scale businesses can gain from. In most cases, small-scale businesses are always at a bigger risk of dropping files which has bad equipment because not many are with backups and integrated storage. When using OneDrive, your small-scale business will be able to store all your files for you safely, and it will make it simple for your operators to get in touch with it from their various systems.

To get started with OneDrive, you have to follow the steps below:

1. **Evaluating fundamental OneDrive information. All you need to do is to** start by revising the elementary OneDrive info obtainable at the **OneDrive help centre**. There will be a response to several questions you wish to ask, even the experience of OneDrive and how it works.
2. **By setting up Microsoft Office 365 subscription,** you must set up a subscription before you can use OneDrive, but truth is that you are not forced to buy every app in Microsoft Office 365 suite.
3. **To Add OneDrive permits,** review your various plan alternatives in **Compare OneDrive plans**, and after then you will add the permits you want.

If you have successfully done the task above, then you are due to planning for, position, and arrange the OneDrive sync app and its applications. For it to be done, you have to complete the following three steps:

1. **Plan to adopt: When dealing with small-scale businesses, if you plan to adopt other operators, it is always easier as when you show your operators how to make use of OneDrive personal. Moreover, small-scale business clients always don't value this step for fresh applications, and this can affect the application's progress very badly.**
2. **To install and arrange:** The applications that are used to sync are always obtainable for macOS and Windows operating systems which gives the operators the experience to interact with their files without stress. In rare cases small-scale businesses start by you downloading and installing of sync app on your operators' systems, after you are done with that you can now think of installing OneDrive mobile app. To be frank, you have the OneDrive customer on your system, especially with devices using Windows 10 operating system and that which is using macOS with Microsoft Office 2016 or another time we will have the OneDrive sync application.
3. **To manage your OneDrive: In so many small-scale businesses, managing OneDrive is not considered very important. You can just install the OneDrive app and configure it without further action being done on it. In a situation where you want to use a model structure of OneDrive or access limitations, you can manage them with ease and change the settings in the OneDrive management focus.**

Managing OneDrive for Businesses

Numerous small-scale businesses use Microsoft OneDrive without alternating some of the alternatives. When you want to add any fundamental device and sharing limitations to OneDrive, you should make use of the OneDrive admin centre. For you to be able to access the fresh OneDrive admin centre, visit **https://admin.OneDrive.com.** Then, you can restrict the people to whom your operators can share files, you can select the devices your workers can use to access Microsoft OneDrive.

The Key OneDrive Structures for Small Scale Businesses

For most cloud storage suppliers, OneDrive does not offer vigorous structures to small-scale businesses belong its limit, but it assists mostly in the availability of several modern structures. This warrants the small-scale businesses with the ability to use modern structures as needed by their establishment.

Adopting OneDrive for Business

Extracting from operators is very necessary concerning the general progress of any fresh application. For a good setting to have the mindset of increasing your investment in OneDrive and Office 365 there is a need for you to increase the level of engagement operators have with them. In the case of small-scale businesses, motivating operator adoption is very easy by introducing OneDrive in the process of installation.

In situations where you show your operators how to share and save the document in Microsoft OneDrive seems to be an important alternative in the case of driving adoption, for the fact that you will be running Manual installation for the main time. The elementary concept for small-scale businesses using OneDrive is the obtainability of files and redundancy. When you save a document in a manual storage device you can easily lose it but for those saved to OneDrive, it gets very difficult to lose. All you need to do is to have this conversation with your operators, demonstrating to them the applications on how to use it, which could bring out profitable results.

The OneDrive Files On-Demand

The OneDrive Files On-Demand enhances the operators to see, search, and also communicate with those files which have been stored in OneDrive from the File Explorer, and you did not have to bother to download every file to your system. This particular character appears as an all-in-one view for OneDrive and local files but does consume enough space on your hard drive. Just like it has been presented to you in the picture below illustratively, those files that have not been downloaded possess a cloud icon to indicate their status. But for those files that were downloaded, it will indicate a checkmark in the color green.

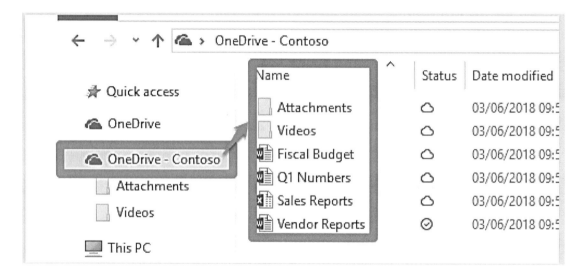

By default, you can only download any files when you want to make use of those files. Moreover, in case you wish to open the files even when you are not connected to the internet what you will do, is to make the files obtainable for you when you are offline. Simply right-click on the file and choose **Always keep on this device.** Another option is when you need some free space on your system and you have to get rid of every copy of the file you download, just right-click on the file and choose to **Free up space**. The picture below provides you with a typical example showing to you the right-click menu of the OneDrive files on a Windows operating system.

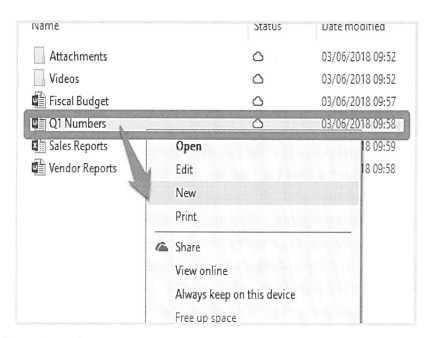

The Modern Attachments

The Microsoft OneDrive assimilates with Microsoft Outlook to enhance sharing of OneDrive files showing merely as an email attachment. This character in particular gives a well-known sharing involvement but it has a unified storage add-on in OneDrive. Its permits all your operator which cooperate on a similar file to avoid to and fro sending of contradictory editions in mails. You can also arrange file sharing permissions straight from the outlook customer.

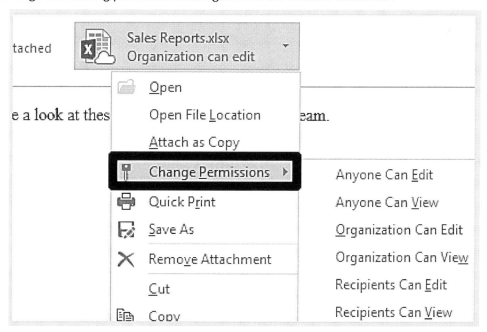

The Known Folder Move

This particular feature enhances the operators to choose Windows-known folders like Documents, Desktop, or pictures to automatically sync it to Microsoft OneDrive. This feature can be added at the beginning of your OneDrive setup or after it has been configured, the work done by this feature grants a changed alternative for those operators seeking to add known folders to their already existing ones that have been synced.

The Recycle Bin

The Microsoft OneDrive also has its own recycle bin that is almost the same as the one which is obtainable on Windows desktop. When you delete any file, it moves automatically to the recycle bin and it will store it for a certain period before it will be deleted finally. For the account made for school or work, files you have deleted will be eliminated after 93 days except you alter the configuration.

How To Restore Files

This feature in OneDrive gives you the ability to restore any files that you have lost for about 30 days. For you to choose a better time to recover your file, OneDrive will give you a histogram that evaluates the activity of the file for you to make a proper suggestion of the exact time you want to recover your files. After that, just click on the file history and select the ones you wish to restore and any other options.

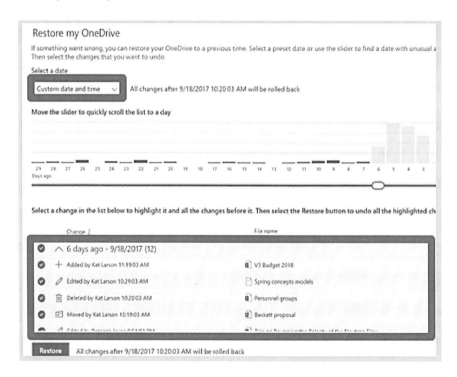

In addition, for the fact that histogram evaluates the work of users on file. This feature can also be used to see the history of your files without much stress.

CONCLUSION ON MICROSOFT ONEDRIVE

With what we have explained so far one should be able to handle any problems concerning Microsoft OneDrive. You should be able to know how to set up Microsoft OneDrive on different operating systems. By now you should know how to share files and documents from your computer to your Microsoft OneDrive account. After going through the book, you will know how to sync, upload and manage your files easily. It is believed that with the aid of this slide you can handle different packages on OneDrive. This small documentation explains in detail how to get more space on your Microsoft OneDrive account. This slide also goes further in giving a detailed explanation of how to manage your OneDrive account. It also throws more light on how to disconnect OneDrive from your computer. There are more things you will gain from these slides even in terms of business.

Finally, if you have patiently gone through this slide, you will also know how to manage the business using Microsoft OneDrive. You will be able to open the OneDrive document both online and offline. This documentation goes with a lot of illustrative examples, which will guide you in completing any task without any form of stress. It will be of much help to those who want the knowledge of Microsoft OneDrive at the elementary level. By following the illustrative example given to you in this documentation, you can manage Microsoft OneDrive with ease. It is believed that as you go through this slide you should be able to understand the basic concept of OneDrive.

Was this book helpful to you?
Are you pleased with the contents of this book?

We would love to hear from you, please kindly leave a review after buying/reading this book.
Thanks

INDEX

Eye Dropper · 473

Z

Printed in Great Britain
by Amazon

79241078R00438